Woolf in the Real World

Selected Papers from the
Thirteenth International Conference on Virginia Woolf

Woolf in the Real World

Selected Papers from the
Thirteenth International Conference on
Virginia Woolf

Smith College, Northampton, Massachusetts
5–8 June 2003

❧

Edited by Karen V. Kukil

CLEMSON UNIVERSITY
DIGITAL PRESS

A full-text digital version of this book is available on the Internet, at the Center for Virginia Woolf Studies, California State University, Bakersfield. Go to http://www.csub.edu/woolf_center and click the Publications link. Works produced at Clemson University by the Center for Electronic and Digital Publishing, including *The South Carolina Review* and its themed series "Virginia Woolf International," may be found at our Web site: http://www.clemson.edu/caah/cedp. Contact the director at 864-656-5399 for information.

Published by Clemson University Digital Press at the Center for Electronic and Digital Publishing, Clemson University, Clemson, South Carolina.

CLEMSON UNIVERSITY
DIGITAL PRESS

Produced at CEDP using Adobe Photoshop Elements CS, Adobe InDesign CS, and Microsoft Word 2000. This book is set in Adobe Garamond Pro and was printed by University Printing Services, Office of Publications and Promotional Services, Clemson University. Copy editing and layout at the press by Christi Conti, assisted by Charis Chapman and Wayne Chapman (Executive Editor).

To order copies, contact the Center for Electronic and Digital Publishing, Strode Tower, Box 340522, Clemson University, Clemson, South Carolina 29634-0522. An order form is available at the digital press Web site (see above) under "SCROLL" and linked to the themed issue page entitled "Virginia Woolf International."

Front cover illustration:
Vanessa Bell (British 1879-1961)
Virginia Woolf, ca. 1912
Oil on paperboard, 14½ x 12 inches
Smith College Museum of Art, Northampton, Massachusetts
Gift of Ann Safford Mandel

Frontispiece:
Virginia Woolf at Garsington, 1923
Original photograph, 3 x 5 inches
Mortimer Rare Book Room, Smith College, Northampton, Massachusetts

Table of Contents

The Afterlife of Virginia Woolf

❧

Introduction

by Karen V. Kukil

The Smith College community was honored to host the thirteenth international conference on Virginia Woolf in Northampton, Massachusetts, on 5–8 June 2003. Generous support for the conference was received from every corner of the campus, as well as from the five-college consortium and from local collectors and museums. As the organizers of the conference discovered, Virginia Woolf is revered in western Massachusetts, a place she never visited but learned about from her British contemporaries. In the 1930s both Vita Sackville-West and Hugh Walpole lectured in Northampton, Massachusetts, for the Hampshire Bookshop.

Smith College is an appropriate place to host a conference on Virginia Woolf. Her work has been an integral part of the curriculum since the early1920s, when authors Mary Ellen Chase and Mina Kirstein Curtiss joined the English faculty. *A Room of One's Own* and other essays by Virginia Woolf have inspired many graduates of the college, from author and aviator Anne Morrow Lindbergh to feminist activist Gloria Steinem, as well as every president of Smith from Jill Ker Conway, the first woman to hold the position, to current president and Victorianist scholar Carol T. Christ. The poetry of Woolf's prose has also influenced aspiring writers, including Smith's most famous poet, Sylvia Plath.

After graduating from Smith, a number of alumnae assembled important collections related to Virginia Woolf and her circle of friends: Frances Hooper purchased Woolf's manuscripts, letters, and first editions of her work directly from Leonard Woolf; Elizabeth Power Richardson purchased and indexed her Bloomsbury iconography collection, including Leslie Stephen's photograph album; and Ann Safford Mandel collected paintings and book-cover designs by Vanessa Bell, in addition to first editions of the Hogarth Press. All of these collections were on display during the conference to the delight of the more than 350 delegates, from eight countries. Most of the exhibitions are now available on the Smith College website (www.smith.edu), fulfilling one of the main goals of the conference: to showcase and share the riches of Smith's special collections with the scholarly community.

An active program committee planned the panels at which nearly 200 papers were presented on the theme of "Woolf in the Real World," a title adapted from Alex Zwerdling's biography of Virginia Woolf published in 1986. The committee was coordinated by Marilyn Schwinn Smith and included conference organizers Stephanie Schoen and Karen V. Kukil; Smith faculty members Robert Ellis Hosmer Jr., Cornelia Pearsall, and Elizabeth von Klemperer; five-college faculty members Laura Doyle and Lee Edwards of the University of Massachusetts at Amherst; and Woolf Steering Committee members Beth Rigel Daugherty of Otterbein College, Jeanne Dubino of Southeastern Louisiana University, Mark Hussey of Pace University, and Vara Neverow of Southern Connecticut State University. Smith alumna Michele Bala and student intern Alyson Shaw assisted with the planning, logistics, and hosting of the conference. The committee was pleased that the event promoted original scholarship and attracted so many new delegates to the proceedings, particularly graduate students, editors, publishers, book artists, creative writers, and feminist activists.

Thirty papers from the proceedings were selected for publication by members of the program and conference committees. The essays were written by an international mixture of seasoned scholars, graduate students, poets, publishers, and "common readers." They represent a variety of scholarship elicited by the provocative theme of the conference, which focused attention on the ways Woolf engaged the "real world" of her time and the ways her legacy continues to engage "real world" issues now.

These papers are divided into three sections: (1) "The Life of Virginia Woolf," (2) "The Writings of Virginia Woolf," and (3) "The Afterlife of Virginia Woolf."

The first section addresses the education of Virginia Woolf as well as aspects of her private and professional life as a publisher and typesetter at the Hogarth Press. President Carol T. Christ opens the selected proceedings with a brief history of Smith College, followed by a history of women's education in England during Virginia Woolf's formative years. The collection's second essay, by literary scholar and plenary speaker Lyndall Gordon, addresses the art of biography. Next comes Catherine W. Hollis's paper on the visual imagery on the dust jackets of Virginia Woolf's books as they were issued by the Hogarth Press. Hollis argues that, in many respects, Vanessa Bell's postimpressionist imagery visually signals the formal innovations Woolf was developing on the textual level. Visual aesthetics are also the subject of Maggie Humm's paper on Virginia Woolf and Vanessa Bell as photographers. According to Humm, Woolf's and Bell's photograph albums provide vivid examples of their ideas about aesthetics, the maternal, the erotic, and identity. Julia Briggs, in contrast, examines Virginia Woolf as the innovative typesetter of Hope Mirrlees's concrete poem *Paris*. Michèle Barrett's essay on Virginia Woolf and pacifism follows. Woolf's reaction to Vita Sackville-West's 1933 lecture tour of North America informs the central argument of Cheryl Mares's essay on British attitudes and assumptions about America and Americans.

Essays on the writing of Virginia Woolf form the heart of these selected proceedings. Thirteen papers are arranged chronologically by the principle work under discussion. Susan Rubinow Gorsky explores Woolf's symbolic use of food imagery in her novels, from *The Voyage Out* to *Between the Acts*. A new nexus of class issues focuses Mary C. Madden's paper on *Night and Day*. Joseph Kreutziger examines Walter Pater's transformation of Darwinian theory to a modern aesthetic and its relation to Woolf's early short stories. Three papers on *Mrs. Dalloway* follow: Cornelia Burian examines the close connection between war trauma and modernist writing, particularly in Woolf's representation of the wounded or vulnerable body; Elizabeth Hirsh illuminates Woolf's encrypted discourse on menstruation and menopause; and Kathryn Simpson discusses the disruptive force of woman-centered gift giving in *Mrs. Dalloway*. The sick body as a vehicle for knowledge organizes Lorraine Sim's paper about Woolf's essay *On Being Ill*. The maternal, the masculine, and death fuse for Woolf in *To the Lighthouse*, according to Dianne Hunter, who sees a double-gendered reality informing Woolf's view of history. McKenzie L. Zeiss's paper on *To the Lighthouse* contributes to our understanding of Woolf's and Vita Sackville-West's complex use of garden and pastoral imagery as metaphors of English prewar identity. Woolf's engagement with the idea of an English homeland for her androgynous protagonist in *Orlando*, according to Erica L. Johnson, stands out in her oeuvre as both a critique and reconfiguration of the concept of national identity. Woolf's travel writing, particularly the sensual Italian section of *Flush,* informs Eleanor McNees's paper. Jennifer-Ann DiGregorio Kightlinger examines fashion as key to the creation and understanding of gender in Woolf's short story "The Introduction" and her novel *The Years.* This middle section concludes in Elizabeth Gallaher von Klemperer's examination of images of needlework in Woolf's novels, culminating with *Between the Acts.*

Ten papers on the afterlife of Virginia Woolf, assembled in the third section of the book, address the ways in which Woolf's legacy continues to influence the world today. Plenary speaker Frances Spalding generously shares an excerpt from her lecture on Vanessa Bell's portraits of Virginia Woolf as the first essay in this section. We are very pleased to reproduce one of these portraits on the front cover of the book. The next paper in part three, by Elizabeth A. Shih and Susan M. Kenney, compares the manuscript and published versions of Woolf's autobiographical essay "A Sketch of the Past," concluding that we need more nuanced editions of Woolf. One such publication, the new Paris Press edition of Woolf's essay *On Being Ill,* a beautiful book featured at the conference, provides the focus of the paper by Jan Freeman, publisher of Paris Press. Freeman documents Woolf's continuing influence on modern presses. William Pryor, also a publisher, discusses in his contribution the influences of Bloomsbury and Neo-Paganism on his private press, Clear Books. The next two papers feature fictional representations of Virginia Woolf. While Drew Patrick Shannon presents an overview of the novels, films, and plays about Virginia Woolf, Laura Francesca Aimone concentrates on Michael Cunningham's novel *The Hours.* Woolf's influence on other writers informs the next two papers. Doryjane Birrer explores Woolf's questions about the representation of reality in fiction through an examination of Woolf's influence on Ian McEwan's novel *Atonement.* In contrast, female imagination as portrayed in Sylvia Plath's novel *The Bell Jar* centers Pamela St. Clair's essay about Virginia Woolf's influence on Sylvia Plath. St. Clair includes an insightful analysis of Plath's annotations of her copies of *Jacob's Room* and *Mrs. Dalloway,* books preserved in the Sylvia Plath Collection at Smith College. Three essays on Woolf and feminism conclude the selected proceedings. Kristin Kommers Czarnecki analyzes Eileen Atkins's interpretation of Woolf in the *Masterpiece Theater* version of *A Room of One's Own,* noting Woolf's feminism in Atkins's translation of the book to film. Joyce Avrech Berkman grapples with the dilemma faced by feminist activists and women's historians who want to preserve and promote the insights and moral integrity of being outsiders while taking on insider positions and roles in academia. Smith Provost Susan C. Bourque brackets the selected essays with a heartfelt reminiscence of her conference interview with Carolyn Heilbrun, one of Heilbrun's last public appearances. Bourque's essay includes an inspiring, comforting history of Heilbrun's long association with Smith College, where Heilbrun's papers now reside alongside those of her feminist friend Gloria Steinem and her literary mentor Virginia Woolf.

These selected papers could not have been published without the support of the Friends of the Smith College Libraries. The expertise of the publishing committee was invaluable: Wayne Chapman, Director of the Clemson University Digital Press, tastefully designed and published the printed book; Merry Pawlowski created the electronic version at the Center for Virginia Woolf Studies at California State University at Bakersfield; and Vara Neverow guided the publishing process, along with Stephanie Schoen and Michele

Bala. The entire manuscript was copyedited by Janet Snow Ritchie. Henrietta Garnett and the Society of Authors graciously extended their permission to reproduce many of the images in this collection. A full list of acknowledgments follows the program at the end of the selected papers. For everyone involved, this conference and the published proceedings have been a more than welcome labor of love.

ক৹

❧

Part One:
The Life of Virginia Woolf

❧

WOOLF AND EDUCATION

by Carol T. Christ

I am delighted to welcome all of you here today—delegates, Smith faculty and staff, and friends from the community. This is the thirteenth annual conference on Virginia Woolf, held in cooperation with the International Virginia Woolf Society and the Virginia Woolf Society of Great Britain. We have guests here from seven countries outside of the United States—Canada, England, Wales, Belgium, Italy, Sweden, and Australia. I'd like to give a particular welcome to you.

The organizers of the conference have asked me to give a short history of the college. Smith College was founded in 1871 with a bequest from Sophia Smith, a resident of Hatfield, Massachusetts, a town very close to Northampton. She was one of seven children of a prosperous farmer and his wife. Like Virginia Woolf, Sophia Smith received little formal education, but she read widely and avidly throughout her life. A story she told her pastor about her childhood has a certain resonance with *A Room of One's Own*. When she was a girl, boys received their lessons at the village schoolhouse in the morning; girls received a few hours' instruction in the afternoon after the boys' lessons were complete. Sophia Smith accompanied her brothers to school in the morning, and sat outside on the steps, trying to overhear the boys' lessons so that she could learn more. When she inherited much of the family wealth, she decided to establish a college for women to provide them with the education she had never received, a schoolhouse of their own. The terms of her will are instructive. They call for the "establishment and maintenance of an Institution for the higher education of young women, with the design to furnish for my own sex means and facilities for education equal to those which are afforded now in our Colleges to young men. It is my opinion that by the higher and more thorough Christian education of women, what are called their 'wrongs' will be redressed, their wages adjusted, their weight of influence in reforming the evils of society will be greatly increased, as teachers, as writers, as mothers, as members of society, their power for good will be incalculably enlarged." She stipulated that the college provide instruction in English Language and Literature, Ancient and Modern Languages, Mathematical and Physical Sciences, the Useful and Fine Arts, Moral and Aesthetic Philosophy, Natural Theology, the Evidences of Christianity, Gymnastics and Physical Culture, the Sciences and Arts, which pertain to Education, Society, and Government, and "such other studies as coming times may develop or demand for the education of women and the progress of the race" (Quesnell 221–22).

The college opened its doors in 1875 with fourteen students and six faculty, under the presidency of Laurenus Clarke Seelye. The founders intended the college to be part of the practical life of the town, choosing to use the town's churches and library and to house students in cottages designed to seem like family homes. President Seelye organized Smith on the principle that it was a college, not a finishing school. The women needed to pass stringent entrance examinations, and the administration turned away unqualified applicants in the college's early years despite its small number of students. President Seelye put in place a demanding curriculum including instruction in Greek, the natural sciences, and the fine arts. He established a botanic garden and an art museum, containing both original paintings and casts of great sculptures. While careful to protect women from too much physical exertion by not constructing any building higher than two and one-half stories, he insisted that no more expenditure of energy was necessary for studying Greek than for ordinary fashionable amusements. In his first annual report, President Seelye wrote that the students accomplished as much and did their work as well as their peers in male colleges. He observed just one difference, that instead of rules to enforce study, they needed rules to diminish it. The college had a closed mark system, which continued until 1912, designed to keep students motivated by the love of learning and protect them from injurious competition.

In the 37 years in which Seelye led the college, it grew to 1,600 students, 122 faculty, and 35 buildings. The next great president in Smith's history was William Allan Neilson, who led the college from 1917 to 1939, enlarging its size, founding the School for Social Work, originally established to help treat shell-shocked veterans of World War I, and developing an international emphasis, founding the second of the nation's junior year abroad programs, and bringing many exiled or persecuted foreign scholars to Smith.

In 1975 Smith celebrated its centennial by inaugurating its first woman president, Jill Ker Conway. The college had earlier responded to the question of coeducation with the decision that it would remain a women's college, and enlarged its mission by beginning the Ada Comstock Scholars Program, designed to recruit older students resuming their education. Jill Ker Conway came to Smith with a vision for women's education, and sharpened its sense of mission, increasing the numbers of women faculty and developing programs for the study of women.

Smith today is the largest of the eastern women's colleges with 2,500 undergraduates and 500 graduate students, about 80 percent of them in the School for Social Work. It is a member of a five-college consortium, including Mount Holyoke, Amherst, Hampshire, and the University of Massachusetts, through which students can take courses on any of the five campuses. Smith has a particularly broad range of majors, including the first major in engineering in a women's college. It strives to fulfill the mission Sophia Smith described in her will, "to develop as fully as may be the powers of womanhood," so that the college might be "a perennial blessing to the country and the world" (Quesnell 222–23).

This short history of Smith provides an apt point of departure for talking about Woolf and education. As I've thought about the subject for the past few weeks, I've framed it as the question: "Why didn't Virginia Woolf go to Smith?" On the surface, of course, the question makes little sense. Virginia Woolf never set foot in the United States, nor did she seem to have much desire to do so. But an American woman with bookish tastes of Woolf's social and economic status at the turn of the century may well have gone to an eastern women's college like Smith. Why did attending college, or university, never seem a possibility for Woolf? And, an even more interesting question, how did Virginia Woolf's lack of formal education shape her work?

College may have seemed a readier opportunity for Woolf's American contemporaries because the development of higher education for women had a very different pattern in the United States than in England. Higher education initially developed in the United States in the form of independent private colleges. When increasingly forceful claims were made, in the second half of the nineteenth century, for women's access to education, this pattern encouraged the founding of private colleges for women. In addition, the land grant colleges founded in the second half of the nineteenth century were largely coeducational. By 1900, when Virginia Woolf reached the age of eighteen, 71 percent of American colleges admitted women, and there were 150 colleges specifically for women. About 36 percent of American college students at the turn of the century were female.

The situation was very different in England, where the movement for the higher education of women had to define opportunities within the existing university structure. Women achieved equal status in the new provincial universities within a short time of their founding, in the last quarter of the nineteenth century, but equal access at Oxford and Cambridge came much more slowly. Although women's colleges were founded at Oxford and Cambridge in the 1860s and 1870s, women did not receive degrees until the early 1920s, and they were not admitted to full privileges at Cambridge until 1948.

Virginia Woolf's family was a Cambridge family. Her father served as an ordained fellow and tutor there from 1855 to 1864; both of her brothers, Adrian and Thoby, went to Cambridge. Why did there never seem to be a thought of sending Virginia to Newnham or to Girton?

When Virginia Woolf writes about women's lack of access to higher education, she talks about money, and the disproportion of the money expended on sons' and daughters' educations. In *Three Guineas,* she symbolizes that disproportion in "Arthur's Education Fund," which figures in household ledgers to the disadvantage of daughters. "[T]he noble courts and quadrangles of Oxford and Cambridge," which family savings provide for the sons, translate into petticoats with holes in them and cold legs of mutton for the daughters (5–7). Could Virginia Woolf's family not have afforded to send her to Newnham or Girton? The fees for students at the Cambridge women's colleges at the turn of the century were less than one hundred pounds per year, including tuition, examination fees, and residence. When Leslie Stephen died in 1904 he left fifteen thousand pounds, a fortune that would seem to permit the several hundred pounds that a university education for Virginia would have required. However, he was irrationally anxious about money, and feared poverty, an attitude he would certainly have communicated to his family. Virginia Woolf felt that she was uneducated because her father didn't want to spend the money (Lee 146).

Some of Virginia Woolf's biographers have suggested that her mental fragility would have prohibited formal education. By 1900 she had experienced the first of her breakdowns, in 1895–96, after her mother's death. Quentin Bell's chronology reports that Virginia Woolf was allowed to start lessons again on 15 February 1897, only to have them stopped on the ninth of May, when Stella fell ill. However, in November of 1897 the chronology reports that she began attending classes at King's College, London, which she continued through 1900 (Bell 1: 190–92).

Finally, there is the question of her preparation. Was her education systematic enough to prepare her for a university course?

All of these questions are sufficiently individual to lead to questions more about the Stephens family than about the general availability of higher education for women. Indeed, when Woolf writes about education for women in *Three Guineas,* she casts it as a family issue. Arthur's Education Fund is a matter of domestic accounts. When she considers the question of whether to contribute to the rebuilding of a women's college in *Three Guineas*, she contrasts the education that the college offers with "the education of the private house" (55). In Woolf's imagination, the daughter's education takes shape from a family drama. In *Three Guineas,* when she considers Sophia Jex-Blake's struggle to enter the Royal College of Surgeons in Edinburgh in 1869 or women's continuing struggle to get degrees at Cambridge, she uses the metaphor of family: "Almost the same daughters ask almost the same brothers for almost the same privileges" (100). It is a contest of siblings. In *The Voyage Out,* Terrence Hewitt imagines the educational needs of his Cambridge friend, St. John Hirst, displacing his sister: "Can't you imagine the family conclaves, and the sister told to run out and feed the rabbits because St. John must have the school-room to himself" (213). The issue is economic. In *Three Guineas,* Woolf imagines the same old song the brothers and fathers sing: "Here we go round the mulberry tree, the mulberry tree, the mulberry tree [. . .] of property, of property, of property" (100). The titles of the two books that Woolf writes centrally concerned with education for women both identify the issue of property in their titles: *A Room of One's Own* and *Three Guineas.*

In *Three Guineas,* Woolf defines herself as an educated man's daughter. Both terms are important in the status that she sees herself possessing. She comes from a class with specific privileges and values—a class in which men have university educations and plan for their sons to have them as well. As Woolf writes in *Three Guineas,* the educated man's sister or daughter will speak with the same accent, have the same table manners, expect maids to do household work, and converse easily at the dinner table about politics and people. However, she does not have an independent identity as an educated woman, but a dependent identity fixed through family relationship. She can only receive the education that her father sees fit and agrees to fund.

With the exception of the lectures she attended in history, Greek, and Latin at King's College, London, and the private lessons she had in Greek starting in 1902 from Janet Case, one of the first Girton graduates, Virginia Woolf received all of her education at home. Leslie and Julia Stephen decided to teach all their children themselves, the boys going off at about the age of eleven to preparatory school. Perhaps Virginia's dependence on her father for lessons intensified her sense that education was a patriarchal dispensation, meted out in accordance with his standards and judgment. Despite her wide reading, and her instruction in Latin and Greek, Virginia Woolf always felt herself to be uneducated. She also felt deeply the lack of intellectual community. After Thoby had gone to Cambridge, she wrote to him, "I dont get anybody to argue with me now, and feel the want. I have to delve from books, painfully and all alone, what you get every evening sitting over your fire and smoking your pipe with Strachey etc. No wonder my knowledge is but scant. Theres nothing like talk as an educator I'm sure" (*Letters* 1: 77).

The sense of contrast that Virginia's letter to Thoby reflects between a woman's and a man's education deeply informs her imagination, and she frequently returns to it, often with considerable anger, particularly evident in her portrayal of men talking about women's education. In *The Voyage Out* she describes the effects of Rachel Vinrace's unsystematic, informal education in terms that must have had personal resonance: "But there was no subject in the world which she knew accurately. Her mind was in the state of an intelligent man's in the beginning of the reign of Queen Elizabeth" (34). St. John Hirst, one of the Cambridge-educated men Rachel meets on the voyage, sees her through the prism of her educational deprivation. He asks her, "About Gibbon, d'you think you'll be able to appreciate him? He's the test, of course. It's awfully difficult to tell about women, how much,

I mean, is due to lack of training, and how much is native incapacity" (154). In *Jacob's Room,* Woolf originally had devoted a section of the chapter about Jacob's Cambridge education to a contrasting portrait of a Newnham student, Angela Williams. (Those pages later became the short story "A Woman's College from Outside.") In *To the Lighthouse,* Woolf pairs the painter Lily Briscoe with Charles Tansley, the philosophical disciple of Mr. Ramsey. *A Room of One's Own* and *Three Guineas* are both structured through the opposition between men's and women's educations. Woolf's early manuscript of *The Years, The Pargiters,* makes the contrast far more prominent than *The Years* ultimately does between the educational opportunities available to the sons and daughters of the Pargiter family. In the second essay that she intersperses with the novel's chapters, Woolf asks, much as I did, why Milly, Delia, and Eleanor Pargiter didn't go to college. Woolf replies to her own question, "But, if you think for a moment, you will remember that the women's colleges were only just in existence; there was a great prejudice moreover against them" (*Pargiters* 28). She goes on to talk about the cost of educating the Pargiters' three sons and the way Delia's desire to be liked would keep her from making demands about her own education. "That was one of the reasons, then, why the Pargiter sisters stayed at home in 1880, and had violin lessons from Signor Morelli, a sad little man with great pouches under his eyes" (*Pargiters* 29). Woolf contrasts the experience of the daughters with that of their brother Edward at Oxford, studying Greek, and in the fourth essay writes at length about the contrast between schools like Eton, Harrow, and Winchester, and Mrs. Beale's day school for girls. The manuscript of *The Pargiters* shows that *Three Guineas* takes its shape from a family drama of the differential opportunities available to sisters and brothers.

In the contrast between men's and women's opportunities, she associates men with two attitudes somewhat in tension with each other. On the one hand, she portrays them as the unconscious and comfortable heirs of centuries of privilege, wearing an easy sense of authority. The chapter of *Jacob's Room* set at Cambridge ends with Jacob returning to his rooms, moving past the sites of male educational privilege:

> He went out into the court. He buttoned his jacket across his chest. He went back to his rooms, and being the only man who walked at that moment back to his rooms, his footsteps rang out, his figure loomed large. Back from the Chapel, back from the Hall, back from the Library, came the sound of his footsteps, as if the old stone echoed with magisterial authority: "The young man—the young man—the young man—back to his rooms." (46)

A Room of One's Own also connects rooms, footsteps, the chapel, the hall, and the library. Unlike Jacob, Virginia Woolf cannot walk freely, just as she cannot share in the easy privilege of the Oxbridge lunch, except by invitation.

In addition to the sense of easy privilege, however, Woolf also associates Oxbridge with an anxious, aggressive misogyny. When Jacob attends service at King's College Chapel, he compares women's taking part in the service to a dog's wandering down the aisle, lifting a leg by a pillar. "[A] dog destroys the service completely. So do these women." And he continues to think, "[T]hey're as ugly as sin" (*Jacob's Room* 33). Lily Briscoe imagines Charles Tansley's thinking, "Women can't write, women can't paint" (*To the Lighthouse* 130). Hirst asks Rachel Vinrace, "[C]an one really talk to you? Have you got a mind?" (*Voyage Out* 154). The men who turn Virginia Woolf off the grass and out of the library in *A Room of One's Own* motivate her own research project on men's beliefs about women's inferiority.

Women's long struggle for degrees at Cambridge and Oxford and for full privileges at the university provided ample justification for Woolf's critique. The timing of the most intense moments of the debate in relationship to Woolf's life and career may explain the role the issue plays in particular books. The debate was particularly bitter at Cambridge; because of the Cambridge ties of Woolf's family, she must have been aware of it. A memorial asking for admission to university membership and degrees at Cambridge was first circulated in the first months of 1896. The proposal was voted down 1,713 to 66, after eighteen months of bitter dispute and what one historian calls "unparalleled disruption of the university's academic life," in which the *Times* reported that "there was a degree of hostility 'previously unknown' in the attitude of the men toward the claims of the women" (Tullberg 112). The undergraduates celebrated the defeat with a night of riotous bonfires, fireworks, and fun, including a noisy procession to Newnham and the suspension from a Cambridge building of an effigy of a woman in bloomers riding a bicycle. The debate became prominent again in the years right after the First World War. In 1919 Parliament passed the Sex Disqualification Act, which permitted the ancient universities to matriculate women. Oxford quickly admitted women to degrees in 1920, but the debate at Cambridge was again protracted and bitter. A proposal admitting women to membership in the university was rejected in 1920; in 1921 a proposal admitting women to more limited rights was also rejected, although one giving women the titles of their degrees passed. The defeat was greeted with a riot, during which undergraduates chanted, "[W]e won't have women," and raced to Newnham, attacking and damaging its bronze gates (Tullberg 165). In 1926, through the intervention of Parliament, women were given a number of privileges, including admission to the library, but they did not receive full membership in the university until 1948. This debate, I believe, shapes Woolf's portrayal of Cambridge and of university privilege more generally.

Woolf characteristically expresses her anger at male educational privilege through caricature and satire. After she represents herself as chased off the grass and forbidden entrance to the library in *A Room of One's Own,* she describes the faculty assembling for chapel: "Many were in cap and gown; some had tufts of fur on their shoulders; others were wheeled in bath-chairs; others, though not past middle age, seemed creased and crushed into shapes so singular that one was reminded of those giant crabs and crayfish who heave with difficulty across the sand of an aquarium" (8). She characteristically moves from her anger to man's anger. In *A Room of One's Own,* she draws a caricature of Professor von X, the author of *The Mental, Moral, and Physical Inferiority of the Female Sex,* and recognizes her own anger in it. While rhetorically dismissing her own anger, she lets the caricature do its work. Indeed, she intensifies it as she dismisses it:

> My cheeks had burnt. I had flushed with anger. [. . .] One does not like to be told that one is naturally the inferior of a little man—I looked at the student next to me—who breathes hard, wears a ready made tie, and has not shaved this fortnight. [. . .] It is only human nature, I reflected, and began drawing cartwheels and circles over the angry professor's face till he looked like a burning

bush or a flaming comet—anyhow, an apparition without human semblance or significance. The professor was nothing now but a faggot burning on the top of Hampstead Heath. Soon my own anger was explained and done with. (32)

Explained maybe, done with, perhaps not. After this passage, Woolf proceeds to analyze male anger and to trace its roots to insecurity. By projecting onto male caricatures the distortion with which misogyny represents women, she at once exercises and exorcises her anger. Although she represents the privilege of education as one of coterie or class, she sometimes uses class prejudice to develop her caricatures of male educational presumption, as in her portrayal in the passage above of the young man sitting next to her or in her portrayal of Charles Tansley.

In her biography of Virginia Woolf, Hermione Lee argues that far from forming her writing under the influence of Cambridge graduates in the early years of Bloomsbury, she forms it in opposition to them (265). Woolf makes the deficiencies of her formal education into shaping elements of her vision. For the most part, Woolf educated herself through books. She was a voracious reader. "[B]ooks are the things that I enjoy—on the whole—most," she writes in her diary. She represented reading through a physical metaphor of incorporation. "I feel sometimes for hours together as though the physical stuff of my brain were expanding, larger & larger, throbbing quicker & quicker with new blood—& there is no more delicious sensation than this." Her consciousness becomes the center of an intellectual web. "I feel as though I had grasped the central meaning of the world, & all these poets & historians & philosophers were only following out paths branching from that centre in which I stand" (*Passionate Apprentice* 178–79).

When she begins to collect her literary essays, Woolf defines herself, as we all know, as "the common reader." Woolf distinguishes the common reader from the critic and the scholar; the common reader has no connection to any organized establishment of learning, or to the critical standards promoted therein. He or she is not well educated. But the common reader is an artist, guided by the instinct to create "some kind of whole—a portrait of a man, sketch of an age, a theory of the art of writing" (*Common Reader* 1). This instinct leads her to a sense of a common mind. She writes in her journal, "I think I see for a moment how our minds are all threaded together—how any live mind today is of the very same stuff as Plato's & Euripides. It is only a continuation & development of the same thing. It is this common mind that binds the whole world together; & all the world is mind" (*Passionate Apprentice* 178–79). Through her concept of the common reader and the common mind, Woolf separates philosophy and literature from an institutional tradition while she conjoins them to her imaginative experience.

It seems that such a concept of education would lend itself to democratic politics, but Woolf was ambivalent about class, and divided in an allegiance to her own class and one to all women. For about two years, from 1905 to 1907, Woolf taught working-class adults history and then composition at Morley College in London, but the experience was a mixed success. Woolf wrote with ambivalence about the project. In her report on the history class, she concludes, "Eight lectures dropped into their minds, like meteors from another sphere impinging on this planet, & dissolving in dust again. Such disconnected fragments will these eight lectures be: to people who have absolutely no power of receiving them as part of a whole, & applying them to their proper ends" (Bell 1: 204).

Yet Woolf's allegiance to her own class is deeply ambivalent. She sees status as a male privilege, conveyed and protected by university education, which controls access to the professions. In *Three Guineas,* she therefore gives the first of her guineas to rebuilding a college for women and the second to a society to help women enter the professions. Yet she does not want to join the procession of educated men, who are leading Europe to war. She defines herself as an outsider, educated by poverty, chastity, derision, and freedom from unreal loyalties. Thus Woolf's exclusion from formal university education leads not only to her concept of the common reader but also to her concept of the outsider. She transforms being locked out to being locked in, finding imaginative and political freedom in defining herself in opposition to the procession of educated men.

Where does that leave women's colleges? Woolf turns to the subject of women's colleges a number of times in her writing—in the original manuscript of *Jacob's Room,* in *A Room of One's Own,* in *Three Guineas,* and in the early drafts of *The Years.* She always associates women's colleges with poverty—the poverty of the institutions themselves, symbolized by the dinner of gravy soup, beef and greens, and prunes and custard at Fernham College in *A Room of One's Own,* and the poverty of the women who attend. Angela Williams, the central character of "A Woman's College from Outside," "was at Newnham for the purpose of earning her living" and could not forget "the cheques of her father at Swansea; her mother washing in the scullery" (*Complete Shorter Fiction* 145). When she returns from lecturing at Girton, where she read an early version of *A Room of One's Own,* Woolf writes in her diary, "Starved but valiant young women—that's my impression. Intelligent, eager, poor; & destined to become schoolmistresses in shoals" (*Diary* 3: 200). Woolf always talks about women's colleges from the outside, as an outsider to them. It's striking that Woolf entitles the cancelled pages from *Jacob's Room* "A Woman's College from Outside." The short story begins with the conceit of a Cambridge wind looking in at the college at night, but develops into a fantasy of the women moving out, free from hours, rules, and discipline, laughing together at night, leaning out of the window to imagine the world at the end of the tunnel. In *Three Guineas,* before Woolf gives the guinea to rebuild the women's college, she imagines burning the current college to the ground with rags, petrol, and matches, so that a new college, a poor college without advertisement, degrees, lectures, or sermons can be built from its ashes. Woolf imagines women's education as having the same values and characteristics as she evolves for her own intellectual life—learning for its own sake, without examinations, degrees, and honors, and the perspective of the outsider. Woolf did not share Sophia Smith's vision of a college for women as the equivalent of one for men. She wrote about women's colleges from the outside, and encouraged them to embrace the values of the outsider.

Woolf's sense of her exclusion from such an opportunity shaped her work in important ways, providing a basis for the opposition between male and female experience that is one of its structuring principles. When Virginia Woolf's nieces, Ann and Judith Stephen, Adrian's daughters, reached college age, they both went to Cambridge, destined for professions. In a generation, the assumptions of the private house, at least that of the Stephens, had changed in regard to women's education. Ann and Judith could have gone to Smith.

Works Cited

Bell, Quentin. *Virginia Woolf: A Biography*. New York: Harcourt Brace Jovanovich, 1972.

Lee, Hermione. *Virginia Woolf*. New York: Alfred A. Knopf, 1997.

Quesnell, Quentin. *The Strange Disappearance of Sophia Smith*. Northampton, MA: Smith College, 1999.

Tullberg, Rita McWilliams. *Women at Cambridge*. Cambridge: Cambridge University Press, 1998.

Woolf, Virginia. *The Common Reader*. New York: Harcourt & Brace, 1953.

---. *The Complete Shorter Fiction of Virginia Woolf*. Ed. Susan Dick. 2nd ed. San Diego: Harvest-Harcourt Brace Jovanovich, 1989.

---. *The Diary of Virginia Woolf*. Ed. Anne Olivier Bell. 5 vols. New York: Harcourt Brace Jovanovich, 1977–84.

---. *Jacob's Room*. New York: Harvest-Harcourt Brace Jovanovich, 1950.

---. *The Letters of Virginia Woolf*. Ed. Nigel Nicolson and Joanne Trautmann. 6 vols. New York: Harcourt Brace Jovanovich, 1975–80.

---. *The Pargiters: The Novel-Essay Portion of The Years*. Ed. and intro. Mitchell A. Leaska. New York: New York Public Library, 1977.

---. *A Passionate Apprentice: The Early Journals of Virginia Woolf, 1897–1909*. Ed. Mitchell A. Leaska. London: Hogarth Press, 1990.

---. *A Room of One's Own*. New York: Harcourt, Brace & World, 1957.

---. *Three Guineas*. New York: Harcourt, Brace and Company, 1938.

---. *To the Lighthouse*. New York: Harcourt, Brace & World, 1955.

---. *The Voyage Out*. New York: Harcourt, Brace & World, 1948.

"This Loose, Drifting Material of Life": Virginia Woolf and Biography

by Lyndall Gordon

Virginia Woolf's diary was like a capacious desk. Into it she would throw a mass of odds and ends: sketches of the great—Katherine Mansfield dragging herself across her room, like a suffering animal, or T. S. Eliot's dropped face hung on a scaffold of private brooding—together with gossip, rows with the cook, broodings over the next book, and always, rising to the surface, elegies for the dead and the insistent memory of summers at St. Ives in the early 1890s, the sound of the sea at night, the children running in the garden—"all built on that, permeated by that: how much so I could never explain" (*Diary* 2: 103).

She began the great diary at the age of thirty-three in October 1917. At the time, reviewing the posthumous volume of Henry James's autobiography, she decided that his memories are yet more wonderful than his novels (*Essays* 2: 168). Reading the first accumulations of her diary on 20 April 1919, she saw looming in her future "the shadow of some kind of form which a diary might attain to. I might in the course of time learn what it is that one can make of this loose, drifting material of life" (*Diary* 1: 266).

Fiction she saw as "the finished article"; the diary was "the raw," and the one was in some indirect way dependent on the fertility of the other. Her fiction depended on her keeping that fount of life going.[1] She castigated herself if she did not catch every drop in the diary. If eleven days went unrecorded, it was a lapse—"life allowed to waste like a tap left running" (*Diary* 1: 239). The diary catches up life as yet unshaped into art; it's life spurting, bathing her with scenes and people. Yet, if she lived indefatigably and recorded hugely, there remained, as she noted in James, "something incommunicable, something reserved"[2] (*Essays* 3: 205). This is the "loneliness of the artist's life" that the diary records every so often in "moments of being" or *non*-being. That essential condition of an imaginative life finds expression in a manuscript quotation from Chaucer's poem "Truth":

> Flee fro the prees,[3] and dwelle with sothfastnesse,
> Suffyce unto thy good, though hit be small. (Chaucer 1: 390)

Truth can't be found on show in the literary marketplace. It lives "[i]n darkness; in silence; where the face is hidden; and only the voice is heard."[4] Biography has not compassed a writer's life unless it takes a measure of this unseen space.

This talk will contrast the "loose, drifting material" of the writer's diary with composed portraits in her fiction, asking two questions: How did Woolf record her own life and what is her legacy to future biographers? She saw biography as a portrait, not as a compendium of fact. Her subject had to be composed as a work of art. Memories and facts were vital of course, but in the end only a guide to questions. Memory gave her the beam of the lighthouse, and using that beam, she asked a difficult question: What was her mother to *herself*? The beam strikes through the façades of the Victorian angel in the house to light up the inner life, the basis of the portrait Lily Briscoe is painting. It was an inspired stroke to let the beam of the lighthouse—"the third stroke"—catch Mrs. Ramsay, in a rare moment, alone. Imaginative truth had to inform remembered truth. When the portrait was published, Woolf's sister, Vanessa Bell, was amazed that such authenticity could be achieved by imagination more than by fact. Vanessa Bell wrote to her sister on 11 May 1927 (six days after publication):

> [I]t seemed to me that in the first part of the book you have given a portrait of mother which is more like her to me than anything I could ever have conceived possible. It is almost painful to have her so raised from the dead. [. . .] It was like meeting her again with oneself grown up and on equal terms and it seems to me the most astonishing feat of creation to have been able to see her in such a way. (Bell 317)

This is not the whole truth. *To the Lighthouse* does not show, for instance, the Mrs. Stephen who was stepmother to Laura Stephen and failed to rescue the girl from being put away for life in an asylum. A portrait as penetrating as that of Mrs. Ramsay has to be selective, and in that sense, subjective. In any case, there is no way, even if one wished, to tell the whole truth of any life: "Full-scale" biography (that formless, baggy monster) has been a delusion of the marketplace.

Given her commitment to the composed portrait, how did Virginia Woolf record her own life? She left nearly four thousand letters, thirty volumes of her diary, and unfinished memoirs. No writer's life can be so fully documented—and yet the writer continues to remain elusive. Her image shifts, and each image on its own can be somewhat reductive. The insistent modernity of the early 1920s was the image Woolf first imprinted on the public, with her jutting Man Ray photograph, all shorn hair, lipstick, and lifted chin. Yet methodological novelty (aligning her with Joyce and Proust) conceals continuity with the nineteenth century: the ordeal of consciousness as developed by George Eliot and Henry James. Everything in Virginia Woolf goes back to George Eliot's attunement to "that roar which lies on the other side of silence."[5] "I want to write a novel about Silence," says Terence Hewet in *The Voyage Out*, "the things people don't say. But the difficulty is immense" (216).

Parallel with modernity is the batty image constructed by Woolf's family. She played up to it, complicit with their agreements that "of course, the Goat's mad." One way of coping with bouts of "madness" was to pass them off as a form of amusing eccentricity. This image was reinforced by Woolf's flights of fancy at Bloomsbury parties, flaunting different colors according to her company. "How queer," she acknowledged, "to have so many different selves." We see this divergent Virginia Woolf in her letters. With their flights, exaggerations, and mockery, the letters are like her talk. This fantastical queen of Bloomsbury, so visible, so much recalled in the Bloomsbury memoirs of the 1960s and 1970s, was often emphasized at the expense of the novelist who is far more difficult to know and almost the opposite in character: not often malicious; rather, tenderly attentive to the recesses and caves behind the public character. The letters are, for the most part, flamboyant performances, the antics of an entertainer. Her correspondents are intimates or butts of her wit who, in an instant's caprice, can change places.

When her reputation began to drop in the mid-1930s, the irrationality of her public image—the hilarity that was modish in the twenties but out of place in the increasingly serious thirties—began to tell against her. With the rise of dictators, followed by the Second World War, she came to appear a frail, batty lady author, out of touch with the brutal world of politics. And so was born the myth of a precious aesthete withdrawn from the real world—the adverse image repeated through the forties, fifties, and early sixties.

This myth seemed to have been reversed with the advent of the women's movement in the 1970s. A new generation of readers appropriated Virginia Woolf for politics, the feminist author of *A Room of One's Own* and *Three Guineas* who promoted the struggle for women's rights. True—and yet, I'd suggest, only partially true. The libbers of the seventies and eighties who seized on her were at times disconcerted when she did not endorse their anti-domestic model.

The justified hurrah for Virginia Woolf as fighter for rights often misses a longer-term issue that suffuses her work from start to finish: the question of women's nature and what it might, in time, contribute to civilization. Women's nature is the subject of "The Mysterious Case of Miss V." (1906), which reappears as a proposition in *The Voyage Out* (1915) that it will take yet six generations for women to come into their own. Her picture of the fisherwoman who fishes for women's submerged desires in a speech of 1931 and the moonlit love-play in her honeymoon-and-after story, "Lappin and Lapinova" (1939), both tell us something about the "Night" in which the elusive Virginia Woolf dwelt.

For all the soaring of her reputation in the last three decades, there remains a curious insistence on narrowing her life to the woes of insanity and suicide, particularly evident in biographical plays, from Edna O'Brien in the late seventies to the movie of *The Hours*. There is a similar bias in treatments of other gifted women—the suicide of Sylvia Plath, that of Carrington in the 1995 movie directed by Christopher Hampton, and the mental decline of Iris Murdoch, going back to the brooding tombstones in Mrs. Gaskell's *Life of Charlotte Brontë*. In each instance, the effect is to distance the work in order to dwell instead on the sufferings that bring greatness down. Only at the end of the Carrington movie is her art trailed as a belated afterthought to sex and death. Seeing this again at Smith, after a passage of years, jolted the audience. This kind of covert misogyny (endorsed by willing females—the actresses who consented to play these parts) is hard to eradicate, as is a concurrent tendency to judge a woman by her flaws: Charlotte Brontë's perceived failure to be a lady by nineteenth-century standards of passionlessness;[6] Plath's excessive ambition by 1950s standards of femininity;[7] and Woolf's self-confessed snobbery and anti-Semitism, at present to the fore. As if this weren't bad enough, the movie of *The Hours* invents a Virginia who is horrid to her husband. It's not that genuine flaws should be ignored, but we need to be aware that flaws in men—say, Wordsworth's desertion of the pregnant Annette Vallon, Dickens's cruel manner of dismissing a wife who had borne him ten children, or Tolstoy's crazed religiosity and pseudo-humility—are still perceived differently, and appear incidental to starry reputations.

So, the woman writing has remained elusive. If the works are what we might go by, what is crucial lies in shadow; in Night as counter to Day; in what she kept out of sight. There, out of sight, was the hard-working professional. Virginia Woolf confided to a friend that she had to "be private, secret, as anonymous and submerged as possible in order to write."[8] In the shadow of legend, she held to herself as the "restless searcher."[9] She liked to imagine a voyage of discovery or the fin of a submerged form lurking in the waves. "Why is there not a discovery in life? Something one can lay hands on & say 'This is it'?" Each afternoon, when she took long walks, London itself beckoned as an unexplored land. Crossing Russell Square, close to home, she sensed "the infinite oddity of the human position" and felt, she said, "my own strangeness, walking on the earth" (*Diary* 3: 62).

Luckily for the biographer, the *Diary* does access that shadow life of the explorer, at least intermittently. As she grew older, in December 1940, it occurs to her that there has never yet been a woman's autobiography with the candor of Rousseau—a hint of what she might have done had she lived to write what she had always intended: to open up that capacious desk at the age of sixty, to find that all the "savings" had cohered into a new form; and then to write a great autobiography of sorts, a "masterpiece." This form would have penetrated the hidden life, as she put it in 1917, "the shadow in which the detail of so many things can be discerned which the glare of day flattens out."[10] *Night and Day* coincides with that focus on "shadow," an awareness of night, which biography too must elicit if it is going to venture beyond the limitations of daylight.

This brings me to the question of Virginia Woolf's legacy for future biographers. We need to balance the twentieth century's stress on Woolf's modernism with biographical aspects of her greatness that have yet to come fully into their own. There is her interest in the undefined elements of women's nature (not the routine feminism). This interest goes back to Mary Wollstonecraft whom Woolf pictures as a dauntless biographic creator who repeatedly makes the effort to invent a new plot of existence.

Woolf's commitment to undefined aspects of womanhood was bound up with a biographic impulse to explore the lives of the obscure. She broke with the march of verifiable fact as practiced by her father, Leslie Stephen, in the 378 lives (amounting to a thousand pages) that he contributed to the *Dictionary of National Biography* from 1885, when Virginia was three, until 1901, when she was nineteen. On 3 December 1923, in her forties, his daughter observes: "I shouldn't have been so clever, but I should have been more stable, without that contribution to the history of England" (*Diary* 2: 277). In a biographical dictionary subjects are chosen, of course, on the basis of public importance. Virginia Woolf inverts this in her essay "The Art of Biography" (1939):

> [T]he question now inevitably asks itself, whether the lives of great men only should be recorded. Is not anyone who has lived a life, and left a record of that life, worthy of biography—the failures as well as the successes, the humble as well as the illustrious? And what is greatness? And what smallness? (*Collected Essays* 4: 226–27)

So, she chose to write on Selina Trimmer who took up her duties as a governess in 1790; on Sara Coleridge who edited the works of her father, the poet; on Flush, the spaniel who shared the sickroom of Elizabeth Barrett and accompanied her when she eloped with Browning; and on Harriette Wilson who, as a courtesan (to, amongst others, the Duke of Wellington) lived the life of an outcast, winding "in and out among the bogs and precipices of the shadowy underworld" (*Collected Essays* 3: 230).

Woolf opened up the challenge of the obscure at the very start of her career in 1906, pushing the question of the unseen woman to its theoretical limit with "The Mysterious Case of Miss V." (It can't go unnoticed that the author, at this time, was herself an unknown Miss V.) Miss V. is a nonentity, the obscurest of the obscure who "cluster in the shade,"[11] a vanishing "shadow"—the word recurs like a refrain—a shadow of an unrecognized life, and one of those "rolled into the earth irrecoverably."[12] Miss V.'s polite platitudes about the weather provide no clue to "the real self." Her reported death seems to close off a biographical blank. Yet that blank reverberates beyond the record, as a challenge—"to track down the shadow, to see [. . .] if she lived, and talk to her" (*Complete Shorter Fiction*, 31). Virginia Stephen calls this a "mysterious case," in the language of Sherlock Holmes. It affirms that there is indeed a mystery to be detected, and she does venture to detect Miss V., if only by circling her absence, as she will go on to circle the absence of that representative of the lost generation of the Great War, Jacob, in *Jacob's Room* (1922). Like her brother Thoby, Jacob dies before his shape is clear. All through *Jacob's Room* his would-be biographer talks directly to the reader: We two push ourselves forward—busy, agog, distractible—while our subject slips from sight. The hopeful biographer is vibrating "at the mouth of the cavern of mystery, endowing Jacob Flanders with all sorts of qualities he had not at all [. . .]; what remains is mostly a matter of guess work. Yet over him we hang vibrating" (73).

The biographic obsession is comic in its futility. The deliberately fragmented narrative, with its gaps and tantalizing glimpses, compels us to share in the searcher's effort and failure. Jacob's room—his space, his leavings—should be full of clues. So it certainly would have been for Sherlock Holmes. The implied question is whether we can realistically deduce Jacob from his room, and the unfortunate answer is no. He remains a resonant absence—the most extreme form of elegiac loss.

Mrs. Ramsay, on the other hand, is all too present and visible in her role as angel of the house. To penetrate her flawless performance presents a different challenge to portraiture. The artist, Lily Briscoe, is visited by her subject at night.[13] Alone with Mrs. Ramsay in the dark bedroom, Lily "imagined how in the mind and heart of the woman [. . .] were [. . .] tablets bearing sacred inscriptions, which if one could spell them out, would teach one everything, but they would never be offered openly, never made public" (*To the Lighthouse* 51). Inscribed in women, written into her DNA in ways we can't yet read, is a hidden nature, tantalizing a biographer. The most original women in the past say this repeatedly. We hear Mary Wollstonecraft declare, "I am then going to be the first of a new genus [. . .]. I am not born to tread the beaten track—the peculiar bent of my nature pushes me on" (qtd. in Gordon 2 and Wardle 163–65). Or we hear, through Charlotte Brontë, Shirley's reply to a friend's questions about her nature: "In showing my treasure, I may withhold [. . .] a curious, unbought, graven stone [. . .] of whose mystic glitter I rarely permit even myself a glimpse" (Brontë 511). Even the advanced Shirley can barely discern certain closely guarded aspects of her self.

Lily paints Mrs. Ramsay as a wedge-shape of darkness. This shape marks a life that is "almost unclassified,"[14] an abstraction beyond the reach of language. What is so original in Woolf's approach to hidden lives is connected with her restraint. She doesn't rush in, at the ready, with modish psychologizing, textbook in hand. Instead, she injects a silence; it circles the untried spaces of character. Her silence is often used to register what is muted in women of the past. In 1930, in her introduction to the writings of working-class members of the Women's Cooperative Guild, she said: "These voices are beginning only now to emerge from silence into half-articulate speech. These lives are still half-hidden in profound obscurity" (*Collected Essays* 4: 148). She tells us how she would go through the alleys of London on her daily walk, "feeling in imagination the pressure of dumbness, the accumulation of unrecorded life."[15]

Virginia Woolf's works propose six biographic possibilities that could transform biography from a plodding genre and make it something of an art.

(1) Choose new, non-celebrity subjects who are worthy of record.

(2) Refuse to elide the gaps in the record with deceptive fullness of documentation. Seamless biography is a sham. We need to observe what lies in "shadow"—often what is most important.

(3) Question the traditional narrative. In *The Waves* Virginia Woolf invented a revolutionary treatment of the lifespan. Here, she is at her farthest remove from the traditional biographic schema, what she calls the Roman road: the public highway from pedigree to grave. Not only are there no pedigrees in *The Waves,* there are no placing surnames and no society to speak of, for here she explores the genetic givens of our existence, unfolding what is innate in human nature against the backdrop of what is permanent in nature: sun and sea. A novelist, Bernard, wishes, he tells his reader, "to give you my life." His life, and those of his five contemporaries, has an internal coherence, derived from innate infant traits. Compared with this, the set form of the lifespan—the chronology of birth, school, marriage, death—is, says Bernard, "a convenience, a lie" because it does not *see* beneath the platform of public action, the half-discernible acts on which a life turns (*The Waves* 238, 255).

(4) Attend to the shared element in lives, not merely predictable influence, but rather the way people create one another. Virginia Woolf brings out forms of creativity that lie beyond public record. Mrs. Ramsay's dinner, it's often said, is a work of art; so too, potentially, is the creative element in friendship, something Woolf gained from the Bloomsbury Group and built into *The Waves.*

(5) She didn't venture to apply her theories to her one formal, full-scale biography, *Roger Fry* (1940), because she felt obliged to the Fry family to present the kind of discreet portrait they would expect. In the course of writing this biography, she groaned under the burden of fact, much as her father had done in the 1880s, locked by his own rulings to the "drudgery" of "Dryasdust." Even so, the daughter, like the father, did exercise the selectivity she advocates in "The Art of Biography": "Almost any biographer, if he respects facts, can give us much more than another fact to add to our collection. He can give us the creative fact; the fertile fact; the fact that suggests and engenders" (*Collected Essays* 4: 228).

(6) "Invisible presences": All Woolf's works alert us to the presence of the dead who break through the limits of the lifespan (*Moments of Being* 80). There is, in truth, no end to the reverberations of far-reaching lives. Virginia Woolf points this out most cogently in her 1929 essay on Mary Wollstonecraft, who can't be dissociated from her daughters (not only her biological daughters, but her political daughters over subsequent centuries). "[O]ne form of immortality is hers undoubtedly: she is alive and active, she argues and experiments, we hear her voice and trace her influence even now amongst the living" (*Collected Essays* 3: 199).

These possibilities for biography suggest that the greater Virginia Woolf's work, the more completely it takes issue with her father's practice of biography as the founding editor of the *Dictionary of National Biography* during the first ten years of this daughter's life. At the age of five her elder brother, Thoby Stephen, produced a box, which he called his "contradictionary box." Asked the reason for its name, he said it was full of rubbish. Leslie Stephen discerned gleams of satire. In a sense, Virginia Woolf's whole oeuvre was contradictionary: her lives of the obscure; the intractable absence of the biographic subject who cannot be deduced from what he leaves behind in *Jacob's Room;* the unseen, inward life of Mrs. Ramsay, lit momentarily by the beam of the lighthouse; and invisible presences, the continuing presence of the dead, blurring the formal limits of the lifespan.

The supposed "golden age of biography" in the latter half of the twentieth century really looked back to the well-worn laborious path from pedigree to grave. By contrast, Woolf, advancing before us, looks to what's ahead: "The art of biography is still in its infancy," she observes in the second draft of *The Waves*, "or more accurately speaking, is yet to be born."

Notes

1. Epitomized later by Rhoda, "the nymph of the fountain always wet" in *The Waves*, by Virginia Woolf (New York: Harvest-Harcourt, 1959) 117.
2. Review in the *TLS*, 8 April 1920, of *The Letters of Henry James*. Reprinted in *The Essays of Virginia Woolf*, ed. Andrew McNeillie, vol. 3 (London: Hogarth, 1987) 205.
3. crowd
4. Draft of an essay on reviewing by Virginia Woolf, Monk's House Papers B11.c, University of Sussex Library.
5. George Eliot, *Middlemarch* (Oxford: Clarendon Press, 1986) 189.
6. Elizabeth Rigby, reviewing *Jane Eyre* soon after its publication in 1847, says that if this novel by Currer Bell is by a woman it must be one who has forfeited the society of her sex.
7. Anne Stevenson's 1989 biography, *Bitter Fame*, whispers, as it were, behind her hand to the reader: She was very *ambitious*.
8. Virginia Woolf, "To Ethel Smyth," 17 Sept. 1938, letter 3443 of *The Letters of Virginia Woolf*, ed. Nigel Nicolson and Joanne Trautmann, vol. 6 (New York: Harcourt, 1980) 272.
9. Virginia Woolf, 27 Feb. 1926 entry of *The Diary of Virginia Woolf*, ed. Anne Olivier Bell, vol. 3 (New York: Harcourt, 1977) 62. Woolf wrote this entry while writing *To the Lighthouse*.
10. Review of *The Middle Years* by Henry James. Reprinted in *Collected Essays* by Virginia Woolf, vol. 1 (New York: Harcourt, 1967) 270.
11. This phrase actually comes from a story of the same year, "Phyllis and Rosamond" in *The Complete Shorter Fiction of Virginia Woolf*, ed. Susan Dick (London: Hogarth Press, 1985) 17.
12. "Memoirs of a Novelist," a story of 1909, in *The Complete Shorter Fiction of Virginia Woolf*, ed. Susan Dick (London: Hogarth, 1985) 72.
13. A parallel scene in *Mrs. Dalloway* is when Mrs. Dalloway *sees* the suicide Septimus Warren Smith at midnight, when she enters the caves behind character, feeling her unaccustomed way into caverns of the hidden life.
14. Virginia Woolf, *A Room of One's Own* (San Diego: Harcourt Brace & Company, 1981) 85.
15. Woolf, *A Room of One's Own* 89.

Works Cited

Bell, Vanessa. *Selected Letters of Vanessa Bell*. Ed. Regina Marler. London: Bloomsbury, 1993.
Brontë, Charlotte. *Shirley.* Ed. Herbert Rosengarten and Margaret Smith. Oxford: Clarendon Press, 1979.
Chaucer, Geoffrey. *The Complete Works of Geoffrey Chaucer.* Ed. Walter W. Skeat. 2nd ed. Vol. 1. Oxford: Clarendon Press, 1899.

Eliot, George. *Middlemarch*. Ed. David Carroll. Oxford: Clarendon Press, 1986.

Gordon, Lyndall. *Vindication: A Life of Mary Wollstonecraft*. New York: HarperCollins, 2005.

Stevenson, Anne. *Bitter Fame: A Life of Sylvia Plath*. Boston: Houghton Mifflin, 1989.

Wardle, Ralph M., ed. *Collected Letters of Mary Wollstonecraft*. Ithaca: Cornell University Press, 1979.

Woolf, Virginia. *Collected Essays*. 4 vols. New York: Harcourt, Brace and World, 1967.

---. *The Complete Shorter Fiction of Virginia Woolf*. Ed. Susan Dick. London: Hogarth Press, 1985.

---. *The Diary of Virginia Woolf*. Ed. Anne Olivier Bell. 5 vols. New York: Harcourt Brace Jovanovich, 1977–84.

---. *The Essays of Virginia Woolf*. Ed. Andrew McNeillie. 4 vols. London: Hogarth Press, 1986–94.

---. *Jacob's Room*. San Diego: Harvest-Harcourt Brace & Company, 1978.

---. *The Letters of Virginia Woolf*. Ed. Nigel Nicolson and Joanne Trautmann. 6 vols. New York: Harcourt Brace Jovanovich, 1975–80.

---. *Moments of Being*. Ed. Jeanne Schulkind. Sussex: The University Press, 1976.

---. "Reviewers," ts. Monks House Papers B11.c. University of Sussex Library.

---. *A Room of One's Own*. San Diego: Harcourt Brace and Company, 1981.

---. *To the Lighthouse*. San Diego: Harvest-Harcourt Brace Jovanovich, 1981.

---. *The Voyage Out*. San Diego: Harvest-Harcourt Brace Jovanovich, 1968.

---. *The Waves*. New York: Harvest-Harcourt Brace Jovanovich, 1959.

Virginia Woolf's Double Signature

by Catherine W. Hollis

I'd like to begin this discussion of Virginia Woolf's double signature by looking at two different dust jackets for Hermione Lee's recent biography of Woolf. Biographies of authors frequently use their subject's name as a title, and dust jackets that use the author's signature as the lettering for the title not only convey the material presence of the author's hand, but also suggest a subtle validation of the biographer's work. The signature in effect "authorizes" the biography.

(Fig. 1: U.K. edition, Vintage, 1997) (Fig. 2: U.S. edition, Knopf, 1997)

The British edition of Lee's biography uses Woolf's handwriting as the lettering for her first name, suggesting intimacy, as though reading the biography would be something like receiving a letter from "Virginia." The dust jacket for the American edition of Lee's biography uses a similar strategy, but with a critical difference: Here the dust jacket uses Vanessa Bell's famous lettering for the Hogarth Press to represent Woolf's signature.

These different jacket designs raise interesting questions about marketing decisions for American and British readers of the Woolf biography. How many readers of the American edition are likely to recognize the lettering as Vanessa Bell's and not Virginia Woolf's? Do British readers—more familiar with Bell's style of lettering from the Hogarth Press editions of Woolf—require an "authentic" Woolfian signature? Although I cannot pursue these questions in this essay, I want to argue that, despite the different "hands," both signatures convey the material presence of Virginia Woolf, not only on the dust jacket, but also within the text itself.

Vanessa Bell's hand has functioned as an extension of Virginia Woolf's signature from the very earliest editions of Woolf's books issued by the Hogarth Press and continues to do so. Bell's lettering and cover designs for Woolf's books in particular and for the Hogarth Press more generally are still used to denote the Bloomsbury Group as a whole.[1] Virginia Woolf's Hogarth Press dust jackets are, in effect, "signed" by Vanessa Bell: sometimes in lowercase, always hand drawn, Bell's lettering functions as Virginia Woolf's authorial signature. Although Bell began initialing her designs in the 1930s, when the Hogarth Press began formally attributing her design on the jacket's inner leaf, some of the early books, such as *Jacob's Room* and *A Room of One's Own,* do not contain any attribution of the designer at all. Other Hogarth books that incorporate elements of design into the presentation of the text (*Kew Gardens, Orlando,* and *Flush* for instance) credit Bell with "decorations," "illustrations," or cover design. As is the case with the dust jacket for the American edition of Lee's biography, Bell's lettering suggests the material signature, or presence, of the author, while cloaking the actual inscriber of the author's name in partial anonymity.

In order to understand this complicated relationship between anonymity and authorship at play in Woolf's double signature, it is worthwhile to briefly review the family dynamics at work in the Hogarth Press. The Hogarth Press books were published by Virginia and Leonard Woolf, wrapped in dust jackets designed by Bell, Duncan Grant, and other artists associated with the Bloomsbury Group, and distributed to booksellers by the Woolfs themselves. From 1917 to 1939, the Hogarth Press was a constant presence in the Woolfs' home, moving from the drawing room to the basement as it grew into a commercial publishing company. The Press was the generative force in the Woolfs' marriage, producing books instead of children, growing at an astonishing rate, and moving with the Woolfs from house to house. J. H. Willis Jr., author of the most complete history of the Hogarth Press, finds the Woolfs "unique" in their physical and "personal need to remain close to their creation" (Willis 3). As a marital collaboration, the Hogarth Press functions both as a triangulating child and as a displaced source of the marriage's fertility, making books explicitly marked as the product of "Leonard and Virginia Woolf."[2]

The Hogarth Press was also an intrinsic component of Leonard Woolf's efforts to keep Virginia Woolf sane and healthy:

> The difficulty with Virginia was to find any play sufficiently absorbing to take her mind off her work. We were both interested in printing and had from time to time in a casual way talked about the possibility of learning to print. It struck me that it would be a good thing if Virginia had a manual occupation of this kind which, in say the afternoons, would take her mind completely off her work. (L. Woolf 233)

Although writing and typesetting are both "manual" occupations, inasmuch as both involve the inscription of words on a page, the former is an act of intellect and creativity, while the latter is repetitive, if not exactly mindless. The daily transition between the spheres of authorship and book production, writing in the morning and typesetting in the afternoon, seems to have given Woolf a mental balance conducive to her main task. Both work and play produced literature, but typesetting allowed Woolf the comparative relief of anonymous labor, of giving someone else's words material form (as in the example of Woolf setting the type for the Hogarth Press edition of T. S. Eliot's *Waste Land*). Further, the bustle of the Press was clearly attractive to Woolf after the solitude of writing:

"[W]e all run about the basement, distracted, henlike, with wisps of string, labels, brown paper, now answering the door—Please come in. Yes I'm the advertising manager. Yes we can give you 33½% on numbers over twelve" (V. Woolf, *Letters* 3: 121). Working at the Hogarth Press offered Woolf both anonymity and community, a relief from the solitary rigors of authorship.

In this relationship between anonymity and community, the Hogarth Press bears a significant relationship with Roger Fry's Omega Workshops (1913–1919). The Omega modernized the legacy of the Victorian Arts and Crafts Movement by producing goods and objects for the home that reflected Fry's belief that "the objects of daily life reveal and perpetuate the social and moral conditions of their creation" (Reed 169). Omega objects were produced anonymously and collectively by artists acting as artisans; similarly, the books of the Hogarth Press were produced by writers acting as publishers. The spirit of anonymity and collectivity, at Omega and at the Hogarth Press, dispenses with issues of credit and attribution. As the painters Duncan Grant and Vanessa Bell alternate between their signed art and their unsigned design, so Woolf alternates between the pressure of authorial creation and the comparative relief of anonymous production. The "making" instinct is exercised, but the ego is removed from the process.

Vanessa Bell's relative anonymity as a book designer is a precondition for Woolf's double signature on the Hogarth Press dust jackets. The scholar Jane Dunn, who along with Diane Gillespie has devoted the most critical attention to Bell's dust jackets, summarizes the relationship between Woolf's text and Bell's cover design as follows: "The book, often the result of years of unremitting labour, anguish and exhilaration, and preferred to her public in trepidation, was protected and promoted by a cover which appeared to be the happy result of an afternoon's work in a summer studio with birds singing" (Dunn 161). I like this description of the tension between the agony of the author and the lightness of Bell's cover designs, which most often featured flowers, birds, and other cheerful objects, and quote it because I think it helps explain why Woolf's authorial signature is written in her sister's hand. The dust jacket literally and symbolically protects the book that it covers: The solitude of the individual author is bolstered by an enmeshment in collaborative production practices. Virginia Woolf may have been notoriously thin-skinned about reviews of her texts, but—as material objects—her books are well armored.

Vanessa Bell's anonymity as the inscriber of her sister's name is relative, not absolute. Despite Vanessa Bell's subordination to Woolf on the dust jackets, her presence is still palpable. Vita Sackville-West evokes this double signature when she writes Woolf a letter about seeing a woman in the street carrying a copy of *To The Lighthouse:* "I saw your name staring at me, Virginia Woolf, against the moving red buses, in Vanessa's paraph of lettering" (Sackville-West 217). A paraph is a flourish made after a signature, specifically to prevent forgery. Bell isn't forging Woolf's signature, but rather uniting the two properties (Woolf's name, Bell's lettering of it) into a recognizable autograph. Woolf's first generation of readers expects the unique book design provided by Bell for the Hogarth Press; and so Bell's lettering functions as a guarantor of the authenticity of Woolf's authorial name. Significantly, as Sackville-West's comment indicates, both Virginia and Vanessa are distinctively present in this emblem of their collaboration, making the signature double.

The convergence of names is most evident (and playful) in Bell's design for the dust jacket for *A Room of One's Own.* This is an example of one of Bell's anonymous cover designs.

Although she had not read the text, she did take great care with this design, filling "a whole sketchbook with ideas" (Bradshaw 17). Both title and author's name are written in lowercase lettering, which accentuates the "amateur" qualities of the Hogarth Press book, its personal, homemade style. Virginia Woolf's comment on this cover design is as ambiguous as the image itself: "I thought your cover most attractive—but what a stir you'll cause by the hands of the clock at that precise hour! People will say—but theres no room" (V. Woolf, *Letters* 4: 81). Woolf's coyness suggests but doesn't directly state what is most often remarked upon, that the hands of the clock form the initial "V," for Virginia, for Vanessa, and for Vita Sackville-West as well. (Jane Marcus, among other scholars, suggests the rich variety of possible readings of the "V.") The "V" on the dust jacket, I would argue, is a collective signature for these three women, for their involvement with the Hogarth Press in general and with *A Room of One's Own* in particular. Vita Sackville-West was the Hogarth Press's best-selling author; Vanessa Bell the designer of its "house style"; Virginia Woolf its founder and beneficiary. Woolf's much-discussed intellectual freedom as a self-publishing author is signified by the central placement of the "V." In my reading, "V" functions as the multiple signature of women

(Fig. 3: Hogarth Press, 1929)

who have access to the means of producing their own work, a small but significant step toward defeating the forces of censorship and commerce that limit women's ability to write and be published. Although Woolf's debt to the Hogarth Press goes unelaborated in the text of *A Room of One's Own,* it is visually inscribed on the surface of the book itself by the "V," which serves as a gendered marker of the convergence of two kinds of literary labor: the creative or intellectual, and the material.[3]

We tend not to associate Virginia Woolf with the idea of literary collaboration. Because Woolf's novels were self-published, and therefore subject to no external editorial intervention, they are, remarkably, the autonomous product of an individual author's mind. But if we define collaboration as the process of signing two names to one work of art, then Woolf's Hogarth books are, as material objects, satisfyingly collaborative. Woolf's double signature on the Hogarth Press editions of her work, as well as on the American edition of Hermione Lee's biography, reminds us of the interrelationship between Woolf the author and Woolf the publisher, and of the collaborative family network that originally produced these books. Further, this double signature is another reminder of the fertile paradox of anonymity and community so compelling to Woolf herself.

Notes

[Illustrations of the jacket covers used by permission of the Random House Group Limited]

1. Tony Bradshaw calls Bell's hand lettering the "house style" of the Hogarth Press and uses it on the dust jacket of his own catalog of the Bloomsbury artists (p. 18).
2. The byline, "published by Leonard and Virginia Woolf at the Hogarth Press," appears on the title page of early Hogarth Press books and is what Gerard Genette calls "paratext": "what enables a text to become a book and to be offered as such to its reader" (p. 1). These kinds of material signifiers are increasingly being examined by book historians and textual scholars as hermeneutically significant.
3. Although Woolf was privately willing to acknowledge that owning and operating the Hogarth Press ensured her intellectual freedom, she does not include a printing press among the catalog of "material things" necessary for women's writing (the infamous room of one's own and £500 a year). This is a striking omission in a text otherwise concerned with encouraging women writers. However, if one reads Woolf's text (i.e., the essay itself) within the context of its material manifestation as a Hogarth Press book, Woolf's argument extends from text to book. This is one reason (among many) why Woolf's texts need to be read and analyzed in conjunction with Bell's cover designs.

Works Cited

Bradshaw, Tony. *The Bloomsbury Artists: Prints and Book Design.* Aldershot: Scolar Press, 1999.

Dunn, Jane. *A Very Close Conspiracy: Vanessa Bell and Virginia Woolf.* Boston: Little Brown, 1990.

Gillespie, Diane F. *The Sisters' Arts: The Writing and Painting of Virginia Woolf and Vanessa Bell.* Syracuse: Syracuse University Press, 1988.

Genette, Gerard. *Paratexts: Thresholds of Interpretation.* Cambridge: Cambridge University Press, 1997.

Lee, Hermione. *Virginia Woolf.* London: Vintage, 1997.

---. *Virginia Woolf.* New York: Alfred A. Knopf, 1997.

Marcus, Jane. Virginia Woolf, Cambridge and *A Room of One's Own.* London: Cecil Woolf Publishers, 1996.

Reed, Christopher, ed. *A Roger Fry Reader.* Chicago: University of Chicago Press, 1996.

Sackville-West, Vita. *The Letters of Vita Sackville-West to Virginia Woolf.* Ed. Louise DeSalvo and Mitchell A. Leaska. New York: Morrow, 1985.

Willis, J. H. Jr. *Leonard and Virginia Woolf as Publishers: The Hogarth Press, 1917–41.* Charlottesville: University Press of Virginia, 1992.

Woolf, Leonard. *Beginning Again: An Autobiography of the Years 1911 to 1918.* New York: Harcourt, Brace and World, 1964.

Woolf, Virginia. *The Letters of Virginia Woolf.* Ed. Nigel Nicolson and Joanne Trautmann. 6 vols. New York: Harcourt Brace Jovanovich, 1975–80.

Virginia Woolf and Vanessa Bell as Photographers: "The Same Pair of Eyes, Only Different Spectacles"

by Maggie Humm

Writing to Vanessa Bell in 1937, Woolf imagined: "Do you think we have the same pair of eyes, only different spectacles?"[1]

I want to start where I left off at a previous Woolf conference when I focused entirely on Woolf's albums, to explore more generally issues of the maternal and the erotic in both sisters' albums. The principles of selection, montage, and tableau in albums are the skeleton of a story. Psychoanalytically speaking, albums are often a testimony to our unconscious pasts rather than the pasts we consciously choose to remember. Memories are the "presence without representation," Jean-François Lyotard calls "the stranger in the house," representing an individual incapacity to "represent and bind a certain something"—a something that "can introduce itself there without being introduced, and would exceed its powers" (16–17). For me, as I have argued elsewhere, it is the 1892 photograph of Woolf's seated mother and father with Woolf in the background mounted as a significant frontispiece in Monk's House album 3 that "exceeds its powers" and shapes Woolf's photography.[2] Bell's albums also focus on the unrepresentable, on the immemorial, as Lyotard argues, "the immemorial [is] always 'present'" (20).

Obviously modernist aesthetics could determine both sisters' sequential montages. The modernity of the albums *is* striking and must owe something to Bell's and Woolf's knowledge of modernism, including Cézanne's painting series and Russian and German cinema. Both sisters' use of composite images, the recognition that the process of construction is part of the content of a constructed piece synchronizes with other modernist developments in the 1920s and 1930s, such as John Heartfield's montages. Techniques of juxtaposition are featured in popular culture, including advertising as well as high art.[3] Cézanne was the central attraction at Roger Fry's 1910 postimpressionist exhibition. Fry claimed that Cézanne sought to express emotion, not mimetically, but precisely through spatial relationships.[4] It is true that the most interesting albums were being constructed during the period of Bell's and Woolf's "strongest commitment to formalism" with its antimimetic aesthetic.[5] Yet, while both sisters' albums, in some respects, reveal them to be enthusiastic modernists, in other respects they are too repetitious, too obsessive to be cataloged simply as modernist. The photomontages in the albums suggest that some other preoccupation, whether conscious or unconscious, informs a modernist façade. Like a palimpsest, the album sequences offer a crucial insight into those psychic mechanisms structuring Woolf's aesthetics. In Lacanian terms, the sisters' continual photographic repetitions would suggest the "return" of a visual event that took place outside their contemporary frames. As Lacan suggests: "The real is that which always comes back to the same place."[6]

I. Virginia Woolf

Woolf's mother, Julia, becomes her "stranger in the house." For Woolf's father, Leslie, and Woolf, Julia "lived in me, in her mother, in her children, in the many relations and friends whom she cheered and helped."[7] Crucially, Stephen explicitly memorializes the exact photograph that Virginia avidly highlights in the opening of Monk's House album 3:

"When I look at certain little photographs—at one in which I am reading by her side at St. Ives with Virginia in the background [...]—I see as with my bodily eyes the love, the holy and tender love" (Stephen, *Mausoleum* 58–59). The connotative power of Julia's image shapes both father's and daughter's "wider circles of reflections."[8] It is the visual language of this particular photograph, what we might call its trauma fragments, I will argue, that determines Woolf's own photographic constructions. Details of the 1892 childhood photograph appear again and again in Woolf's photo sequences. Many contain a tall flower, usually a lily, placed immediately behind the head of the subject mirroring the flowers behind the Stephens at St. Ives.

There are similar quiet connections and discontinuities between the sisters' albums. Both Vanessa and Virginia are drawn to the maternal. Pregnant, Vanessa fantasizes to Virginia that "I [. . .] shall see you every day and gaze at the most beautiful of Aunt Julia's photographs [that of their mother] incessantly" (Bell, *Selected Letters* 67). Later, in 1927, she pleads with Virginia to "write a book about the maternal instinct. In all my wide reading I haven't yet found it properly explored" (315). Both shared a Bloomsbury party visit to a film of a caesarean section. Vanessa wrote to her son Quentin in 1931: "Really it was quite the oddest entertainment I've ever been to [. . .] Leonard felt very ill" (361–62).

All photographs are a language and Woolf's language was maternal. "She has haunted me," Woolf wrote to Vita Sackville-West in 1927 (*Letters* 3: 374). Woolf literally wrote "through" the maternal. "Here I am experimenting with the parent of all pens—the black J. *the* pen, as I used to think it, along with other objects, as a child, because mother used it" (*Diary* 1: 208). Woolf realized that this pictorial enthusiasm raised complex epistemological questions about the psychoanalytic: "[I]t is a psychological mystery why she should be: how a child could know about her; except that she has always haunted me" (*Letters* 3: 383). Julia Stephen's early death meant that, to Woolf, she became the phantasmic mother, that is a mother who can exist only as an image, who can be seen or mirrored only in identifications and who might incite the imagination (of a photographer) into hallucinatory significations.[9] Hermione Lee argues that the family was Woolf's "political blueprint" and I would argue that the death of her mother gave Woolf a visual blueprint (52). In *Moments of Being,* Woolf describes how it was her mother's death that "made me suddenly develop perceptions" (Woolf, 1985, 93). In a chapter entitled "The Dead Mother" (which includes depressed and absent mothers), André Green suggests that the "mirror identification" with the mother "is almost obligatory" (151). Green suggestively discusses the history of psychoanalytic concepts in relation to the arts. The mother is a "framing-structure" for the child who projects its feelings back onto the mother through "revivifying repetitions" (159).

II. VANESSA BELL

Frances Spalding suggests that Vanessa Bell's paintings similarly revive the maternal. *The Nursery* (inspired by *To the Lighthouse*) and *Nursery Tea* have two groups of female figures contained within a circle creating "a nostalgic evocation of motherhood" (Spalding 251). Bell evokes the maternal with spatial arrangements of objects, strong verticals, and monumental figures of women very like Virginia's photo sequences. It could be argued that both sisters "refuse" their mother's death by constantly revivifying the maternal in art. In addition, Bell's photographs disrupt their own singular authority through the narrative contexts of the albums and through the kind of psychic stories that meta-texts like albums can tell. In a sense, Bell's very eclecticism, together with her devotion to seriality, provides a key to answering questions about gender and modernism. What I think we witness in the albums of Virginia and Vanessa are the tensions of gendered modernism. Reality is a necessarily more contingent force in the thinking of women artists and writers and in the ways in which this contingency might be represented artistically in repetitive, as well as eclectic forms, particularly in photography. Family albums fit uncomfortably into the conventions of photographic theory, which tend to fetishize the individual photograph and the photographer. Albums are repetitive, feminine forms (inasmuch as albums are most often constructed by women) not collections of seminal, masculine images.[10] In addition, as Walter Benjamin suggests, the enlargement of snapshots (Bell's constant album activity), reveals "entirely new structural formations of the subject [. . .] the camera introduces us to unconscious optics as does psychoanalysis to unconscious impulses" (238–39).

Bell's photographs are familial and autobiographically revealing because they project psychological intensity. Two photographs vividly encapsulate this theme. Album 1 in the Tate Archive contains photographs of Clive Bell, Vanessa's husband, together with Virginia Woolf taken at Studland Beach in 1910 (Humm fig. 22–23). In both photographs, Clive and Virginia collude with Vanessa's gaze, but both Clive and Virginia are passive and unsmiling. If we take the idea of each photograph as an image operative in terms of psychic signs we can look at what the patterns and arrangements of signs might reveal about Bell. In each scene the figures almost exactly mirror each other in positionality. Both sitters have right arms parallel to lower legs and both bend their right legs at the same angle, reinforced by a pairing of shoes to the right of the frame. In one photograph the raised seams of Virginia's gloves parallel the swollen veins of Clive's downward pointing hands. Such parallelism and repetition suggest a psychic "excess."

In "Perverse Space," an essay about fetishism, the "gaze," and Helmut Newton's photograph *Self-portrait with wife June and models, Vogue Studio, Paris 1981,* the photography theorist Victor Burgin calls a similar parallelism in Newton's photograph "the subsidiary and 'combined figure' of chiasmus ('mirroring')" or a rhetorical structure in a photograph, which Burgin argues we sometimes recognize only "intuitively" (224). Similarly, Bell's photographs depict Clive's and Virginia's bodies not only realistically but also indexically as if Clive and Virginia's relationship is being represented by Bell. After the birth of Vanessa's first child, Julian, in February 1908, Clive and Vanessa interrupted their sex life and Clive began to flirt with Virginia. Hermione Lee suggests that from this time—May of 1908—they began to play a game of intimacy and intrigue that lasted for perhaps two years, that is until the Studland photographs of 1910 (249). W. J. T. Mitchell suggests in *Picture Theory,* an account of the literary and textual aspects of picture theories, that photographs can materialize a "memory trace embedded in the context of personal associations" (289).

Family tableaux and window framing are common pictorial devices that show Bell's understanding of artistic codes. But Bell's repetitions and enlargements of particular photographs suggest the presence of other tensions than simply Bell's facility in translating painting codes into photography. Why did Bell need to represent herself as Madonna so frequently? Why are window frames so deliberately evident? As Frances Spalding points out, the window motif "may reflect on her need for domestic security and on the protected position from which, because of her sex and class, she viewed the world" (153). But also the photograph of her mother, Julia Stephen, which Bell treasured most of all, is a photograph in which Julia is leaning against a window (Richardson pl. 5). There is a constant synchronization of the psychic, the pressure of the autobiographical, together with art conventions throughout Bell's work. To try to fit Bell's repeated photographic and pictorial motifs neatly within a formal modernism negates the pressure of the psychic, which equally shapes Bell's work. It is as if two languages often coexist in the photographs. As Roland Barthes argues in his analysis of photographic messages, photographs can create a "free exchange" of messages. Barthes examines the way in which photographs always contain "denotation," that is, mythical encoded messages, and "connotation" or specific messages (19). Bell's photographs problematize modernist connotations with autobiographical denotation.

The maternal and the erotic also inform Bell's photographs of her children. A fresh and powerful engagement with issues of childhood in literature, the arts, and education marks Bell's moment of modernity. As Jonathan Fineberg points out in *The Innocent Eye,* there were many exhibitions of children's art at the turn of the century and artists looked at how children drew "as a stimulus to their own work" (12). The American modernist photographer Alfred Stieglitz promoted an exhibition of children's drawings in 1912 at his Little Galleries, Fifth Avenue, which "was like a commentary on modern art ideas, it recalled some elemental qualities that art has lost and which might do much, if attainable at all, to imbue it with a fresh and exquisite virility."[11] In 1917 Roger Fry wrote articles and exhibition catalogs promoting children's drawings collected by their tutor, Marion Richardson. Almost all the modernist artists, including expressionists, cubists, futurists, and the artists of the avant-garde Russian movements, hung the art of children alongside their own pioneering exhibitions in the early years of the century. Modernist photography shared this enthusiasm. For example, Edward Weston made nude studies of his children, particularly *Torso of Neil* (1925). Clarence White placed naked boys in classical settings in his *Boys Wrestling* (1908) and Alice Boughton made nude compositions of children in *Nude* (1909).

Bell was intensely interested in early childhood development and education and attempted to set up and teach a nursery school at Charleston. Together with Clive Bell, Vanessa painted a nursery at 33 Fitzroy Square. But the first and most important thing to say about Bell's photographs of her naked son Julian, as well as those of her other children, Quentin and Angelica, is that Bell only really begins to photograph her son naked as a young male, approximately seven or eight years old. In album 2 there are erotic photographs of Julian alone spread-eagled across the French windows at Asheham, emphasizing the spectacular quality of his to-be-looked-at young, firm body (Humm fig. 28). Other powerful photographs, again taken at Asheham in 1914, place Julian in chiaroscuro, half-hidden under a shadow of dappled leaves just touching his penis (Humm fig. 29). Sunlight falls on Julian's belly, and his face is partly in shadow. The photograph does foreground what Abigail Solomon-Godeau calls a typical erotics of the fragmentary. That is to say, the photograph isolates parts of Julian's body in a sexually coded way—a common convention in pornographic photography.[12] Two slightly later photographs continue to utilize these devices. In one, Julian stands, legs apart, pensively looking downwards away from the camera while sunlight falls fully on his naked figure (Humm fig. 30). In the other, Julian and Quentin are rolling naked together on the lawn with Julian poised over Quentin, lips distended as if to kiss (Humm fig. 31). The whiteness of both boys' bodies gives each child a further to-be-looked-at specular quality. Such photographs evoke what Jacqueline Rose describes as "the necessary presence of the one who is watching" (31). In a later photograph, Angelica's friend Judith Bagnell is photographed lying prone, her arm obscuring her face (Humm fig. 32). She is objectified, as it were "available" to a spectator's gaze since Bell obliterates any specificity of daily objects and clothes. Quentin Bell remembers the chemist Boots's refusal to print certain of Bell's photographs: "Would Mrs Bell please mark those rolls of film which contained images unsuitable for the eyes of the young ladies."[13]

The last decade dramatically highlighted issues about the representations of children's naked bodies and how we should spectate or not spectate such bodies. The problematic nature of spectating naked children currently occupies many disciplines, including psychoanalysis and legal studies, as well as art history. Many contemporary women photographers, such as Sally Mann, Alice Sims, and Susan Copen Oken, also frequently use their own children and friends' children as naked models. Sally Mann photographs the daily lives of her three children in intimate poses and scenes. Mann's photographs, like Bell's, "explore the nature of family love, *maternal* love and child response" through sequencing the developmental processes of childhood.[14]

Similarly, Bell's children are clearly comfortable in her world. Bell's photographs of childhood narcissism could as easily be read as reflecting back to the child the narcissism he or she so earnestly desires and needs to perform. Jacqueline Rose argues that writing for children "is an act of love. It is a way of 'knowing' the child. Loving the child and knowing the child—the idea is one of an innocent attachment" (20). Bell photographs reciprocal moments, interconnections between her children and between Bell and her children. Each child seems to exchange what anthropologists would call the intersubjective moment. There is no soft focus, no glycerin, and no muslin obscuring their world. Bodies are not isolated in tight spaces, subjected to harsh illumination or an unreturnable gaze.

Often in Bell's photographs it is children, not adults, who have an active gaze; for example, in the photograph of a naked Angelica standing next to the fully clothed Roger Fry (Humm fig. 34). Angelica looks actively at Fry while Fry is carefully *not* observing the naked girl. The photograph does not center any implied relation between clothed adult male and naked girl since Fry avoids the gaze. Kaja Silverman describes how, psychoanalytically, the mother/daughter relationship is one of identification and desire and the endless interchangeability of their positions.[15] Reading Bell's photograph from within Silverman's framework it could be said that the photograph rather than being voyeuristic shows the possibility of interchangeable subject/object viewing positions with Angelica *substituting* for Bell. Vanessa might be describing Angelica as a self-surrogate in a letter to Roger Fry in 1923: "I send you a photograph of myself and Angelica to remind you at any rate that there is *one* very lovely *and* witty *and* brilliant *and* charming creature to be seen in Gordon Square" (Bell, *Selected Letters* 273). Modernism offered Bell aesthetic coordinates, and by aestheticizing the potential voyeurism of camera/spectator Bell is able to safely handle the potentially erotic image.

Woolf's and Bell's albums are marginal to conventional art history but are a particularly pertinent site of the struggle between the public and the private, between the formally expressive and the everyday moment, which occur in other modernist women's work. Their photography brings into modernism's formalism and aesthetic unity the autobiographically repetitive and other identifications. As Luce Irigaray suggests, identification is never simply active or passive, but rather frustrates that opposition by the economy of repetition that it puts into play.[16] From a feminist perspective, it could be argued that the sisters perhaps turned so frequently to photography because photography allowed them the freedom of vision.

Notes

[Vanessa Bell's 1892 photograph of a young Virginia Woolf behind her parents reading reproduced courtesy of Henrietta Garnett © 1961 Estate of Vanessa Bell]

1.   Virginia Woolf, "To Vanessa Bell," 17 Aug. 1937, letter 3294 of *The Letters of Virginia Woolf*, ed. Nigel Nicolson and Joanne Trautmann, vol. 6 (New York: Harcourt, 1980) 158.
2.   Maggie Humm, *Modernist Women and Visual Cultures: Virginia Woolf, Vanessa Bell, Photography and Cinema* (Edinburgh: Edinburgh University Press, 2002) 44.
3.   Diane Collecott, "Images at the Crossroads: The 'H.D. Scrapbook,'" *H.D.: Woman and Poet*, ed. Michael King (Orono, ME: National Poetry Foundation, 1986) 321–67.
4.   Simon Watney, *English Post-Impressionism* (London: Studio Vista, 1980) 7.
5.   Christopher Reed, "Through Formalism: Feminism and Virginia Woolf's Relation to Bloomsbury Aesthetics" *The Multiple Muses of Virginia Woolf*, ed. Diane F. Gillespie (Columbia: University of Missouri Press, 1993) 21.
6.   Jacques Lacan, *The Four Fundamental Concepts of Psychoanalysis*, ed. Jacques-Alain Miller, trans. Alan Sheridan (New York: Norton, 1978) 42.
7.   Leslie Stephen, *Mausoleum Book* (Oxford: Clarendon Press, 1977) 58.
8.   Shoshana Felman and Dori Laub, *Testimony: Crises of Witnessing in Literature, Psychoanalysis, and History* (New York: Routledge, 1992) 71.

9. Mary Jacobus, *First Things: The Maternal Imaginary in Literature, Art and Psychoanalysis* (New York: Routledge, 1995).

10. *Family Snaps: The Meaning of Domestic Photography*, ed. Jo Spence and Patricia Holland (London: Virago, 1991).

11. Sadakichi Hartmann, "The Exhibition of Children's Drawings" *Camera Work: The Complete Illustrations 1903–1917*. Ed. Simone Philippi and Ute Kieseyer (Köhn: Taschen, 1997) 644.

12. Abigail Solomon-Godeau, *Photography at the Dock: Essays on Photographic History, Institutions, and Practices* (Minneapolis: University of Minnesota Press, 1991).

13. *Vanessa Bell's Family Album*, comp. Quentin Bell and Angelica Garnett (London: Jill Norman & Hobhouse, 1981) 10.

14. Reynolds Price, "Afterword" *Immediate Family* (London: Phaidon, 1992).

15. Kaja Silverman, *The Threshold of the Visible World* (New York: Routledge, 1996).

16. Luce Irigaray, *Speculum de l'autre femme* (Paris: Editions de Minuit, 1974) 77.

Works Cited

Barthes, Roland. *Image, Music, Text*. Trans. Stephen Heath. New York: Hill and Wang, 1977.

Bell, Vanessa. *Selected Letters of Vanessa Bell*. Ed. Regina Marler. London: Bloomsbury, 1993.

Benjamin, Walter. *Illuminations*. Ed. Hannah Arendt. Trans. Harry Zohn. [London]: Fontana/Collins, 1973.

Burgin, Victor. "Perverse Space." *Sexuality & Space*. Ed. Beatriz Colomina. New York: Princeton Architectural Press, 1992.

Family Snaps: The Meaning of Domestic Photography. Ed. Jo Spence and Patricia Holland. London: Virago, 1991.

Felman, Shoshana, and Dori Laub. *Testimony: Crises of Witnessing in Literature, Psychoanalysis, and History*. New York: Routledge, 1992.

Fineberg, Jonathan David. *The Innocent Eye: Children's Art and the Modern Artist*. Princeton, NJ: Princeton University Press, 1997.

Gillespie, Diane F. *The Multiple Muses of Virginia Woolf*. Columbia: University of Missouri Press, 1993.

Green, André. *On Private Madness*. Madison, CT: International Universities Press, 1986.

Humm, Maggie. *Modernist Women and Visual Cultures: Virginia Woolf, Vanessa Bell, Photography and Cinema*. Edinburgh: Edinburgh University Press, 2002.

Irigaray, Luce. *Speculum de l'autre femme*. Paris: Editions de Minuit, 1974.

Jacobus, Mary. *First Things: The Maternal Imaginary in Literature, Art, and Psychoanalysis*. New York: Routledge, 1995.

Lacan, Jacques. *The Four Fundamental Concepts of Psychoanalysis*. Ed. Jacques-Alain Miller. Trans. Alan Sheridan. New York: Norton, 1978.

Lee, Hermione. *Virginia Woolf*. London: Chatto & Windus, 1996.

Lyotard, Jean-François. *Heidegger and "the jews."* Trans. Andreas Michel and Mark S. Roberts. Minneapolis: University of Minnesota Press, 1990.

Mann, Sally. *Immediate Family*. Afterword Reynolds Price. London: Phaidon, 1992.

Mitchell, W. J. Thomas. *Picture Theory: Essays on Verbal and Visual Representation*. Chicago: University of Chicago Press, 1994.

Richardson, Elizabeth P. *A Bloomsbury Iconography*. Winchester: St Paul's Bibliographies, 1989.

Rose, Jacqueline. *The Case of Peter Pan, or The Impossibility of Children's Fiction*. London: Macmillan, 1984.

Spalding, Frances. *Vanessa Bell*. London: Weidenfeld and Nicolson, 1983.

Stephen, Leslie. *Mausoleum Book*. Oxford: Clarendon Press, 1977.

Stieglitz, Alfred. *Camera Work: The Complete Illustrations 1903–1917*. Ed. Simone Philippi and Ute Kieseyer. Koln: Taschen, 1997.

Watney, Simon. *English Post-Impressionism*. London: Studio Vista, 1980.

Woolf, Virginia. *The Letters of Virginia Woolf*. Ed. Nigel Nicolson and Joanne Trautmann. 6 vols. New York: Harcourt Brace Jovanovich, 1975–80.

---. *Moments of Being*. Ed. Jeanne Schulkind. 2nd ed. San Diego: Harvest/Harcourt Brace and Company, 1985.

"Printing Hope":
Virginia Woolf, Hope Mirrlees, and the Iconic Imagery of Paris

by Julia Briggs

I. The Compositor

As Eleanor Pargiter walks through Bloomsbury, glancing automatically into the basements, she stops:

> There was a man in an apron [. . .] working at a case of type. She watched him [. . .] fascinated by the way he flicked type into a great box with many compartments; there, there, there; rapidly, expertly; until, becoming conscious of her gaze, he looked up over his spectacles and smiled at her. She smiled back. Then he went on, making his quick half-conscious movements. (*The Years* 390)

Could the man who smiles back at her be Leonard? And is this a moment that is uniquely public and private, at the same time? It is part of the deleted "1921" sequence of *The Years,* and interestingly, Woolf altered this scene from a carpenter's shop in the first draft (Berg Ms. 42, notebook 6: 13) to give us this tantalizing glimpse of Leonard "dissing."

This passage is exceptional in several ways, and not least in being one of the rare references to printing in Woolf's writings; yet, though she seldom discusses printing, the impact of the Hogarth Press on her sense of what writing might be, as well as on her material practice of it, is widely acknowledged. Moreover, the Press served to introduce her to modernist writers, notably Katherine Mansfield and T. S. Eliot, whose work was among the first to be published by the Press. To their names we should now add that of Hope Mirrlees, author of the extraordinary poem *Paris,* dated 1919 but published by the Woolfs in May 1920.

Paris is a description of the city in the spring of 1919, at once mourning its war dead, yet animated by the presence of the postwar Peace Conference, which has brought to the city the world's most influential statesmen—Woodrow Wilson and David Lloyd George, who join Georges Clemenceau, the old French prime minister and chairman of the Peace Conference. In response to this international moment, Mirrlees wrote her poem in the language of international modernism, in a macaronic blend of (mainly) English and French, in a style whose key influences were contemporary and French, that of poets who read their work at Adrienne Monnier's bookshop—Guillaume Apollinaire, Blaise Cendrars, and Jean Cocteau.

We don't know when or where Hope met the Woolfs, though it was almost certainly through her close friend Karin Costelloe (the daughter of Mary Berenson), who had married Adrian Stephen in 1914—but Hope also numbered the Stracheys and Ottoline Morrell among her friends. In September 1918 the Woolfs asked her to write a story for the Press.

By June 1919 she had become a friend of Virginia's, and the Woolfs were expecting the manuscript of *Paris*. We don't know when the manuscript (as it is likely to have been) arrived, but by 6 March 1920, the Woolfs were "printing Hope" (*Diary* 2: 22). This was to be the single most difficult task Woolf would ever undertake as a printer.

By the time Woolf printed *Paris,* she was comparatively experienced as a typesetter of poetry (which poses far more of a challenge than prose, obviously): Her first attempt, with the poems of Cecil Woolf (Leonard's younger brother, killed in World War I) had been attended by "all sorts of accidents," but Eliot's poems, printed in March 1919 were "our best work so far by a long way, owing to the quality of the ink" (*Diary* 1: 124, 257). The selection of Eliot's poems printed were quatrain or couplet poems, so comparatively straightforward to set, and when, in 1923, Virginia set *The Waste Land,* it had previously been published in *The Criterion,* making her task significantly easier. Mirrlees's *Paris,* on the other hand, was not merely free verse—it actively used typography and spacing as part of its system of representation.

By chance, three proof sheets have survived (in the E. J. Pratt Library, Victoria University, Toronto), on which Mirrlees not only has made a number of substantive textual changes, but also gives detailed instructions for adjustments in the typesetting, several of which were impossible for even the most willing typesetter to achieve, since there was no extra space on the page in which to make them. Clearly Hope "saw" her poem quite as vividly as she "heard" it.

The difficulties Woolf confronted are reflected in the large number of typographical errors evident in the poem—a number of these occur in French words (and may have been copied from the original), but not all; for example, "carryl ong" for "carry long" (17) and "leisuerly" (19)—and when the print run was finished and the book bound, Woolf spent a trying afternoon going through 160 copies and making two further corrections by hand in each (*Diary* 2: 33). Mirrlees had learned something about "shape" poems from her reading of such seventeenth-century English poets as Herbert and Vaughan, but more influential predecessors were Mallarmé's poetic meditation on the nature of art, "Un coup de dés jamais n'abolira le hasard" (first published in 1897 and reprinted in 1914), and Apollinaire's *Calligrammes* (1918). Mirrlees had also learned from Apollinaire, Cocteau, and Reverdy that the placing of a line of poetry itself constituted a form of punctuation, and that the spaces on the page were a crucial part of a poem's rhythm. Can it be a coincidence that Woolf's next two novels used spaces to separate individual sections? *Mrs. Dalloway* is divided into its twelve sections by lines left between them, and though *Jacob's Room* includes numbered chapters, there are also (as Edward Bishop points out), two-, three-, and four-line spaces in the text, whose precise significance has yet to be investigated.

II. THE POEM

The poem's typographical features are only the most obvious aspect of its exploration of space and vision, aspects that are also apparent in its figure of a journey through Paris (and through a day, from morning to night), in the many references to posters, street signs, paintings, statues, monuments, and architectural features of the city, and, behind that, what is imagined, or seen with the inner eye, in trance or dream states. The poem makes use of a wide range of sign systems, not only employing several languages, but using roman and italic type, in upper- and lowercase to represent the range of signs—of words—encountered in the city: These may be bordered with black, like a votive plaque; memorial plaques to the famous dead; metro names or brand names; eight bars of music or a star sign. Three lines typographically image the Tuileries by imitating Le Notre's layout of the gardens (4), three lines represent queuing taxis (21), and on 1 May 1919, when daily life was interrupted by a general strike and demonstrations in the street, the horizontal lines of print turn to become vertical, representing the marching columns of strikers and perhaps also the stems of lily of the valley, normally sold in the street on May Day but not available that year (13–14).

The poem begins (as it will end) by invoking Hope's muse and close friend, the Cambridge classicist Jane Harrison, famous for her research into the Greek mysteries and the powers of female deities in ancient Greece. "I want a holophrase" (3) reflects the poem's search for a single word that will encompass the complex range of experiences it comprehends (in *Themis,* Harrison defined the holophrase as a primitive stage of language in which long words expressed complex relationships more fully and less analytically). From there the poem descends into the "NORD-SUD" metro line (now known as line 12), which will carry the narrator from "Rue du Bac," underneath the Seine, to her arrival at (the significantly named) "Concorde," a version of the classical descent into the underworld, as a quotation from Aristophanes' chorus in *The Frogs* indicates. This descent acknowledges the poem's central concern with mourning the war dead, a theme that runs through the whole poem. The Nord-Sud had a further significance as the line from Montmartre to Montparnasse, reflecting the cultural shift that had brought so many artists and writers from the north to the south of the city, and as such was commemorated in the avant-garde journal of that name published in 1917 and edited by Pierre Reverdy (it printed poetry and discussed contemporary poetry and painting).

In the metro (then as now), the traveller encounters a range of posters, and those mentioned here introduce further themes of (French) imperialism and "négritude": ZIG-ZAG was (and is) a cigarette paper advertised by the head of a Zouave (French Algerian) soldier, who was supposed to have rolled the first-ever cigarette; LION NOIR was a make of (black) shoe polish; CACAO BLOOKER was a Dutch drinking chocolate—the reds and blacks of the posters suggesting "[b]lack-figured vases in Etruscan tombs" (and so anticipating the themes of descent and burial). Other posters for Dubonnet and "Byrrh" are mentioned: The latter, with its picture of a shouting drummer girl, dressed in scarlet, in turn evokes the Scarlet Woman from the Book of Revelation with St. John's role as witness, and his concern with the "logos" (another version of the all-embracing, holophrastic word), drawing him into the poem (3).

The poem seeks comprehensiveness by reducing traditional boundaries, between different languages and literatures, as well as between different kinds of discourse and different levels of culture, so that it slips easily from the posters in the metro to the paintings in the Louvre, rehung in February 1919, after being stored underground during the First World War. Those mentioned by name include the famous *Pieta of Avignon* (whose Virgin mourning her Son evokes the bereaved mothers of France) and Manet's *Olympia,* one of a sequence of allusions to Georges Clemenceau, who in 1907 spearheaded a campaign for this painting to be displayed in the Louvre (8).

As well as alluding to familiar posters and paintings, the poem imagines a series of nonexistent paintings, as part of an extended meditation on the relationship between art and the violence of history, and of experience:

> Whatever happens, some day it will look beautiful:
> > Clio is a great French painter (15).

As originally drafted (the Toronto proof-pages reveal), Mirrlees had envisaged her paintings thus:

> Cézanne's *Quatorze Juillet*,
> David's *Prise de la Bastille*,
> > Poussin's *Fronde*,

> Hang in a quiet gallery. (15)

Whether "Cézanne's *Quatorze Juillet*" was intended to show the later celebration of Bastille Day or the actual taking of the Bastille itself is unclear, but it was evidently too close to the *"Prise de la Bastille,"* so Mirrlees altered it to *"Manet's Massacres des Jours de Juin,"* thus creating within the poem a historical sequence of acts of French political resistance, running back from the strike of 1 May 1919, through what is more often referred to as "les journées de Juin" of 1848 (when protesters were rounded up, disarmed, and shot by the army), through 1789 to the popular rising of the Fronde in 1648 (Manet was also a more appropriate choice than Cézanne as the painter of such a scene, since, though he did not paint that particular event, he did paint *The Execution of Maximilian* in 1867, as well as the executions of communards—*The Barricade*—in May 1871).

In addition to imagining pictures, the poem recreates Paris itself in visual terms, so that the Eiffel Tower, with its crosshatched lines, becomes an etching, and the soldiers in the Tuileries waiting to be demobbed, in their "ciel bleu" uniforms and their *"Terre de Sienne"* packs, become a chalk drawing, to be printed and sold to tourists "in the rue des Pyramides at 10 francs a copy" (15). Perception takes a variety of forms, the "tranced" states, which have been appearing intermittently, begin to make themselves felt, as dreams rise, first knee-deep, and then, as the atmosphere grows heavier, waist-deep (16, 19). They are linked with the figure of the river Seine, itself associated initially with the underworld, and later with the unconscious:

> If through his sluggish watery sleep come dreams
> > They are the blue ghosts of king-fishers. (14)

Finally, from behind the "ramparts of the Louvre" (holding the unconscious of the river at bay?) emerges the great analyst of dreams, perhaps making his début in an English poem:

> Freud has dredged the river and, grinning horribly,
> waves his garbage in a glare of electricity. (21)

This is Paris as the city of dreams, as Baudelaire described it in "Les sept Vieillards":

> Fourmillante cité, cité pleine de rêves,
> Où le spectre en plein jour raccroche le passant! (140)

And indeed "the famous dead of Paris" pass one another on the Pont Neuf, invisible to each other—the nineteenth-century critic Sainte-Beuve and the seventeenth-century duc de la Rochefoucauld (who appears in Sainte-Beuve's great study of Jansenism, *Port-Royal).* Such hallucinatory states may have their origin in mind-altering drugs. The poem alludes to cigarette papers and Algerian tobacco (twice), while the Duchess of Alba in Goya's 1795 painting of her is

> Long long as the Eiffel Tower
>   Fathoms deep in haschich (5).

Mirrlees's fantasy novel *Lud-in-the-Mist* (1926) would tell the story of a town near the borders of Fairyland, where magic fruits inducing ecstatic states were washed down river, driving the staid burghers to frenzy. Her novel looks back to Rossetti's *Goblin Market,* and forward to its current status as a cult novel, read as encoding the social problems of drug-taking. Yet the artificial paradise of drugs is less significant than the mysterious moment of creativity as

> From the top floor of an old Hôtel,
>   Tranced,
> I gaze down at the narrow rue de Beaune. (17)

The old Hôtel (in the traditional French sense of a substantial townhouse) is also a modern hotel, the Hotel de l'Elysée, where Hope Mirrlees regularly stayed when she was in Paris: Its address at "3 Rue de Beaune" is given as the author's address at the end of the poem. The hotel stands on the street corner with the Quai de Voltaire, and it is a question whether, from a high window, the poet could have seen the sun "sinking behind le Petit-Palais," and the crowds crossing the Solférino bridge, silhouetted like flies against the apricot sky in the early evening haze (20). More importantly, she could see these things in her mind's eye, and it may be that this tranced moment was the actual point of genesis, the matrix of the entire poem, written not in the act of travelling from the rue de Bac to the Tuileries, from the rue Saint-Honoré to the Grands Boulevards, but rather in the act of imagining herself travelling those routes.

Whether or not these lines constitute the poem's starting point, they are exceptional in their use of the first person. Though the poem is narrated, we learn extraordinarily little about its narrator, who records the various events, both visual and aural, going on around her and relates her experiences to a wide range of classical, literary, and modern allusions and instances, yet is present herself mainly as the poem's recorder—she is its camera. In 1919, the year of the poem, Woolf described Mirrlees as having "a view of her own about books & style, an aristocratic & conservative tendency in opinion, & a corresponding taste for the beautiful & elaborate in literature" (*Diary* 1: 258); yet while Woolf identified some aspects of her tastes, she failed to see others—and in particular, she failed to recognize Hope's intense interest in the current scene, both politically and culturally speaking, and her irony at the expense of the narrower or more constraining features of social life in the city. *Paris* was to end with Mirrlees's own version of Nighttown in a curious, if apparently unconscious, anticipation of Joyce. The narrator ascends to Montmartre to find floorshows being staged for the Americans, Black jazz musicians, and even alternative sexualities:

> *"I dont like the gurls of the night-club—they love women."* (21)

As the night wears on, Verlaine and Rimbaud, sitting up late, smoking and drinking "Absynthe," are juxtaposed with the respectably married president of the Republic, Raymond Poincaré, and his wife, while in the maternity hospital at Port-Royal, "babies are being born" (22), in a final reworking of the poem's ritual conflict between the Virgin, figuring the ordered and disciplined world of art and religion, and "the wicked April moon," standing for the happenstance and accident of life (14). And the poem comes full circle to close, as it had opened, with a salutation to the city of Paris as "Notre-Dame," Our Lady, in a variant on the familiar words of the prayer *Ave Maria:*

JE VOUS SALUE PARIS PLEIN DE GRACE (22).

But the poem's final line is wordless: It is the star sign of the seven stars, the constellation of the Great Bear, Ursa Major, which Mirrlees also used as the tailpiece to her three novels. It was a coded message, dedicating the poem to another great lady—Jane Harrison. The star sign was part of a private game played between Jane and Hope, in which they became the wives of Jane's teddy bear, comically endowed with totemic significance as "the Old One." Later they would celebrate their private myth by translating a number of folktales from Russian in *The Book of the Bear* (1926). But there are few simple or single meanings in this poem, and the sign of the Great Bear, the seven stars of the Book of Revelation, perpetually pointing toward the Pole Star at the highest point of the night sky, also stand for art's aspiration to permanence in that foundational work of modernism, Mallarmé's "Un coup de dés jamais n'abolira le hasard." As the poem ends, its semantic and typographical schemes, as well as its private and personal meanings and its traditional and classical references, clasp one another and kiss.

Works Cited

Baudelaire, Charles. *Les Fleurs du Mal.* Paris: Editions Fernand Roches, 1929.
Harrison, Jane. *Themis: A Study of the Social Origins of Greek Religion.* 2nd ed. London: Merlin Press, 1989. 473–75.
Mirrlees, Hope. *Paris: A Poem.* Richmond: Printed by Leonard & Virginia Woolf at the Hogarth Press, 1919.
Woolf, Virginia. *The Diary of Virginia Woolf.* Ed. Anne Olivier Bell. 5 vols. New York: Harcourt Brace Jovanovich, 1977–84.
---. *The Years.* Ms. 42. Henry W. and Albert A. Berg Collection, New York Public Library.
---. *The Years.* 1937. Ed. Jeri Johnson. London: Penguin, 1998.

Virginia Woolf and Pacifism

by Michèle Barrett

Virginia Woolf famously claimed that in the Great War, her circle was one of conscientious objectors: "We were all C.O.'s in the Great war" (Bell 2: 258). As the run-up to the Second World War intensified and her pacifism became more and more beleaguered, she articulated her incomprehension of the increasingly militarist attitudes of friends and colleagues. A lengthy correspondence with Ben Nicolson, by then in the army, mirrors the earlier impassioned argument with Julian Bell that is *Three Guineas*. The "we" of Woolf's remark is in an obvious sense generational—it refers to these young men rejecting the pacifism of their parents. This paper looks at other aspects, too, of whom were the "we" that Woolf thought of as COs in the First World War.

Firstly, this "we" is a surprisingly small group of people. A total of around 16,500 conscientious objectors are recorded. Studies of the data on these cases, by John Rae and Martin Ceadel, suggest that of these the most important category was those who were pacifist according to religious belief, the Quakers or Society of Friends being the best-known example. The breakdown of what happened to these 16,500 recorded cases is given by John Rae (71): Approximately 5,000 were exempted altogether; 1,000 were exempted conditional on doing work of national importance; 3,000 were exempted but required to serve in noncombatant (support) roles; 2,000 refused this option and were court-martialed. Rae notes that 4,500 men were therefore dissatisfied with the results of their hearings. These tribunals dealt with around 14,000 cases, and another 1,500 were exempted by the Army Council.

Martin Ceadel concludes that the largest single group to be exempted as COs was the Christadelphians, which accounted for over ten percent of the total. He suggests that "the common pre-war assumption that pacifism was largely the preserve of small Christian sects had a considerable degree of truth in it" (Ceadel 43). Gilbert Thomas, a convicted CO, complained on the basis of his neighbor in prison: "It was assumed that every pacifist . . . was a narrow-minded religionist, basing his creed upon the literal reading of Biblical texts. . . . And indeed, there *were* many conscientious objectors of this type, as I soon discovered" (Ceadel 43–44).

Virginia Woolf's "we," referring to the pacifism of the Bloomsbury Group, touches on a tiny number of cases, so small that although they figure in the historical analyses of Great War pacifism, it is usually in terms of the individuals involved. Ceadel regards their position as elitist in that it rested on an "entitlement to be recognized as C.O.s" on the basis of a "higher personal obligation, as creative artists, to Beauty and Truth" (44). Alternatively, a belief in "'Reason' and 'beauty' recoiled from a conflict that appeared ugly and irrational" (Rae 81–82). It must be said that Lytton Strachey's "Madam, *I* am the civilization they are fighting for" (the new Holroyd-approved exact wording), while offering a cheap target, contains a grain of truth. The people who went to prison for their beliefs were the real COs of the war; the "we" of Virginia Woolf's memories was far more ambiguous. Strachey was exempted on medical grounds, as indeed was Leonard Woolf. The hand tremor that secured his exemption was evidently part of a more systemic shakiness. In 1911 Woolf had written to James Strachey, asking for medical help—"could they cure me of a trembling hand and shaking body?" he asked (Strachey Correspondence, British Library).

The attitudes underlying this stance have been subjected to diplomatic criticism. "What enabled these 'Bloomsbury' quasi-pacifists [. . .] to stay so cheerful was the confidence that they possessed the necessary connections and influence—J. M. Keynes appeared for both [David] Garnett and [Duncan] Grant, for example—to impress the tribunals and to provide a congenial environment, such as existed [. . .] at [. . .] Garsington [. . .] to carry out work of national importance" (Ceadel 45). Nowhere is the social class affiliation of this orientation shown more strongly than in Duncan Grant's reply when asked if he objected to war so much that he would refuse to make a pair of boots; apparently "he 'was a gentleman and objected to making boots'" (Ceadel 45).

Woolf's colleagues took a variety of positions on these issues—E. M. Forster joined the Red Cross, for example. Many of the "we" to whom she refers, including her own husband, were not actually pacifists in belief or COs on principle. What is true is that they did not join the initial enthusiasm for the war that saw enlisted so many men of her class and generation—and indeed they were rather critical of the Brookes and Sassoons for that early commitment to the war. As the criticism of war advanced (let us say by 1917 certainly) there was less distance between these two initially opposed sets of attitudes.

Initial enthusiasm for the war was shared by a rather unlikely person, namely Sigmund Freud. For a fortnight in August 1914 he felt and wrote: "All my libido is given to Austro-Hungary" (Jones 2: 171). He then came to his senses, according to his biographer Ernest Jones. Leaving aside more general questions about psychoanalysis and the war, since there is a complex and unsatisfactory debate about the purchase of Freudian ideas on the psychopathologies of the war, I want to focus on one particular issue relevant to the question of Woolf's pacifism. How did the new psychoanalytic thinkers interpret pacifism? Their understanding of pacifism was, to my mind, curious. Edward Glover, then director of research at the Institute of Psycho-Analysis in London, took up a position in an essay on "War, Sadism and Pacifism" in 1931. Pacifism, he said, was not the product of rational considerations, but was the product—as was war—of individual unconscious needs; in particular it was the product of infantile sadism.

Glover's position is identified in the following passage:

In its most official form warmongering is simply the aggressive aspect of international diplomacy but, of course, it is concealed to a large extent by the manifestly pacific nature of much diplomatic activity. The man in the street has not the same reason to cover his bellicose imaginings. And in the ordinary way preoccupation with international rights and wrongs is a useful substitute activity, a vicarious discharge of emotional tension, the original source of which is infantile sadism. *During actual crises, however, this vicarious discharge may bias the person towards war or peace.* You will observe that we cannot immediately predict in what direction the balance will swing. Knowledge of many other factors is necessary for any such prognostication. The fact remains, however, that the bias is dictated by individual unconscious needs and not by rational considerations of social necessity." (Glover, 1933, 24)

Not surprisingly, perhaps, Glover comments in a subsequent edition that a well-known pacifist "takes exception to the view that the energies of war and pacifism have much in common." Glover concludes:

[T]he facts remain that *infantile* love tendencies *are* closely related to hate reactions, that conscious love is an excellent 'cover' for unconscious hate and that the energies driving the most active part of unconscious conscience are certainly sadistic in origin. Perhaps the best way of expressing the relation is to say that whereas a sufficient excess of love will certainly help to promote peace and a sufficient excess of hate will certainly promote war, the *uncertainties* of war and peace are due to various mixtures of unconscious *love and hate* which are well described as unconscious 'ambivalence.'" (Glover, 1946, 66)

The historical figure Virginia Woolf does not jump out at me from this rendering of the psychology of pacifism. The energetic business of the campaigner and the effortful committee work were scarcely to be borne by her, as we know from her irritated toe dippings into these activities, such as the For Intellectual Liberty project in the 1930s, the archives of which at Cambridge have now been helpfully made public by David Bradshaw's work. Even Leonard Woolf ran out of energy for it—"I admit that I am impotent and a sparrow, but even a sparrow should refuse to twitter," he said in a letter to Miss Gardiner, the secretary of the group, in August 1936 (For Intellectual Liberty Archives, Cambridge University).

If infantile sadism and aggression doesn't seem to fit Virginia Woolf, perhaps ambivalence is nearer the mark. Virginia Woolf's autobiographical writings make the well-known claim, attached to the date of 19 June 1940, that "only the other day" she started to read Freud "for the first time." Thinking about her relationship with her father, she wrote: "I discovered that this violently disturbing conflict of love and hate is a common feeling; and is called ambivalence." The comment is editorially noted to her diary entry of 2 December 1939, "Began reading Freud last night" (*Moments of Being* 108).

Leaving aside the interpretation of her fiction in terms of psychoanalytic concepts, Woolf herself (in "the real world") in 1936 put her name to the proposition that "We, the undersigned, who cannot imagine our mental world without Freud's bold lifework [. . .]" in going on to wish him a happy eightieth birthday in the company of Thomas Mann, Romain Rolland, and other writers. She was also at the Savoy Hotel on 8 March 1939, at a dinner to celebrate the twenty-fifth anniversary of the British Psycho-Analytical Society.

Here I turn to a final connection, not so much between Woolf and psychoanalysis, but on the psychology of passivity. In "A Sketch of the Past," in a passage from her childhood at St. Ives, she recalls the following shock:

I was fighting with Thoby on the lawn. We were pommelling each other with our fists. Just as I raised my fist to hit him, I felt: why hurt another person? I dropped my hand instantly, and stood there, and let him beat me. I remember the feeling. It was a feeling of hopeless sadness. It was as if I became aware of something terrible; and of my own powerlessness. I slunk off alone, feeling horribly depressed. (*Moments of Being* 71)[1]

This speaks to a passivity or quietism that is rather different from pacifism. Pacifism and passivity have different Latin roots; there is *pacificus,* meaning peacemaking, which gives rise to a proponent or advocate of pacifism: one who believes in resort to peaceful alternatives to war as a means of settling disputes. This is a rejection of war and a belief in peaceful alternatives—true of Woolf, of course. In the writings of the Great War period, a distinction was often drawn between pacifist, the belief that war is always wrong, and pacificist, the view that war is best avoided (Ceadel 3).

Close but distinguishable is the Latin *passivus,* meaning capable of suffering or feeling, from which we get the first meaning of passivity, which is the capability of suffering (now, interestingly, obsolete). Present-day meanings focus on the quality or condition of being subject to external force, a state of being affected by an external agent, from which we see a tendency to submit to force, or to another's will. Next passivity denotes inertness, want of activity, quiescence.

It is tempting to read some significance into the gendered sibling conflict of the children, and the girl Virginia Stephen's adoption of the stoic-suffering characteristic of the archaic hermeneutic of passivity. Lack of agency and the feminine situation are an element of the adult woman Virginia Woolf's political abdication. "Happily," she is "uneducated and voteless," and "not responsible for the state of society" (*A Writer's Diary* 247). Of war, she says, it is "like sitting in a sick room, quite helpless" (*Letters* 6: 33). *Jacob's Room,* in which uncertainties of gender, and social class, are played out against a backdrop of the Great War, brings some of these themes together in one extraordinary passage of narration. We are at the opera house, it is Wagner's *Tristan and Isolde,* and the commentator is overwhelmed at the class system in operation: a "classification which is simplicity itself; stalls, boxes, amphitheatre, gallery. The moulds are filled nightly." How attractive, says the narrator, to sit and listen and observe these different people, not to be them but to sit next to them and talk to them for an evening. "But no—we must choose. Never was there a harsher necessity! or one which entails greater pain, more certain disaster; for wherever I seat myself, I die in exile: Whittaker in his lodging house; Lady Charles at the Manor" (*Jacob's Room* 69).

"Wherever I seat myself I die in exile" ("I" here being the narrative consciousness of a woman acutely aware of the implications of existential choice). A mere two pages later Mrs. Durrant is wondering how to describe Jacob Flanders; he is so awkward, but so distinguished-looking. She thinks that "distinction was one of the words to use naturally, though, from looking at him, one would have found it difficult to say which seat in the opera house was his, stalls, gallery, or dress circle" (*Jacob's Room* 70).

Jacob does not have to die in exile. His masculinity enables him to transcend the class system in ways that the women of *Jacob's Room* cannot. But let's not forget that he does die in Woolf's novel, not in social exile but in war. The aborted fisticuffs with Thoby may have left the child depressed, but the philosophy of a quietist endurance of violence, whether near or far to a more formal pacifism, is shown to have the greater value.

Note

1.   I am grateful to Alison Light for drawing my attention to this passage from "A Sketch of the Past."

Works Cited

Bell, Quentin. *Virginia Woolf: A Biography.* London: Hogarth Press, [1990].

Ceadel, Martin. *Pacifism in Britain 1914–1945: The Defining of a Faith.* Oxford: Clarendon Press, 1980.

Glover, Edward. *War, Sadism and Pacifism: Three Essays.* London: George Allen and Unwin, [1933].

---. *War, Sadism and Pacifism: Further Essays on Group Psychology and War.* London: George Allen and Unwin Ltd., [1946].

Jones, Ernest. *The Life and Work of Sigmund Freud.* New York: Basic Books, [1953–57].

Rae, John. *Conscience and Politics: The British Government and the Conscientious Objector to Military Service 1916–1919.* London: Oxford University Press, 1970.

Woolf, Leonard. Letter to James Strachey. 1911. Strachey Correspondence. British Library.

---. Letter to Miss Gardiner. August 1936. For Intellectual Liberty Archives. Cambridge University.

Woolf, Virginia. *Jacob's Room.* San Diego: Harvest-Harcourt Brace, 1978.

---. *The Letters of Virginia Woolf.* Ed. Nigel Nicolson and Joanne Trautmann. 6 vols. New York: Harcourt Brace Jovanovich, 1975–80.

---. *Moments of Being.* Ed. Jeanne Schulkind. 2nd ed. San Diego: Harvest-Harcourt Brace, 1985.

---. *A Writer's Diary.* Ed. Leonard Woolf. New York: Harvest-Harcourt Brace Jovanovich, 1954.

WOOLF AND THE AMERICAN IMAGINARY

by Cheryl Mares

Courtesy of HonusWagner.com   Walking in Cornwall, 1916

I was recently at the New York Public Library, in the Office of Special Collections, waiting in line for a reader's card when a man in front of me with two small children in tow asked where they could find "the rare Honus Wagner baseball card." Later I learned that this is the most valuable baseball card in history, selling at last report for $1.1 million.[1] The library's copy was supposed to be on display that day in a special exhibit of baseball memorabilia. When the man was told that that display case had not been set up yet, he frowned, glanced at the brochure in his hand, and asked, "Well, what about Virginia Woolf's walking stick, then? Can we see that?" No, he was told, that item was a recent acquisition and was not yet ready for the public.[2] At that, the man gave up and left, dragging the children behind him.

Virginia Woolf thought of America as a land of bizarre juxtapositions, but would she ever have imagined her name being invoked in the same breath as that of a legendary baseball player, her walking stick being sought after, in the New York Public Library of all places, as a consolation prize by a man who had really hoped to see, and to show his children, a very special baseball card? How unlikely. And yet, as Woolf wrote in 1925, American culture is "a mosaic of incongruous pieces," a culture made up of "odds and ends [. . .] loosely tied in temporary cohesion" (*Collected Essays* 2: 120, 112). Category crossings, collapsing distinctions—this is, for better or worse, what America is all about, to judge from Woolf's writings.

My paper explores Woolf's America by drawing primarily upon her correspondence with Vita Sackville-West during Vita's 1933 tour of the United States and Canada, the travel diary Vita kept at the time, and Woolf's 1938 essay "America, Which I Have Never Seen." Toward the end, I briefly speculate about why Woolf never visited America, an intriguing question since she repeatedly said that she intended to come here, and, as Andrew McNeillie observes, "[t]here is no reason why she might not have crossed the Atlantic to North America" ("Virginia Woolf's America" 41).

Surprisingly, Vita's 1933 travel diary was first published in 2002 (*Vita Sackville-West: Selected Writings* 146–66). I was also surprised by her diary entry for 17 March 1933. After staying in Ashfield, Massachusetts, with Mina Kirstein Curtiss (associate professor of English at Smith College), she writes:

> Back at Northampton, I dine with Marion Dodd [proprietor of the Hampshire Bookshop] and Esther Dunn [English professor at Smith College]. Robert Frost there, a handsome man who goes in for good conversation. He has a professorship at Amherst. He pays me compliments about "The Land," which I return in kind. I lecture afterwards—not very well—to Smith College, "Modern Spirit in Literature." (164)

This is one of the moments when Vita became more real to me, less remote. It seems that I had unconsciously compartmentalized her. I had been to Knole years ago. It was easy to imagine Vita there or, for that matter, in Italy, France, and Greece. But in Buffalo? In Des Moines? In Hollywood, being shown around by Gary Cooper? Vita finally became real to me when she described herself seated at a drugstore counter in Philadelphia, eating chicken salad while waiting for a train to Wilmington, Delaware. It was a kind of epiphany. From then on I was hooked.

I have no evidence that Woolf read Vita's travel diary, though parts of it reappear in some fashion in Vita's letters to Woolf in 1933, and it is clear from other letters that they talked afterward about Vita's trip. Certain images and observations from both Vita's travel diary and her letters to Woolf from America also appear in Woolf's 1938 article "America, Which I Have Never Seen." It would be hard to prove that Vita's experience directly influenced Woolf's ideas and images of America after 1933, since these may have come from other sources. Still, as Alex Zwerdling points out, Woolf often used her friends and acquaintances to learn about various aspects of the "real world" (*Virginia Woolf and the Real World* 112–13). She directed Vita to "[d]escribe everything" she experienced on her tour of North America (*Letters* 5: 149). In fact, Vita may have kept the travel diary in part to preserve memories detailed enough to satisfy Woolf. "Please, please, write down every scrap for me," Woolf urged her; "I cant bear to think of all you're doing and seeing, and I not there, and I not there" (*Letters* 5: 153). As did other friends and acquaintances, Vita seems to have served Woolf at times as "[a]n extra pair of eyes" (*Letters* 5: 350).

In "America, Which I Have Never Seen," written four or five years after Vita's tour of the United States, Woolf conveys a much more vivid sense of the heterogeneity of American culture and geography than she had in her 1925 essay "American Fiction."[3] It is as if she now has more images and details at her command and, freed from the role of the critic, can put them together in new ways that dramatize her sense of the American "mosaic." Despite its brevity, this essay is packed with detail. But the effect is not an increase in conventional realism; instead, Woolf's imaginary America seems surreal. The scenes and images in her letters as she tries to imagine what Vita must be seeing on her tour of America are also often fantastic, but they are too vague or hackneyed to resonate. We don't feel the tie to the real in them, whereas her 1938 vision of America, however fantastic, also seems prophetic: "America, Which I Have Never Seen" conveys a sense of postmodern America and hints at a future in which America is the dominant world power.

Both Vita's travel diary and Woolf's 1938 essay convey a sense of speed, of perpetual motion, of contents under high pressure, so disparate that they threaten to fly apart. In Vita's diary, glimpses of jarringly different kinds of people, places, landscapes, architectural styles, and realms of experience are quickly juxtaposed as Vita proceeds on her whirlwind tour: "33,000 miles [. . .] 72 different cities [. . .] 63 nights in the train" (*The Letters of Vita Sackville-West to Virginia Woolf* 368). Woolf's technique in "America, Which I Have Never Seen" seems cinematic, its swoops and plunges recalling jump cuts, close-ups, pans, and montages. But the manic pace and tremendous spatial compression her essay achieves, and the sense of abrupt cultural discontinuities it conveys, may also indirectly reflect Vita's experience of America.

Of course, there were other English travelers to America to whom Woolf could, and on occasion did, turn for firsthand impressions of this country through English eyes. Many British writers and artists went back and forth to America in the 1930s, in part because of the lucrative lecture circuit. More than a few of them knew Woolf, and they talked with her or wrote to her about the American scene. The long tradition of transatlantic travel writing as well as other literary and nonliterary sources must also have contributed to Woolf's conception of this country.

Although Woolf seems largely sympathetic toward the American experiment in "American Fiction" and "America, Which I Have Never Seen," she is equivocal enough for us to sense that she is not, at present, particularly impressed with the results. Nigel Nicolson maintains, somewhat enigmatically, that Woolf was "as prejudiced against the United States as she would have been against Liberia" (*Virginia Woolf* 126). Had she gone to America to see for herself, he suggests, she would have thought differently about it and its citizens (Introduction, *Letters* 5: xii). But would firsthand experience so dramatically have altered Woolf's views?

Class differences, cultural elitism, and vestigial colonialist attitudes enter into Woolf's so-called prejudices. Many Woolf scholars have discussed these matters at length. I will simply suggest that Raymond Williams's essay "The Bloomsbury Fraction," about the fractured relationship of Bloomsbury members to their class and culture, bears rereading. Alex Zwerdling further developed this notion of divided loyalties resulting in ambivalent stances toward modernization and social change, forces that America obviously came to epitomize. This ambivalence affects Woolf's attitude toward the very idea of America, not just toward most of the Americans she met, conceived of, or read about. This ambivalence also helps to explain why Woolf never made it to America, in spite of her expressed interest in doing so, and in spite of Vita's writing to her at the end of her North American tour that she felt "[b]attered but enriched,—not only by dollars" (*The Letters of Vita Sackville-West to Virginia Woolf* 367).

Vita may have felt "enriched" by her American tour, but she was not as responsive to American culture as Nigel Nicolson wishes she had been. He suggests that circumstances—the weather, the financial crisis (the Great Depression), her grueling itinerary—prevented Vita from being "emotionally aroused" by America, as she had been by France, Italy, Greece, and Persia (Foreword, *Vita Sackville-West: Selected Writings* xiv). But class differences, cultural elitism, and Vita's political conservatism also must have chilled her responses to Americans and American society. Mary Ann Caws points out the signs of Vita's disdain in her travel diary, her "more than unfortunate" sensitivity to "the looks, the background, the lack of conversational ability, and the mental and aesthetic shortcomings of certain new acquaintances" (*Vita Sackville-West: Selected Writings* 146). This sensitivity she shared with Woolf, despite differences in their class backgrounds and political orientations. Perhaps it even formed part of what Woolf thought of as Vita's "truthfulness," which Woolf prized[4] and feared she herself might lose should her situation require her to court American approval[5] or, as in Vita's case, to endure American adulation.

And yet, Vita did feel "enriched" by her American experience and "not only by dollars." In fact, she was "emotionally aroused" by America, but not so much by the people as by the land, and not even by the land until she reached the West. Up until then, American landscapes generally seemed to her "unspeakably hideous" or, at best, merely monotonous, though she did note that she had seen some patches of "[p]retty country, very like England."[6] Vita's attitude started to shift just outside of Denver. "It is all, quite suddenly, un-American and subtly Spanish," she wrote to Woolf. The approach to the Rockies, the views of the "distant ranges," and the deserts of Arizona reminded her of her beloved Persia (*The Letters of Vita Sackville-West to Virginia Woolf* 363–64). "The Grand Canyon," she wrote to Woolf, "is the most astonishing thing in the world" (369). She would return to her memories of it a decade later for the setting of her novel *Grand Canyon* (1942). During her tour, Vita dreamed of returning to this "un-American" America with Woolf and even sent her a proposed itinerary. Accompanied by their husbands, they would "motor all through Texas, Arizona, California, and Mexico," camp in tents in the desert, and sail back home from New Orleans (*The Letters of Vita Sackville-West to Virginia Woolf* 369).

Woolf knew that Vita was captivated by parts of the American West and Southwest. Dorothy Brett, whom Vita had visited in California's Big Sur country, wrote to Woolf from New Mexico later on in 1933, asking whether she should leave America and return to London. Woolf told her no, satirized the London scene, and then turned serious:

> But if I'm sincere, then of course I love London and couldnt live with your splendours [in New Mexico], not forever. One of these days I shall pounce or sweep through them and knock at your door as Vita did. She's back, entirely delighted with America, your part, that is; not the other. (*Letters* 5: 202)

But would Woolf have been "entirely delighted" by Vita's un-American America, if she had managed to swoop over? It's doubtful.

"[D]amn America," Woolf wrote to Vita from Crete in 1931, only two years before Vita's tour of the United States. "We must at all costs come here [Crete] next year. [. . .] Seriously, its a folly to waste one's prime acquiring gold when there's this perfectly wild and yet very civilised and entirely beautiful place without an Englishman or woman in it" (*Letters* 5: 62). What Woolf meant by the word "civilised" is subject to debate, but most likely the Grand Canyon and Smoke Tree Ranch in California were not what she had in mind and would not have appealed to her as they did to Vita. This difference between Vita's and Woolf's sensibilities is important and makes itself felt, for example, in fundamental differences between Woolf's *Between the Acts* and Vita's *Grand Canyon*.

The ocean Vita had put between them while on her American tour and the sheer size of the country ("vast" is a recurrent word in Woolf's evocations of America) made Woolf anxious for her return. The difficulty she had imagining Vita there (which is obvious in her letters) and her negative associations with America must have added to her anxieties. Dizzying heterogeneity, a frenetic pace, provincialism, lack of privacy, "frank commercialism," and "[m]oney—money—money" (*Diary* 5: 95)—all are noted in Vita's travel diary and in references to America in Woolf's essays, letters, and diaries.

When writing to Vita in the United States, Woolf invariably referred to Sissinghurst and to the vivid signs of seasonal change occurring in the English countryside, culminating in this final note: "Ah but you've missed the spring of one thousand years, all gone now [. . .] lovelier than any desert sewn with roses and Brett into the bargain" (*Letters* 5: 178). She is admittedly trying to make Vita "jealous of the English fields" (*Letters* 5: 147), but also is reminding her of who she is, what (and whom) she loves, and where she belongs. These reminders reveal as much about Woolf's own attachment to the land and strong sense of place[7] as they do about Vita's, lending support, in their own way, to McNeillie's claim that Woolf is "the most English of the modernists" ("Virginia Woolf's America" 41).

Ultimately, it seems that while Woolf wished she had gone to America, she never actually wanted to come here. "I wish I'd got it over now," she wrote in 1927 after twice turning down invitations (*Letters* 3: 338). Over the years she gave a wide range of reasons for not making the trip: the expense (*Letters* 3: 320, 328); her unwillingness to lie to her hosts about her impressions of their country (*Letters* 3: 325); Leonard's commitments (*Letters* 3: 532); the time it would take (*Letters* 5: 405); her sense that American literary agents and publishers were trying to exploit her (*Diary* 5: 95–96); her duties at the Hogarth Press; her unwillingness to lecture about literature; "politics"; and her need to finish her own work (*Letters* 5: 439). These are good reasons, but they are so numerous and various that one may be tempted to agree with Nigel Nicolson when he claims that Woolf's "preconceived notions" of America and "her unconcealed prejudices about the character of its people" are what kept her from crossing the Atlantic (Introduction, *Letters* 5: xii).

Nevertheless, not all of Woolf's "preconceived notions of America" were negative. By the late 1930s, her sense of being an outsider in her own country had deepened while the political situation in Europe had steadily worsened. "America, Which I Have Never Seen, Interests Me Most in This Cosmopolitan World of Today," the full title of her 1938 essay proclaims. Here she uses America in part as a foil. In the closing paragraphs, she pits America, faced toward the future, against Europe, trapped in the past. McNeillie notes that she is more interested in the "idea of America" than in the actual place. He emphasizes (as does Woolf) that the America she is invoking is "imaginary" ("Virginia Woolf's America" 45). Still, her essay's conclusion gets its force from Woolf's allusion there to the very real historical and political crisis that was overtaking Europe and her anticipation of the coming shift of power to the United States.

Hermione Lee mentions that, as war engulfed Europe, the Woolfs, unlike many others, never attempted to escape to America (694). But what if they had? Would Virginia Woolf have found there the conditions she needed in order to write? In 1920 she wrote in her diary that she couldn't "imagine anything less desirable than to be a person who may stay permanently in America" (*Diary* 2: 38). By the end of the 1920s, she was announcing that she would "jump off Waterloo Bridge," rather than suffer such a fate (*Letters* 4: 113). In April 1939, when war had broken out in Europe and England's involvement seemed nearly inevitable, her response is more subdued. "[L]ike so many people[,]" Christopher Isherwood and W. H. Auden "have gone to America," she wrote to Ling Su-Hua. "They dont like it, I hear; but at any rate there is more feeling of security there; and they can work better so they say" (*Letters* 6: 328). The qualifying "so they say" hints at her own reservations.

Wouldn't Woolf have felt even more alien in America than she did as an outsider in her own country, even more alien than she imagined Americans felt in England?[8] Not only would she have been personally deracinated, but also America, as she understood it, is, by definition, essentially and perpetually deracinated. It is not only a relatively new nation, but also a nation distinguished by its commitment to the idea of the new. As a rebel, progressive thinker, and experimental writer, Woolf endorsed that idea,[9] but her attachment to her own country—to London, the landscape, the language, the literary tradition—is everywhere apparent in her work.[10] The strength of that attachment can be felt even in the casual note she sent when Vita, her American tour behind her, had come home at last. "Lord," Woolf wrote, "how I envy you the pink tower [of Sissinghurst] after all America" (*Letters* 5: 178).

Notes

1.   15 July 2000: "A 1909 Honus Wagner baseball club is auctioned for a record $1.1 million on eBay." <http://www.baseballlibrary.com/baseballlibrary/ballplayers/W/Wagner_ Honus.stm>.
2.   "The New York Public Library Opens Its Cabinet of Curiosities." Press release. 28 February 2002. <http://www.nypl.org/press/curiosities.cfm>.
3.   Andrew McNeillie and Melba Cuddy-Keane commented on "America, Which I Have Never Seen" in their papers for Voyages Out, Voyages Home: The Eleventh International Conference on Virginia Woolf, University of Wales, Bangor, 14–15 June 2001. Jane Garrity also briefly discusses this essay in *Step-Daughters of England* (New York: Manchester University Press, 2003) 17. My sense is that Woolf is more deeply ambivalent toward even the "idea" of America in this piece than these writers suggest.
4.   See *The Diary of Virginia Woolf*, ed. Anne Oliver Bell, 5 vols. (New York: Harcourt Brace Jovanovich, 1977–84) 3: 57 and 4: 248.
5.   See *The Letters of Virginia Woolf*, ed. Nigel Nicolson and Joanne Trautmann, 6 vols. (New York: Harcourt Brace Jovanovich, 1975–80) 3: 325.
6.   *Vita Sackville-West: Selected Writings*, ed. Mary Ann Caws. (New York: Palgrave, 2002) 155 and 162.
7.   See Garrity 303.
8.   See *Diary* 3: 95.
9.   See Andrew McNeillie "Virginia Woolf's America" *Dublin Review* 5 (winter 2001–2002): 44 and Garrity 17.
10.   See Hermione Lee, *Virginia Woolf* (New York: Alfred A. Knopf, 1997) 728–32 and Garrity 302–3, 307.

Works Cited

BaseballLibrary.com. "Honus Wagner. Chronology. July 15, 2000." <http://www.baseballlibrary.com/baseballLibrary/ballplayers/W/Wagner_Honus.stm>.
Cuddy-Keane, Melba. "Flexible Englishness: Woolf Reads the Americans." Voyages Out, Voyages Home: The Eleventh International Conference on Virginia Woolf. University of Wales, Bangor. 14 June 2001.

Garrity, Jane. *Step-Daughters of England: British Women Modernists and the National Imaginary*. New York: Manchester University Press, 2003.

Lee, Hermione. *Virginia Woolf*. New York: Alfred A. Knopf, 1997.

McNeillie, Andrew. "Virginia Woolf's America." *Dublin Review* 5 (winter 2001–2002): 41–55.

---. "Woolf in America and America in Woolf," Voyages Out, Voyages Home: The Eleventh International Conference on Virginia Woolf. University of Wales, Bangor. 15 June 2001.

New York Public Library. "The New York Public Library Opens Its Cabinet of Curiosities." Press release. 28 February 2002. <http://www.nypl.org/press/curiosities.cfm>.

Nicolson, Nigel. Foreword. *Vita Sackville-West: Selected Writings*. Ed. Mary Ann Caws. New York: Palgrave, 2002. xiii–xiv.

---. *Virginia Woolf*. New York: Viking Penguin, 2000.

Sackville-West, Vita. "Lecture Travel Diary (January to March 1933)." *Vita Sackville West: Selected Writings*. Ed. Mary Ann Caws. New York: Palgrave, 2002. 146–66.

---. *The Letters of Vita Sackville-West to Virginia Woolf*. Ed. Louise DeSalvo and Mitchell A. Leaska. New York: William Morrow and Company, 1985.

Williams, Raymond. "The Bloomsbury Fraction." *Problems in Materialism and Culture: Selected Essays*. London: Verso Editions, 1981. 148-69.

Woolf, Virginia. "American Fiction." *Collected Essays of Virginia Woolf*. 4 vols. New York: Harcourt, Brace & World, 1967. 2: 111–21.

---. "America, Which I Have Never Seen." *Hearst's International—Cosmopolitan* (April 1938): 21, 144-45. Rpt. in *Dublin Review* 5 (winter 2001–2002): 56–60.

---. *The Diary of Virginia Woolf*. Ed. Anne Olivier Bell. 5 vols. New York: Harcourt Brace Jovanovich, 1977–84.

---. *The Letters of Virginia Woolf*. Ed. Nigel Nicolson and Joanne Trautmann. 6 vols. New York: Harcourt Brace Jovanovich, 1975–80.

Zwerdling, Alex. *Virginia Woolf and the Real World*. Berkeley: University of California Press, 1986.

❧

Part Two:
The Writings of Virginia Woolf

❧

The Mask/Masque of Food: Illness and Art

by Susan Rubinow Gorsky

To both Virginia Woolf and her characters, food mattered. The way Woolf writes about food and its significance reveals her struggle with an eating disorder. Yet, as she often observed, illness lets one perceive the world in new ways. Thus, eating issues in the novels reflect Woolf's vision, her strength, and her creativity, as she transformed the substance of illness into the symbols of art.

I. Disordered Eating and Eating Disorders

There are profound differences between disordered eating and an eating disorder such as anorexia (self-starvation) or bulimia (binging and purging). Each has social, emotional, and physical elements, and each appears to offer a solution to a problem. The first might; the second never does.[1]

Disordered eating is common; it manifests itself in the woman who has dieted most of her life or the young wrestler who periodically starves himself to make his weight class. It can be a coping mechanism or a strategy for success (the woman's perception of beauty, the boy's trophy), but it can lead to difficulties from self-image to health, and it is a sign of *dis*ease.

Eating disorders often begin as an attempt to mask or solve a problem, reflecting a desire to achieve perfection or control, with body image as an actual or symbolic goal. However, when the effort to regulate food intake crosses into psychological illness, the *dis*ease takes control. Perceived or real expectations can precipitate an eating disorder, and society's emphasis on thinness can play a role. More complex causes include sexual repression, abuse, and illnesses such as depression.

Eating disorders differ from disordered eating less in the causes than in the results. If she chooses her food well, the perpetual dieter can live a healthy life; after his season, the wrestler can return to "normal" eating. But someone with anorexia or bulimia is not solving a problem; he or, far more frequently, she is ill. She may lose her hair, her teeth, and one-fourth of her weight, stop menstruating, suffer abnormal blood pressure, and damage her kidneys or heart. She may die.

II. Virginia Woolf

Little of this was known in Woolf's day. Women were considered physically, emotionally, and morally weak, subject to the ironic conclusion that what made them *female* also made them *ill*. Neurasthenia, the most common psychological diagnosis, was one of the nervous (i.e., emotional) disorders to which women were believed especially vulnerable. As a "wasting disease," it could involve weight loss.

Although anorexia nervosa was medically described in 1869 and named in 1873, several years before neurasthenia, it was not officially recognized as a diagnosis. Anorectic behaviors grew naturally from contemporary attitudes toward women's health and the ideal of genteel femininity. People associated food preparation with the lower classes and eating with digestion. A good appetite for food implied other, even less genteel, appetites, while dainty eating communicated personal fastidiousness and moral restraint. These factors, along with sexual and behavioral repression, led girls to avoid food or mask their intake through secret eating. Those behaviors alone do not define disease, but some girls progressed from supposedly refined eating habits to potentially fatal practices, and some exhibited the psychological distress we associate with anorexia.

In the last few decades, thanks to increased understanding of eating disorders as well as increased knowledge about Woolf, a number of scholars have recognized her personal issues with food and the manifestations of those issues in her writings.[2]

Certainly Woolf had reason to develop an eating disorder. Her patriarchal and difficult father was extremely demanding; her mother was absent, first in their relationship and then through her death. Sexually repressed and sexually abused, Woolf may have been genetically predisposed to depression or manic-depression. Her parents severely limited her options when she was a girl; her husband and doctors did so when she was a woman.

In her life and writings, Woolf displayed many signs of an eating disorder. Relishing food and its preparation, she could describe a meal with lavish pleasure or be found in the kitchen baking bread. Yet she always tried to control her eating, for what it literally meant (a sign of the physical, a threat to body image) and for what it might symbolize (external control, sexual relations). These attempts reveal the pride, frustration, powerlessness, and self-loathing of an anorectic person.

Compounding the problem, a symptom of her illness became a supposed cure, since her medical treatment included replacing the stimulation of company or work with rest and food. Although Vanessa, Leonard, and some of her doctors probably knew the underlying causes for her abnormal relationship with food, they still relied on this standard treatment and measured her health by her weight. Urged to eat, Woolf could not, or would not, obey. She might feel gluttonous if she desired food and fat if she ate. Sometimes Woolf acceded to their view of her illness; sometimes she capitulated or manipulated or mocked—all reactions typifying someone with anorexia.

III. THE NOVELS

In Woolf's fiction, we see the effects of her issues with eating, and we see her turn illness into art. Ultimately, it is the art that matters: not why Woolf writes about food the way she does, but the significance and effect of what she says. When she insists that novelists must transform themselves from "materialists" to "spiritualists," presenting "life" by focusing on the "spirit," not the "body," some take this to mean she avoids the physical, but that's not true.[3] Rather, when she includes something "material," she does so for a purpose. Each reference to food conveys significance.

Some characters struggle to eat ordinary foods at the usual times, some overeat, and others avoid food. Those who find a healthy relationship with food can successfully participate in the pageant of life. What people eat, when, how, why, and with whom, always matters.

"A SOUR, YELLOW FRUIT" AND "A FLOWERING BRANCH OF ORANGES": THE ABILITY TO EAT

In real people, physical and emotional health can affect the desire or ability to eat. In *Flush*, Woolf shows how eating can symbolize well-being. Trapped in a sterile life in a paternalistic home, the sickly Elizabeth Barrett finds most visitors exhausting. Even when her father "commands" (51) her to eat, she surreptitiously feeds her dog. But when Robert Browning visits, her appetite returns. In England she can barely manage "a thimbleful of port"; in Italy, fulfilled in marriage and motherhood, she "tossed off a tumbler of Chianti"; the single "denuded, sour yellow fruit" decorating her table in England grows into "a flowering branch of oranges" (122). Her health is symbolized by a healthy attitude toward food.

"SILVER DISHES" AND "PARTY RELICS": THE SOCIAL AND POLITICAL SIGNIFICANCE OF FOOD

The social and political significance of food begins in its definition of physical and emotional status. In *The Waves*, Louis, by birth and nature an outsider, finds he "cannot read [his] book, or order [his] beef" even in a cheap "eating-house" (239). Bernard, steady and self-possessed, can readily assert himself with waiters and enjoy a good meal. In *The Years*, the impoverished Sara and Maggie cook for themselves, Kitty is banned from an exclusive college dinner, and solid middle-class Martin dines well at a restaurant. In *Night and Day*, contrasting Mary's sense of futility with Cassandra's rich life, Woolf allows only the latter to see the beauty in a table set with napkins folded like "lilies," glasses with "flakes of gold," and silver dishes (345).

Food also defines social power, connected to gender. Contrasting the opulent lunch at a men's college with the paltry dinner at a women's school in *A Room of One's Own*, Woolf asserts that the meals symbolize the relative richness and opportunities granted each sex and also influence the abilities of each to benefit from those opportunities.

She makes the point more subtly in *Jacob's Room*, where food is always available for men: Sopwith feeds undergraduates cake and ideas; Mr. Clutterbuck eats plum tart, indulged by Mrs. Durrant; Jacob need only pack his jacket to be assured of a dinner invitation. Men may be fed at women's expense, as when Jacob unthinkingly eats so much mutton that his hostess and her daughters will go hungry at lunch.[4] Depending on social status, women may spend ten-pence on a roll for lunch, dine in a dingy hotel, or pour tea at home. Their hunger reveals their lack of power, so that no woman can ever say, as Jacob does, "I have more than I can eat already" (62).

The most obvious and horrific example of food used as a tool of masculine power is when meat is "crammed down [the] throat" (232) of the suffragist Rose in *The Years*, with painful echoes of Woolf's medical treatment. In *The Pargiters*, Woolf makes overt the link between the intake of food and sexual assault when the nurse attributes Rose's nightmares following the flasher's assault to eating "rich cake" (45). In the finished novel, Rose develops food issues: Feeling "dirty," she chooses a bath rather than food after a political rally (156), and she becomes very obese.

Yet women also use food, the traditional feminine sphere, for their own ends. In *Mrs.*

Dalloway, Lady Bruton's lunch is exclusive and political. After feeding Hugh Whitbread and Richard Dalloway a distasteful-sounding meal of fish with a "mask" of brown cream and "severed" chickens, which "swim" in casseroles (158), she in turn is fed by them as they agree to help her write a letter.[5]

"LET'S FINISH OUR PUDDING" OR "MEDICINE AND MILK": FOOD AS "CHARACTER"

What one eats can demonstrate character. Casually suggesting, "let's finish our pudding" and "have some wine" after a bombing raid, Maggie and Renny prove their emotional and physical strength (*The Years* 291). However, obesity signifies either a problem (like Rose's) or moral weakness: In *The Voyage Out,* Mrs. Paley is so greedy, so bogged down by selfishness and excess flesh, she can eat even when hearing of Rachel's death.

In *To the Lighthouse, not* eating is a sign of fortitude to Mr. Ramsay, who brags that he once walked all day with a biscuit in his pocket. The sandwiches he provides for the long-delayed trip to the lighthouse are barely edible: mere sustenance, nothing more.

Defining the characters in *The Waves* by their relationships with food, Woolf contrasts the earth mother Susan, the sensual Jinny, and the anorectic Rhoda. Susan, who eats as naturally as she reproduces, can frankly state, "I am hungry" (243). Her rising bread dough imitates the fecundity of her body and the springtime. Jinny eats with the same joyous abandon with which she embraces anything physical. In contrast, Rhoda can "hardly drink" her tea and "choke[s]" on food (204). Woolf connects Rhoda's problems to her self-image and discomfort with sex; her body is "ill-fitting" (248) and she "feared embraces" (318). So powerful is Rhoda's self-effacement that she repeatedly says, "I have no face" (197). Starving herself is a step toward death.

Also failing to define a place for herself is Rachel in *The Voyage Out,* and she too develops anorexia. First seen "laying forks severely straight by the side of knives" (14), Rachel is trapped in a paternalistic world whose "rigid bars" are the established daily meals (214). Observing the role models around her, she sees no satisfying life. Sexually and emotionally repressed and quite immature, she is innocent of love and ignorant about sex. Her engagement is filled with tension; she and her fiancé are "impotent" (303). Perhaps she falls ill because of the trip up the Amazon, perhaps because of contaminated food, as one man suggests. But Rachel's illness is more likely her escape; living on "medicine and milk" (335), she can avoid meals as she evades all the demands of the people around her, including her fiancé. Her illness frees her from society's expectations, but it also kills her.

Those characters who maintain a healthy relationship with food, like Jinny and Susan, have healthy self-images. In *Between the Acts,* Mrs. Manresa may represent a personal wish: Like Woolf, she marries a Jew and befriends homosexuality, but Mrs. Manresa further defies convention by refusing to diet or wear stays, helping herself to cream, and glorying in the sensual. Though an outsider and "vulgar" (41), she offers a healthy counterpart to the repressed and unhappy Isa and Miss La Trobe.

"HOW GOOD TO EAT":
MEALS THAT PARTAKE OF ETERNITY

Glimpsing the seductive Sasha, Orlando thinks of melons and pineapples; later, he describes something beautiful in the gypsies' phrase, "how good to eat" (*Orlando* 142). In this opulent love letter to Vita Sackville-West, Woolf associates food with beauty, the antithesis of an eating disorder.

In the pageant in *Between the Acts,* the villagers chant about the old ways of planting and gathering food. Despite the intrusions of modern life, the refrain recalls the ceremonial significance of food in a world where people aligned themselves with the eternal verities of mother earth.

In the contemporary world, Clarissa Dalloway's party touches the eternal. She may be ill or frigid, yet her party proves she is unlike Miss Kilman or Septimus, for she conveys life, not death. In the pageant of the party, she creates moments of significance beyond the mundane. Despite his disdain, Peter Walsh acknowledges her central role: "What is it that fills me with extraordinary excitement?" he asks. "It is Clarissa" (*Mrs. Dalloway* 296).

The Waves goes further in asserting the ceremonial power of a shared meal. Although locked in their parallel soliloquies, at the first dinner the characters manage a startling level of communication. Initially insisting on their separateness, they gradually share images and ideas until they achieve a nearly mystical communion. That unity cannot survive Percival's death, so the second party lacks the intensity of the first.

The mystical significance they almost achieve is fully realized in *To the Lighthouse* over a shared meal. Just as Lily uses art and Mr. Ramsay uses ideas to attempt to find—or impose—order on the existential chaos, so Mrs. Ramsay uses relationships, symbolized by the party. Each method is limited; each has value.

Mrs. Ramsay embraces traditional roles of matchmaker, social organizer, wife, and mother, and, through her dinner party, she feeds and heals those around her. She gains as well, for her art defines her identity and gives her meaning. Using a dining room as her canvas and people as her subject, she creates an "island" that transcends the ephemeral (240). This world, described in language derived from art and religion, requires food.

Mr. Bankes does not want to dine, for he frets about improperly cooked vegetables. Charles Tansley wants to be alone. Lily dislikes the role of female guest. The children wear "mask-like faces" (164). Mr. Ramsay is annoyed that Mr. Carmichael wants more soup. Yet by the end of the dinner, these disparate individuals have been brought together. Their masks are gone, revealing the underlying human connections.

All this happens because of Mrs. Ramsay and her dinner. The meal is a "masterpiece" not just because the food is a "perfect triumph" but also because the gathering "partook [. . .] of eternity" (158). Perhaps she casts "a spell" on the others or creates an "illusion" (151–52). Still, by giving "shape" and "order" to the "chaos" in which they live, she creates a community and, as Lily says a decade later, makes "of the moment something permanent" (240–41).

Mrs. Ramsay values women's traditional relationship with food as a symbol of her pragmatic, mythical, and eternal roles. But it is only by joining the fecundity of the female to the force of the male that she establishes a place for herself that neither submits to nor dismisses tradition. The mix of phallic and maternal imagery in a key scene conveys this:

Comforting her husband, she "raise[s] herself" to "pour erect" a "column of spray," and he leaves well-fed, "like a child who drops off satisfied" (58–60).

Knowing that food nourishes people physically and makes life possible, and that it can nourish their hearts and spirits as well, Mrs. Ramsay uses actual and metaphoric food to create order and celebrate life. Unfortunately, Virginia Woolf could not sustain such a vision for herself. Her relationship with food remained too complex and ultimately too unhealthy. Yet, as she showed her strength in living with and learning from depression, so she showed her strength here. Intuiting a comprehension of eating disorders that medical professionals did not have, Woolf turned illness into art.

Notes

1. For a history of eating disorders, see Joan Jacobs Brumberg, *Fasting Girls: The Emergence of Anorexia Nervosa as a Modern Disease* (Cambridge: Harvard University Press, 1988).
2. Roger Poole, in *The Unknown Virginia Woolf* (Cambridge, [Eng.]: Cambridge University Press, 1978), was among the first to note that Woolf "feared" and "hated" food (54). Allie Glenny offers a thorough study in *Ravenous Identity: Eating and Eating Distress in the Life and Work of Virginia Woolf* (New York: St. Martin's Press, 2000). In *Word of Mouth: Body Language in Katherine Mansfield and Virginia Woolf* (Charlottesville: University Press of Virginia, 1996), Patricia Moran suggests that female characters who avoid food are freer and less confident, while eating aligns women with heterosexuality and the father. Harriett Blodgett considers Woolf's literary use of food in "Food for Thought in Virginia Woolf's Novels" (*Woolf Studies Annual* 3 [1997]: 45–60).
3. Virginia Woolf, "Modern Fiction," *Collected Essays*, ed. Leonard Woolf, vol. 2 (London: Chatto & Windus, 1967) 103–110.
4. In *The Years* (New York: Harvest-Harcourt, Brace, & World, [1969, c1965]), women also eat the "relics" from a party (77).
5. See also Molly Huff, "A Feast of Words in *Mrs. Dalloway*" (*Woolf Studies Annual* 1 [1995]: 89–105).

Works Cited

Woolf, Virginia. *Between the Acts*. New York: Harvest-Harcourt Brace Jovanovich, 1969.

---. *Flush*. New York: Harcourt, Brace and Company, 1933.

---. *Jacob's Room & The Waves*. New York: Harvest-Harcourt, Brace and World, 1959.

---. *Mrs. Dalloway*. New York: Harvest-Harcourt, Brace and World, 1953.

---. *Night and Day*. New York: Harvest-Harcourt Brace Jovanovich, 1973.

---. *Orlando*. San Diego: Harvest-Harcourt Brace Jovanovich, 1973.

---. *The Pargiters*. New York: New York Public Library, 1977.

---. *To the Lighthouse*. New York: Harvest-Harcourt, Brace and World, 1955.

---. *The Voyage Out*. New York: Harvest-Harcourt Brace and World, 1948.

---. *The Years*. New York: Harvest-Harcourt, Brace and World, [1969, c1965].

WOOLF'S INTERROGATION OF CLASS IN *NIGHT AND DAY*

by Mary C. Madden

It seems axiomatic that Woolf's corpus of writing (and indeed her very corpus or bodily presence in life) is refracted through the lens of class. After examining a nexus of class issues in *Night and Day* (1919)—issues that seem encased by border and identity questions quite possibly related to her experience of alleged sexual abuse, war, and mental illness—I suggest that in this novel a subterranean lesbian theme challenges the idea of gender as a "class" and questions whether women themselves constitute a distinct class. As a childless, married woman inclined toward "Sapphism," Woolf was conscious of a deep contradiction between her desire for radical social reform of constricting class codes and her own complicity (and enjoyment) in maintaining and sustaining the privileges of class. Sustaining class boundaries may at times have been a psychological necessity and may have aided Woolf in shaping an identity that enabled her to retain—or at times regain—her sanity in periods of great rupture. On the other hand, certainly Woolf also found at times that class boundaries were exactly what were driving her mad. In *Night and Day*, Woolf initially employs a fairly gentle, Horatian mode of satire to interrogate the restrictive lifestyles of young men and women engaging in the still-Victorian dance of courtship, marriage, and drawing-room civilities. Nonetheless, Katharine Hilbery retains (like Woolf herself) a solid nostalgia for the past—partly perhaps as a guarantor of class structures, which appear to support the British concept of "civilization." The tray that brings her cup of tea in the morning, along with her mother's note stating that she will travel to Stratford-on-Avon to visit the site of the Bard, is metonymic: the assumption of the continued material support of servants for a privileged lifestyle, the leisure to support contemplation of the great tradition of English literature, and a general involvement with the ideological and practical continuum of the British Empire. However, Katharine Hilbery is in some ways quite unlike the average Victorian young woman, and she engages in behavior that places both her class and her personal identity in question. Her cousin Cassandra exclaims in exasperation near the end of the novel: "How queer, how strange, how unlike other people you are, Katharine" (*Night and Day* 427). Yet, even in this early novel, Woolf seems to recognize her heroine's complicity in perpetuating some form of an imperialist will-to-power, and Katharine is satirized for her obvious delight in dominating both William and Ralph with her charms—as well as Cassandra, who searches frantically under the barely concealed, scornful eye of Katharine (acknowledged as Cassandra's intellectual superior) for the volume of Macaulay's *History of England* so that she may impress William by tea time with her fifteen-minute foray into intellectual life. Katharine is glorified in a moment of possible Woolfian self-satire as another kind of society angel: the savior, the reformer, the independent artist whose vision incorporates a mountain in the north of England—a mountain nonexistent on any map, but which represents a vision possibly linked with that of Lily Briscoe in *To the Lighthouse*. Katharine's "mountain" is also the serious and solitary place of the artist, the "narrow room" of Clarissa Dalloway, providing the solitude needed for work of the imagination. Though supposedly based upon Vanessa, Katharine periodically seems to reincarnate instead a Virginia who craves this essential space for her personal, novel dialectic of class and identity, and who recognizes that this space depends upon income related to either inherited class wealth or one's own work (as exemplified by Mary Datchet).

Night and Day signals the concentric circles of class, which encompass all of Woolf's work and could be viewed as a lesson in coordinate geometry presented by its mathematically inclined heroine. The novel presents a plot graph of spatial complexity: line tracings of "star-crossed" couples crossing street after London street, unexpected negative and positive encounters at zoo and home, opposing movement of emotions in scenes with the engaged (then unengaged) couples, reflections upon the conflicting prospects of married and single life, the divergent agonies of comparing suitors, opposing lines of heterosexual and homosexual desire, and the oppositions of the nineteenth and twentieth centuries.

Michael Whitworth's presentation on "*Night and Day* and National Efficiency" at the Thirteenth Annual Conference on Virginia Woolf (6 June 2003) corroborates my sense of the novel as very much an interconnected web. Whitworth points out that prewar Britain was engaged in a major national efficiency debate that emphasized a rational business model for government, the centralization of charitable work, a plan for physical fitness (after the realization that Boer War recruits were often unfit), and street straightening and slum demolition. The vision of the state as an interconnected web began to dominate. Streets became more gridlike, and a strong model of rationality was endorsed as a means for, among other things, preventing the horror of war. Ironically, this very emphasis upon rationality may have led to war. Did Virginia Woolf, writing in this national context, perhaps mean to suggest this very contradiction? Such an effect would render Katherine Mansfield's criticism of *Night and Day* for ignoring the war perhaps a bit less potent.[1]

"It was a Sunday evening in October, and in common with many other young ladies of her class, Katharine Hilbery was pouring out tea" (*Night and Day* 1). In the very first sentence Woolf presents the tradition of tea and company, striking a chord emblematic of the British aristocracy, which will reverberate throughout this novel. Ralph Denham, pointedly introduced to the reader as a member of a lower class, enters the room full of people "much at their ease, and all launched upon sentences" (2). Katharine, keenly aware of her pretense of enjoyment of this required ritual, feels the discord represented in her "sentencing" (in a darker sense) by her social class, and by her "class" as a woman, to a birdcage of expectations that constrict her true desires as an individual. As Alex Zwerdling notes, Woolf was convinced that a novelist must acknowledge that class differences were real and not to be ignored. He quotes E. M. Forster on Woolf: "'Her snobbery—for she was a snob—has more courage in it than arrogance. It is connected with her insatiable honesty'" (89).

Night and Day might be seen as a fleshing out of Woolf's own essay "Am I a Snob?" by means of Katharine Hilbery, who strikes a note of duality consonant with the novel's title. Her inner life does not match her outer life. Secrecy appears necessary in order to preserve some core of her individual self; she may also be furtive (we discover later) because of an initially dimly recognized attraction for women, or at least for the life of a permanently single woman—not an option generally sanctioned by her class.

The Hilberys comprise an intellectual aristocracy, which sees itself as caretakers of Britain's literary and cultural past—a fact that both attracts and repels Katharine as she seeks to clarify her vocation in life. Her job has been defined by her family: to help her mother write a biography of her famous grandfather, the poet Richard Alardyce—a project hopelessly bogged down in an overwhelming mass of materials and one that remains unfinished throughout the novel. Katharine secretly studies math at night and hides her work, Austen-like, at the sound of a step on the staircase. She professes to have no aptitude for literature and to dislike expressing herself in words—preferring silence and absorption in some vision of her own. Ironically, according to Julia Briggs, her fantasy visions of taming wild ponies on the American prairies and saving a vast ship in a hurricane seem to come from book scenes influenced by masculine ideas of power, and to signal a concern in the novel with issues of dominance and subordination (Briggs xxviii). These issues are related to class as well as to gender.

Although Katharine envies Mary Datchet's "rooms of her own," she also plays the role of a dominant female (partially because of class difference) in lesbian-nuanced scenes related to Mary. However, Katharine is also able to analyze her own desire for control of her possible marriage to William Rodney: Caring about his happiness but not *really* loving him actually may provide for the kind of independence she senses as necessary for her in a long-term marital relationship, if she is to have one at all.

Shirley Nelson Garner points out that *Night and Day* represents a tentative exploration of lesbian love, one disguised because of events like the banning of *The Well of Loneliness* in 1928 (331). Garner also observes that *Mrs. Dalloway* (1925) contains a lesbian-nuanced scene between Sally Seton and Clarissa, which exactly replicates in its structure the scene where Katharine and Mary meet for the first time. *Mrs. Dalloway* suggests even more clearly that lesbian love may threaten heterosexual love (326). Garner also analyzes Katharine's recognition of the privacy she will lose in marriage, for she is often depicted as wanting to be away from even Ralph, desiring her own space (330-31).

When Katharine attends a gathering at the rooms of Mary Datchet, the suffragist, Woolf sounds more strongly the counterpoint of another "class" or category: that of the single woman, possibly that of the Sapphist. Although Katharine leaves the meeting with William Rodney, who is soon to become involved in a serious courtship with her, it is not before she inquires about the room in which Mary sleeps and registers a "momentary flush of pleasure" (*Night and Day* 56) in coming perceptibly nearer to another person by repeating Mary's first name four times. Mary and Katharine also join each other in staring out the window at the moon and are linked as "star-gazers"[2] by others in the room—an image frequently associated with Katharine. When Mary finds herself affectionately placing a hand on Katharine's knee for an instant, the reader begins to realize that there is possibly more physical spark between the two women than between Katharine and William.

Mathematical graphing, webbing, and net imagery pervade this novel. Although the underlying web seems to be one of class identity, which inextricably complicates individual identity (both physically and psychically), other enmeshing and related structures are also apparent. Mary Datchet sits amid her growing pile of letters at the suffragist center and feels at last that she is in control, that she is the "centre ganglion of a very fine network of nerves which fell over England" and which would eventually emit a "splendid blaze of revolutionary fireworks" (*Night and Day* 78). The center's office equipment and tactics are presented as operating like spider webs flung down upon the torrent of street life below. The suffragist aim of egalitarianism is a threat to established class structures.

Katharine calls out later in the novel, raising her voice to Mary: "'Remember, I want to belong to your society—remember'" (382). She is repelled by some aspects of the society's work (such as shabby material surroundings), but attracted strongly by the sense of vocation, of deeply felt work giving meaning to one's life, and by the society of Mary herself. Curiously, Katharine leaves her purse behind at Mary's, necessitating a return whereupon she jingles the coins in her purse and remarks to Mary, "'I think being engaged is very bad for the character'" (183), a seeming acknowledgment of the marital monetary/class-based commodity exchange system she has recently agreed to in becoming engaged to William Rodney. William has also just alluded to Katharine as *being* Shakespeare's Rosalind, who in *As You Like It* is disguised as a boy. Has Woolf coded an unspoken contemplation by Katharine of the possibility of an intimate relationship with a woman instead of a man? Are the characters also enmeshed in a cage of heterosexuality? Is not heterosexuality indispensable for the replication of class structures solidly based on Victorian family life models? Perhaps Katharine's "turbulent map of the emotions" (351) registers a space for unexpressed Sapphist desire. Throughout the novel, various "border crossings" seem to signify irruptions from the logic of class boundary markers (as when William regularly registers annoyance at Katharine's lack of conventional womanly behavior).

In some ways Woolf's webbing structural technique in this novel is ironically similar to Peter Lurie's description of a computer Web: contingent, associative, antiauthoritarian, suggestive of links to other times and even to other starlike worlds, and subversive because of the very *structure* itself. The traditional, linear happy ending is subverted by the satiric, mathematical webbing structure, where the technology of the telephone also lurks in the background as destructive of the old order. In *Night and Day* issues of class become endlessly referential and seem to spiral off to the stars in Derridean fashion.

In a seminal article, Mark Hussey asserts that *Night and Day*, was written partially as a response by Virginia to Leonard Woolf's *The Wise Virgins* (1914)—a bitter, misogynistic novel revealing the negative effects of convention and class divisions upon heterosexual relations (Hussey 129).[3] Hussey points out that a character in this novel, Arthur, is distressed over Camilla's refusal to play her expected role in the social order: "'What she really wants, only she doesn't know it, is to be a man; and—damn, damn, damn—she never will be'" (134). Or does Camilla, like Virginia, simply desire the same opportunities afforded to men for development of human potential? Hussey also notes the class-related disgust with physical demonstration of emotions reflected in letters exchanged between Lytton Strachey and Leonard and in *The Wise Virgins;* he further calls attention to Roger Poole's claim that Virginia's fear of physical sex was related to her experience of sexual abuse as a child (132). Hussey additionally highlights class issues related to Leonard's Jewishness, observing that both novels involve male characters who aspire to (but also despise) the social class to which they could gain entry by way of marriage. Hussey even suggests heterosexuality issues in quoting a letter to Lytton in which Leonard expresses attraction for Thoby, Virginia's brother (135). Of course, Lytton himself was a rather public homosexual. Interestingly, one can see aspects of Lytton Strachey, who proposed marriage to Virginia before Leonard did, in the character of Rodney, Katharine's rejected suitor. Hussey also notes that DeSalvo reveals a general association for Virginia in both the *Melymbrosia* manuscript and in *The Voyage Out* (1915) of heterosexual love with death. Throughout the article Hussey analyzes the differing narrative perspectives of Virginia and Leonard in representing the economy of sexual exchange of women between fathers and husbands and its importance to British society's patriarchal structure.

Hermione Lee in her biography of Woolf insists that Woolf resisted being identified as a Sapphist or lesbian because she despised all simplistic categories and delighted in sexual amorphousness and complexity (484-85). Is *Night and Day* an early exploration of the turmoil involved in realizing that the categories of class and heterosexuality are inadequate? Woolf wrote *Night and Day* while recovering from a serious bout of mental illness and later told Ethel Smyth that she wrote the novel as an academic exercise, as a kind of protection against her own insanity, which terrified her (*Letters* 4: 231). She may also reveal in this novel some of the irruptions of emotional imbalance experienced either before or during her recovery. She may have begun to consider herself as part of the "class" of the mentally ill. One example of a trigger to a "night" experience not brought to daylight until many years later may be revealed in Katharine's assertion to Ralph: "In fact, there never was a family so unable to take care of itself as ours is. [. . .] Once I was left in a field with a bull when I was a baby" (*Night and Day* 247). This odd remark leads the reader to suspect an allusion to Woolf's early experience of sexual abuse by her Duckworth half brothers and the family's failure to stop it. Mark Hussey observes that the families in both Leonard's *The Wise Virgins* and Virginia's *Night and Day* are drawn from the Stephen family at Hyde Park Gate (129).

References abound in *Night and Day* to Katharine's frequent habit of being abstracted, withdrawn, and even undemonstrative regarding emotions (except with Mary Datchet!). She abruptly decides to visit Mary Datchet in the middle of the night after she has been musing on the dream nature of life, the world as an antechamber to reality, "as if, lately dead, she heard the living talking" (*Night and Day* 373). Later she holds out an empty cup to a visitor, having forgotten to pour tea into it, and then gets dressed to go out, still holding her unfinished bread and butter in her hand. The portrait of Katharine here may reflect Woolf's own possible undiagnosed dissociative disorder due to earlier emotional trauma. Dr. Marlene Steinberg, a Harvard-trained psychiatrist specializing in treatment of trauma victims, observes that feelings of separation from reality, of having lost pieces of time, feeling "spacey," and feelings of impersonality—all experienced by both Katharine and Woolf—are symptoms of trauma (Personal Interview). In a related observation, Hussey references Woolf's early title for the novel ("Dreams and Realities") as representing Woolf's scrutiny of advantages and disadvantages of the unembodied dream world versus the world of heterosexual relations (133).[4] Katharine appears alternately in this novel as someone strong and yet, ironically, in need of care, someone who periodically is removed (or removes herself) from the real world of fact to a place offering another vision. Is the single life practical for one inclined toward mental illness? Surely Woolf must have speculated about her need for a somewhat less conventional marriage, much as Katharine does, and may have decided that marriage was very much both a personal and a political act.

The term "queer" occurs at interesting junctures in the novel. In addition to Cassandra having labeled Katharine as "queer" on several occasions, later when visiting Mary Datchet alone, Katharine describes her own dress in terms of "the queer look of her blue silk skirt and blue shoes upon the stone" (*Night and Day* 375). Cassandra later admits that perhaps William is queer as well, but she makes this remark while looking "with shy devotion at her cousin's beautiful face" (385), a scene marking her attraction toward

Katharine. Hermione Lee observes that "[q]ueer was certainly a known code word for homosexuality by the 1930s" (*Virginia Woolf* 487). Though *Night and Day* was published in 1919, Woolf easily could have been familiar with the term by that date and did, in fact, use the term in 1927 in telling Vita that "Moments of Being: Slater's Pins have no Points" was "a nice little story about Sapphism" (qtd. Lee 487). Ralph Denham characterizes marriage as "a very queer business" (*Night and Day* 405), a comment perhaps suggestive of Woolf's speculation (via Katharine) on the advantages of marriage to a homosexual male—or a relationship with another female—as less complicated and more rewarding than the conventional emotional turmoil of heterosexual coupling. Toril Moi and others demonstrate the manner in which Woolf undermines the notion of a unitary self; I maintain that inevitably Woolf also undermines the notion of a unitary social class.

Woolf appears to deconstruct the category of class along several fault lines, suggesting that it may not be simplistically determined by one's socioeconomic status at birth but may involve gender, education, and even health issues. Katharine, for example, anticipates Woolf's argument in *Three Guineas* that the daughters of educated men may in some respects be worse off than the daughters of the poor or relatively poor (like Mary Datchet) who perform honest (and even socially useful) labor and who support themselves. What, then, does the category of class signify for women if they remain essentially dependent upon father or brother? For Katharine to have a "house of her own" in practical terms, she must marry; otherwise, she will be trapped as a single woman working interminably on the Alardyce family biography project. Men in the novel, particularly because they are given opportunities for a college education, are not so dependent, even when they are born into a lower class (like Ralph Denham and Leonard Woolf). Granted, a woman could inherit wealth, but constricting class expectations would still deter her from living alone—and certainly from living with another woman. Marriage and family life, the crucible for producing more subjects of the British Empire (and fodder for war, as Woolf demonstrates in *Three Guineas*), were certainly the expectations for women, negating in many instances the kind of independence that both Katharine and Virginia seem to dream about. And what about the question of mental illness? One might speculate about Virginia's probable recognition, after several episodes of mental breakdown, that she could not easily live alone, that her disability placed her in an additional class of dependency despite her birth as a Stephen. I do not suggest that she married Leonard primarily for security, but do propose that her own experiences of dependency because of her gender (and related lesbian issues), her lack of formal education, and her emotional disability caused her to view the category of class through a kaleidoscopic lens that shifted with circumstance and perspective.

Shirley Nelson Garner reports that the Bloomsbury Group, though tolerant of homosexuality, regarded lesbianism with suspicion. Garner quotes Quentin Bell as reporting that Virginia's good friend E. M. Forster (a homosexual) told Virginia that he "'thought Sapphism disgusting: partly from convention, partly because he disliked that women should be independent of men'" (332). Garner believes that some of Woolf's evasiveness in portraying lesbianism in *Night and Day* is related to Woolf's fear of losing Forster's good critical opinion or friendship or both; furthermore, Forster's response to *Night and Day* was unenthusiastic.

Silences in the text may represent spaces in the web or graph structure of the novel, particularly regarding homosexuality and mental illness. In several instances, Mary Datchet provocatively fingers the fur on the edge of Katharine's skirt, which may function as a kind of border she longs to cross. Mary is also swept on the "breast of a wave" to tell Katharine that Ralph loves her (291). Shortly thereafter, Mary and Katharine sit *in silence* as Mary again fingers the fur on Katharine's dress. Later Katharine feels lonely and longs to be with Mary Datchet; in doing so, she draws the curtains so that the draperies meet in deep folds in the middle of the window—a possible psychosexual reference (373). Does Katharine speculate about whether Sapphists constitute a special "class" of people?

Just earlier, Katharine and Rodney have decided *not* to marry, and Katharine is flooded with *Antigone* imagery (anticipating Woolf's later, related "novel of fact," *The Years*) as she muses upon a lonely, "sealed away" existence (346). Mary Datchet has also resorted to *Antigone* imagery of living an "immured life" in her loneliness, a state she both treasures and fears (289). Perhaps indicative of the deep duality theme of the novel, Mrs. Hilbery confides to Katharine that she had once considered naming her "Mary." The single life chosen by Mary is one Woolf herself seriously considered before deciding to marry Leonard. Did Woolf decide, however, that living alone as a person subject to bouts of mental illness might not be a smart choice? Choosing a marriage partner on the basis of a larger shared vision (as Ralph and Katharine do) rather than simply upon the basis of sexual compatibility, desire for children, or other conventional reasons eventually seems eminently rational in this novel. It solves the problem of loneliness to a degree (Katharine invites Ralph to share her loneliness in a profound sense, for she believes that reality can be apprehended only in loneliness and that this recognition is a more honest approach to a marital relationship than one based upon conventional class expectations). Katharine has had her vision of being alone on a mountain in the north of England, the vision of an outsider, a vision subversive of her society's class structure. Toward the end of the novel, Ralph and Katharine are finally alone at the *bottom* of the house, "which rose, story upon story, upon the top of them" (445)—a curious inversion of an image for a new relationship for "The Third Generation," another early title for this novel (Briggs xiii), and one suggesting a new foundation for the "house" of civilization that Woolf seems to be trying to preserve yet modernize in *Night and Day*.

Notes

1. Julia Briggs discusses Mansfield's criticism of *Night and Day* in her introduction to the 1992 Penguin edition of the novel (xi).
2. Mark Hussey discusses the star-gazer reference in fascinating detail in "Refractions of Desire: The Early Fiction of Virginia and Leonard Woolf." *Modern Fiction Studies* 38 (1992): 127–46.
3. Although the date of composition of *Night and Day* is uncertain, Hussey reminds us in this article of Elizabeth Heine's belief that it was early in 1915, which would have been soon after Virginia's suicide attempt in 1913.
4. Hussey in this article also quotes Leonard's depiction of Virginia as Aspasia: a woman like "a snow-covered hill, as probably having no heart, but possessed of a pure and clear mind interested only in the pursuit of reality" (130).

Works Cited

Briggs, Julia. Introduction. *Night and Day*. By Virginia Woolf. New York: Penguin, 1992. xi–xxxv.

Garner, Shirley Nelson. "'Women Together' in Virginia Woolf's *Night and Day.*" *The (M)other Tongue: Essays in Feminist Psychoanalytic Interpretation.* Ed. Shirley Nelson Garner, Claire Kahane, and Madelon Sprengnether. Ithaca: Cornell University Press, 1985. 318–33.

Hussey, Mark. "Refractions of Desire: The Early Fiction of Virginia and Leonard Woolf." *Modern Fiction Studies* 38 (1992): 127–46.

Lee, Hermione. *Virginia Woolf.* New York: Knopf, 1997.

Lurie, Peter. "Why the Web Will Win in the Culture Wars for the Left: Deconstructing Hyperlinks." CTHEORY A125 (15 Apr. 2003) <http://www.ctheory.net/text_file.asp?pick=380>.

Moi, Toril. *Sexual/Textual Politics: Feminist Literary Theory.* London: Methuen, 1985.

Poole, Roger. *The Unknown Virginia Woolf.* 3rd ed. Atlantic Highlands, NJ: Humanities Press International, 1990.

Steinberg, Marlene, M.D. Personal Interview. 6 June 2003.

Whitworth, Michael. *"Night and Day* and National Efficiency." Woolf in the Real World: The Thirteenth Annual Conference on Virginia Woolf. Smith College, Northampton, MA. 6 June 2003.

Woolf, Virginia. *The Letters of Virginia Woolf.* Ed. Nigel Nicolson and Joanne Trautmann. 6 vols. New York: Harcourt Brace Jovanovich, 1975–80.

---. *Melymbrosia: An Early Version of "The Voyage Out."* Ed. Louise A. DeSalvo. New York: New York Public Library, 1982.

---. *Night and Day.* London: Duckworth and Company, 1919.

Zwerdling, Alex. *Virginia Woolf and the Real World.* Berkeley: University of California Press, 1986.

DARWIN'S TEMPORAL AESTHETICS:
A BRIEF STRETCH IN TIME FROM PATER TO WOOLF

by Joseph Kreutziger

Heraclitus says, "All things are in motion and nothing is at rest."
—Plato's *Cratylus*, 402A

Pater begins his "Conclusion" to *The Renaissance* (1873) with the epigraph of Plato quoting Socrates quoting Heraclitus, the same epigraph he translated in *Plato and Platonism* as "All things give way: Nothing remaineth" (9). This notion resonates through four voices and two millennia, still giving way but gathering, in Pater's customary way, more than the nothing that remains. If we remember Pater's counsel in his "Conclusion" that "our one chance lies in expanding that interval" (220) of the moment in art and song, we should also remember he sets artistic vision against this "continual vanishing away" (219) of ourselves *in time:* "[E]xperience dwindles down" impressions to "a single moment, gone while we try to apprehend it, of which it may ever be more truly said that it has ceased to be than that it is" (218). This is Heraclitus's theory of perpetual flux set forth in Pater, and the idea has in an era spanning what we loosely call modernism its myriad variations and negotiated responses. Rescuing the moment from the river of time becomes the substance of literary and philosophical works announcing almost ubiquitously a modern aesthetic perplexed by the present.

But before giving the age away to Heraclitus we should also note how that supposed antiquarian and aesthete Walter Pater makes Heraclitus his contemporary: "The entire modern theory of 'development,' in all its various phases, proved or unprovable,—what is it but old Heracliteanism awake once more in a new world, and grown to full proportions?" (*Plato and Platonism* 13). The seeds of Heraclitus, Pater argues, are only now expressing their full germinating power through this "formula, not so much new, as renovated by new application" (13): most prominently, Darwin's theory of evolution. What I wish to explore here today is *how* Pater's reconstitution of this perpetual flux, his particular rescue of the moment in time, responds to Darwin's *On the Origin of Species* in creating such an aesthetic—what I think is a remarkable translation of evolutionary and scientific theory into an aesthetic vision and a historical sensibility of reimagined temporality for literature. Doing so will help elucidate Virginia Woolf's own first forays into those moments of vision set against Darwin's great stretch of time: most explicitly, her early short fiction—"The Mark on the Wall" and "Kew Gardens"—which are not coincidentally the pieces Woolf herself attributes to her "discovery of technique" that would lead to the more experimental forms of temporality in the novels beginning with *Jacob's Room*.

&

Billie Andrew Inman has exhaustively researched and cataloged Pater's readings of evolutionary theory that came to inform his writing the "Conclusion" of *The Renaissance*, including, among many, Darwin, Herbert Spencer, George Henry Lewes, and Thomas

Huxley.[1] In his introduction to *Marius the Epicurean,* Michael Levey notes Pater "lived to write coolly, almost uncontroversially, that evidence for the Darwinian theory—that the identifying forms of life, immutable as they seem 'as of old in the Garden of Eden', are fashioned by slow development—was constantly increasing" (10). By the late date of *Plato and Platonism* (1893), Pater had fully appropriated Darwinian theory for his aesthetic needs. The revelation in Pater's chapter on "Plato and the Doctrine of Motion" is that Plato's types or ideal forms are established against Heraclitean flux, and after twenty-three centuries of stony sleep, "Darwin and Darwinism" answers back "'type' itself properly *is* not but is only always *becoming*" (14). What I've gathered from my reading of Pater is how essential this *idea of becoming* is to his aesthetics of the moment. The "long argument" of *On the Origin of Species,* which begins with Darwin's claim "that species are not immutable" (6), arranges about it example after example of the slippage between organic forms if seen through time, so that type indeed opens up to a transitional and continuous *becoming.* Only always *becoming* because evolution, if understood through Darwin's lapses of geological time and the slow, graduating steps of natural selection, "implies the continual supplanting and extinction of preceding and intermediate gradations" (203) that Darwin first posited in *On the Origin of Species.* Hence Pater transforms a few fragments of Heraclitus into a Darwinian figure of "full proportions," but such investment more crucially reveals how Darwin's theory of descent leads Pater, among so many contemporaries and heirs, to believe that we are not assured of the hard outline of final form in art or in life.

Especially malleable becomes the human form, now seen as less divine in Pater though by necessity always refining. How differently Pater's most regarded passage on *La Gioconda* reads, his own "symbol of the modern idea" an aesthetic of evolutionary characteristics ("Leonardo da Vinci" 150). To break up Pater's Lady Lisa rudely to foreground the point, she is: "expressive of what in the ways of a thousand years men had come to desire"; "the deposit, little cell by cell, of strange thoughts and fantastic reveries and exquisite passions"; "[a]ll the thoughts and experience of the world [. . .] in that which they have of power to refine and make expressive the outward form"; she is "older than the rocks among which she sits" (150). Pater's hyperbolic language, at first simply setting her for a moment beside Greek statuary, passes her through time with increasing extension, "dead many times, [. . .] a diver in deep seas," until Pater returns her to modern philosophy's conception of "humanity as wrought upon by, and summing up in itself, all modes of thought and life"—and that idea of perpetual motion, we are reminded, is "an old one" (150). Those "changing lineaments" (150) of her form, which so inspired Yeats when he read Pater's prose, embody the dynamics through which Pater will write down, again and again, the moment's impression even as it becomes, adds to, disappears into, the past. Or, in Pater's words, worth hearing against the Darwinian tenor, "[t]hat clear, perpetual outline of face and limb is but an image of ours, under which we group them—a design in a web, the actual threads of which pass out beyond it. This at least of flame-like our life has, that it is but the concurrence, renewed from moment to moment, of forces parting sooner or later on their ways" ("Conclusion" 217-18). Pater's "moment" in art becomes significant not simply because life is significantly short but because time under Darwin's tutelage is now stretched to inconceivably significant lengths. Darwin muses that the thought of evolution impresses his mind almost "as does the vain endeavour to grapple with the idea of eternity," but it is an eternity without the consolation of eternal forms, the descent long and disappearing, the ascent uncertain and accidental. Darwinism creates of the present a transitory state in the Modernist aesthetic. Pater will spend it "getting as many pulsations as possible into the given time" ("Conclusion" 220).

But perhaps the temporal difficulty never reconciled by Pater and his moment is the twin-born problem of a perpetual flux operating over all of physical life (after Darwin so fully extended it theoretically) and the passage of such varying temporality through the individual mind. It is the paradox Pater introduces in "Conclusion" by juxtaposing the elemental forces of which we are made that extend beyond us—transformation that "rusts iron and ripens corn"—and the more eager and devouring internal flow of our "inward world of thought and feeling [. . .] the race of the midstream" (217–18). At first Pater will give us cohesion over our sensations and impressions, a suspension of the flux "like some trick of magic," but Pater contracts the mind to its narrow chamber where he finds it impenetrable, each mind "keeping as a solitary prisoner its own dream of the world" ("Conclusion" 218). It informs the charges of solipsism which have been levied against Pater ever since publication of *The Renaissance*. Taken fully, Pater's aesthetic example proves especially taxing when applied to fictional forms. How can the evolutionary expansion of flux and the inward, contracted flow of consciousness find a form adequate to their expression when character itself, the presentation of another individual, is locked inside Pater's dream of heady solitude, especially given his famous aspiration for a fusion of matter and form? He had not realized that narration itself had become a problem. A problem, that is, if his unhinging of fixed ideas in the time of Darwin were to find an approximate form of expression in writing and presentation of character. We must turn to Virginia Woolf to discover that struggle undertaken.

∞

Virginia Woolf's most Darwinian plot is her first, *The Voyage Out*, which takes the heroine Rachel Vinrace to South America, often read as a kind of Darwinian or Conradian voyage without the benefit of a return. Gillian Beer's excellent essay on "Virginia Woolf and Prehistory" does more to flesh this out than I could begin to do here, but the novel shows a careful reading of Darwin, especially *The Voyage of the Beagle*, in which Beer finds many correspondences with Woolf.[2]

I'm more interested, though, in where Woolf departs from more established forms of the novel, how her own record of "descent" begins with a discovery of technique. Woolf recalls the unforgettable day in 1917, "the day I wrote The Mark on the Wall—all in a flash, as if flying, after being kept stone breaking for months" (*Letters* 4: 231). The quarry of her frustration was *Night and Day*, by Woolf's own estimate her most conventional novel, useful to her as compositional exercise but possessing none of the immediacy or departure provided by those first "little pieces"—the short stories eventually published in *Monday or Tuesday* (1921). Her diary describes this breakthrough as a "new form for a novel," her three short stories—"The Mark on the Wall," "Kew Gardens," and "An Unwritten Novel"—taking hands and stretching to two hundred pages or so—"doesn't that give the looseness & lightness I want: doesnt that get closer & yet keep form & speed, & enclose everything, everything?" (*Diary* 2: 13–14). This experiment would develop by *Mrs. Dalloway* into what Woolf would call her "method," "how I dig out beautiful caves behind my characters [. . .]. The idea is that the caves shall connect, & each comes to daylight at the present moment" (*Diary* 2: 263), a technique she also calls her "tunnel-ling process, by which I tell the past by instalments, as I have need of it" (*Diary* 2: 272). Throughout the diary entries during this germinative period, Woolf marvels at the success of tunneling, as her tropes for technique inevitably descend into the caverns of her mind; "I am laboriously dredging my mind" (2: 189); "I may have found my mine this time [. . .]. And my vein of gold lies so deep, in such bent channels" (2: 292); "it seems to leave me plunged deep in the richest strata of my mind" (2: 323).

Those early digs, though, the three short stories that join hands around Woolf's fu-ture experiments in temporal form, uncover Woolf's early intimations of this "method." In these few pages I want to touch upon two of these three short stories—"Kew Gardens" and "A Mark on the Wall"—the two of them written in quick succession in the summer of 1917, which we might too preciously describe as Woolf's "tales of the snails." Perhaps of both biographical and biological interest is that the most famous curator of the actual Kew Gardens was the famous botanist Joseph Dalton Hooker, the close friend of Charles Darwin, to whom Darwin first revealed in 1844 that he was "almost convinced (quite contrary to opinion [Darwin] started with) that species are not (it is like confessing a murder) immutable." Darwin helped make Hooker's career by presenting him with all his botanical specimens from the Galapagos Islands from the voyage of the *Beagle,* which are still today stored at Kew Gardens. While this can only be speculative, it is a happy coinci-dence for the historical imagination to envision Virginia Woolf walking through the floral arrangements and botanical specimens culled from Darwin's voyage. My little reverie even has plausibility, given Woolf's diary accounts of frequenting Kew Gardens while living at the time in nearby Richmond.

What need not be speculative is the significance Woolf gives to her characters' fic-tional visits to Kew Gardens. Katharine Hilbery and Ralph Denham meet in Kew Gardens in a pivotal chapter of *Night and Day,* where they stroll through "these legendary gardens" (330). Ralph shows off a bit, prodding the flowers, Woolf writes, "with the peculiar touch of the botanist," calling them by their Latin names. He speaks to her of bulbs and seeds, of living things endowed with sex, "and susceptibilities which adapted themselves by all manner of ingenious devices to live and beget life [. . .], by processes which might reveal the secrets of human existence" (330). Katharine wishes "he would go on for ever talking of plants, and showing her how science felt not quite blindly for the law that ruled their endless variations" (331), but also perhaps more significantly, how it allows her contem-plation "of that other part of life where thought constructs a destiny which is independent of human beings" (331). Woolf embeds Katharine's deepest capacity for happiness in this contemplative region that "entirely lacked self-consciousness" (332).

When we turn to the short story "Kew Gardens," written concurrently with *Night and Day,* this vegetative life and its unself-conscious existence is given a voice entirely outside any of the characters' thoughts and sensations, revealed and shared only by the narrative. Hidden below the oval-shaped flowerbed and its protrusion of stalks, which Woolf's varied human couplings pass by "with much the same irregular and aimless move-ment" ("Kew Gardens" 89), is Woolf's snail. Interspersed between the quickened, flicker-ing voices and the curiously irregular movements of her human beings are these interludes of the snail's lapsed progress, the goal before it only to trespass the "arched tent of a dead leaf" (86). Its presence at once registers Katharine Hilbery's contemplation of "a destiny which is independent of human beings" (*Night and Day* 331). But it also registers the temporal process external to human will, an expanded time, which slows existence to a snail's pace that has occupied all organic forms for millions of years. Against this Darwinian pace Woolf measures the progress embodied by the drone of the "aeroplane"—always in Woolf the intrusive suggestion of war—and the mechanical movement of London's "wrought steel turning ceaselessly" (89).

When the snail moves from the garden into the even more domesticated spaces of a house interior, the perspective is inverted. The first-person narration of "Mark on the Wall" focuses upon this splotch of seeming insignificance, which refracts prismlike the light of so many thoughts shot through it by the perceiving narrator. Withheld until the final sentence is the fact that the mark is a snail. Her narrator's reverie begins by attempting to fix a date and a beginning to the mark, musing over "[h]ow readily our thoughts swarm upon a new object" ("The Mark on the Wall" 77). The internal flow of her consciousness is given abundant free play over an associational sequence of moments *even as* the momentary thoughts comment upon the rapidity of thought and life, likening it to "being blown through the Tube at fifty miles an hour" (78). If what the narrative describes as "the perpetual waste and repair; all so casual, all so haphazard" (78), recalls Pater's "Conclusion," the mediating presence of this narrated consciousness still traverses vast stretches of time. We move in no preexisting order from the dust that covered Troy and the mantelpiece to seeds "sown in the reign of Charles the First" ("The Mark on the Wall" 79); from the masculine point of view, which establishes tables of precedency and fields of war to our "learned" descendents of witches and hermits crowded in caves. Finally, there is relief in the thought of trees. The solidity of our lives—these discernible marks, this solid wooden furniture with which we cover our interior spaces to give some semblance of stability and order—after all comes from trees. "Wood," Woolf writes, "is a pleasant thing to think about. It comes from a tree; and trees grow, and we don't know how they grow." And when they die, when "the highest branches drive deep into the ground again," Woolf continues, "[e]ven so, life isn't done with; there are a million patient, watchful lives still for a tree [. . .] in bedrooms, in ships, on the pavement, lining rooms" ("The Mark on the Wall" 82–83).

What I am arguing here is that this tree of life is the very metaphor Darwin made famous in his *On the Origin of Species*. The difficulty Pater presented as a "Conclusion" between the perpetual flux operating through the individual moments of the mind is not reconciled in Woolf so much as it is more convincingly represented. Woolf's moments are not pared down or refined out of existence into art as Pater would have us do; they are enveloped even as they are expanded, though not enclosed in fixity or final forms, as Woolf's assertion on aesthetics has us repeat that "life is a luminous halo, a semi-transparent envelope surrounding us from the beginning of consciousness to the end" (*Collected Essays* 2: 106). That assertion leaves open the temporal divergences of narrative never fully circumscribed. Gillian Beer has argued that evolutionary theory "does *not* privilege the present," that it sees the present as "a moving instant in an endless process of change. Yet it has persistently been recast to make it seem that all the past has been yearning towards the present moment and is satisfied now" (*Darwin's Plots* 10). Pater yearns for that satisfaction where Woolf will not fully restore it. The ethical questions, the feminist necessity, the war that keeps interrupting these short pieces, will not allow Woolf to rest on even the illusion of restoring it. "[I]f you can't be comforted," her narrator thinks, "if you must shatter this hour of peace, think of the mark on the wall" ("The Mark on the Wall" 82). Even there is relief in thinking on life beyond our own design on it. The male voice that both curses the war and interrupts her reverie doesn't see why we should have a snail on the wall. Woolf does.

Notes

1. Billie Andrew Inman, "The Intellectual Context of Walter Pater's 'Conclusion,'" *Prose Studies* 4 (May 1981): 12–30.
2. Gillian Beer's book *Darwin's Plots* is perhaps the one indispensable study for anyone interested in the impact of evolutionary narrative on fiction.

Works Cited

Beer, Gillian. *Darwin's Plots: Evolutionary Narrative in Darwin, George Eliot and Nineteenth-Century Fiction.* 2nd ed. Cambridge: Cambridge University Press, 2000.
---. "Virginia Woolf and Prehistory." *Virginia Woolf: The Common Ground.* Ann Arbor: University of Michigan Press, 1996. 6–28.
Darwin, Charles. *On the Origin of Species.* London: John Murray, 1859.
Levey, Michael. Introduction. *Marius the Epicurean.* By Walter Pater. Harmondsworth, Middlesex, England: Penguin Books, 1985.
Pater, Walter. "Conclusion." *Walter Pater: Three Major Texts.* Ed. William E. Buckler. New York: New York University Press, 1986.
---. "Leonardo da Vinci." *Walter Pater: Three Major Texts.* Ed. William E. Buckler. New York: New York University Press, 1986. 134–52.
---. *Plato and Platonism: A Series of Lectures.* New York: Macmillan, 1895.
Woolf, Virginia. *Collected Essays.* 4 vols. New York: Harcourt, Brace and World, 1967.
---. *The Diary of Virginia Woolf.* Ed. Anne Olivier Bell. 5 vols. New York: Harcourt Brace Jovanovich, 1977–84.
---. "Kew Gardens." *The Complete Shorter Fiction of Virginia Woolf.* Ed. Susan Dick. London: Hogarth Press, 1985. 84–89.
---. *The Letters of Virginia Woolf.* Ed. Nigel Nicolson and Joanne Trautmann. 6 vols. New York: Harcourt Brace Jovanovich, 1975–80.
---. "The Mark on the Wall." *The Complete Shorter Fiction of Virginia Woolf.* Ed. Susan Dick. London: Hogarth Press, 1985. 77–83.
---. *Night and Day.* New York: Harvest-Harcourt Brace Jovanovich, 1973.

MODERNITY'S SHOCK AND BEAUTY: TRAUMA AND THE VULNERABLE BODY IN VIRGINIA WOOLF'S *MRS. DALLOWAY*

by Cornelia Burian

Trauma theory can provide valuable insights into Woolf's fiction by elucidating how intricately intertwined experiences of World War I and other, seemingly more personal traumata, namely the childhood abuse and other forms of gendered oppression Woolf suffered, register in *Mrs. Dalloway*. Abject images of physical vulnerability indicate the psychic splitting that often accompanies traumatic experience.[1] More surprising, perhaps, is the traumatic content of another set of images: Woolf transforms and intensifies the sense of trauma in her use of beautiful flower imagery,[2] which suggests a paradoxically close interconnection of modern beauty and shock.

The trauma of modernity registers in *Mrs. Dalloway* on the level of metaphor. The wounded, broken body is written into the pages of Woolf's novel. Clarissa Dalloway, we learn, is "over fifty, and grown very white since her illness" (4). The fact that she has aged quickly since her illness—apparently influenza—is repeated several times. Peter Walsh thinks, "[s]ince her illness she had turned almost white" (36), reinforcing the sense of buried psychic pain. Clarissa often appears frail and seems to suffer from an unspecified ailment, which she experiences like some kind of demonic physical and psychic possession:

> It rasped her, though, to have stirring about in her this *brutal monster!* to hear twigs cracking and feel *hooves* planted down in the depths of that leaf-encumbered forest, the soul; never to be [. . .] quite secure, for at any moment *the brute* would be stirring, this hatred, which, especially since her illness, had power to make her feel scraped, hurt in her spine; gave her physical pain, and made all pleasure in beauty, in friendship, in being well, in being loved and making her home delightful rock, quiver, and bend as if indeed there were *a monster* grubbing at the roots. (*Mrs. Dalloway* 12, emphasis added)

The "monster" here could be read as a metaphor of Clarissa's illness, which may, like Woolf's own periods of psychic and physical breakdown, strike again at any time. The term "brute" also suggests her vulnerability to being preyed on by a predator, and thus hints at the psychological scars that Woolf's own early abuse probably inflicted.

Clarissa's physical fragility in the face of aging and illness signifies the fragmentation of her identity, as becomes obvious early on in the novel's mirror scene. Clarissa appears as a coherent self only in front of others; when alone, she feels shattered into irreconcilable fragments. Sitting at her dressing table, she sees "the delicate pink face of the woman who was that very night to give a party; of Clarissa Dalloway; of herself" (37). The strangely impersonal way in which she perceives her face as first that of "a woman" or "Clarissa Dalloway" before she recognizes it as "herself" suggests deep self-alienation caused by a traumatic shattering of her identity. She is, however, able to temporarily unite the fragments into a hard unity: "She pursed her lips when she looked in the glass. [. . .] That was her self—pointed; dart-like; definite. That was her self when some effort, some call on her to be her self, drew the parts together" (37). Despite her sense of psychic disintegration, Clarissa is able to piece together her shattered self into "one centre, one diamond, one woman" (37), which suggests a defense against trauma.

The fragmentation of Clarissa's identity has much to do with the conflict between her lesbian desire and the conflicting social roles forced upon her. Clarissa "could not resist sometimes yielding to the charm of a woman" (31–32). When younger women turn to her for moral support and advice, she "did undoubtedly then feel what men felt" (32). Obviously, Clarissa is bisexual. For her, there was "this falling in love with women. Take Sally Seton" (32), for instance, whom Clarissa adored. When they first met, "she could not take her eyes off Sally. It was an extraordinary beauty of the kind she most admired, dark, large-eyed" (33). Moreover, Sally was wild, funny and unconventional; she discussed subversive political theories with Clarissa, and made her feel truly alive. Societal pressures of postwar British society in the early 1920s, however, smothered this kind of love.

Modern life, and modern war in particular, threatens not only the female but also the male body. When Peter Walsh leaves Clarissa's house, he observes "[b]oys in uniform, carrying guns, march[ing] with their eyes ahead of them, march[ing], their arms stiff, and on their faces an expression like the letters of a legend written round the base of a statue praising duty, gratitude, fidelity, love of England" (51). Their stony appearance, obvious emotional coldness, and mechanical movements bring Jacob Flanders to mind. Like him though, too, these boys are vulnerable: "[T]hey did not look robust. They were weedy for the most part, boys of sixteen," wearing "the solemnity of the wreath which they had fetched from Finsbury Pavement to the empty tomb" (51). Many of these boys will die in the war; others will return home maimed or deeply emotionally scarred, like Septimus Smith.

Septimus has indeed been deeply wounded. He survived the trenches apparently unharmed. His physician Dr. Holmes thus insists that there is nothing serious "the matter with him" (21). Dr. Holmes of course greatly underestimates the devastating effects of trench warfare. As a soldier, Septimus had to witness his friend Evans's death, and he himself only narrowly escaped being killed. He suffers from what we call today posttraumatic stress disorder:[3] He is dysphoric, feels completely numb and separated from the world that "normal" human beings inhabit. According to Sue Thomas, Woolf was familiar with the War Office Committee of Enquiry's close examination into the phenomenon of shell shock and the debate about its causes and cures. Her characterization of Septimus hauntingly shows that for traumatized veterans, the war never ends: "For now that it was all over, truce signed, and the dead buried, he had, especially in the evening, these sudden thunder-claps of fear. He could not feel" (87). Septimus remains forever trapped in the trenches; he does not regain his feeling, nor can he rid himself of involuntary flashbacks.

The threat of total physical annihilation on the battlefield caused Septimus's psyche to dissociate. As Robert J. Lifton explains, "[i]n extreme trauma, one's sense of self is radically altered. And there is a traumatized self that is created" (Caruth, "Interview" 137); a form of "doubling" takes place as the psyche splits. This is clearly the case for Septimus; he has retained some of his prewar personality insofar as he can still recall how he felt, for instance, about literature, or what kind of aspirations he had. Yet the war has profoundly changed his personality. Before he volunteered, he was an ambitious young writer, leaving his hometown to make it in London. He was deeply passionate. At night, he would devour his favorite writers, or dream about his literature teacher, Isabel Pole, with whom he had fallen in love (85). He had great hopes for the future—he was sure that he would become a great man, a famous writer (84). The war changed all this; it destroyed Septimus's ability to feel. His wife, Rezia, loves him, but no matter how movingly she tells him that she is "so unhappy" (70), wants children, or wishes him to speak to her, he hardly ever replies. Only at the very end does he join her in making a hat, perhaps in an attempt at reparation.

Septimus's injured psyche, moreover, generates images of bodily disintegration. He believes that he can "see through bodies" (68), and anticipates that his own body will go to pieces: "Scientifically speaking, the flesh was melted off the world. His body was macerated until only nerve fibres were left. It was spread like a veil upon a rock" (68). These frightening images of physical pain and dissolution, however, are closely intertwined with images of desire and beauty. As Henke observes, "[h]is visions are poetic, even seductive, as he fantasizes the dissolution of his ego in a benevolent, pantheistic universe" ("Virginia Woolf" 151). This kind of bruised beauty becomes especially obvious in the many passages of *Mrs. Dalloway* containing flower imagery. Susan Gallagher's cover illustration for the 1981 edition shows a woman, probably Clarissa, before a grayish-brown background adorned with pale roses. We already encounter flowers in the novel's famous opening sentence: "Mrs. Dalloway said she would buy the flowers herself" (3). Flowers take on very different meanings in the novel, depending on who perceives, buys, or arranges them. Sometimes, they offer respite from the hectic life in the city. To some, flowers are a symbol of English formality and tradition, and even of the British army. For still other characters, however, flowers signify just the opposite; they become a means of breaking with convention and striving for a more liberated life. Different characters interpret the meanings of flowers differently, based on their gender, age, nationality, and personal experience. Most striking is Septimus Smith's relation to flowers.

Flowers remind Septimus of the war and its tremendous losses. He remembers his employer "Brewer at the office," whose "geraniums" were "ruined in the War" (89). Such memories of flowers destroyed by bombs still appear relatively sane; yet elsewhere, the frightening magnitude of Septimus's affliction becomes evident. The war has fractured his psyche; flashbacks of his commanding officer (and perhaps lover), Evans, resurface everywhere. The sights and sounds of "normal" life—his wife's voice, the pleasant sight of an urban park—have taken on ominous meanings. No cultural sign is any longer what it once was. Before the war, Septimus was fond of literature, and Shakespeare in particular: "That boy's business of the intoxication of language—*Anthony and Cleopatra*—had shrivelled utterly. How Shakespeare loathed humanity [. . .]! This was now revealed to Septimus; the message hidden in the beauty of words" (88). The beauty of flowers, too, can no longer conceal the world's ugliness.

For Septimus, flowers have become harbingers of death. Significantly, it is right before he commits suicide that he helps his wife to arrange the "artificial flowers" (143) she uses for making hats. Moreover, one day, when Rezia takes him to Hampton Court, "they were perfectly happy. All the little red and yellow flowers were out on the grass, like floating lamps he said, and talked and chattered" (66). Yet suddenly he says, to his wife's horror, "'Now we will kill ourselves'" (66). Or, looking at his wife, he finds her "pale, mysterious, like a lily, drowned, under water" (89). Even more disturbing is his delusion of physical penetration that becomes closely associated with flowers; he believes that "[r]ed flowers grew through his flesh" (68). And there are further "roses" that "hang about him"—"the thick red roses which grow on [his] bedroom wall" (68). The flowered wallpaper reminds him that he is "like a drowned sailor on a rock. I leant over the edge of the boat and fell down, he thought. I went under the sea. I have been dead, and yet am now alive" (68–69). Like a ghost, Septimus seems to have overcome the life-death boundary.

Moreover, flowers become Septimus's means of speaking to the dead. While his psyche is clearly disturbed, the idea of communicating with the dead through flowers is ancient. In grave sites around the world, archeologists have found pollen; even thousands of years ago, our ancestors adorned their dead with flowers. And today, too, we lay down wreaths and other floral arrangements on graves to honor those who have passed on. Via flowers, Septimus hears and sees messages from beyond. In the park, he imagines hearing his friend: "Evans answered from behind the tree. The dead were in Thessaly, Evans sang, among the orchids" (70). Even more unsettling is a later scene:

Rezia came in, with her flowers, and walked across the room, and put the roses in a vase, upon which the sun struck directly, and it went laughing, leaping around the room. She had had to buy the roses, Rezia said, from a poor man in the street. But they were almost dead already, she said, arranging the roses. So there was a man outside; Evans presumably; and the roses, which Rezia said were half dead, had been picked by him in the fields of Greece. (*Mrs. Dalloway* 93)

These flowers have many layers of meaning. Almost dead, they are reminders of the brevity of life. Yet they also bridge the world of the living and the world of the dead; they are, Septimus believes, a message from Evans. The roses thus symbolize, as for Clarissa (recall the scene of their first kiss right after Sally rips off the flowers' heads), homosexuality. The rose imagery here establishes an interesting link between war trauma and the trauma inflicted by rigidly heterosexist standards; for Septimus and Clarissa, flowers express the traumatic aftereffects felt by those who are unable to live out their true sexual identity. Roses have traditionally been objects of desire and an expression of love. If Evans sends Septimus roses picked in "the fields of Greece," a country that has, since antiquity, been associated with the free expression of male homosexuality, then they clearly express a man's sexual desire for another man.

Septimus's attraction to Evans is evident elsewhere, too; many of his reminiscences are homoerotic. Attraction between men at the front was certainly not unusual. As Paul Fussell describes in the chapter "Soldier Boys" of his study *The Great War and Modern Memory:*

Since antiquity everyone who has experienced both war and love has known that there is a curious intercourse between them. [. . .] Given this association between war and sex, and given the deprivation and loneliness and alienation characteristic of the soldier's experience—given, that is, his need for affection in a largely womanless world—we will not be surprised to find both the actuality and the recall of front-line experience replete with what we can call the homoerotic. (270–272)

Fussell's observations about male bonding at the front correspond to Woolf's depiction of Septimus's feelings for Evans.

Septimus admits to himself that "he had married his wife without loving her; had lied to her; seduced her" (91). We learn that "he drew the attention, indeed the *affection* of his officer, Evans by name" (86, emphasis added). The two men "had to be together, share with each other, fight with each other" (86). Rezia has seen Evans only once; she finds him quiet and "*undemonstrative in the company of women*" (86, emphasis added). Yet surprisingly enough, when Evans is killed, "Septimus, far from showing any emotion or recognising that here was the end of a friendship, congratulated himself upon feeling very little" (86). Soon he becomes engaged to Rezia, the youngest daughter of an Italian innkeeper: He "was bound to survive. He was right there. The last shells missed him. He watched them explode with indifference" (86). Septimus's lack of feeling can be accounted for in several ways. As Cathy Caruth and other trauma theorists explain, what is traumatic in near-death experiences is on the one hand the realization that one has *almost* died, and on the other the fact that one has survived in unlikely circumstances. Septimus's indifference can thus easily be explained in terms of the numbness of trauma. *If* Septimus and Evans were more than fellow soldiers, more than friends—if they were lovers—then his numbness may be intensified beyond survivor guilt, becoming guilt over sexual desires that the society of his day condemned as perverse. Septimus's case thus forcefully illustrates how closely intertwined sexual and war trauma become in Woolf. The seemingly odd connection between Clarissa and Septimus at the novel's end, when Clarissa "felt somehow very like him—the young man who had killed himself" (186), gains a new dimension if we consider both characters, who seem to have little else in common, as bisexual. If we regard both as oppressed by societal standards of sexual conduct, then Clarissa's intuitive understanding of his despair suddenly makes perfect sense.

The experimental imagery in *Mrs. Dalloway* captures the shock of modernity. Woolf conveys sexual and war trauma via disturbing images of bodily wounding and disintegration. At the same time, however, she represents the trauma of modernity in beautiful language. Like the early psychoanalyst Pierre Janet, who used hypnosis to substitute a patient's "traumatic death images with those of flowers" (van der Kolk and van der Hart 179), Woolf, too, employs flower imagery. Her goal, however, unlike Janet's, is not to make the trauma "fade away altogether" (179). Instead, in *Mrs. Dalloway*, flowers become the insistent images of both Eros and Thanatos.

Notes

1.   Geoffrey H. Hartman argues that a "traumatic event" is "registered rather than experienced," bypassing the psyche and causing it to "split" or dissociate (537). The clinical experiences of psychiatrists like Judith Herman (*Trauma and Recovery* 107), Henry Krystal ("Trauma and Aging" 85), and Lynne Layton ("Trauma, Gender Identity and Sexuality" 109), to name only a few, seem to confirm that trauma fragments the sufferer's personality.

2.   I am indebted to Lyndsey Stonebridge's discussion of rose imagery in Henry Green's novel *Caught*. Her claim that Green's account of the Blitzkrieg uses roses as pivotal images of trauma inspired me to take a closer look at flower imagery in Woolf.

3.   Caruth explains that posttraumatic stress disorder (PTSD) is commonly agreed to be "a response, sometimes delayed, to an overwhelming event or events, which takes the form of repeated, intrusive hallucinations, dreams, thoughts or behaviors stemming from the event, along with numbing that may have begun during or after the experience" ("Introduction" 4).

Works Cited

Caruth, Cathy. "An Interview with Robert Jay Lifton." *Trauma: Explorations in Memory.* Baltimore: Johns Hopkins University Press, 1995. 128–47.

---. Introduction. *Trauma: Explorations in Memory.* Baltimore: Johns Hopkins University Press, 1995. 3–12.

---. *Trauma: Explorations in Memory.* Baltimore: Johns Hopkins University Press, 1995.

---. *Unclaimed Experience: Trauma, Narrative, and History.* Baltimore: Johns Hopkins University Press, 1996.

DeSalvo, Louise A. *Virginia Woolf: The Impact of Childhood Sexual Abuse on Her Life and Work.* Boston: Beacon, 1989.

Fussell, Paul. *The Great War and Modern Memory.* New York: Oxford University Press, 1975.

Hartman, Geoffrey H. "On Traumatic Knowledge and Literary Studies." *New Literary History* 26.3 (1995): 537–63.

Henke, Suzette A. *Shattered Subjects: Trauma and Testimony in Women's Life-Writing.* New York: St. Martin's, 1998.

---. "Virginia Woolf and Post-Traumatic Subjectivity." *Virginia Woolf: Turning the Centuries: Selected Papers from the Ninth Annual Conference on Virginia Woolf.* Ed. Ann Ardis and Bonnie Kime Scott. New York: Pace University Press, 2000. 147–52.

Herman, Judith Lewis. *Trauma and Recovery.* New York: BasicBooks, 1992.

Hussey, Mark, ed. and introd. *Virginia Woolf and War: Fiction, Reality, and Myth.* Syracuse, NY: Syracuse University Press, 1991.

Krystal, Henry. "Trauma and Aging: A Thirty-Year Follow-Up." *Trauma: Explorations in Memory.* Ed. Cathy Caruth. Baltimore: Johns Hopkins University Press, 1995. 76–99.

Layton, Lynne. "Trauma, Gender Identity and Sexuality: Discourses of Fragmentation." *American Imago* 52.1 (1995): 107–25.

Lee, Hermione. *Virginia Woolf.* London: Chatto & Windus, 1996.

Stonebridge, Lyndsey. "Bombs and Roses: The Writing of Anxiety in Henry Green's *Caught.*" *Diacritics* 28.4 (1998): 25–43.

Thomas, Sue. "Virginia Woolf's Septimus Smith and Contemporary Perceptions of Shell Shock." *English Language Notes* 25.2 (1987): 49–57.

Van der Kolk, Bessel and Onno van der Hart. "The Intrusive Past: The Flexibility of Memory and the Engraving of Trauma." *Trauma: Explorations in Memory.* Ed. Cathy Caruth. Baltimore: Johns Hopkins University Press, 1995. 158–82.

Woolf, Virginia. *Jacob's Room.* London: Hogarth, 1990.

---. *Mrs. Dalloway.* San Diego: Harcourt Brace, 1981.

Mrs. Dalloway's Menopause:
Encrypting the Female Life Course

by Elizabeth Hirsh

Just before learning of the death of Septimus Warren Smith, Clarissa Dalloway surveys her party from the staircase and reflects as follows:

> It was too much like being—just anybody, standing there; anybody could do it; yet this anybody she did a little admire, couldn't help feeling that she had, anyhow, made this happen, that *it marked a stage,* this post that she felt herself to have become, for oddly enough she had quite forgotten what she looked like, but felt herself a stake driven in at the top of her stairs. (*Mrs. Dalloway* 170, emphasis added)

Concealed in the compounding ambiguities of Virginia Woolf's syntax is a straight-forward declaration—"it marked a stage"—that invites us to join Clarissa in seeing the party as something other than pure diversion—to see it instead as a particular kind of ritual, specifically a rite of passage from one *stage of life* to another. The transformation in question—despite its profound importance in the lives of most modern women—is one for which Clarissa's society, like our own, has evolved no positive form of recognition, let alone any shared ritual like those that routinely accompany birth, death, or marriage. It is, of course, the aptly termed "silent passage" of menopause. In *Mrs. Dalloway* (1925) Woolf registers this dimension of female experience as a true "climacteric" or crisis whose existential specificity warrants careful delineation. She does so, however, in a deliberately cryptic way, at once publicly marking and prudently concealing her menstrual theme. Where Elizabeth Abel's frequently anthologized reading of *Mrs. Dalloway* uncovers a con-cealed narrative of female development tracing a violent rupture between pre-Oedipal and post-Oedipal sexuality, I suggest that Woolf's text encrypts another transformation in the female life course: the passage between premenopausal and postmenopausal identity, and specifically Clarissa's successful mourning for the end of her menses and of biological fertility.

Woolf's fiction is full of concealments, as we know. Her widely read essay "Modern Fiction"—substantially revised from an earlier piece and republished almost simultane-ously with *Mrs. Dalloway* in the first *Common Reader* (1925)—famously notes that in modern novels "the accent falls differently from of old; the moment of importance came not here but there" (*Common Reader* 150), repeating that "the emphasis is upon some-thing hitherto ignored" or is "laid upon such unexpected places that at first it seems as if there were no emphasis at all" (*Common Reader* 152). No doubt the parenthesized, brack-eted, or grammatically subordinated catastrophes of "Time Passes" (in *To The Lighthouse*) constitute Woolf's most celebrated use of such semantic displacements, but a similar logic operates less overtly and to varying effect throughout her fiction. In the passage quoted at the beginning of this paper, the embedded assertion—"it marked a stage"—exemplifies the same technique. When the narrator of *A Room of One's Own* (1929) takes a second look at the awkwardly "broken" sentences and sequences of the experimental novelist Mary Carmichael, she illustrates the kind of reading that Woolf both solicited and saw as corollary to the modern writer's, and especially to the modern *woman* writer's, work. It is a hallmark of Woolf's critical thought that there could be no literary innovation without the active collaboration of writer and reader. This is a permissive as well as a demanding doctrine, but as practiced by Woolf it also implies certain exclusions. Thus lesbian and feminist critics have excavated from Woolf's text sexual themes that often lay hidden, as it were, in plain view, awaiting only the responsive ear of the knowing reader. Woolf's inscription/encryption of Mrs. Dalloway's menopause elicits a comparable pact between writer and reader.

In the early pages of *Mrs. Dalloway* at least two elements signal the cryptic nature of Woolf's text: The airplane's ambiguous and evanescent skywriting is interpreted by each member of the London crowd according to his or her vantage point and disposition; and similarly, just a moment before the plane's appearance, an anonymous but authoritative "male hand" discreetly draws the blind of a passing limousine, concealing "a face of the very greatest importance" from the crowd's prying gaze (*Mrs. Dalloway* 14). Woolf practices a similar discretion vis-à-vis male onlookers (and perhaps also youthful onlookers) in her treatment of Mrs. Dalloway's menopause. Clarissa, she tells us, "had just broken into her fifty-second year" (36) and felt at one moment "very young; at the same time unspeakably aged," and "shrivelled, aged, breastless" the next (8, 31); she suffers from insomnia and may often be found reading at three a.m.; and she walks through London feeling "invisible, unseen; unknown; there being no more marrying, no more having of children now, but only this astonishing and rather solemn progress with the rest of them, up Bond Street" (11).

Throughout the novel, meanwhile, floral imagery alludes to the old euphemism "to have one's flowers" (to menstruate), linking it with the idea of the female life course. Clarissa's seventeen-year-old daughter, Elizabeth, is "a bud" or "buds on the tree of life" (29); a slightly older young woman delightfully named Nancy Blow merges beautifully in her green dress with the ambient flowers of late June; and Clarissa receives from her husband a bunch of red and white roses in full bloom. Nubile young women like Elizabeth, Rezia Warren Smith, the young Clarissa, and the young Sally, as well as Clarissa's sister Sylvia who died, it is said, "on the verge of life" (78) are coupled with middle-aged and elderly women like Miss Kilman, Lady Bradshaw, Lady Bruton, and of course the present-day Clarissa and Sally. A certain Mrs. Dempster sits in Hyde Park watching the unknown nineteen-year-old Maisie Johnson, and thinks:

> You'll get married, for you're pretty enough [. . .]. Get married, she thought, and then you'll know. Oh, the cooks, and so on. Every man has his ways. [. . .] For it's been a hard life, thought Mrs. Dempster. What hadn't she given to it? Roses; figure; her feet too. (She drew the knobbed lumps beneath her skirt.)
> Roses, she thought sardonically. [. . .] Pity, for the loss of roses. (*Mrs. Dalloway* 27)

The juxtaposition of Maisie and Mrs. Dempster is paralleled in another class by that

of mother and daughter, Clarissa and Elizabeth. While Elizabeth reflects, "[I]t was beginning. . . . People were beginning to compare her to poplar trees, early dawn, hyacinths,
fawns, running water, and garden lilies, and it made her life a burden to her, for she so
much preferred being left alone to do what she liked in the country" (134), we are told
that her mother, going upstairs to change clothes, "paused at the window, came to the
bathroom. There was the green linoleum and a tap dripping. There was an emptiness
about the heart of life; an attic room. Women must put off their rich apparel. At midday
they must disrobe" (31).

The dignity and lyricism of Woolf's language of menopause stands against the pathol-
ogizing of the female that turns Clarissa's friend Evelyn Whitbread into a perennial invalid. Meeting Evelyn's husband, Hugh, in the park, Clarissa learns that Evelyn "had some
internal ailment, nothing serious, which, as an old friend, Clarissa Dalloway would quite
understand without requiring him to specify" (6). At this news Clarissa feels "sisterly"
and anticipates settling down with Evelyn "for the usual interminable talk of women's
ailments" (10). Clarissa's encounter with Hugh Whitbread is treated rather differently
in Woolf's short story of 1923, "Mrs Dalloway in Bond Street," from which her novel
gradually "branched," as Woolf wrote in her diary. In the short story Evelyn is called Milly
Whitbread and the suggestion about what ails her is more emphatic:

> "Milly?" said Mrs Dalloway [. . .]
> "Out of sorts," said Hugh Whitbread. "That sort of thing." [. . .]
> Of course, [Clarissa] thought [. . .] Milly is about my age—fifty—fifty-two. So
> it is probably *that*. (*Mrs Dalloway's Party* 20)

Along with this allusion to Evelyn Whitbread's menopause, the story contains another fairly explicit reference to menstruation. While shopping for gloves, Clarissa hesi-
tates to trouble the so-called shop-girl because "it seemed tiresome to bother her—perhaps
the one day in the month, thought Clarissa, when it's an agony to stand" (*Mrs Dalloway's
Party* 26). In the text of the novel these references to the menstrual cycle have been muted
or suppressed, and the shop-girl has become Miss Pym, proprietor of Mulberry's florist,
whom Clarissa thinks "looked older, this year, turning her head from side to side among
the irises and roses" (*Mrs. Dalloway* 13).

According to Victorian and Edwardian models of the female life cycle, "looking
older" was the least a menstruating *or* menopausal woman had to fear. The Victorian
gynecologist Edward J. Tilt had pioneered medical recognition of the menopausal syn-
drome by enumerating one hundred and twenty different infirmities, subdivided into
"seven distinct modes of suffering," that characterized the change of life in women
(Jalland 281). As the medical historians Pat Jalland and John Hooper demonstrate, ideas
about the fate of postmenopausal women were deeply contradictory during the period of
Clarissa Dalloway's lifetime. In medical discourse it was customary to see the female life
cycle in terms of epochs, which might number as few as three or as many as seven. Four
widely recognized stages were prepuberty; menstruation; marriage and childbirth; and
finally menopause, with the transition from one epoch to another representing a point
of physical and psychological vulnerability. The climacteric was sometimes compared to
puberty as a critical point in the life cycle, wherein women were especially at risk for all

kinds of "perturbation," up to and including both insanity and suicide. Thomas Laycock wrote, for example, "The vigour of the reproductive system begins to decline about the age of forty or forty-two; and from this period to the age of forty-nine, there is a state of system exceedingly analogous to that of the period during which it was first developed" (Jalland 287). In short, both entering into and exiting from the state of womanhood were seen as fraught with peril, in keeping with the logic that pathologizes the female body as such. Also parts of the negative stereotype of menopause were such familiar complaints as nervous irritability, headache, perspiration, insomnia, and flushes. Most gravely, since "the primary meaning of female life was achieved through maternity," according to the experts, it followed that "the woman's world after reproduction was necessarily characterized by the loss of meaning" (Jalland 281).

But contradicting the negative stereotype of menopause was the recognition that "women lived longer than men, and generally survived in better health than elderly men" (Jalland 281)—provided they had been able to weather the illness and the risk of death so often associated with childbirth. Moreover, since menstruation was "seen as a major cause of ill-health, the menopause allowed good health to be re-established" (Jalland 283)—a view again in keeping with the broader pathologization of the female. In fact, it was said that after menopause women entered into a sexually "neutral" or even a masculine state that was generally salutary. Dr. J. Braxton Hicks nuanced this view by underscoring the persistence of the feminine. "[I]t is quite certain," he wrote, in *The British Medical Journal* (21 April 1877),

> that all the tendency to various troubles, to which I have partly alluded as belonging to females, principally after puberty, now cease [. . .] and then, when the change is complete, the woman passes much into the state of one who has had her ovaries removed, having a tendency to revert to the neutral man-woman state; yet not entirely so, because there remains impressed upon the mind, memory, and nervous system the reflection of the woman; in manifold ways recalling to her actions and movements that manner and style she had earlier in life. (Jalland 293)

Mrs. Dalloway echoes the medical discourse insofar as it underscores a connection between nubile young women in their teens and twenties just entering the "epoch" of marriage and maternity, and those over forty who have left or are in the process of leaving it. In this context Woolfians may speculate whether the menopausal Clarissa represents a kind of androgyne—albeit not exactly of the Woolfian variety—but one who has reverted to "the neutral man-woman state" of the prepubescent subject. I would argue, on the contrary, that *Mrs. Dalloway* affirms the persistence of feminine identity in "the mind, memory, and nervous system," as J. Braxton Hicks writes. But it is against the essentialist, heterosexist reduction of the feminine to marriage and maternity entailed in prevailing medical formulations that Woolf inscribes the menopausal Clarissa as a specifically feminine subject-in-process.

In *Mrs. Dalloway*, red roses and red carnations, as well as Sally Seton's red cloak and ruby ring, all connote passion as distinct from the purity or deathliness of Clarissa's white dress as a girl, or her pale complexion in middle age as a newly recovered invalid. Within the novel's imaginary, this color coding also dovetails with the representation of the menstrual cycle. Importantly, the book's most explicit image of "having one's flowers" is displaced onto the male Septimus, who imagines that "[r]ed flowers grew through his flesh" (68)—an image in which the blood of menstruation and the wounds of battle merge.[1] By the same token, Clarissa's menopausal mourning here rejoins the novel's elegy for the lost sons of the war, and for their grieving mothers.

When Septimus flings himself from the boarding-house window and is impaled on the iron railing below, these hallucinatory "red flowers" again metamorphose into real wounds. His impalement also recalls the rape of Clarissa Harlowe, at once feminizing Septimus and identifying him as a guardian of innocence and the soul. In effect, he dies resisting the medicalization of the soul enforced by Drs. Holmes and Bradshaw, symbolically redressing the soul murder of Evelyn Whitbread effected through the medicalization of her female body. The epistemic violence of medical science drives a wedge between body and soul, objectifying "life" and "the body" at once, as does Miss Kilman's religiosity, with its demonizing of "the flesh" (*Mrs. Dalloway* 128). Her desire to be pure soul—"a soul cut out of immaterial substance; not a woman, a soul" (134)—is also a denial of her sexed body, which she mortifies by shrouding it in a sweaty green mackintosh. Against any such carceral logics (Evelyn is confined to a nursing home; Septimus would have been confined to a rest home), Septimus's flight through the air posits the freedom of the birds that populate the text of *Mrs. Dalloway* as well as the flight of the airplane above London, which one Mr. Bentley "vigorously rolling his strip of turf at Greenwich," sees as "a symbol [. . .] of man's soul; of his determination [. . .] to get outside his body, beyond his house, by means of thought" (28).

Septimus's *earthward* flight suggests that freedom is won not so much by thinking oneself "outside" the body as by thinking oneself into it: by embracing the fact of embodiment, including its corollary—and Clarissa's recurring reflection—"how it is certain we must die" (175). *Mrs. Dalloway* suggests that, by heralding the inevitable process of *dis*embodiment, the climacteric proffers an opportunity to encounter one's embodiment in a distinctive, historically new, and specifically feminine way. As articulated by Woolf, Clarissa's "crisis" is an experience enormously more complex than can be fathomed within the prevailing discourses of mainstream medicine, Orthodox Christianity, classical metaphysics, or any logic that polarizes body and soul—or indeed, life and death (Peter Walsh reminds us that the soul too can die [58]). When Clarissa identifies with Septimus in the moment of his bloody death, she also rises to the occasion cryptically marked by her ongoing party, symbolically embracing her new, postmenopausal status—embracing, as Elizabeth Abel writes, "a positive commitment to development—not to any particular course, but to the process of change itself" (110). The passing of her menses, merging in Clarissa's mind with the festivity of her ongoing party, releases her to another stage of life: "No pleasure could equal, she thought, straightening the chairs, pushing in one book on the shelf, this having done with the triumphs of youth" (185).

Note

1. The image perhaps specifically recalls a line from Isaac Rosenberg's poem "Break of Day in the Trenches": "Poppies whose roots are in men's veins / Drop, and are ever dropping" (lines 23–24).

Works Cited

Abel, Elizabeth. "Narrative Structure(s) and Female Development: The Case of *Mrs. Dalloway.*" *Virginia Woolf: A Collection of Critical Essays.* Ed. Margaret Homans. Englewood Cliffs, NJ: Prentice Hall, 1993. 93–114.

Jalland, Pat, and John Hooper. *Women from Birth to Death: The Female Life Cycle in Britain 1830–1914.* Atlantic Highlands, NJ: Humanities Press International, 1986.

Woolf, Virginia. *The Common Reader: First Series.* Ed. Andrew McNeillie. San Diego: Harcourt, Brace and Company, 1986.

---. *Mrs. Dalloway.* San Diego: Harvest-Harcourt Brace, 1981.

---. *Mrs Dalloway's Party.* Ed. Stella McNichol. London: Hogarth Press, 1973.

THE PARADOX OF THE GIFT:
GIFT GIVING AS A DISRUPTIVE FORCE IN WOOLF'S WRITING

by Kathryn Simpson

As co-owner of the Hogarth Press and as a woman writer intent on making money from her pen, Virginia Woolf was interested in markets and profit margins. Sales figures feature significantly in her diaries as both a marker of her artistic achievement and an indication of her financial success. However, she also felt considerably uncomfortable about her own place in the commercial world.[1] Participation in mass consumer culture—characterized as feminized, fluid, shifting, and in which flows of desires are equated with commodity flows—can be experienced as positive and pleasurable. But Woolf is resistant to the sexual politics of the marketplace. As critics Bridget Elliot and Jo-Ann Wallace argue, for Woolf "the exchange of commodities in a capitalist economy" and "the exchange of women in a patriarchal sexual economy" are interrelated (73). Participation in market economies is always in tension in Woolf's work with a resistance to the rational male-dominated capitalist system, based as it is on possession of things, money, and people; focused on calculation and fixing of value; and rigorously organized by the laws of profit and loss.

What I want to explore here, however, is another economy at play in Woolf's work. That is the gift economy, which can be read as running counter to, but also contiguous with, capitalist systems. Hélène Cixous characterizes the gift economy as feminine, and as one that offers a resistance to the commodifying impulse of capitalism.[2] It emphasizes fluidity, indeterminacy, a destabilization of hierarchies and rational systems, and a disturbance of property rights. It doesn't try to recover its expenses or to recuperate its losses—in fact giving, excess, and overflow are recognized as sources of pleasure and *jouissance*.

Gifts and gift giving figure quite significantly in Woolf's writing and her fiction has many instances of gifts exchanged between her female characters. These gifts are sometimes literary texts, but other, often erotically charged, gifts are also made, which mark the bond between women, notably Sally's "diamond" kiss in *Mrs. Dalloway* and the ambiguously coded bottle of crème de menthe in *The Voyage Out*. Woolf also famously made a gift of her own writing—the original manuscript of *Orlando*—to Vita Sackville-West. However, what is in Nigel Nicolson's estimation the "longest and most charming love-letter in literature" may possibly be Woolf's most ambiguous gift (Nicolson 192). It has been seen simultaneously as a sign of Woolf's love and desire for Sackville-West and as a punishment for her infidelity (as Suzanne Raitt and Anna Snaith have argued). Sackville-West's thank-you letter suggests both gratitude and a sense of entrapment, as she tells Woolf that she feels like "one of those wax figures in a shop window, on which you have hung a robe stitched with jewels."[3]

Gift giving, then, can be ambiguous and problematic: The issue of motivation and reciprocation (for Cixous "the paradox of the gift that takes") is one problem that we see in the giving of *Orlando* ("The Laugh of the Medusa" 263). But there is also the danger of colluding with heteropatriarchal power structures, which identify woman *as* a gift to be exchanged between men.[4] However, gift giving also creates a utopian and liminal space; it has a disruptive effect in suggestively and ambiguously sidestepping the calculation of market exchange and eluding the fixity of heterosexual economies.

I want to explore here the interrelation of capitalist commodity economies (focused on the marketplace and commercial exchange) and libidinal economies (the structures of desire) in relation to Woolf's short story "Mrs Dalloway in Bond Street." Located in commercial London, this story encapsulates Woolf's ambivalence about consumerism, capitalism, and commodity culture. Initially intended to be the first chapter of *Mrs. Dalloway*, the story is premised on Clarissa's shopping trip to buy a pair of gloves. In her essay "Collecting, Shopping and Reading: Virginia Woolf's Stories about Objects," Ruth Hoberman identifies shopping in this story as good but problematic (84). She argues that shopping promotes relationships and social exchanges; "human contact is the story's subject" (92).

In particular, though, the subject of this story is *female* contact, of bonds between women that differ from the bonds implied in the street's name. What seems significant in this story is Clarissa's ability to empathize with other women, to feel admiration and possibly attraction for them. I'm interested in the ways the usual bonds (of exchange in business and personal relationship) can, in Cixous's words, "function otherwise" in this story so as to destabilize market and heterosexual economies ("Castration or Decapitation?" 50). Shopping in Bond Street provides opportunities for Clarissa's bonds with other women to surface in an ambiguous way through what she *almost* purchases, and, importantly, through the idea of gift giving. At odds with capitalist consumerism and the flow of cash and commodities, Clarissa's actual concerns for most of the story focus on "flows" of other kinds as she expresses her wishes to give gifts to women.

In her essay on "Castration or Decapitation," Cixous outlines the ways in which a masculine social, psychic, and libidinal economy 'decapitates' women, silencing the feminine voice. But she also considers how this system could be disrupted through, in her words, "resistance to masculine desire conducted by woman as hysteric, as distracted" ("Castration or Decapitation?" 50). In "Mrs Dalloway in Bond Street" Clarissa isn't exactly an "hysteric" but she is distracted from her participation in the masculine market economy by a preoccupation with the womb and menstrual flows.[5] Significantly, this preoccupation is what seems to motivate her desire to give gifts to women. She seems to want to compensate Milly Whitbread for the difficulties with her menopause and to compensate the shop assistant for the pains and discomfort of her monthly losses. The roots of Clarissa's generosity and sympathy, then, are physical as well as emotional, and they are exclusive to women. However, like the Clarissa Dalloways of Woolf's other texts (*The Voyage Out, Mrs. Dalloway,* and several short stories), Clarissa here remains an ambiguous character. She isn't firmly located in one or another economy but moves between gift and market economies, between homoerotic possibility and heterosexual certainty.

The gifts Clarissa considers giving to Milly and the shop assistant offer an escape from daily life, and involve Clarissa in recollections of her past. Standing outside Hatchard's bookshop, Clarissa contemplates buying a copy of Elizabeth Gaskell's *Cranford* for Milly. For Clarissa this novel conjures up a simpler, idyllic world and she becomes lost in a reverie about her youth—a time of transition, a liminal state in which her desires and mature emotional bonds were emerging and in a state of possibility. Although Clarissa's choice of novel here signals her conventionality and lack of modern sensibility, this text, centered firmly on a community of women ("Amazons") from which men are largely excluded, helps to emphasize the female-specific space of Woolf's story (*Cranford* 1).

Once inside the glove shop, the flow of empathy and generosity extends to the shop assistant, for whom menstrual flows seem to be causing discomfort. Clarissa considers giving a gift of a holiday to this woman, a holiday better than any the shop assistant would be able to afford. It would give her experiences and pleasures beyond the scope of her class-bound situation. Like the gift for Milly, this imagined gift for the shop woman is also prompted by a sense of connection to the past. Clarissa remembers the woman but is surprised at how much older she looks, again recalling an earlier period of Clarissa's own life, and possibly a premarital state.

There is a parallel scene in *Mrs. Dalloway* that takes place in a florist shop. It is, on the whole, more explicitly erotically charged (the shop is full of flowers that are more evidently sensual and sexual). However, there is eroticism implicit in the glove shop too, and this context adds greater significance to the idea of gift giving. Like the florist shop of *Mrs. Dalloway*, the glove shop is a feminine space. The masculine economy, signaled by Bond Street, is marginalized, merely a distant hum, a sound that can intrude only in a dulled way, apparently stifled by the atmosphere of expectation and the female-specific commodities (the gloves and silk stockings) for sale. It is a space of female intimacy and has a potentially erotic atmosphere as gloves are fitted and removed by the shop assistants, and as the women shoppers look at each other, exchanging glances. It's also a space in which Clarissa expresses her admiration and implicitly her desire for women as she gazes at them "through the hanging silk stockings quivering silver," an image vibrating with sexual suggestion ("Mrs Dalloway in Bond Street" 151).

Clarissa's entry to the shop is also suggestive as she makes an instant, possibly flirtatious, connection with the shop woman:

> "Good morning," said Clarissa in her charming voice. "Gloves," she said with her exquisite friendliness and putting her bag on the counter began, very slowly, to undo the buttons. "White gloves," she said. "Above the elbow," and she looked straight into the shop woman's face. ("Mrs Dalloway in Bond Street" 150)

The unnecessary lingering over removing her gloves, her bag on the counter, and her direct gaze add a sense of suggestiveness to this exchange. It seems significant too that the *specific* context in which Clarissa imagines and rules out the gift of a holiday is the intimate one of having a glove fitted and drawn off. This context is only implicit in the story—the fitting isn't "present" at the textual surface—but in this feminine space, in which eroticism is already evoked, this detail makes Clarissa's fantasy of a gift even more subversive.

That Clarissa doesn't buy *Cranford* and doesn't pay for a holiday for the shop assistant might suggest her lack of commitment to the feminine gift economy—her lack of investment in such bonds. However, this could also indicate a refusal to participate in a system of property and possessions. The fact that she only considers buying Milly a "little *cheap* book" could indicate that the gift and the bond it represents are trivial ("Mrs Dalloway in Bond Street" 149, emphasis added). However, it is also significant in representing only a minimal investment in a masculine capitalist economy. The paradox of the gift here is not that it is given with the expectation of a return, but that the gift *isn't* given.

However, Clarissa's *imagined* gift giving still retains a disruptive potential. On their honeymoon, Clarissa's husband, Dick, dismisses her desire to give impulsively and asserts that trade with China is "much more important" ("Mrs Dalloway in Bond Street" 151). Dick's economic lesson, presumably forcefully delivered given the long-term impact on Clarissa, hints at a sense of threat and draws attention to the idea that gift giving does have the potential to scupper the economy and trade. It threatens the economic system by undermining the notion of a fixed hierarchy and certain measurement of value, and by disrupting the controlled flows of profit and loss. In a sense, the exchange of gifts between women also scuppers the heterosexual economy in which women are the gifts exchanged between men, not the givers or the receivers. In gift exchange between women, then, women are agents with the power to negotiate their own pleasures, and to give pleasures to other women. The promise of Clarissa's gifts in both cases is pleasure and escape.

Dick's choice of the word "folly" is quite apt when we consider its meaning in the architectural sense—that is, of a mock building constructed to satisfy someone's fancy or conceit—or, here, to satisfy other kinds of longing. In this sense, a folly can function as a mocking imitation (and subversion of) the "architecture" of the capitalist economy. The "folly" of giving impulsively, then, can mockingly undermine the foundations of capitalist and heterosexual economies. That Dick tries to prohibit Clarissa's impulsive behavior on their honeymoon seems to be a recognition that such "impulses" have the potential to bring the disorder of flux and fluidity to market and sexual paradigms. In this story the flow of people and commodities, the bodily flows of women (menstrual blood and also tears), and the more fluid economy of the gift have the potential to blur and to even dissolve capitalist and heteropatriarchal structures.[6]

"Mrs Dalloway in Bond Street" explicitly puts the market and gift economies into opposition, but Clarissa's negotiation of and participation in the two economies remains ambiguous. Dick's system keeps everyone in his or her place—in terms of class, gender, and role in the process of capitalist exchange, and Clarissa seems to agree. In many ways, Clarissa's gift is problematic anyway—it is patronizing and motivated by class prejudice, and it's also a possible slight on the shop woman's hard-earned independence. It too could be considered as a means of maintaining social hierarchies and keeping hierarchies of value in place.

In reneging on her gift, Clarissa seems to comply with a masculine economy that silences the feminine and, in Cixous's theory, denies women's erotic and emotional needs and desires. Clarissa stifles her impulse to give a gift to the shop assistant (and presumably to Milly) and, seeming to favor Dick's economic sense, also becomes more "business-like" in her attitude to the shop assistant, more "thrifty" with her time and attentions, more focused on bringing the transaction to a close:

> At last! Half an inch above the elbow; pearl buttons; five and a quarter. My dear slow coach, thought Clarissa, do you think I can sit here the whole morning? Now you'll take twenty-five minutes to bring me my change! ("Mrs Dalloway in Bond Street" 153).

However, the ambiguity and potential for destabilization of heteropatriarchal systems continue *as part of* the capitalist transaction, as part of the process of purchasing the gloves. Clarissa's impulses toward the shop assistant dissipate, but her serial desires for women continue and her attention is diverted by the entrance of a woman she recognizes. This woman's entrance is announced by the roar of traffic as the door opens (a reminder of the busy city and the operation of the masculine economy), but also by the brightening of the silk stockings in the shop. Immediately this woman "distracts" Clarissa, a certain "ring in her voice" triggers emotive memories for Clarissa; again she recalls a premarital state, a youthful pastoral idyll of female intimacy before the death of her sister. This memory immediately leads to thoughts of an imagined future, after the death of her husband. Although apparently this is Clarissa's fantasy about her own stoicism, both remembered and imagined times are, significantly, times when Clarissa is at a remove from heterosexual structures.

Following this stream of thought, and still immersed in her fantasy of a future free from marital bonds, Clarissa's gaze lingers admiringly on this "sensual, clever" woman, objectifying her as a "Sargent drawing," and trying to find a point of connection in order to capitalize on this momentary meeting. The end of the story is Clarissa's recollection of the woman's name, Miss Anstruther, but this is clearly only the beginning of further exchanges between them. The final words affirm her connection with this unmarried woman, and the pleasure this affords Clarissa, as she smilingly says this woman's name.

Significantly, by the end of the story the capitalist transaction is incomplete—her participation in the masculine monetary economy continues to facilitate Clarissa's activities in a feminine libidinal economy, beyond the ending of this narrative. Earlier in the story we're told that Clarissa takes great pleasure in the "endless—endless—endless" stream of people and sights in the city; equally what we see in this story is the endless flow of Clarissa's desires ("Mrs Dalloway in Bond Street" 148). The story ultimately resists closure: The transaction is not closed and a bond with another woman just renewed.

Clarissa's participation in gift and market economies is not fixed and specific. She isn't constrained by a masculine (capitalist and heterosexual) economy or limited to a feminine, potentially lesbian, gift economy, but she shifts between the two. Indeed, her "proper" participation in the market economy provides a space for other "improper" economies to function. She takes erotic pleasure from shopping and window shopping, gazing at women and "bonding" with them, but ultimately she stakes no claim. She neither gives gifts nor makes a purchase, but takes pleasure in the possibility and processes of both. Certainly the story provides plenty of scope for "speculation" and Clarissa's activities in the marketplace give rise to a good deal of "interest." What seems to be the case is that whether participating in market or gift economies, Clarissa's bonds with women are invested with desire in a way that has the potential to threaten and bring disorder to both capitalist and heterosexual economies.

Notes

1. See Jane Garrity and Leslie Kathleen Hankins.
2. See "Castration or Decapitation?" and "The Laugh of the Medusa," for example.
3. Letter, 11 Oct. 1928 of *The Letters of Vita Sackville-West to Virginia Woolf,* ed. Louise DeSalvo and Mitchell A. Leaska (New York: William Morrow and Company, 1985) 288.
4. In her influential essay "The Traffic in Women: Notes on the 'Political Economy' of Sex," Gayle Rubin takes issue with the work of structural anthropologist Claude Lévi-Strauss on the importance of gift exchange in

primitive societies, notably the exchange of women as gifts to consolidate bonds of kinship in his study *The Elementary Structures of Kinship*. Writing from a feminist perspective, Rubin argues that because women are "sexual semi-objects—gifts" rather than "exchange partners" or "sexual subjects," they cannot "realize the [social] benefits of their own circulation" (542–43). She suggests that the practice of the "'exchange of women'" is "more pronounced and commercialized in more 'civilized' societies" and goes on to discuss such practice as fundamental to the constitution of dualistic gender identities, socioeconomic relations and "obligatory heterosexuality" in a range of male-dominated societies (543, 545, 548). Significantly, she argues that "[t]he asymmetry of gender—the difference between exchanger and exchanged—entails the constraint of female sexuality" (548).

5. Hoberman also notes that "menstruation is a running theme" in the story (81–98).
6. Similarly, Jennifer Wicke argues that in *Mrs. Dalloway* consumption is reformulated as "the possibility of the gift" and as such has the potential to liquefy or collapse distinctions and hierarchies (19).

Works Cited

Cixous, Hélène. 1975. "The Laugh of the Medusa." Translated by Keith Cohen and Paula Cohen. *New French Feminisms: An Anthology*. Ed. and introd. Elaine Marks and Isabelle de Courtivron. Amherst: University of Massachusetts Press, 1980. 245–64.

---. "Castration or Decapitation?" 1976. Trans. Annette Kuhn. *Signs: Journal of Women in Culture and Society* 7.1 (1981): 41–55.

Elliot, Bridget and Jo-Ann Wallace. *Women Artists and Writers: Modernist (Im)positionings*. London and New York: Routledge, 1994.

Garrity, Jane. "Virginia Woolf, Intellectual Harlotry, and 1920s British *Vogue*." *Virginia Woolf in the Age of Mechanical Reproduction*. Ed. Pamela L. Caughie. New York and London: Garland Publishing, 2000. 185–218.

Gaskell, Elizabeth. *Cranford*. Ed. Elizabeth Porges Watson. London: Oxford University Press, 1972.

Hankins, Leslie Kathleen. "Virginia Woolf and Walter Benjamin Sellig Out(Siders)." *Virginia Woolf in the Age of Mechanical Reproduction*. Ed. Pamela L. Caughie. New York and London: Garland, 2000. 3–35.

Hoberman, Ruth. "Collecting, Shopping and Reading: Virginia Woolf's Stories about Objects." *Trespassing Boundaries: Virginia Woolf's Short Fiction*. Ed. Kathryn N. Benzel and Ruth Hoberman. New York: Palgrave Macmillan, 2004. 81–98.

Nicolson, Nigel. *Portrait of a Marriage*. Ill. ed. London: Weidenfeld and Nicolson, 1990.

Raitt, Suzanne. *Vita and Virginia: The Work and Friendship of V. Sackville-West and Virginia Woolf*. Oxford: Oxford University Press, 1993.

Rubin, Gayle. "The Traffic in Women: Notes on the 'Political Economy' of Sex." *Literary Theory: An Anthology*. Ed. Julie Rivkin and Michael Ryan. London: Blackwell, 1998. 533–60.

Sackville-West, Vita. *The Letters of Vita Sackville-West to Virginia Woolf*. Ed. Louise DeSalvo and Mitchell A. Leaska. New York: William Morrow and Company, 1985.

Snaith, Anna. *Virginia Woolf: Public and Private Negotiations*. Basingstoke, Hampshire: Macmillan Press, 2000.

Wicke, Jennifer. "*Mrs. Dalloway* Goes to Market: Woolf, Keynes, and Modern Markets." *Novel: A Forum on Fiction* 28.1 (1994) 5–23.

Woolf, Virginia. "Mrs Dalloway in Bond Street." *The Complete Shorter Fiction of Virginia Woolf*. Ed. Susan Dick. London: Hogarth Press, 1985. 146–53.

Ailing Dualisms:
Woolf's Revolt against Rationalism in the "Real World" of Influenza

by Lorraine Sim

This paper explores the role that common forms of illness assume in Woolf's account of our knowledge of the "real world." In an abridged version of her 1926 essay "On Being Ill," Woolf refers to common illness as an "unexploited mine," and argues that the significant effects of the sick body on thought are generally ignored.[1] In "On Being Ill" she discusses the effect that the pain and social isolation associated with common ailments, such as headache, influenza, and toothache, have upon the perspectives, values, and beliefs she attributes to everyday, healthy consciousness, which is represented in the essay by the "army of the upright" (*Collected Essays* 4: 196). This paper focuses upon "On Being Ill" as a critique of rationalism and looks more widely at Woolf's representation of illness through the spatial imagination. I argue that, for Woolf, physical illness instigates an unmaking of the real world as it is known and experienced by healthy, rational consciousness. This unmaking occurs in relation to rationalist views of the subject and society, which I will discuss in the context of Plato's dualism and the Enlightenment values of reason and progress. The second part of this paper considers the relationship between illness, imagination, and the creation of new worlds. Estranged from the now "remote" world of healthy consciousness, Woolf discusses the internal and external topographies that, she writes, are "disclosed" to the "invalid" (*Collected Essays* 4: 193, 195). Thus in "On Being Ill," Woolf presents the sick body as a vehicle for knowledge and suggests that common illness poses a challenge to many of our everyday assumptions about self and the world.

I. Illness as "Common" Experience

Woolf's motivation for writing "On Being Ill" stems from her conviction that illness is "common" to everyone, yet it is a mode of experience that remains "ignored" by "literature," which, she claims, is concerned only with the "doings of the mind" (*Collected Essays* 4: 193, 194). Ailments such as a headache, toothache, and fever are indeed "common" experiences. However, a complexity arises regarding the shared or private nature of common illness, due to the inexpressibility of physical pain. In *The Body in Pain,* Elaine Scarry discusses the political and social consequences of pain's inexpressibility. Pain is rendered unsharable not only through its resistance to language, but its capacity to actively destroy "language, deconstructing it into the pre-language of cries and groans" (Scarry 4, 172). In her introduction, Scarry refers to "On Being Ill," in which Woolf also discusses the "poverty of the language" to express physical pain, how language "runs dry" when a "sufferer" tries to "describe a pain in his head to a doctor" (*Collected Essays* 4: 194; Scarry 3–6). We need, Woolf claims, a "new language," "more primitive, more sensual, more obscene" (4:

194–95). However, if the "experience" of, for example, influenza, "cannot be imparted" in terms of physical sensation, the effects of pain or a "little rise of temperature" on perception and thought can be communicated (4: 195, 193). Thus, while "On Being Ill" does not represent physical pain through language, it does seek to explicate the ways in which illness transforms the relations between the sick person and language, body and mind, self and others, and self and nature. It is this aspect of common illness that can be shared in a language that privileges mind.

II. Ailing Dualisms: Illness and Rationalism

Woolf suggests in "On Being Ill" that some of the fundamental beliefs and values of normal, healthy consciousness are challenged during illness. Healthy consciousness, she suggests, is dictated by reason and the values of economic and social progress, which motivates the "army of the upright" as they "[march] to battle" with the "heroism of the ant or the bee" (*Collected Essays* 4: 198). During illness, the experience of intensified physical sensations dominates consciousness and directs thought. Social "responsibility" is "shelved" and "reason" put in "abeyance" (4: 199). It is this "shelving" of reason that enables the "invalid" to perceive self and world in new ways and reflect skeptically upon the limits of healthy understanding.

Woolf claims her gripe is with literature's failure to account for the "daily drama of the body":

> People write always of the doings of the mind; the thoughts that come into it, its noble plans; how the mind has civilized the universe. They show it ignoring the body in the philosopher's turret; or kicking the body, like an old leather football, across leagues of snow and desert in the pursuit of conquest or discovery. (*Collected Essays* 4: 194)

The descriptions of the mind-body relation Woolf critiques in the essay are, however, derived less from literature than philosophy. They refer to what Elizabeth Spelman calls the tradition of "somatophobia," or fear of the body, which has dominated notions of subjectivity in Western philosophy since pre-Socratic times (119–29).[2] Several feminist critics have traced this tradition back to Plato, who discoursed at length on the relationship between the soul, the body, and knowledge (Lloyd and Spelman). The Manichaean model of soul-body relations critiqued in "On Being Ill" can be read, I argue, as a critique of Platonic rationalism. Woolf was equally interested in Plato's literary style as in his ideas, so this interpretation does not conflict with her avowed critique of "literature."[3] She learned Greek from the age of fifteen and translated several of Plato's dialogues in her twenties. As Emily Dalgarno observes in *Virginia Woolf and the Visible World*, Woolf's notes on the *Phaedrus, Protagoras, Euthyphro,* and *Symposium* are preserved, and there are strong indications that Woolf also read the *Republic* (43). If, as Dalgarno argues, Woolf's interest in Plato was predominantly as a "poet and image-maker," several of the images and metaphors used to describe the soul-body relation in "On Being Ill" are based on those in Plato's dialogues (43). Woolf had translated two of the relevant dialogues, the *Phaedrus* and *Symposium,* by the time she wrote "On Being Ill" and had previously explored the mind-body relation in the context of the *Phaedrus* in *Jacob's Room.*[4]

Plato viewed the body as a deceptive and morally corrupting entity, a part of the ever-changing, unknowable realm of phenomena (Spelman 111). "On Being Ill" reiterates Plato's notion of the body as a site of flux and desire. It goes through an "unending procession of changes, heat and cold, comfort and discomfort, hunger and satisfaction, health and illness" (*Collected Essays* 4: 193). Plato contrasts matter with form, the forms constituting real, immutable, and perfect knowledge accessible through the rational soul. Thus, Plato distinguishes the realm of matter seen through the senses and the realm of forms known rationally through intellect. The body is a deceptive and distracting creature that must be disciplined by the rational soul if the subject is to attain real knowledge and thereby achieve ethical ascendancy. In book three of the *Republic,* the body is described as a hindrance to the soul, and an obstacle to virtue (Plato 651–52: sec. 407b–c), while in book four, Socrates describes how the appetitive part of the soul can be infected by the pleasures of the body and must be guarded and ruled over by the rational part of the soul (Plato 683–85: sec. 441–42). In the *Phaedrus,* in which Socrates describes the nature of the human being through the myth of the chariot and charioteer, the pleasures of the body are deemed to be "slavish" (Plato 504: sec. 258e) and the body is described as the "prison house" of the soul (Plato 497: sec. 250c). Woolf parodies this Platonic and later Christian concept of the body as tomb or prison, and transfers animal and primitive status from body to soul: "The creature within can only gaze through the pane—smudged or rosy; it cannot separate off from the body like the sheath of a knife [. . .] until there comes the inevitable catastrophe; the body smashes itself to smithereens, and the soul (it is said) escapes" (*Collected Essays* 4: 193–94). Plato's view of the body as an ethically corrupt creature that must be ruled over by sovereign mind is also reversed in "On Being Ill." Woolf rejects the view that the body's significance is limited to a few corrupt passions "such as desire and greed," beyond which it is "null, and negligible and non-existent" (4: 193). "On the contrary," she claims, "the very opposite is true." "All day, all night" the body perpetually "intervenes" upon the soul, it cannot "separate off from the body like the sheath of a knife," but is itself a "slave" to the body, particularly during the "great wars" of illness (4: 193–94). Here, Woolf inverts Plato's image of the body as a slave to be mastered by mind.

In the *Phaedo,* Socrates claims that sickness, as a time of intensified bodily sensation, hampers the pursuit of "reality" to an even greater extent: "[T]he body provides us with innumerable distractions in the pursuit of our necessary sustenance, and any diseases which attack us hinder our quest for reality" (Plato 48: sec. 66b–c). By contrast, Woolf explores how the sick body functions as a catalyst for skeptical insights about the "real" world and how the "act of illness" uproots several of the "ancient and obdurate oaks" of reason (*Collected Essays* 4: 193). Illness, Woolf suggests, alters the subject's social relations, due to the physical isolation integral to convalescence and the social ostracism she claims ensues. Society's lack of willingness to bestow "sympathy" on the sick is interpreted as a result of the negative effect such a "burden" would have on social and economic progress. If the healthy attempted to imaginatively grasp the "pains" of another, "buildings would cease to rise; roads would peter out into grassy tracks; there would be an end of music and painting." Thus, the healthy will always find "some little distraction" to avoid the burden of "sympathy" (4: 195). Illusions about our common humanity and the possibility of shared experience are also challenged in sickness as questions regarding our knowledge of others are displaced by a skepticism regarding the limits of self-knowledge. The "illusion [. . .] of human beings so tied together by common needs and fears that a twitch at one wrist jerks another [. . .] where however far you travel in your own mind someone has been there before you" are, Woolf claims, dismantled. "We do not know our own souls, let alone the souls of others. Human beings do not go hand in hand the whole stretch of the way" (4: 196). The limits to shared experience are represented through images of disrupted physical connection, isolation, and estrangement: "They march to battle. We float with the sticks on the stream; helter-skelter with the dead leaves on the lawn." All the "genial pretence[s]" that motivate the "army of the upright"—"to communicate, to civilize, to share, to cultivate the desert, educate the native, to work together by day and by night to sport"—are no longer perceived as "genial" but rather as the insidious and self-gratifying "illusions" of imperialism (4: 196). Thus, in illness several forms of "make-believe" cease. The "sick-deserter," no longer a soldier in the "army of the upright," becomes estranged from the so-called real world and discovers new landscapes in self and the world.

III. ILLNESS AND THE SPATIAL IMAGINATION

Illness is imagined in the essay as a process of physical estrangement from normal life. In the tradition of romantics such as De Quincey and Coleridge, the sick body initiates an imaginative voyaging into self, during which new landscapes of the "soul" become visible. Woolf imagines illness through ideas of space, both as the interaction of the physical on psychical spaces and as the respective spaces inhabited or perceived during sickness and health. As illness alters the subject's perceptions and relations, a shift occurs in the perceived connections between things. The pattern of life changes, proportions alter: "[T]he world has changed its shape; the tools of business grown remote [. . .] the whole landscape of life lies remote and fair, like the shore seen from a ship far out at sea" (*Collected Essays* 4: 195). The estrangement from common systems of meaning and value are represented through an increased physical space between the sick person and "life." Physical pain focuses attention away from the familiar landscapes in the external "world" and reveals new landscapes within the "soul." At the beginning of the essay Woolf refers to the "spiritual change" that sickness induces. As opposed to being in conflict with the soul as Plato maintained, the sick body illuminates new areas of "soul"; "how astonishing [. . .] the undiscovered countries that are then disclosed, what wastes and deserts of the soul a slight attack of influenza brings to view" (4: 193).[5] Woolf imagines a spiritual topography composed of precivilized landscapes. In illness, she claims we journey alone into the "virgin forest" or "snowfield" of self "where even the print of birds' feet is unknown" (4: 196). Woolf materializes the soul, and links it to the sphere of nature and matter, which are historically associated with the body. Illness is consistently linked to the precivilized subject. It unmakes civilized language and reduces the subject to a series of cries and groans. Illness estranges the subject from the external landscapes of community and work, and compels attention inward to private landscapes within the self. Illness opposes itself to civilization, to Enlightenment rationalism, imperialism, and progress. Woolf therefore reappropriates imperialist tropes of "discovery" and travel in this essay in order to launch an attack on capitalism and imperialism. Linking the subjectivities of the invalid and precivilized subject, Woolf argues that bodies and their effects matter but that that matter is repeatedly reappropriated or undermined by rationalism.

In *Illness as Metaphor,* Susan Sontag critiques traditional metaphors, such as war and spiritual journey, used to describe illness, because she claims they distract from the physicality of illness and romanticize the condition of the sick person. Judith Shulevitz, in her review of the 2002 Paris Press edition of "On Being Ill," refers to Sontag's essay and claims that "being ill, in 'On Being Ill,' looks a lot like a Romantic's idea of being interesting" ("The Poetry of Illness"). However, I would argue that this reading fails to consider the ways in which Woolf redeploys these old metaphors of illness in new ways, and examines their ethical and philosophical consequences. Metaphors of war and conflict in "On Being Ill" do not focus on the relationship between the body and the invading illness, but rather on the conflicts of understanding and interest between the sick person and the community and the conflicts between bodies and minds. Tropes of travel do not, as Woolf warns in the essay, result in a metaphysical flight into "the raptures of transcendentalism" (*Collected Essays* 4: 194). Rather, metaphors of space and travel function to represent the epistemological and physical space that illness creates, a space in which the assumptions and values she attributes to healthy, rational consciousness can be critically reassessed. The essay engages with romantic tropes of travel, nature, and poetry, in order to interrogate aspects of the romantic ideology. For example, Wordsworth's account of nature as a source of truth and companionship is questioned in the essay. Nature, Woolf claims, does not comfort through its capacity to sympathize with human suffering, but through its "indifference" and "forgetfulness" (4: 198). The romantic view of nature and humanity as a harmonious organic unity, a "world so shaped that it echoes every groan," and human beings "tied together by common needs and fears," are here deemed "illusions" (4: 196). While romantic literature and ideology were very important influences on Woolf's thought and writing, "On Being Ill" argues that the more idealistic and utopian social and ontological theses of romanticism are challenged during times of physical illness.[6] Illness therefore rejects both Platonic and romantic attempts to rationalize the universe. Knowledge in this essay is not grounded in rational speculation, but stems from the experience of the sick body and its effects on thought and perception.

Notes

1.   "On Being Ill" was originally published in T. S. Eliot's *New Criterion* in January 1926. In an abridged version of the essay it is renamed "Illness—An Unexploited Mine" (*Essays of Virginia Woolf* 4: 581–89).

2.   In Orphic mythology the body is viewed as a nuisance, an evil, and a hindrance to the soul's grasp of truth. This association of the body with evil and spiritual defilement reappears in Socratic accounts of the body (for example, *Phaedo*) and later in St. Paul's distinction between body (*soma*) and flesh (*sarx*), the latter of which cannot enter the kingdom of God and is the domain of sin (MacDonald 37–54; 89–107).

3.   In a letter to her tutor Janet Case on 4 November 1920 on reading Plato's *Symposium,* Woolf expresses greater admiration for Plato's style than thought: "[I]f I could write like that!" (*Letters* 2: 446).

4.   In *Jacob's Room* (1922), Jacob fails to have satisfying relations with women whom he physically desires but intellectually disrespects: "The problem is insoluble. The body is harnessed to a brain. Beauty goes hand in hand with stupidity" (81–82). Earlier, Jacob reads Plato's *Phaedrus,* in which Socrates describes the myth of the charioteer who seeks to control the virtuous and vicious parts of the soul. Erotic love is designated here as one of the four types of divine madness. The narrator of *Jacob's Room* states the dialogue is "very difficult," as it contradicts Jacob's own views, and is further contradicted by the conspicuous absence of Jacob, both body and soul, at the end of the novel after he dies in the war (110).

5.   As Hermione Lee notes in her introduction to the Paris Press edition of the essay (xxx), the "undiscovered countries" is a reference to Shakespeare's *Hamlet* (III.i.76–82). For Woolf, the undiscovered countries refer not to death but the soul.

6.   Woolf read a great deal of romantic literature and wrote several critical essays on the life and writings of William and Dorothy Wordsworth, Samuel Taylor Coleridge, Thomas De Quincey, and William Hazlitt, among others. While I acknowledge the influence of romantic thought elsewhere in Woolf, for example, her interest in the creative imagination and her secular "moments of being," my discussion here is concerned with the ways in which, according to Woolf, sickness forces us to challenge both our common sense and more idealistic views and assumptions.

Works Cited

Dalgarno, Emily. *Virginia Woolf and the Visible World*. Cambridge: Cambridge University Press, 2001.

Lee, Hermione. Introduction. *On Being Ill*. Ashfield, MA: Paris Press, 2002.

Lloyd, Genevieve. *The Man of Reason: "Male" and "Female" in Western Philosophy*. Minneapolis: University of Minnesota Press, 1984.

MacDonald, Paul S. *History of the Concept of Mind: Speculations about Soul, Mind, and Spirit from Homer to Hume*. Aldershot, Hants: Ashgate, 2003.

Plato. *The Collected Dialogues of Plato Including the Letters*. Ed. Edith Hamilton and Huntington Cairns. Princeton: Princeton University Press, 1963.

Scarry, Elaine. *The Body in Pain: The Making and Unmaking of the World*. New York: Oxford University Press, 1985.

Shulevitz, Judith. "The Poetry of Illness." *New York Times*. 29 Dec. 2002, late ed.: sec. 7, p. 19.

Sontag, Susan. *Illness as Metaphor*. New York: Farrar, Straus and Giroux, 1978.

Spelman, Elizabeth. "Woman as Body: Ancient and Contemporary Views." *Feminist Studies*. 8.1 (1982): 109–31.

Woolf, Virginia. *Collected Essays*. Ed. Leonard Woolf. 4 vols. New York: Harcourt, Brace and World, 1967.

---. *Jacob's Room*. San Diego: Harvest-Harcourt Brace and Company, 1978.

---. *The Essays of Virginia Woolf*. Ed. Andrew McNeillie. 4 vols. London: Hogarth, 1986–94.

---. *The Letters of Virginia Woolf*. Ed. Nigel Nicolson and Joanne Trautmann. 6 vols. New York: Harcourt Brace Jovanovich, 1975–80.

Objects Dissolving in Time

by Dianne Hunter

The peroration of *A Room of One's Own* mentions two orders of reality. The speaker says that female literary genius will someday get expressed unimpeded "if we [. . .] see human beings not always in their relation to each other but *in relation to reality;* and the sky, too, and the trees [. . .] in themselves; [. . .] if we face *the fact* [. . .] that there is no arm to cling to, but that we go alone and that our relation is to *the world of reality* and not only to the world of men and women" (114, emphasis added). The "fact" cited here can be connected to the factuality of death in *To the Lighthouse,* where we find vindicated Mr. Ramsay's insistence on the "passage to that fabled land where our brightest hopes are extinguished, our frail barks founder in darkness" (4); but the "reality" the speaker of *A Room of One's Own* points to is the reality of the sky, opened to the view of the speaker thanks to the financial security supplied by an inheritance. Woolf writes, "[M]y aunt's legacy unveiled the sky to me, and substituted for the large and imposing figure of a gentleman, which Milton recommended for my perpetual adoration, a view of the open sky" (39). This open sky is the reality of the energetically moving clouds that become objects of contemplation in *On Being Ill. A Room of One's Own* says that women must look past "Milton's bogey"—the patriarchal literary tradition, the patriarchal God, in order to think back through our mothers and create a women's literature. A page earlier the text urges access to "the common life which is the *real life*" (113, emphasis added), collective female creativity, which historically has been channeled into child rearing and domestic art. The "real life," "the common life" here are evidently a different order from the sky and cloud reality beyond human relations and the world of men and women.

In the mid-to-late 1920s, Woolf's works articulate several distinct realities: (1) reality inherent in objects made and used by human beings, such as a table, a house, a painting, a book; (2) the reality of the natural world as revealed in the sky, trees, and seasons; (3) the reality of the communal life of human beings as it unfolds in economic and political history. Although she believed her unique gift was a capacity to express her lonely sense of the abstract reality she saw residing around her in the downs and sky quite apart from human relationships and patriarchal social organization, Woolf also wished, she says in her diary, for a "closer and thicker knowledge of life" (*Writer's Diary* 132). She wished, she reports to herself, "to deal with real things sometimes" (132), and theorized on how social history and the material conditions of the production and sales of her books affected her literary creativity. Once the Hogarth Press was established, Woolf was pleased to think of herself as the freest writer in England, unhindered by editors or publication series. Freedom from editorial scrutiny and academic or marketplace opinion converged in Woolf's middle age with an autumnal sense that, she wrote at the age of forty-six, "one will turn cold and silver like the moon" (*Writer's Diary* 129). She felt as if the sun were sinking on her physical being and that of her friends, as her energy cooled down into the privacy of death. In summer stays at Monk's House in the late 1920s, generating thoughts for what became *A*

Room of One's Own, Woolf experienced the agony and terror of loneliness, "of seeing to the bottom of the vessel" and "got then to a consciousness" of what she calls reality:

> a thing I see before me: something abstract; but residing in the downs or sky; beside which nothing matters; in which I shall rest and continue to exist. Reality I call it. And I fancy sometimes this is the most necessary thing to me: that which I seek. But who knows—once one takes a pen and writes? How difficult not to go making "reality" this and that, whereas it is one thing. Now perhaps this is my gift: this perhaps is what distinguishes me from other people: I think it may be rare to have so acute a sense of something like that—but again, who knows? I would like to express it too. (*Writer's Diary* 129–30)

Here Woolf articulates her uniqueness as an acute sense of death opening to a revelation of permanent, abstract residence. There is a reality she intuits, and her sense of it and wish to express it she introspects as her uniqueness, but taking a pen and writing transforms the "one thing" into this and that, subjective variations concretizing the abstract. In the completion of Lily's painting on which *To the Lighthouse* ends, the maternal, the masculine, art, and death fuse in a working through of grief for the lost mother, anger at the surviving patriarch, and resolution of oedipal frustrations and resentments into a vision of objects dissolving in time and the inspirational power of their loss.

Andrew Ramsay tells Lily Briscoe that his father's work concerns "[s]ubject and object and the nature of reality" (23). The representations of gender in the novel as well as in the feminist manifesto *A Room of One's Own* inflect and complicate the desire in "Time Passes" for "something alien to the processes of domestic life, single, hard, bright, like a diamond in the sand, which would render the possessor secure" (*To the Lighthouse* 132). The persistence of Mrs. Ramsay's female creativity, her capacity to create moments of interpersonal significance that lodge in memory counterpoints Mr. Ramsay's linearity and insistence on "facts." This creativity counters the objectivism and death orientation of the "Time Passes" break in the novel's narrative. In the completion of Lily's painting, Woolf's mystical sense of reality joins family history, art, and the world of women and men. The subjective vision integrating Lily's ambivalent feelings for the Ramsays includes the reality of death; it depends on awareness that, like the deteriorating house in "Time Passes," Mr. Ramsay is going to join Mrs. Ramsay in death, and so are their remaining children.

The beach-walker passages from sections VI and VII of "Time Passes" address, in the context of war, the issue of whether human life has purpose. "Time Passes" asks whether nature supplements what human beings advance, whether there is a serenity in the natural world mirroring the beauty in the contemplative mind of a person who walks by the sea and marvels at reflected light on water, sunset, dawn, fishing boats, and children at play on the beach as tokens of "divine bounty" (133). The silent apparition of an ashen-colored ship on the seascape horizon and the bloody stains of warfare rising to the sea's surface change the significance of the landscape—not only are human beings revealed in warfare to be preying on one another, but the sea itself seems to harbor Hobbesian leviathans to remind us that life is meaningless, "as if the universe were battling and tumbling, in brute confusion and wanton lust aimlessly by itself" (135). Without Mrs. Ramsay to supply maternal support and in the face of the chaos of the First World War, consciousness shatters like a broken mirror to reveal irrational, terrible monsters in the depths of nature and of human nature. But then peace follows the war and "the beauty of the world" (36) is heard murmuring once again, calling sleepers to notice "night flowing down in purple; his head crowned; his sceptre jewelled; and how in his eyes a child might look" (142). This anthropomorphized natural beauty—like a benevolent King of Night, the antidote to the "insensibility of nature" (138), provides comfort. A child might look and see night as a bejeweled monarch looking at him; perhaps it is only as a child that one can see darkness thus. "Time Passes" suggests that we live in an idiot universe where we find refuge from deeply brutal realities by appreciating the splendors of the physical world as revealed to the senses when we are in states of contemplation that recreate the protective mirroring supplied by a loving maternal force. This idea supports the opening of the novel, where the child James sits cutting pictures of objects out of an Army and Navy Stores catalog. His mother's presence and the sound of her voice saying yes to the prospect of a trip to the lighthouse endow "the picture of a refrigerator, as his mother spoke, with heavenly bliss" (3). Subjective desire and the sense of being emotionally supported create bliss, a token of divine bounty no less real for James because his father is about to puncture it by insisting on the uncompromising facts of adverse weather. Mr. Ramsay may tell the truth, but he does not define reality. His thought processes remain stalled at "Q," before "R" (reality). James, in contrast, endows representations of objects with subjective bliss and may combine them into a new reality in the form of a collage, similar to the way the narrative form of the overall novel creates a matrix of continuous though disparate consciousnesses.

The family dynamics of the novel remind us that when psychoanalysts speak of the "object," as in the phrase "object relations theory," "object" means person significant to the subject or perceiving consciousness being analyzed, as in the phrase "the object of her affection." This object is usually internalized, part of the subjectivity of its beholder. In this regard, we must rethink the meaning of Andrew's phrase "subject and object and the nature of reality" as it bears on Lily's mourning and demystification of Mrs. Ramsay.

In part one of the novel, Mrs. Ramsay acts as a patriarchal imprinter, differentiating genders through the social identities she confers on her daughters and sons. For example, as Rose clasps her mother's necklace in the scene before dinner, Mrs. Ramsay divines

> through her own past, some deep, some buried, some quite speechless feeling that one had for one's mother at Rose's age. Like all feelings felt for oneself, Mrs. Ramsay thought, it made one sad. It was so inadequate, what one could give in return; and what Rose felt was quite out of proportion to anything she actually was. And Rose would grow up; and Rose would suffer, she supposed, with these deep feelings, and she said she was ready now, and they would go down, and Jasper, because he was the gentleman, should give her his arm. (81)

Rose is in love with her mother, as her mother recognizes from her own past, helpless adoration for an inaccessible mother; but Jasper is a model of his mother's social partner.

In the opening scene of the novel, we see James Ramsay standing stiffly between his mother's legs, resentful of the barren plunging male beak of his father. She strokes James's head, transferring to him what she feels for her husband. Mrs. Ramsay imagines her son dressed in the red and ermine trappings of his future patriarchal role, and she feels that she has the whole male sex under her protection "for their chivalry and valour," their conquest of India and control of finance, and their childlike reverence of her as a mother (6). The Ramsay daughters meanwhile dream of "a life different from hers, in Paris, perhaps [where in the 1920s lesbian artists and their female muses were congregating]; a wilder life; not always taking care of some man or other; for there was in all their minds a mute questioning of deference and chivalry, of the Bank of England and the Indian Empire, of ringed fingers and lace, though to them all there was something in this of the *essence of beauty, which called out the manliness in their girlish hearts*" (7, emphasis added). Lily Briscoe, a father's daughter apparently without a mother with whom to identify, looks longingly from a distance, in part one, at mother *and son* framed by the window, wishing to fling herself at Mrs. Ramsay's knee and declare love. "[B]ut what could one say to her?" Lily thinks. "'I'm in love with you?' No, that was not true. 'I'm in love with this all,' waving her hand at the hedge, at the house, at the children" (19). This scene epitomizes an oedipal daughter's dilemma. The mother figure Mrs. Ramsay is an object of desire, but she is also a model of femininity; she thinks Lily will miss the best of life unless she marries a man. On the one hand, Lily would like to be at Mrs. Ramsay's knee in a masculine role; on the other hand, there would be no Mrs. Ramsay and no such family life as hers without feminine socialization.

The final image of *To the Lighthouse,* where Lily completes her painting while watching Mr. Ramsay standing in the boat with his two children, suggests that Lily sees that he is symbolically traveling to rejoin his wife in death, and on a second level, that Mrs. Ramsay as a maternal figure who is Lily's object of desire depends on the intruding male for children. Death and creation are fused in the final passages of the novel, as in what psychoanalysis calls "primal scene fantasy," the parents in sexual intercourse understood as a struggle ending in a deathlike sleep. Woolf thought of creativity as mental nuptials celebrated in darkness, and she wrote in her diary that without the death of her parents she would not have conceived her novels. On the anniversary of what would have been Leslie Stephen's ninety-sixth birthday, Woolf confides to her diary, "I used to think of him and mother daily; but writing the *Lighthouse* laid them in my mind" (*Writer's Diary* 135). Lily finishes her painting only after Mrs. Ramsay has died. Woolf's "Professions for Women" states that she felt she had to kill the phantom of the mother in herself in order to be a successful writer:

> I discovered that if I were going to review books I should need to do battle with a certain phantom. And the phantom was a woman, and when I came to know her better I called her after the heroine of a famous poem, The Angel in the House. It was she who used to come between me and my paper when I was writing reviews. It was she who bothered me and wasted my time and so tormented me that at last I killed her. [. . .] She was intensely sympathetic. She was immensely charming. She was utterly unselfish. She excelled in the difficult arts of family life. [. . .] I turned upon her and caught her by the throat. I did my best to kill her. My excuse, if I were to be had up in a court of law, would be that I acted in self-defense. Had I not killed her she would have killed me. She would have *plucked the heart* out of my writing. (*Essays* 2: 285–86, emphasis added)

Mrs. Ramsay represents a version of this domestic goddess, the persona of Victorian poet Coventry Patmore's *The Angel in the House,* and Prue Ramsay, based on Stella Duckworth, in *To the Lighthouse* calls her a "second angel." Both the primary domestic angel and the second angel die of their female role. The image of a phantom who *plucks* the heart out of creativity connects to Lily's blocked creativity in the first part of the novel: "[I]n that moment's flight between the picture and her canvas [. . .] demons set on her who often brought her to the verge of tears and made this passage from conception to work as dreadful as any down a dark passage for a child." She struggles to clasp "her vision to her breast, which a thousand forces did their best to *pluck* from her" (19, emphasis added). In this moment of frustrated creativity, Lily feels "her own inadequacy, her insignificance, keeping house for her father off the Brompton Road" (19), in contrast to Mrs. Ramsay's motherhood. In death, Mrs. Ramsay proves more enabling to Lily's vision than she had in life.

Throughout the novel, Lily hates having her painting seen, and she imagines that when it is finished, it will be rolled up and forgotten in an attic. Her difficulty in completing her picture is a problem of relating the masses so that the composition balances (May 91–98). During the dinner party in part one, Lily moves the saltcellar and seems to have an illumination, simultaneously thinking, "she need not marry, thank Heaven" and deciding to "move the tree rather more to the middle" (102). On one side of her canvas is the wall of the house and its most significant feature, the image of the Madonna and child. Moving the tree to the center does not provide a solution; and as the final section of the book unfolds, it becomes apparent that the structural difficulty with the painting links with Lily's attitudes toward Mr. and Mrs. Ramsay. Up until part three, Mr. Ramsay has not figured in the design; instead, he has been an irritating distraction, "bearing down upon her" (30) and demanding sympathy. But as the morning wears on, Lily's thoughts alternate between her painting and Mr. Ramsay making his way across the bay to the lighthouse. The painting on the land and Mr. Ramsay on the water begin to act on Lily as two opposing forces: "For whatever reason she could not achieve that razor edge of balance between two opposite forces; Mr. Ramsay and the picture" (193).

As Mr. Ramsay nears the lighthouse, Lily continues to recall Mrs. Ramsay, her limitations and her capacity to bring moments of stability to the household. The painter passes through brief periods of not needing Mrs. Ramsay. "Yes [. . .] the drawing-room step was empty, but it had no effect on her whatever. She did not want Mrs. Ramsay now" (195). But, while Lily thinks she is free of her desire for Mrs. Ramsay, a wave of white appears in the house windowpane and recalls Mrs. Ramsay with all the old longing and frustration: "'Mrs. Ramsay! Mrs. Ramsay!' she cried, feeling all the old horror come back—to want and want and not to have" (202). Here Lily is in the midst of what the novel represents as a mother-daughter dilemma and a set of contradictory oedipal ambivalences. Because the novel works within a matrix of multipersonal consciousness involving the reader in several minds simultaneously, Lily's design problem clarifies itself in the reader's mind via the dynamics of father-son and father-daughter relationships in the boat (Auerbach 536). At first the boat is stalled, but then the wind picks up, just as, at the dinner party ten years before, the social atmosphere failed to flow until Mrs. Ramsay animated the group like a sailor seeing the "wind fill his sail" (84). While Lily struggles artistically on land, Cam and James in the boat work from their initial resentment of their father's tyrannical neediness toward gendered oedipal resolutions that bring them closer emotionally to their father. Cam notices her father's beautiful hands and magnificent head as he declares how we perish, each alone; she appreciates how much he can teach her in his library. Mr. Ramsay coaxes a smile from her by asking about her puppy. James remains determined to hold out against his father in spite of what he sees as his sister's defection from the cause of defying tyranny; but at last receiving praise from his father for landing the boat on the lighthouse island, James realizes that paternal praise is what he has wanted, and that the lighthouse close-up and the lighthouse seen from a dreamy distance are both subjective objects, and both real, a matter of perspective, like his attitude toward Mr. Ramsay. Meanwhile, Lily's emotional recognition of her continuing need for Mrs. Ramsay is followed by a sudden awareness that she needs Mr. Ramsay as well: "Lily went past Mr. Carmichael holding her brush [erect] to the edge of the lawn. Where was that boat now? And Mr. Ramsay? She wanted him" (202). This revelation comes to Lily: She needs Mr. Ramsay because without him, there can be no Mrs. Ramsay to be an artistic mother figure for her. Although she momentarily imagines herself independent of the mother figure, Lily's completed painting depends on the family image; and like the overall novel, Lily ends by memorializing motherhood. Shortly after Mr. Ramsay lands at the lighthouse, Lily transmutes her revelation into the form of a line in the center of the painting, and in so doing, balances the masses. This line suggests the father as linear, as both phallic separator and connector of mother and child. The balancing of the masses suggests androgynous creativity as an image of the mother, father, son, and daughter unified within—subjective objects celebrating nuptials, ultimately in death.

Overcoming obstacles to creativity in this novel depends on getting a distanced perspective on this inner fusion and recognizing that all objects, including self-objects, dissolve in time. By having the occurrence of Lily's vision, the oedipal resolutions on the boat, the completion of the painting, and the novel's end coincide, the narrating matrix communicates an experience of simultaneity and communication of minds across time and space, from the dead who lived before the Great War to those surviving into part three of the novel, to the current moment in which the book is being read (on oedipal resolution in *To the Lighthouse*, see Abel 45–67). Woolf's vision of objects dissolving in time composes a reality that is at once transient and transcendent, visual and artifactual, intrapsychic and interpersonal.

Works Cited

Abel, Elizabeth. *Virginia Woolf and the Fictions of Psychoanalysis.* Chicago: University of Chicago Press, 1989.

Auerbach, Erich. *Mimesis: The Representation of Reality in Western Literature.* Trans. Willard R. Trask. Princeton: Princeton University Press, 1953.

May, Keith M. "The Symbol of 'Painting' in Virginia Woolf's *To the Lighthouse*" *A Review of English Literature* 8.2 (1967): 91–98.

Woolf, Virginia. *Collected Essays.* Ed. Leonard Woolf. 4 vols. New York: Harcourt, Brace & World, 1967.

---. *A Room of One's Own.* San Diego: Harcourt Brace Jovanovich & Company, 1981.

---. *To the Lighthouse.* San Diego: Harvest-Harcourt Brace Jovanovich, 1981.

---. *A Writer's Diary.* Ed. Leonard Woolf. New York: Harvest-Harcourt Brace Jovanovich, 1954.

The Political Legacy of the Garden: (Anti)Pastoral Images and National Identity in Virginia Woolf and Vita Sackville-West

by McKenzie L. Zeiss

Both Virginia Woolf and Vita Sackville-West use land and gardens to explore English identity and experience in relationship to a prewar past. Sackville-West's long poems *The Land* and, later, *The Garden* use the pastoral setting for an ongoing examination of English identity. Garden imagery is also woven into family history and national imagination in Woolf's *To the Lighthouse*. Most critics have taken Woolf's work as serious critique of the social system and have read Sackville-West's as a celebration of conservatism. The condescension inherent in such a reading relies on a failure to take Sackville-West's work beyond face value. However, it is not at all clear that Woolf is so simply the radical to Sackville-West's conservative. Both women partook of a Victorian heritage that largely shaped their work; both sought to construct, in the aftermath of World War I, a new form of English identity in relationship to that past. Woolf's critique of the ideals of the past as untenable is inseparable from her sorrow over their failure. *To the Lighthouse*, though not primarily pastoral in either form or content, offers an opening into Woolf's ambivalent use of pastoral imagery to simultaneously critique and eulogize a lost prewar sense of order and identity.

I. *To the Lighthouse:* The (Anti)Pastoral Lament

To the Lighthouse uses the Ramsays' garden as a means of exploring gender and national identity. At the most obvious level, characters are consistently identified with specific garden plants; Mr. Ramsay and Lily Briscoe are identified with, respectively, geraniums and exotic specimens. Mrs. Ramsay, as the emblem of the old order, is identified with native violets.

Mr. Ramsay's association with geraniums comes into play consistently when he debates his own status (intellectual status) in British society. Thinking to himself that his is "a splendid mind" (*To the Lighthouse* 33), he pauses by an urn of geraniums. As he continues his ruminations, "[t]he geranium in the urn bec[omes] startlingly visible" (34). Later, "seeing again the urns with the trailing red geraniums which had so often decorated processes of thought" (42), he "slipped, seeing all this, smoothly into speculation" on whether or not Shakespeare's existence has truly made any difference in the world. With this shift from his own intellectual status to the grander significance of his country's greatest thinkers, Mr. Ramsay takes the geranium as an emblem not only of his own position but also of the growing question of England's character and her position in the world at large.

The geranium is an interesting choice, as it links his desire for a dominant English identity to his estrangement from that identification. "Geranium" is actually a very broad term, encompassing both the smaller, less flashy native English plants and the more familiar large-leaved, bright-flowered South African pelargoniums. Thus, the name of the plant itself establishes the vacillation between a nativist and a colonialist English identity. Most likely Woolf has the pelargonium in mind, both from her focus on the display of flowing leaves and red flowers, and from the likelihood of it being the pelargonium rather than the somewhat weedy native geranium, that one would find in a decorative urn.

Mr. Ramsay's use of an imported specimen to characterize his place in the world, like his constant repetition of "The Charge of the Light Brigade," links his intellectual career to the military career of Britain herself. However, his exotic identifier has been present so long and has become so familiar as to appear a specimen of English traditionalism. This ambiguity captures exactly the ambiguity Woolf explores in *To the Lighthouse:* England no longer seems to have a steady definition or place in the world, torn as it is between its external conflict and its internal sense of self, the two of which have become (especially for those in ruling positions) impossible to sort out.

Whereas Mr. Ramsay holds an intermediary position embodying the question of British identity, Lily Briscoe's identification with more obvious exotics positions her as rebelling against British traditionalism. She is first introduced standing at her easel as "the jacmanna beyond burnt into her eyes" (*To the Lighthouse* 17). As Mr. Ramsay bellows—"Some one had blundered"—her opposition to him is emphasized with the following phrase: "The jacmanna was bright violet" (18). "Jacmanna" is most likely the *Clematis x jackmanii.* Though some species of clematis are native to England, this particular hybrid ("raised by Messrs Jackman's nursery at Woking in 1860") was developed from stock imported from China, and was largely responsible for the Victorian-era boom in the popularity of the genus (Phillips 199). This mixed provenance—derived from China, but bred in England to suit Victorian floral tastes—repeats the themes captured in Mr. Ramsay's geranium, yet now it "burns" Lily's eyes, forcing a confrontation with the Victorian nostalgia portrayed through exoticism. As the text continues, Lily gazes on "the house starred in its greenery with purple passion flowers" (19). Passion flowers, a South American species also popularized in England as part of the Victorian rage for imported plants, further signify both the Victorian tradition in which Mrs. Ramsay functions and the foreignness of Lily's refusal to contain herself within that tradition.

As Lily leaves the enclosed garden, her association with exotic plants continues: "past the pampas grass, to that break in the thick hedge, guarded by red-hot pokers" (*To the Lighthouse* 19–20). Here Lily is indiscriminately placed within sight of any non-English plant—the Argentinean pampas grass, the South African red-hot poker. Lily sees these plants as she leaves the garden thinking that "[i]t was absurd, it was impossible" to go to Mrs. Ramsay and announce: "I'm in love with this all" (19). Thus, Lily's exotics, like Mr. Ramsay's, signify a complex relationship with Mrs. Ramsay's comfortable domesticity; along with the break in the hedge, they mark the boundary between Lily's longing for the traditionalism of the past and her rejection of it.

The emphasis upon the aloe in this opening moment of rupture sets up one of the central images of "Time Passes." After Mrs. Ramsay's wartime death, the garden runs amok, with the English plants coming to signify wildness and danger and the aloe alone serving as a reminder of the past. In this fantasy of decay, "briars and hemlocks would have blotted out path, step, and window, would have grown, unequally but lustily over the mound, until some trespasser, losing his way, could have told only by a red-hot poker

among the nettles, or a scrap of china in the hemlock that here once some one had lived"
(138–39). The red-hot poker, precisely because it could have arrived only through human
intervention, serves as the sign of civilization, putting an ironic twist on Lily's identification of it as the sign of her rebellion. Woolf's transformation of the English plants into
stinging and poisonous interlopers shades her perspective into an antipastoral, privileging
the legacy of colonialism, not the native English landscape, as the sign of the eulogized
past. Thus, Woolf's antipastoral leanings in *To the Lighthouse* inscribe a form of colonialist
conservatism ultimately as disturbing as that which she critiques.

II. Sackville-West: The Self-Disrupting Pastoral

Sackville-West's uses of garden and pastoral images are actually much more complex
and internally disruptive. The wife of a colonial administrator, and therefore intimately
aware of the political side of the exoticism of foreign plants, she insists upon using the garden as a means of tracing the legacy of colonialism as it shapes English identity in a postwar period. In her gardening articles as well as her poetry, Sackville-West pays scrupulous
attention to the origin of plants. A prime example is her discussion of roses, often taken
as the symbol of England (and pervasive as such in Woolf's *Mrs. Dalloway*): "You have to
consider the Gallicas, the Damasks, the Centifolias or Cabbage, the Musks, the China,
the Rose of Provins . . . all more romantic the one than the other. Take this phrase alone:
'In the twelfth century the dark red Gallic rose was cultivated by the Arabs in Spain with
the tradition that it was brought from Persia in the seventh century'" (*V. Sackville-West's
Garden Book* 80). Yet at the same time, she identifies the actual cultivation of roses with
their place in English tradition and their unique ability to evoke nostalgia: "Dead-heading
the roses on a summer evening is an occupation to carry us back into a calmer age and a
different century. Queen Victoria might still be on the throne" (121).

In *The Garden,* Sackville-West uses roses as emblematic of the order disrupted by war.
Evoking, in "Winter," a scene very similar to the overgrowth of Mrs. Ramsay's garden in
"Time Passes," she describes "neglected gardens in these years of war," with the owner
longing "to cut and trim / Having a vision of his roses prim / As they should be" (*The
Garden* 127). However, she describes this scene in order to warn against overpruning, arguing that "[n]eglect may hold a beauty of her own" (127). Thus, the rose evokes English
traditionalism and order only to critique it, quite contrary to Woolf's lament over the loss
of imposed order in the landscape. The function of the rose as emblem of Sackville-West's
criticism of traditional pastoral symbolism grows even more explicit. "Summer" is largely
an exploration of the symbolic and cultural meanings of the rose. Sackville-West speaks
of "June of the iris and the rose. / The rose not English as we fondly think" (*The Garden*
148). She goes on to describe the genealogy of the rose, making it a figure for her critique
of English conceits of British culture as supreme: "Asia and Europe to our island lent /
These parents of our rose, / Yet Albion took her name from her white rose / Not from her
cliffs, some say" (149). Here, English identity even at the level of name becomes derivative
of Asian and southern European forerunners.

Sackville-West also insists on using the pastoral to question rather than to solidify
English identity in the earlier poem *The Land*. Its most often cited lines come in the
introduction: "I sing once more / The mild continuous epic of the soil" (*The Land* 15).

However, to take these lines at face value is to ignore the rest of the poem, which renders profoundly ironic any description of the pastoral setting as "mild." Sackville-West characterizes the country life as "A loutish life, but in the midst of dark / Cut to a gash of beauty" (18). Calling beauty of the pastoral a "gash" asserts that it is precisely the opposite of anything either "mild" or "continuous." She continues by asserting that she "Will sing no songs of bounty, for I see / Only the battle between man and earth" (18). Pastoral forms can serve as an answer to war because they reproduce it, and Sackville-West's focus on the origins and histories of plants suggests the ways in which the political history of the nation is bodily inscribed in the land itself.

Having thus explained her project in "Winter," Sackville-West proceeds to explore the deadly conflict embodied in the land in each of the seasons. In "Spring," the farmer's orchards are pictured as riddled through with danger and pestilence at their literal roots. Blossom-weevil, grubs, and root-louse, respectively, "bore," "tunnel," and are "tucked beneath" the trees, and "Canker, rot, scab, and mildew blight the tree; / There seems an enemy in everything" (*The Land* 37). Spring becomes the season not of rebirth but of re-engagement with old, insidious enemies, who do not attack from without but are instead nestled inside the orchard itself.

When Sackville-West turns to "Summer," she describes two shepherds carrying a dead man, whom she had known, and she stops to gaze in the hope of learning from his death. However, she "could not learn from him, for there's no learning / Either from alien or familiar dead" (*The Land* 58). Her language here replicates the futility expressed by other World War I writers, for whom war becomes not a site of enlightenment but an illustration of the meaninglessness of death. It does not matter that the dead man is English; it does not even matter that she knows him. The reality of death supersedes the importance of identity or familiarity. As "Summer" continues, Sackville-West describes a farmer's crops burning. Like the dead man carried by his comrades, the hypothetical fire pictured as "[a] blood-red feather flaming on the west" (*The Land* 60) echoes the imagery of war literature. The passage suggests the fire as an image of the war's impersonal destruction brought home to the countryside itself. As the summer harvest continues, she describes the desperate flight of a rabbit to escape the reaper; however, "odds too heavy end the frantic race; / There's nothing but a twitching body cast / Down by a jacket, as 'twere nothing worth / But shillings to the farmers' frugal wife" (*The Land* 62). Again and again, Sackville-West distills her idyllic pastoral imagery to a moment of meaningless death and destruction.

As she moves into "Autumn," Sackville-West sums up the glut of deadly images: "Nature's an enemy who calls no armistice" (*The Land* 74). The language confirms the growing hints that, throughout the poem, she has been reproducing the image of the war in the land itself. For Sackville-West, the land cannot exist as a remembered space outside of war, as something preexisting conflict and lost in the ruins of war. Land is itself the site of an ongoing war, and therefore is the proper site in which to formulate a response to World War I.

Compared to Woolf's elegiac use of the pastoral to evoke a lost and beloved, even if also deeply resented and often-mocked past, Sackville-West's injunction to "[t]he land and not the waste land celebrate" (*The Garden* 131) comes to seem far more deeply demanding of the reader. Despite Woolf's inherent critiques of the imagined past she explores, ultimately, it is far more progressive, even disruptive, to demand a concept of English identity that revises isolationist representational traditions to incorporate a history of colonialism and conflict within the land itself than to mourn the passing of a simultaneously idealized and discredited past and to condemn the pastoral as an archaic and untenable form.

Works Cited

Phillips, Roger, and Martyn Rix. *The Random House Book of Shrubs*. New York: Random House, 1989.
Sackville-West, Vita. *V. Sackville-West's Garden Book*. Ed. Philippa Nicolson. New York: Atheneum, 1969.
---. *The Land & The Garden*. Ed. Nigel Nicolson. Ill. Peter Firmin. Exeter, Devon: Webb & Bower, 1989.
Woolf, Virginia. *To the Lighthouse*. San Diego: Harvest-Harcourt Brace Jovanovich, 1981.

WRITING THE LAND: THE GEOGRAPHY OF NATIONAL IDENTITY IN *ORLANDO*

by Erica L. Johnson

From his hilltop "crowned by a single oak tree" (18), Orlando "count[s], gaze[s], recognise[s]" the English landscape before him. On a clear day, he sees forty counties, the English Channel, and the houses of his father and uncle. Although Orlando's quantifying, proprietary gaze undergoes revision over the course of Virginia Woolf's extraordinary biography, his relationship to the land remains elemental, for "[h]e loved, beneath all this summer transiency, to feel the earth's spine beneath him [. . .] for he felt the need of something which he could attach his floating heart to" (19). Indeed, Orlando floats, tethered only lightly and in passing to such markers of identity as gender and historical period. Yet the topography of Orlando's identity remains constant, and it remains English.

Given her later problematization of an exclusive, masculine model of national identity in *Three Guineas*, Woolf's assertion of an English homeland for her androgynous protagonist in *Orlando* stands out in her writing as both a critique and reconfiguration of the concept of national identity.[1] *Orlando* provides critical leverage on national identity insofar as the experience of Englishness is shown to be quite different depending on Orlando's gender status; as a woman, Orlando is chastised and disinherited by the same country that endows him with admiration and property as a man. Thus it is all the more interesting that Woolf maintains an English home for her hero/ine, for clearly, adherence to a static ideological or historical narrative of English identity cannot function equally for Orlando in his/her different forms. Rather, it is through geography that Woolf is able to observe national identity in such a way that she builds continuity between Orlando's possession of England and English identity as a man, and her more adjacent relationship to England as a woman.

In the introduction to *The Geography of Identity*, Patricia Yaeger credits Woolf with inserting "ghostly gendered imaginings" (6) into what we now understand to be the "imagined community" of national identity. Yaeger notes that Woolf accomplishes this conceptual paradigm shift through her engagement with geography, citing Woolf's entombment of Judith Shakespeare in the very foundations of London in *A Room of One's Own*. Yaeger chooses Woolf to articulate a move that Brian Osborne also makes when he reflects on recent models for understanding national identity as either an "imagined community" (Benedict Anderson) or an "invention of tradition" (Eric Hobsbawm) by adding that "nation-states occupy imagined terrains that serve as mnemonic devices" (Osborne 39) for national identity. While Osborne is interested in the extent to which these terrains are imbricated with "myths and memories, monuments and commemorations, quotidian practices and public ritual" (40), it is terrain itself that Woolf reveals to be a signifier of national identity in *Orlando*.

Within the body of Woolf criticism, much has been written on the role of the pastoral, whether as a neo-romantic chronotope through which Woolf critiques English tradition and ideology (Susan Bazargan), or as a means of destabilizing the feminization of nature in the context of masculine poetics (Roger Hecht). These analyses take as an underlying assumption the idea that landscape poses as an objective entity that is in fact inscribed with ideological agendas; by extension, the status of an *imagined geography*—like imagined community—is central to the formation of national tradition and identity. As a mnemonic device for national identity, the geography of England is central to Orlando's identity, although as a woman Orlando occupies the space of the "ghostly gendered imagining" that Yaeger identifies as Woolf's contribution to understanding the poetics of national space.

How is national space not only imagined, but gendered in *Orlando?* Woolf offers us the cultural contact zone of Constantinople, in the feminized Orient, as an exemplary answer to this question. The landscape of Turkey initially appears to Orlando as a field of absence: "[P]arsonage there was none, nor manor house, nor cottage, nor oak, elm, violet, ivy, or wild eglantine. There were no hedges for ferns to grow on, and no fields for sheep to graze. The houses were bare and bald as egg-shells" (121). That Orlando senses a strange affinity for this landscape in spite of the fact that the same passage identifies him as "English root and fibre" (121), signals his fluid sexuality in that the landscape is not only feminized by orientalist discourse, but by its status as "lack"—which mirrors seventeenth-century (as well as later psychoanalytic) constructions of women as lack. Thus Orlando's sex change in Constantinople occurs at least in part as a consequence of his response to orientalized terrain. Furthermore, it must be noted that the terrain to which he responds is not only gendered, but it is an imagined geography, for if Orlando sees absence before him, Woolf makes it clear that the inhabitants of this landscape view it through an entirely different ontological lens. These clashing points of view lay bare the nature of Orlando's orientalizing English gaze as he views the landscape of the exotic and hence unknowable East.

Constantinople is feminized not only through the concrete details of Orlando's existence there, during which he wears unisex costumes while carrying out his vocation of paying polite calls to Turkish families—a ritual that places him firmly in the domestic sphere—but by the altered shape of the novel's discourse as well. Imitating the landscape of absence, Woolf's narrative of Orlando's voyage out disintegrates into traces and outlines: "It is with fragments such as these that we must do our best to make up a picture of Orlando's life and character at this time. There exist, even to this day, rumours, legends, anecdotes of a floating and unauthenticated kind about Orlando's life in Constantinople" (124). The dismantling of space, subject, and narrative in this section of the novel compels a reading of the Constantinople trip as an interregnum during which a certain narrative and bodily anarchy ensues. Orlando's sex change is the most obvious consequence of this interregnum, and her nomadic travels with the gypsies further signify Orlando's anarchic subject status in that her nomadism dismantles the overarching and implicitly imperial narrative of travel that places her in Turkey in the first place. Unlike Orlando the ambassador, the gypsies know no nation states; indeed they recognize no geographical boundaries save that between land and sea, and their company provides Orlando with the opportunity to trade in her orientalist understanding of her environs for a more hermeneutic principle of understanding geography. As Susan Bazargan notes, however, "[t]he radical changes in Orlando's life in Constantinople—her passage from male to female, from the center of power to the margins of nomadic life—do not enhance her self-awareness or alter her sense of English superiority" (50).

The primary barrier to Orlando's shift in perception is that of terrain, as we see when she attempts to embark on a hermeneutic understanding of her location: "There were mountains; there were valleys; there were streams. She climbed the mountains; roamed the valleys; sat on the banks of the streams" (143). So far so good. But her primary imagined geography surfaces almost immediately, as the landscape then disappears into an English fog of metaphor: "She compared the flowers to enamel and the turf to Turkey rugs worn thin. Trees were withered hags, and sheep were grey boulders. Everything, in fact, was something else" (143). Again, the Eastern landscape is displaced, its absence reinstated. The othered geography of the Orient ultimately reorients Orlando's gaze toward her English homeland. Her powers of perception are subsumed by the imagined geography of England quite literally when, "gazing rather disconsolately at the steep hill-side in front of her," Orlando is suddenly possessed of a vision of England's "undulating and grassy lawn[s]" (150), oak trees, and thrushes. At the sharp return to her perception of her immediate Middle Eastern landscape, "she burst into a passion of tears, and striding back to the gipsies' camp, told them that she must sail for England the very next day" (151). The quick resolution to Orlando's interregnum is precipitated by the confrontation between the two imagined geographies of the Orient, on the one hand, and England, on the other. Her identity re-coalesces as English through the dynamic of geographical othering, through which English terrain asserts itself over orientalized terrain in an imperial fashion. While the oriental terrain is gendered as female, the female Orlando's refusal of Turkey for her fatherland speaks to the role of geography as a mnemonic device for national identity, yet provokes the question of how Orlando *can* reenter national space given what Woolf reveals about the extent to which imagined geographies are gendered. The female Orlando clearly cannot "return" to the England of her boyhood; she must find another point of entry or, rather, she must engage England's "ghostly gendered imaginings," to reiterate Yaeger's phrase, for she arguably returns to her ancestral house as a ghost, only to haunt the corridors from which she is disinherited as a woman.

The paradoxical position Orlando occupies upon her return to England results from her engagement with "foreign" terrain, and the extent to which she is marked and marginalized by the same geographical discourse that she espouses while in Turkey. That is, the fact that Orlando's sex change reflects a landscape characterized by the imperial eye as "lack" does not mesh with her internal English compass in spite of the fact that Woolf parodies this discourse of "lack" precisely by insisting on the continuity of Orlando's character, nationality, and geographical orientation. As Karen Lawrence points out, Orlando defies the discourse of lack insofar as Woolf "comically deflates the symbolic power and horror of the sight of castration upon which psychoanalysis builds its theory of sexual difference" (268) in the scene of her composed and confident unveiling as a woman. However, just as the landscape of the Orient remains a tabula rasa for the contesting geographical narrations of Orlando and the gypsies, the female Orlando is subject to others' readings of her in a way that the male Orlando is not. Her experience of repatriation thematizes her displacement: "[A]s the chalky cliffs loomed nearer, she felt culpable; dishonoured; unchaste; which, for one who had never given the matter a thought, was strange" (162). The same geographical space that comprises Orlando's "home" bars her reentry in the sense that she is now marked by an absence, and is hence more susceptible to being scripted by others. In spite of the narrator's claim that "[t]he change of sex, though it altered their future, did nothing whatever to alter their identity" (138), Orlando's national identity does undergo change between her departure from England as one who reads other landscapes, and her return as one who is read by her homeland.

Hence we see how Orlando assumes what I referred to earlier as a more adjacent relationship to national identity as a woman. This is not to say that Woolf dispenses with national identity as a principle of Orlando's subjectivity, for given Orlando's compulsive return to English terrain and her romantic tendency to ground her writing in the land, her Englishness is consolidated throughout the novel. Yet her repatriation as someone who is read in dominant discourse as a partially absent subject means that she acquires a ghostlike quality through which she haunts, rather than participates in, a certain discourse of national identity. This is not to say that she becomes politically irrelevant, for as Avery Gordon argues, "[t]he ghost is not simply a dead or a missing person, but a social figure, and investigating it can lead to that dense site where history and subjectivity make social life" (8). Orlando's ghostlike qualities derive not only from the narrator's use of absence as a signifying trope for her existence, but from narrative events as well, including her symbolic withdrawal from life during her transformative sleeps and her pronouncement of her own death on three different occasions as a woman. As Orlando says in introducing herself to Shelmerdine, "I'm dead, Sir!" (250). The fact that she says this while literally clinging to the earth, suggests that however corporeal she may be and however profound her literal and literary connection to the land may be, as a woman she is a ghost in the machine of national identity. Orlando's identification of herself as dead articulates her legal and social status as we see in the pending lawsuits, which charge "(1) that she was dead, and therefore could not hold any property whatsoever; (2) that she was a woman, which amounts to much the same thing" (168).

Orlando haunts her ancestral house and land quite effectively in the sense that she is still able to draw upon land as a means of mapping out her writing endeavor, and here we get to the heart of the reason for which Orlando's maintenance of a national, geographical identity is of such profound importance. Cut out of the role of political subject as a woman, Orlando has recourse to geographical subjecthood as a writer. Her manuscript, "The Oak Tree," is grounded in England; thus Orlando needs to continue her relationship with this place from which she writes, for an organic connection between space and literary representation emerges throughout her great work—"the age of prose was congealing [. . .]. The very landscape outside was less stuck about with garlands and the briars themselves were less thorned and intricate" (113). Orlando's dilemma of needing to maintain a place from which to write, on the one hand, and of being cast into what Woolf in *Three Guineas* calls the "Outsider's Society" of nationless women, on the other, poses important questions with regard to national identity. In speaking of the marginalization of women by the masculine discourse of political nationalism, Woolf notes in *Three Guineas* that the "cawing of rooks in an elm tree [. . .] the splash of waves on a beach" (106) may herald continued attachment to England even for members of the "Outsider's Society." This same scenario, of the outsider's adjacency to national identity, is manifest in Orlando's haunting and writing. Woolf identifies the role of geography as a mnemonic device for national identity and shows how imagined geographies are both inhabited by national subjects and haunted by outsiders.

Note

1.   Jaime Hovey argues that Woolf creates a quite specific "positive" configuration of national belonging—for the "polymorphously sexual" white woman. I am interested in the other side of the coin, in the sense that my focus is on the haunting absences of national belonging. While I introduce the idea of haunting in this paper, I work these themes out more explicitly in a longer essay entitled "Giving Up the Ghost: National and Literary Haunting in *Orlando*" *Modern Fiction Studies* 50.1 (2004): 110–29.

Works Cited

Bazargan, Susan. "The Uses of the Land: Vita Sackville-West's Pastoral Writings and Virginia Woolf's *Orlando*." *Woolf Studies Annual* 5 (1999): 25–52.

Gordon, Avery F. *Ghostly Matters: Haunting and the Sociological Imagination.* Minneapolis: University of Minnesota Press, 1997.

Hecht, Roger. "'I Am Nature's Bride': *Orlando* and the Female Pastoral." *Re: Reading, Re: Writing, Re: Teaching Virginia Woolf: Selected Papers from the Fourth Annual Conference on Virginia Woolf.* Ed. Eileen Barrett and Patricia Cramer. New York: Pace University Press, 1995.

Hovey, Jaime. "'Kissing a Negress in the Dark': Englishness as a Masquerade in Woolf's *Orlando*." *PMLA: Publications of the Modern Language Association of America* 112.3 (1997): 393–405.

Lawrence, Karen R. "Orlando's Voyage Out." *Modern Fiction Studies* 38.1 (1992): 253–77.

Osborne, Brian S. "Landscapes, Memory, Monuments, and Commemoration: Putting Identity in its Place." *Canadian Ethnic Studies* 33.3 (2001): 39–78.

Woolf, Virginia. *Orlando.* San Diego: Harvest-Harcourt Brace Jovanovich, 1973.

---. *Three Guineas.* New York: Harcourt Brace and Company, 1938.

Yaeger, Patricia, ed. *The Geography of Identity.* Ann Arbor: University of Michigan Press, 1996.

THE GUIDEBOOK AND THE DOG: VIRGINIA WOOLF AND ITALY

by Eleanor McNees

I n an 1869 essay in the *Cornhill Magazine,* Leslie Stephen indicts the British tourist who, blindly following one of Murray's guidebooks, never deviates from the beaten track and has "no independent judgment":

> [H]e admires what the infallible Murray orders him to admire [. . . and] never diverges one hair's breadth from the beaten track of his predecessors [. . .]. The tourist, in short, is notoriously a person who follows blindly a certain hackneyed round; who never stops long enough before a picture or a view to admire it or to fix it in his memory; and who seizes every opportunity of transplanting little bits of London to the districts which he visits. ("Vacations" 174)

Stephen reinforces an opposition between the traveler and the tourist that became popular in the nineteenth century when middle-class workers, with limited time but aspirations to acquire culture, booked tours through Cook's Travel Company and spent several weeks seeing major European sites. These tourists began to replace the former century's aristocratic grand tourists who had had months, sometimes years, at their disposal.

A member of that middle class himself, Leslie Stephen, like Charles Dickens several decades earlier, disdained any sense of camaraderie with tourists who adhered to the popular Murray's handbooks for instruction on where to go and what to see. An avid mountain climber, Stephen believed that to have an authentic experience of landscape and scenery, one must cultivate a personal acquaintance with place that could not be procured from any guidebook. Stephen echoes Coleridge, intimating that it is impossible for a city dweller to respond intuitively to landscape: "To take a raw Londoner and, with no previous training of mind or eye, to place him in the midst of the finest scenery, is to subject him to an unfair trial. He has not acquired the inward sense to which it appeals" ("Vacations" 175).

Acquisition of this "inward sense" distinguishes the true traveler from the tourist. Although throughout her diaries, letters, and essays, Virginia Woolf calls herself a tourist, her desire to develop an inward sense of place that corresponds to an external view demonstrates her struggle between touristic sensibilities and a traveler's appreciation. In her travel writing she searches for a means of conveying authenticity of place. Nowhere is this search more convoluted than in her attempts to describe her experiences in Italy from her first trip after her father's death in 1904 to her last one with Leonard Woolf in 1935. From her earliest journal entry to her last, she worries about the efficacy of words to embody authentic experience, particularly when she confronts Italian (and Grecian) sites laden with classical and literary connotations. Only when she is momentarily able to stray from the beaten track, to drop the self-consciousness of the "superficial traveler" (*Passionate Apprentice* 355), can she merge impression with reality.[1] The antiself-consciousness of the traveler open to impressions and experiences culminates in Woolf's depiction of

Elizabeth Barrett Browning's dog Flush in Italy; the most successful because it is the least mediated of her travel sketches. There, unself-consciously, she moves from sensual impression to scene instead of the reverse, and the conflict between external reality and internal response temporarily abates.[2]

Over the past several decades, spearheaded by Dean MacCannell's cultural analysis of tourism in *The Tourist: A New Theory of the Leisure Class* (1976; rpt. 1999), a substantial body of criticism on theories of tourism has arisen. Most pertinent to Woolf's writing are, on one hand, historical surveys of the origins of sightseeing (Adler 1989; Buzard 1993) and, on the other, a search for an unmediated authenticity (MacCannell; Culler 1988; Urry 1990). These studies illuminate the debate between the tourist and the traveler in Woolf's work and stress the ultimate impossibility of unmediated authenticity in any encounter between sightseer and site/sight. Woolf struggles with this dilemma from her abortive attempts to describe the scene in *The Voyage Out* (1915) to her journal accounts of her last trip to Italy in 1935 when, after describing the Campagna di Roma and the bay in which Shelley drowned near Lerici, she concludes, "But that kind of perfection no longer makes me feel for my pen—Its too easy" (*Diary* 4: 314).

In his analysis of the twentieth-century tourist, Dean MacCannell attributes the search for authenticity to the experience of living in an increasingly inauthentic and fragmented world. Thus sightseeing becomes "a kind of collective striving for a transcendence [. . .], a way of attempting to overcome the discontinuity of modernity, of incorporating its fragments into unified experience" (13).

In "The Semiotics of Tourism" (1988), Jonathan Culler builds on MacCannell's discussion of authenticity by focusing on the mediating relation between the tourist marker and the actual site. For Culler, all sites are cultural signs with the tourist transformed into a sign reader who needs markers to understand the significance and the authenticity of a particular place.[3] Most conscious of herself as such a sign reader during her first trip to Greece in 1906, Virginia Woolf vacillates between succumbing to the guidebook (now Baedeker instead of Murray) to mark the significance of particular ruins and rejecting the guidebook as a barrier against authentic impression. Of the ancient theater at Olympia, she concludes, "[O]nce more we might quote the Guidebook: for our purposes it is simply a flat circle of grass, scattered with innumerable fragments of stone. [. . .] Still this is not what the vagrant mind dwells on most" (*Passionate Apprentice* 319). The "vagrant mind" exchanges the intermediary role of sign reader for the immediacy of sense impression, but is aware that it sacrifices any cultural significance of the scene to the personal eye. In the same journal entry, she abandons Baedeker's account of the statues at Olympia in order to see them with her own eyes: to "let the eye spring like a creature set free along those curves & hollows; for it has secretly craved such beauty!" (319).

Relying on the work of MacCannell and Culler, but analyzing the history of tourism and sightseeing in previous centuries, Judith Adler and James Buzard explore the evolution of the tourist from the impartial surveyor and chronicler to the romantic seeker of sublimity. In "The Origins of Sightseeing" (1989), Adler argues that early tourists of the seventeenth and eighteenth centuries (many of the original grand tourists) approached European sites first through discourse (by learning the language and entering the aristocratic circles of the country) and later through naturalistic observation. With the advent of guidebooks in the late eighteenth and early nineteenth centuries, discourse and naturalistic observation ceded ground to the elevation of aesthetic over impartial observation. This shift marked the transition to the romantic emphasis on sublimity and personal impression: "In its aesthetic transformation, sightseeing became simultaneously a more effusively passionate activity and a more private one" (Adler 22). James Buzard's *The Beaten Track: European Tourism, Literature, and the Ways to Culture, 1800-1918* (1993) is the first major discussion of tourism to focus on specific literary figures (Wordsworth, James, and Forster). After a discussion of the tourist versus the "anti-tourist" (Leslie Stephen's *traveler*), Buzard's most pertinent point for analyzing Woolf's attitude toward the tourist and travel writing is his characterization of Forster's "view of tourism *from within*" (292) instead of from the outside perspective of the guidebook. Buzard discusses the discontinuity between Forster's tourists' expectations and their actual experiences. The only opportunities for authenticity, Buzard implies, reside in the disruption of the romantic expectations of Forster's tourists.

From her earliest trips abroad Woolf tries to unite the tourist with the traveler, thus bridging the gap Judith Adler perceives between eighteenth- and nineteenth-century sightseers. During her second trip to Italy in 1908, Woolf expresses an aesthetic that will dictate her future travel writings. She resolves to "write not only with the eye, but with the mind; & discover real things beneath the show" (*Passionate Apprentice* 384).[4] All future attempts to describe Italy in her letters and diaries demonstrate a singular inability to execute this double vision. Only in *Flush,* where reality is purely sensual and not reflective, is she able to resolve this dilemma.

In her 1928 introduction to the World's Classics edition of Laurence Sterne's *A Sentimental Journey through France and Italy,* she praises Sterne's substitution of a mental journey for a guided tour. This new "angle of vision" (*Second Common Reader* 80) seems to allow Woolf to abandon traditional descriptions of major sites and landscapes. Only thus, she implies, can one achieve any sense of authenticity or, "the essence of things" (81). Sterne sanctions Woolf's decision to record impressions over external description. Speaking of his movement "from the outer to the inner," she states, "It is no use going to the guide-book; we must consult our own minds [. . .]. In this preference for the windings of his own mind to the guide-book and its hammered high road, Sterne is singularly of our own age" (81).

In her first contribution to *Times Literary Supplement* in 1905, "Literary Geography," a review of two books on the countries of Thackeray and Dickens, Woolf was already mapping her attitude toward travel writing as a mirror of mind over eye. She states that "[a] writer's country is a territory within his own brain; and we run the risk of disillusionment if we try to turn such phantom cities into tangible brick and mortar" (*Essays* 1: 35). But in 1908 in a review of Vernon Lee's *The Sentimental Traveller,* Woolf cautions against a purely impressionistic description of place, perhaps seeing her own tendencies reflected in one she considers an inferior writer. Unfortunately, only very few authors possess the artistic talent "to give such perishable matter an enduring form" (*Essays* 1: 158). Of these select few, Henry James stands preeminent, though, as she suggests elsewhere, this may be because as a non-European, he is a less biased observer and more open to "picturesque attitudes and impressions" (*Essays* 1: 125).

Woolf's diagnosis of E. M. Forster's conflict between external description and symbolic significance reveals her frustration with her own attempts to depict Italy. She halts frequently at simile, evincing a struggle between an urge to witness scenery and a retreat into subjective impression. She faults Forster for failing to achieve a "single vision" (*Collected Essays* 345) through a combination of "realism and mysticism" (346), for being too realistic and too symbolic so that the reader is buffeted between the two. Employing the same image of "bricks and mortar" from "Literary Geography" to signify Forster's realism, she states that "his brick must be lit up; we must see the whole building saturated with light" (346). How to illuminate the material with the spiritual, to fuse the Edwardian with the Georgian, becomes Woolf's principal concern in her own writing. Central to her attempts to describe Italian landscape and cities is the crux she identifies in Forster's novels: "how to connect the actual thing with the meaning of the thing and to carry the reader's mind across the chasm which divides the two without spilling a single drop of its belief" (346).

Especially in her journal entries and in her letters to Vanessa, Woolf strives to find the bridge that will carry the reader's mind across this chasm. In her descriptions of landscape this effort is strained. The pictorial quality of her writing either collapses into a series of subjective impressions lacking any unified panorama, or she pauses self-consciously at the edge of the pictorial, reverting to simile or apologizing for the guidebook quality of her writing. As early as her first visit to Italy in 1904, she writes to Violet Dickinson of the trip over Gotthard Pass: "There was a snowstorm on the St. Gotthard: we came down into brilliant sun shine, and the lakes were pure blue. The mountains had snow all over them. Isnt this like a guide book?" (*Letters* 1: 137). And on the same trip, this time from Florence, she assures Emma Vaughan, "I wont write a dissertation upon the Italian landscape because I know it would bore you" (*Letters* 1: 138). In her comparison of Vanessa Bell's painting and Virginia Woolf's writing, Diane Gillespie devotes a chapter to the sisters' methods of depicting landscape. While Vanessa's paintings adopt an unmediated perspective, Gillespie suggests Virginia's writing about landscape always contains a consciousness of the viewer. Woolf is keener to fuse outer and inner, to turn "from beautiful but lifeless surfaces to the complexities of people's inner lives and relationships with each other" (*Sisters' Arts* 277).[5]

In her diary from Florence in 1909 and again from Pisa in 1933, Woolf emphasizes the difficulty of descriptive writing. Pure description is too derivative of the guidebook: "Descriptive writing is dangerous & tempting. It is easy, with little expense of brain power, to make something. [. . .] As a matter of fact, the subject is probably infinitely subtle, no more amenable to impressionist treatment than the human character. What one records is really the state of ones own mind" (*Passionate Apprentice* 396). She laments the "lapidary inscriptions" (396) that make her writing tense and strained. The same problem—how to select a picturesque aspect and illuminate it from within—besets her in Siena in 1933 on her first automobile trip to Italy. Reading Henry James's *The Sacred Fount,* she essays a descriptive method reminiscent of Dickens in its rapid piling of image upon image, and with this technique she is able momentarily to effect a sense of immediacy and authenticity. During this next-to-last trip to Italy, Woolf seems acutely aware of color and eager to infuse her descriptions with a deeper sense of reality. She is also, as she emphasizes in a letter to Ethel Smyth, trying to see the Italian landscape, significantly near the spot where Shelley drowned, as it really is, without forcing fiction to overtake fact. In spite of her query, "[W]hats the use of writing?" she proceeds, but how describe the hills, the tall pink yellow white houses, and the in fact, not fiction, purple brown sea, not rolling in waves, as I made my sea [in *The Waves*], but now and again giving a little shiver, like that which runs through a field of corn, or the back of a race horse! [. . .] Italy beats me. (*Letters* 5: 186)

The process by which Woolf merges descriptive fact with fiction is best effected through her abandonment of a self-conscious mediator, of the tourist-following-the-guidebook, for the complete submersion of self into sense. Adopting the persona of an animal allows her to bypass the problem of external versus internal and to achieve an inward connection with place her father had advocated for the true traveler. A 1927 letter to Vanessa from Rome hints at the method Woolf was to choose in *Flush*. Describing Rome and the Vatican, she moves from the lush vegetation to the costumes of Italian nurses, when suddenly, thinking of Proust, she shifts perspective, abandoning herself through a simile to a fish.

She had adopted a similar angle of vision in her story "Kew Gardens" in 1919 when she assumed a snail for her persona. Surrendering human self-consciousness to animal consciousness allowed her to express an authentic connection with the land, to avoid the beaten track of the tourist for the receptive eye of the traveler. *Flush,* though ostensibly a "joke," had serious implications for her style and point of view. According to Quentin Bell, "[h]er dog was the embodiment of her own spirit, not the pet of an owner. *Flush* in fact was one of the routes which Virginia used [. . .] in order to escape from her own human corporeal existence" (410). *Flush* achieves an undeniable if ironic authenticity in its choice of a dog's perspective.

In *Flush* Woolf satirizes the literary pedigree of her predecessors as Flush, newly shorn in Italy, realizes a new freedom where all dogs are equally mongrels. Whereas in London he had been relegated to the "back room" and taken everywhere on a leash, in Pisa and Florence he is free to roam, to experience what Dean MacCannell calls the "back regions" off the beaten track where one can "share in the real life of the places visited, or at least [. . .] see that life as it is really lived" (*The Tourist* 96). According to this theory of tourism, the traveler who seeks these back regions as opposed to the guidebook sites comes closer to experiencing the authentic culture or seeing behind the scenes.

Throughout the Italian section of *Flush,* as Susan Squire indicates, both Flush and Mrs. Browning achieve an independence denied them in London society. As their interests begin to divide them, Woolf and the reader clearly side with Flush, who ceases to be an observer and plunges into the sensuous midst of Florence. While Mrs. Browning "observes" pictures and cathedrals, Flush abandons himself to the back regions of the marketplace and other dogs. The true traveler who, as Woolf had averred years earlier, must lose oneself in the slums of Constantinople, Flush

went in and out, up and down, where they beat brass, where they bake bread, where the women sit combing their hair, where the bird-cages are piled high on the causeway, where the wine spills itself in dark red stains on the pavement [. . .]—he ran in and out, always with his nose to the ground, drinking in the essence. (*Flush* 139)

The sightseer's vision gives way to the primal, unmediated senses of smell and touch as the narrative voice expresses the inadequacy of words to depict scenery. The narrator mocks Mrs. Browning's futile attempt to describe the Apennines in contrast to Flush's dumb enjoyment of landscape: "She [Mrs. Browning] could not find words enough in the whole of the English language to express what she felt. [. . .] But the baby and Flush felt none of this stimulus, none of this inadequacy. Both were silent" (*Flush* 136).

Between completion of the serialized version of *Flush* for the *Atlantic Monthly* and its publication in book form in October 1933, the Woolfs took a driving trip to Italy where Virginia, probably remembering the description in *Flush,* is self-consciously reticent about the Apennines. She notes in her diary, "Of the Apennines I have nothing to say—save that up on the top theyre like the inside of a green umbrella: spine after spine: & clouds caught on the point of the stick" (*Diary* 4: 159). Characteristic of her descriptions of Italian land-scape is her tendency to strain after simile until the image becomes a kind of metaphysical conceit, far removed from, yet strangely suggestive of, the actual scene.

In a nod to the inadequacy of Victorian literary figures' depictions of Italy, the nar-rator contrasts Flush's blissful, wordless experience with mediated accounts: "[H]e knew Florence as no human being has ever known it; as Ruskin never knew it or George Eliot either. He knew it as only the dumb know. Not a single one of his myriad sensations ever submitted itself to the deformity of words" (*Flush* 140). In her allusions to John Ruskin and George Eliot, Woolf emphasizes the inability of such literary genres as the aesthetic essay (*Stones of Venice*) and the historical novel (*Romola*) to convey a true sense of Italian life. Such genres are finally little better than guidebooks in revealing the essence of Italy.

The distinction between the literary Elizabeth Barrett Browning/Virginia Woolf and Flush, the voiceless embodiment of sensuous experience, signifies the split between self-conscious description and unconscious revelation. By reflecting the antitouristic, antiself-conscious state of Flush the traveler, Woolf was able to abandon the guidebook and imagine an authentic confrontation with Italian culture where language no longer guided perception.[6]

Notes

1. On her second visit to Europe in 1906, she worries that "[her] efforts to rid [her]self of certain precon-ceptions have taken my attention from the actual facts" (*Passionate Apprentice* 351). Consequently, she determines to stray from the beaten track in Constantinople, to "lose [her] way in the unrecorded slums," where "even a stranger & a tourist may stumble upon something that is quite without self consciousness; & then the town for the first time will become a real town of flesh & blood" (353).

2. Woolf's conflict between impression and external reality finds its aesthetic roots in Walter Pater's famous 1873 conclusion to *The Renaissance,* where he denies the possibility of any objective view of experience (151). Numerous critics have discussed the subjective/objective split in Woolf's writings in relation to the perceiving eye/I of the narrator. James Naremore's *The World Without a Self: Virginia Woolf and the Novel* (New Haven: Yale University Press, 1973) was one of the first to tackle this crux; his study was followed by Alex Zwerdling's *Virginia Woolf and the Real World* (Berkeley: University of California Press, 1986) and, most recently, by Ann Banfield's *The Phantom Table: Woolf, Fry, Russell and Epistemology of Modern-ism* (Cambridge: Cambridge University Press, 2000). In her study of Woolf's literary and philosophical investment in the aesthetic and epistemological philosophies of Fry and Russell, Banfield devotes a chapter, "How describe the world seen without a self?" to Woolf's struggle to find "a language of sensibility" (297) equivalent to a Cézanne painting (296).

3. Culler notes the irony of the search for authenticity since the tourist often cannot know whether or not

the site is authentic without the aid of a marker: "The paradox, the dilemma of authenticity, is that to be experienced as authentic it must be marked as authentic, but when it is marked as authentic it is mediated, a sign of itself, and hence lacks the authenticity of what is truly unspoiled, untouched by mediating cultural codes" (164). In *The Tourist Gaze: Leisure and Travel in Contemporary Societies* (1990), John Urry argues against MacCannell and Culler that the search for authenticity rests on a comparison between "one's normal place of residence/work and the object of the tourist gaze" (11).

4.   Mitchell Leaska terms this "a new prismatic quality" that he observes in Woolf's responses to her trip to Greece and Turkey two years earlier (*Passionate Apprentice* xxiii).

5.   Diane Gillespie speculates that Vanessa and Virginia had already by 1910 discussed the latter's limitations as a descriptive writer, Vanessa asserting that she preferred her sister's depictions of characters to those of landscape (*Sisters' Arts* 275–76).

6.   Quentin Bell notes that Woolf began twice-weekly Italian lessons in the winter of 1933 when she was writing *Flush*. Not surprisingly, she is acutely conscious when in Italy of her limited fluency. To Elizabeth Bowen in May 1933, she writes of the Italian peasants: "They are charming people [. . .] offering one wine, or 6 dead fish—I've only 10 words of Italian, but I fire them all perpetually; and so we get led into all kinds of queer places" (*Letters* 5: 184).

Works Cited

Adler, Judith. "Origins of Sightseeing." *Annals of Tourism Research* 16 (1989): 7–29.

Banfield, Ann. *The Phantom Table: Woolf, Fry, Russell and Epistemology of Modernism.* Cambridge: Cambridge University Press, 2000.

Bell, Quentin. *Virginia Woolf: A Biography.* New York: Harcourt Brace Jovanovich, 1972.

Buzard, James. *The Beaten Track: European Tourism, Literature, and the Ways to Culture, 1800–1918.* Oxford: Oxford University Press, 1993.

Culler, Jonathan. "The Semiotics of Tourism." *Framing the Sign: Criticism and Its Institutions.* Norman: University of Oklahoma Press, 1988. 153–67.

Gillespie, Diane F. *The Sisters' Arts: The Writing and Painting of Virginia Woolf and Vanessa Bell.* Syracuse: Syracuse University Press, 1988.

Lawrence, Karen R. *Penelope Voyages: Women and Travel in the British Literary Tradition.* Ithaca: Cornell University Press, 1994.

MacCannell, Dean. *The Tourist: A New Theory of the Leisure Class.* 1976. Berkeley: University of California Press, 1999.

Pater, Walter. *The Renaissance: Studies in Art and Poetry.* 1873. Ed. Adam Phillips. Oxford: Oxford University Press, 1986.

Squier, Susan Merrill. *Virginia Woolf and London: The Sexual Politics of the City.* Chapel Hill: University of North Carolina Press, 1985.

Stephen, Leslie. "Vacations." *Men, Books, and Mountains.* Ed. S. O. A. Ullmann. London: Hogarth Press, 1956. 168–81.

Urry, John. *The Tourist Gaze: Leisure and Travel in Contemporary Societies.* London: Sage Publications, 1990.

Woolf, Virginia. *Collected Essays.* Ed. Leonard Woolf. 4 vols. New York: Harcourt, Brace & World, 1967.

---. *The Common Reader: Second Series.* London: Hogarth Press, 1932.

---. *The Diary of Virginia Woolf.* Ed. Anne Olivier Bell. 5 vols. New York: Harcourt Brace Jovanovich, 1977–84.

---. *The Essays of Virginia Woolf.* Ed. Andrew McNeillie. 4 vols. London: Hogarth Press, 1986–94.

---. *Flush: A Biography.* New York: Harcourt Brace and Company, 1933.

---. *The Letters of Virginia Woolf.* Ed. Nigel Nicolson and Joanne Trautmann. 6 vols. New York: Harcourt Brace Jovanovich, 1975–80.

---. *A Passionate Apprentice: The Early Journals 1987–1909.* Ed. Mitchell A. Leaska. London: Hogarth Press, 1990.

Sex Costumes:
Signifying Sex and Gender in Woolf's "The Introduction" and *The Years*

by Jennifer-Ann DiGregorio Kightlinger

In much of Virginia Woolf's fiction, a gap exists between her characters' clothing and sense of self; that gap becomes a space for critical reflection. Insofar as clothing performs an identity that is in conflict with a character's physical body and/or sense of self, Woolf's characters may be seen as drag performers. When considering Woolf's "frock consciousness,"[1] many critics discuss *Orlando*. It seems important to note that Woolf's more realist works similarly explore gender in innovative and complex ways.[2] In both "The Introduction" and *The Years*, fashion subverts the heterosexual hierarchy, deconstructing sex and sexual signifiers. Woolf's treatment of clothing becomes its own discourse—one that permits a reexamination of traditional understandings of gender and encourages a reappropriation of traditional male/female signifiers. This paper will briefly discuss the presentation of dress as central to the creation and understanding of manliness/womanliness in Woolf's short story "The Introduction" and in her novel *The Years*. It will also explore the relationship between Woolf's treatment of costume and Judith Butler's gender performance theory.

Lily Everit, the protagonist of "The Introduction," feels like she is "being flung into a whirlpool where either she would perish or be saved" (185). Lily's reflections reveal the whirlpool is womanhood and the threat of being overpowered by patriarchal institutions—the Church, Parliament—and by societal expectations of femininity and fashion. Prior to her arrival at Mrs. Dalloway's party, Lily feels confident in her sense of self. Fashion preparations for the party are distinct from her identity. The narration describes "her essay on the character of Swift," which lay "untouched" beneath her dress, as "fact" (184). The dress and Lily's "going out" are considered "fiction" ("The Introduction" 184).

Upon her arrival at Mrs. Dalloway's, her sense of self begins to fade. The self—represented by the essay—is transformed by social context:

> [A]t the very first sight of people moving up stairs, down stairs, this hard lump (her essay on the character of Swift) wobbled, began melting, she could not keep hold of it, and all her being [. . .] turned to a mist of alarm, apprehension, and defence as she stood at bay in her corner. This was the famous place: the world. ("Introduction" 184)

Lily's once solidified "essay" self is destabilized; Lily's new self—one marked by traditional notions of womanliness—is constructed by the social situation: "[T]he dress [and] all the little chivalries and respects of the drawing-room—all made her feel that she [. . .] was being proclaimed [. . .] a woman" (185). Lily's womanhood is constructed by her dress and the presence of the people "moving up stairs, down stairs" that "seemed to menace her and mount over her" (185). Here, Woolf suggests costume constructs reality.

Woolf's treatment of fashion questions what is "real" or "true." Is reality the subject's sense of self? Is reality society's perception of the subject based on her costume? How does the subject's reaction to societal perception influence what is "real"? Lily's dilemma lies in the inability to know or hold onto a fixed reality—a definitive truth. This is the fashion dilemma. Woolf's ambiguousness and her refusal to locate the "real" suggest reality is dependent upon the contextual moment. This seems to reflect Butler's theory that gender identity is purely performative.

For Judith Butler, recognizing gender as a construction constituted by repetitive acts permits a challenge to the institutions that have constructed gender hierarchies and presents opportunities for a "cultural transformation of gender" ("Performative Acts" 403). Woolf's short story acknowledges womanhood as constructed by Lily's dress and calls attention to social institutions—represented by Mrs. Dalloway's party—that perpetuate gender hierarchies. In doing so, Woolf challenges the reader to reimagine gender. What fashion might represent the intellectual Lily—the Lily represented by the essay?

Yet, while Woolf's examination of costume and identity resonates with Butler's, it is markedly different in its suggestion of an underlying true identity. The narrator recognizes Lily's new womanly self as a falsehood; womanhood is carefully scripted onto her body. The signifiers of womanhood—the "finery," the "coiled and twisted hair," the "delicacy" of costume—the narrator admits, are "not hers after all" ("Introduction" 186). They are artificial; they are implemented to disguise (what Lily considers to be) the true self. The narrator suggests Lily "accepted the part which was now laid on her and, naturally, overdid it a little as a soldier, proud of the traditions of an old and famous uniform might overdo it, feeling conscious as she walked, of her finery" (186).

It is interesting that Woolf analogizes the delicacy of woman with the pride of a soldier. Drawing the parallel between Lily and a masculine figure signifies something not explicitly stated. The soldier imagery lends masculine qualities to Lily—it plays with the notions of her anatomical sex and traditional sex signifiers. Woolf's equating of the performative nature of womanhood with masculine pride reveals Lily's underlying androgyny. At one and the same time, Lily is a soldier and a "delicate" woman of "finery." (This is not the last time Woolf draws the analogy between a female character and masculine soldierly traits. In *The Years,* Rose's lesbianism is marked largely by soldierly signifiers.)

In Mrs. Dalloway's presence—the presence of seemingly genuine femininity—Woolf suggests there is some objective reality beneath costume. It is important to note the interactions between gender, costume, and narration as central to "The Introduction." The contrast between the gendered identities of Mrs. Dalloway and Lily are, perhaps, an effect of narrative perspective. Mrs. Dalloway may feel as if she too is performing. But the reader is not provided with her interiority.

Woolf complicates things further when she reveals Lily's sense of oneness with the male romantic identity. Before the party, the narrator informs us, Lily's "ordinary being, by which she knew and liked herself," preferred to "ponder on long solitary walks," enjoying the "ecstasy of loneliness," and the discovery of "little ceremonies which had no audience, private rites, pure beauty offered by beetles and lilies of the valley" ("Introduction" 186). Lily has a Wordsworthian sense of self. This seemingly androgynous self (one that is sexed female but self-identified by traditionally masculine intellectual activities) "[creeps] into the heart of mother and father and brothers and sisters" (186).

Woolf's suggestion that Lily's true self is hidden beneath female-sexed costumes is mitigated by societal pressures. Lily's somewhat masculine identity cannot hold up against the suggestive power of her dress, the social context of the party, and the embodied presence of the male romantic—the academic, Bob Brinsley. Brinsley's presence is destructive; it damages Lily's androgynous Wordsworthian self, "her ordinary being, by which she knew and liked herself" ("Introduction" 186). The narrator asks, "What had [Lily] to oppose to this massive masculine achievement? An essay on the character of Dean Swift! [. . .] [W]hat could she do but lay her essay, oh and the whole of her being, on the floor as a cloak for him to trample on, as a rose for him to rifle" (186-87). Ultimately, Lily is reduced to the clothing that signifies her femininity, a femininity that is subordinate to the supremacy of the male intellectual in Victorian England.

In "A Rose for Him to Rifle," Jane Marcus notes that while Brinsley's trampling of the metaphorical cloak marks a reversal of gender roles—one that plays on "chivalry," "gallantry," and "obeisance as she [Lily] plays Walter Raleigh to his [Brinsley's] Queen Elizabeth" (2)—the reversal seeks to maintain patriarchal power dynamics. Marcus explores "The Introduction" as an "allegory for survival" (1); Lily "emerges from battle shouldering her feminist responsibilities: 'this civilization . . . depends on me'" (4). But Lily does not emerge unscathed; "[t]he rifled rose and the trampled cloak suggest male violence and rape of woman's textuality and sexuality" (3).[3] Lily's symbolic "battle with Brinsley" as representative of "patriarchal civilization" (4), Marcus argues, points to Woolf's "intellectual and political commitment to a socialist feminist attack on the family" patriarchy (9),[4] and implicates Mrs. Dalloway in her acceptance of Victorian femininity. Marcus suggests betrayal: "Lily is literally handed over to Bob Brinsley by Mrs. Dalloway, her surrogate mother" (3).

In Mrs. Dalloway's society, Lily's body—her female physiology—demands the performance of proper femininity. The performance of femininity—the dress—feels unnatural, is challenged by the presence of her hostess, and threatens the Wordsworthian self Lily values. The performance of masculinity—the essay—is crushed by Brinsley. The tension between the identity that prides itself on the essay and the identity created by the dress makes a space available for critical reflection on society's sex roles and gender formation. Woolf's treatment of Lily's identity crisis points toward a naturally formed androgynous self that is challenged and ultimately compromised by society's demand for traditional gender performances.

Several Woolf scholars have suggested that some of the characters in *The Years* serve to challenge traditional gender constructs. For example, Claire Hanson proposes that Sara Pargiter's speech patterns "[stitch] together echoes of poems and stories from high and popular culture, and creates a pastiche of gender roles," "undercutting" or undermining the dominant heterosexual discourse (61). Sara's speech, Hanson argues, reveals gender as "not stable but tenuously constituted through a stylized repetition of acts [. . .] opening up the possibility, at least, of gender transformation" (62).

I'd like to suggest "the stylized repetition of acts" that may "open up the possibility [. . .] of gender transformation" is not limited to speech acts but might also include "acts" of costume manipulation. Several characters in the novel undermine the dominant heterosexual "language" of dress. Characters that refuse to participate in the dominant mode of dress resist gender identification. Their unusual choice of clothing flies in the face of fashion and may be seen as a pastiche of old and new styles, male and female signifiers.

Sara's fashion choices recall Butler's suggestion that imitations of the myth of "original" genders are "characteristic of pastiche" (*Gender Trouble* 176). "[P]arodic proliferation deprives hegemonic culture and its critics of the claim to naturalized or essentialist gender identities" (176). On the night of Delia's party, North visits Sara and finds her in "shabby" dress (*The Years* 338). Later, when Sara emerges from the bedroom, "she had changed; she was in evening dress; [yet] there was something odd about her—perhaps it was the effect of the evening dress estranging her?" (349). Sara's evening dress imitates the fashion norms, but her "odd" imitation is in tension with those norms. Woolf's treatment of costume resonates with Butler's call to "affirm the local possibilities of intervention" through which traditional gendered constructions of identity may be challenged (*Gender Trouble* 188).

Butler suggests "[t]he notion of an original or primary gender identity is often parodied within the cultural practices of drag, cross-dressing, and the sexual stylization of butch/femme identities" (*Gender Trouble* 174), and "is subversive to the extent that it reflects" the ways in which traditional notions of male and female genders are produced through imitation (*Bodies That Matter* 125). In her evening dress, Sara imitates the "myth" of "original" female gender. Sara's body—though female sexed—is enacting a type of drag performance; her appearance does not conform to the laws of traditional femininity, it displaces traditional notions of gender and points to the possibility of resignification.

Butler's treatment of drag generally addresses male-sexed bodies performing female genders or female-sexed bodies performing male genders. Sara enacts a drag performance that is not in direct conflict with her sexed body. Yet Woolf manages to create a chasm between the body and the performance that—at times—seems more disorienting to the onlooker than the tension between the physiological sex and dress of a traditional drag performance (male performing femininity or female performing masculinity).

Determining what is subversive and what perpetuates hierarchical structures is sometimes difficult. "Sometimes," Butler suggests, "it is both at once; sometimes it remains caught in an irresolvable tension" (*Bodies That Matter* 128). Eleanor—*The Years*'s angel in the house—abandons her Victorian dress, and assuming the dress of the Indian other, embodies the ambivalence of drag. North compliments Eleanor's dress upon his arrival at Delia's. "'You're looking very young. You're looking extraordinarily handsome. I like you in those clothes,' he said, looking at her Indian cloak" (*The Years* 371). Eleanor's appropriation of Indian dress may be a celebration of Indian culture—certainly a subversive act. It may be a celebration of the nation's colonizing power—a perpetuating act. Her body, cloaked in Indian garb, refuses a definitive reading.

Eleanor's untraditional dress at Delia's party reminds Woolf's reader of her refusal to attend Lady Lasswade's party where, the narrator reveals, in the midst of "the groups of beautifully dressed women" (*The Years* 262), Kitty is certain "Eleanor would have found herself out of it" (257). While Kitty recognizes parties as social imperatives for women of her standing, she seems almost envious of Eleanor's ability to resist expectations. *The Years'* narrator reveals, Kitty "did not like being alone with women after dinner; it made her shy" (256). "Always after dinner women paid each other compliments about their clothes or their looks" (256). And, after all, Kitty "did things on the sly that they—the ladies over there—did not approve" (258). While Kitty "was formal; fashionable" (249), a vision of propriety, there is some rebellious quality that is not signified by her dress or outward appearance—something that keeps Kitty "evading the shrewd old eyes" (258) of traditional society women.

While Kitty's performance of traditional femininity (what Butler calls a "literalizing fantasy" or literalizing fiction) seems successful, her frustration with societal expectations for femininity cannot be consciously suppressed. Her thoughts—presented in much the same way Lily's are—reveal resentment toward the Victorian tradition and the women who represent it.

Rose Partiger, a lesbian and leader in the feminist movement, uses clothing (like Sara) as pastiche. Her ensemble seems the result of various items haphazardly thrown together. A female-sexed character Woolf often likens to a military general, Rose is a conscious nonparticipant in the fashion game. She wears "[a]lways reach-me-downs, coats and skirts [. . .] they saved time, and the years after all—she was over forty—made one care very little what people thought" (*The Years* 161).

When Rose discovers Maggie sewing her own clothes, Woolf's narrator suggests, she "begin[s] to feel at her ease. She [takes] off her hat and [throws] it on the floor" (*The Years* 170). Rose begins to feel at ease because she recognizes that Maggie too has rebelled against the fashion game. Maggie does not buy the latest fashion; she creates her own. While Maggie may do so out of financial necessity, she does so nonetheless. She and Rose share a fashion kinship. Tossing her hat aside, Rose communicates her unwillingness to participate in social proprieties. "Maggie look[s] at her with approval" and thinks she is "handsome, in a ravaged way; more like a man than a woman" (170). Rose's identity—in its refusal to subscribe to the fashion norms—resists fixed reading, and reflects a constant renegotiation of identity.

The possibility of effective and continuous renegotiation of identity in *The Years* (1937) reflects a historical optimism not present in 1923, the year of "The Introduction." While Kitty's presence confirms the existence and pressures of traditional gendered identities, Eleanor, Rose, and Sara's costumes reflect greater freedom of expression. The optimism in *The Years* may be attributed in part to the characters' age and class, but also seems indicative of social change that challenged traditional gendered identities and of Woolf's desire for continued positive change in the political and social standing of women.

Woolf's costumes—at one and the same time—signal sex and gender and resist stable, fixed signification. Lily's female costume, her interiority, and her interactions with others encourage a reexamination of sex and gender roles. Rose, Sara, and Eleanor's sexed costumes reveal sexual signifiers as constructs and work toward subverting traditional heterosexual hierarchies. And while Kitty's costumes signify gender, the narrative treatment of those costumes reveals their inadequacy in reflecting identity. Woolf's fashions become discourse—a discourse that recognizes the need to resist traditional gender construction/convention and understands the obstacles to resistance, specifically societal pressures, the veiled nature of the true self, and individual interpretations of costume as subversive or complicit.

"Gender"—the concepts it signifies—was not an analytical category available to Woolf. And Woolf certainly could not have anticipated the importance of the gender studies movement in contemporary academia. Needless to say, associating Butler with

Woolf is quite slippery. While acknowledging these difficulties, reexamining Woolf's "frock consciousness" with contemporary gender consciousness may inform the history of the gender studies movement and open Woolf's texts to a new critical audience. Woolf seems to have understood that bodies do matter, as do the costumes they are cloaked in. Woolf's gender performances do not permit a solidified sense of self. Rather, they defy definition and place individual selves and the larger community on shaky ground—the ideal foundation for self-reflection and responsible communal change.

Notes

1.   Katheryn Laing's "Addressing Femininity in the Twenties: Virginia Woolf and Rebecca West on Money, Mirrors and Masquerade" is particularly successful in presenting "frock consciousness" as a personal challenge for Woolf (as illustrated by letters/diary entries).
2.   Marcus suggests that Woolf's more "'factual novels'" provide "explicit evidence, less buried than in her other novels" of "Woolf's battle with the tyranny of the patriarchal family" (5). Despite this suggestion, and others like it, Woolf's realist fiction remains largely unexplored.
3.   "Rifle," Marcus notes, "uncannily suggests rape in its Old French origin" (3).
4.   While Marcus's "A Rose for Him to Rifle" informs the "costume" focus of this essay, her examination moves beyond the gendered implications of Lily's "cloak" to fully explore Woolf's critique of the patriarchy in various texts. Marcus discusses the ways in which Woolf placed "herself as a writer in relation to the powerful community of women artists" (Marcus 5), suggesting, "Woolf spent her life trying to write 'the feminist sentence'" (16), a "mother tongue" spoken by "the outsider woman, the crone, the charwoman, or the lesbian" (15). Marcus reminds, "Woolf's work is not simply a feminist valorization of woman but [. . .] is always marked with a socialist or class analysis" (17).

Works Cited

Butler, Judith. *Bodies That Matter: On the Discursive Limits of "Sex."* New York: Routledge, 1993.
---. *Gender Trouble: Feminism and the Subversion of Identity.* New York: Routledge, 1999.
---. "Performative Acts and Gender Constitution: An Essay in Phenomenology and Feminist Theory." *Writing on the Body: Female Embodiment and Feminist Theory.* Ed. Katie Conboy, Nadia Medina, and Sarah Stanbury. New York: Columbia University Press, 1997. 401–17.
Hanson, Clare. "Virginia Woolf in the House of Love: Compulsory Heterosexuality in *The Years.*" *Journal of Gender Studies* 6.1 (1997): 55–62.
Laing, Katheryn S. "Addressing Femininity in the Twenties: Virginia Woolf and Rebecca West on Money, Mirrors and Masquerade." *Virginia Woolf and the Arts: Selected Papers from the Sixth Annual Conference on Virginia Woolf.* Ed. Diane F. Gillespie and Leslie K. Hankins. New York: Pace University Press, 1997. 66–75.
Marcus, Jane. "A Rose for Him to Rifle" (introd.). *Virginia Woolf and the Languages of Patriarchy.* Bloomington: Indiana University Press, 1987. 1–17.
Woolf, Virginia. "The Introduction." *The Complete Shorter Fiction of Virginia Woolf.* Ed. Susan Dick. 2nd ed. San Diego: Harcourt Brace & Company, 1989. 184–89.
---. *The Years.* San Diego: Harvest-Harcourt Brace & Company, 1969.

"THE WORKS OF WOMEN ARE SYMBOLICAL"

by Elizabeth Gallaher von Klemperer

In *Aurora Leigh,* published in 1857, Elizabeth Barrett Browning makes sewing "symbolical" of the subjection of girls and women:

> The works of women are symbolical.
> We sew, sew, prick our fingers, dull our sight,
> Producing what? A pair of slippers, sir,
>
> To put on when you're weary [. . .] (1: 456–59)

In her essay on the poem, published in 1931, Virginia Woolf deals mainly with the difficulty of writing a novel in verse, of putting modern life into iambic pentameter. Being a literary anomaly, she concludes, Aurora Leigh has had no successors. The poem is powerful mainly as a period piece: It seizes "what it felt like to be a Victorian" (*Collected Essays* 1: 217). Yet Woolf does remark on the "torture of women's education" (1: 211) inflicted on the passionate Aurora, complete with awful cross-stitching, thus recalling Shakespeare's sister in *A Room of One's Own,* told to mend stockings and stir the pot. Does Woolf see sewing, then, as "symbolical" of women's continuing difficulties?

In her own novels, what does Woolf make of sewing? Not much, perhaps, if by sewing one means as I do here a hand and mind directing the movements of a needle and thread, and not textile work in general—not even Mrs. Ramsay's knitting. Woolf writes about sewing just enough, however, to make one wonder whether it plays a part in her feminist texts and subtexts.

In Victorian novels a woman's "work," unless otherwise specified, means some sort of needlework. And in Victorian literature sewing, though not conspicuous, partakes in the preoccupation with work that characterizes Victorian culture. Behind this preoccupation lurks the twofold conception of work derived from Genesis. Work is first a prerogative of God—that is, creation. But it becomes the punishment visited on the fallen Adam and his descendants. Is woman's quintessential work, sewing, creative or oppressive? Until the spread of the sewing machine, sewing fell into two categories: plain sewing, which was useful but tedious, and fancy sewing, which included embroidery and involved inventiveness and taste.

Fancy sewing did not, however, fulfill the aspirations of women like Aurora Leigh, who found such work demeaning. She did not object to poor women doing plain sewing to support themselves: What offended her was the fancy sewing designed, along with "a score of books on womanhood," to shape girls into young ladies (*Aurora Leigh* 1: 427). The making of cross-stitched slippers trivialized the needlewoman: These were neither actual necessities, nor art.

When Virginia Woolf was growing up, three generations after Aurora Leigh, the spread of the sewing machine had altered plain sewing—with the important exception of mending. But fancy sewing was encouraged by women's magazines that featured directions for embroidering slippers and other frippery. Wouldn't Virginia Woolf have considered such work demeaning, and used it to carry on the protest voiced by Mrs. Browning's heroine?

She might have had she been American. In a comprehensive study of textile work in writings by American women, Ellen Hedges has shown that in America the late nineteenth and early twentieth centuries saw an "increasingly negative treatment of sewing," which was a "ready signifier of a set of repressive cultural attitudes" (345, 346). In England cultural attitudes were not identical, although Englishwomen had much to complain about.

Even before the publication of *Aurora Leigh*, the Victorian sage John Ruskin had preached the honor and joy of manual work, including needlework. For him the "accomplished phase" of textile work was sewing, "directing the serviceable stitch, to draw the separate into the inseparable" (*The Works of John Ruskin* 29: 511). Ruskin's disciple William Morris launched the Arts and Crafts Movement, which during the 1880s and 1890s gave pride of place to minor but nonetheless creative arts including embroidery. This movement created a subculture that overlapped Virginia Woolf's early environment, and she continued even in the 1920s to meet Morris's associates and to visit houses decorated according to his teachings. Morris himself she called "a great man" (*Passionate Apprentice* 221).

The Arts and Crafts Movement, which furthered the serious appreciation of needlework, probably favored Woolf's early, unrecorded use of the needle. But her interest in sewing matured in a different context—during the revolution initiated in 1910 by Roger Fry's exhibition promoting the postimpressionism of Matisse and Cézanne, and carried on in the Omega Workshops he founded in May 1913, in which the new postimpressionist aesthetic was realized in interior design. Here curtains and cushions recalled not the High Middle Ages, but rather the paintings of Matisse, with their forceful colors and insistent patterns. With her sister, Vanessa, Woolf embroidered cushions in this modern style. This interest in needlework coincided with her protracted work on her first novel, *The Voyage Out*, which finally appeared in March 1915. It lasted at least a decade: In 1925 Woolf wrote Vita Sackville-West, "[W]oolwork is my passion," and threatened to send her a tea cozy worked with parrots and tulips (*Letters* 3: 207). Insofar as Woolf wrote about needlework, then, she did so from direct experience.

The heroine of *The Voyage Out*, Rachel Vinrace, is no second Aurora Leigh. No sewing is mentioned in connection with her sheltered upbringing. The needlewoman in this novel—a willing one—is Rachel's aunt, Helen Ambrose, who sets out to complete both a piece of embroidery and Rachel's education in the course of two voyages, the eponymous voyage out—across the ocean to a tropical resort, and the more important voyage in—up a river into the jungle. Beautiful and experienced, Helen brings to mind Woolf's sister, Vanessa, and also Homer's Helen. Early in the ocean voyage she sets up her embroidery frame on the steamer's deck and chooses thread from a "vari-coloured tangle" of wool on her lap (*The Voyage Out* 33). In book four of the *Odyssey*, Helen, home again in Menelaus's hall, has her maidens bring her a silver basket full of colored wools. Later, on the deck of the riverboat, Helen Ambrose reminds a fellow passenger of Greek mythology when she draws a long thread through her canvas, as if "spinning the thread of fate" (*The Voyage Out*

208). This allusion to the Parcae is hardly necessary: Homer's Helen herself is sufficiently associated with disaster.

Helen Ambrose's embroidery, mentioned several times in the draft of the novel, *Melymbrosia,* is described in detail in the finished text. Its "great design," presumably in the barbaric colors of French *Fauve* painting, centers on "a tropical river running through a tropical forest" and features masses of ripe fruit and a troupe of naked natives (*The Voyage Out* 33) that seem to represent primal instincts and appetites, like "Aunt Jennifer's tigers" in Adrienne Rich's poem ("Aunt Jennifer's Tigers" 2). But Helen is no Aunt Jennifer.

Her embroidery does not absorb her entirely. Between stitches she dips into a book of philosophy, or more often engages in conversation with young people, especially Rachel, whose unformed mind she focuses on the possibilities of life and on "[v]isions of a great river, now blue, now yellow in the tropical sun and crossed by bright birds" (*The Voyage Out* 86). These visions, created both verbally and in colored wool, induce Rachel to remain at the tropical resort instead of sailing on with her father.

In the last quarter of the book the river of Helen's embroidery and Rachel's imagination becomes a reality as a boat takes them and several other characters—including Rachel's suitor, Terence Hewet—into the lush, wild interior. There Rachel and Terence follow a path into the depths of the forest, where they have what comes closest in the novel to a sexual encounter. Back on the boat another young man complains about the landscape: "What sane person could have conceived a wilderness like this, and peopled it with apes and alligators? I should go mad if I lived here—raving mad" (*The Voyage Out* 275). Helen quickly tames the wilderness for him by changing the primal into the aesthetic, nature into a verbal tapestry: "[L]ook at the amazing colours, look at the shapes of the trees" (275). Meanwhile the two lovers are deep in nature itself, sunk mentally to "the bottom of the world" (274).

It's in these psychological depths that Rachel, rolled around in a forest of green, imagines looming over her the heads of Helen and Terence, which come together and kiss in midair. This perplexing passage suggests that Rachel's voyage in has been a voyage toward sexual knowledge, which as the novel ends proves fatal. Helen Ambrose, like Homer's Helen calm despite all her experience, has indeed played the role of fate, her embroidery accompanying Rachel's voyaging from beginning to end, representing both a confusion of art and life and the fusion of vitality and danger.

In *The Voyage Out* needlework consists of making; in Woolf's later fictions it consists more often of mending, as it does in her next novel, *Night and Day* (1919). Back in her London flat after a day at the office, Mary Datchet finds she has time for a bit of darning before receiving a few guests. Her workbasket, "containing balls of differently coloured wools," is inviting, and while her hands work with yarn her mind goes happily wool gathering (*Night and Day* 43). These mingled pleasures are interrupted by the early arrival of one guest, a young man surprised to discover her darning, and even more surprised to hear that she reads Emerson. "[B]ooks and stockings," he says, "[t]he combination is very odd." Pleased, Mary feels she is stitching with "singular grace and felicity." "The only thing that's odd about me," she tells her guest, "is that I enjoy them both—Emerson and the stocking" (45).

This slight scene anticipates the great one in which Clarissa Dalloway, mending her dress, is interrupted by Peter Walsh. In both scenes the needlework consists of mending;

in both the needlewoman is preparing for a party; in both she is interrupted by a male who doesn't really understand what she's doing or thinking; and in both hand and mind work in harmony, though not in unison, with each other.

Before going on to *Mrs. Dalloway* (1925), however, one should glance at *Jacob's Room* (1922), the saddest of Woolf's novels and the only one in which sewing seems dreary. What we first see of Betty Flanders's sewing is its paraphernalia separated from their owner, as we will finally see Jacob's shoes after his death. The light of an oil lamp reveals no needlewoman, only a bleak *nature morte:* "her large reels of white cotton and her steel spectacles; her needle-case; her brown wool wound round an old postcard" (*Jacob's Room* 12). We actually see Betty sewing only when she sits on the remains of an old Roman camp patching Jacob's britches (19). Along with a lost brooch, the needles she drops there will be all of her that lasts (132). In *Jacob's Room,* then, sewing not only bespeaks the straitened circumstances of a widowed mother; it also helps convey the theme of discon-nectedness realized in the novel's form.

In *Mrs. Dalloway* sewing plays a larger part in the fabric of the novel as a whole. Clarissa is not, like Helen Ambrose, producing a new artifact, but repairing a tear in her dress. In both cases, however, the item being sewn has womanly implications, female in one case, feminine in the other. Helen's represents primal fulfillment, Clarissa's something like chastity—the tear in her dress recalls the stain on a new brocade in *The Rape of the Lock.* For Clarissa the torn dress is something so private that she declines her devoted maid's offer to mend it for her. Meanwhile sewing with silk clearly gives her the sensuous pleasure coupled with imaginative freedom rendered in one of the novel's most lyrical passages:

> Quiet descended on her, [. . .] as her needle, drawing the silk smoothly to its gentle pause, collected the green folds together [. . .]. So on a summer's day waves collect, overbalance, and fall; collect and fall; and the whole world seems to be saying, "that is all" [. . .]. Fear no more, says the heart, committing its burden to some sea, which sighs collectively for all sorrows, and renews, begins, collects, lets fall. (*Mrs. Dalloway* 39–40)

Whereas wool and needles matched the formal disconnectedness of *Jacob's Room,* in *Mrs. Dalloway* sewing matches the novel's connectedness. Gathered together in this scene are thematic filaments that extend throughout the text, often intertwined with each other. These include the color green, part of the novel's pronounced color scheme. Green is associated with water, a motif introduced on the first page in the word "plunge," and related to the novel's varied marine imagery (*Mrs. Dalloway* 3). In turn, the collecting of waves and silk is related to other modes of assembling—Rezia's millinery; the party for which Clarissa is preparing her dress, and which will bring together present and past; and finally life and death. Meanwhile the rhythmic movement of her hand recalls both vertical movement elsewhere in the book and the song from Shakespeare's *Cymbeline* that she was murmuring earlier that morning. With the sound of the song comes its sense, the promise of peace in death, in the phrase that links her with Septimus—"Fear no more the heat of the sun" (*Mrs. Dalloway* 186).

This tranquility is interrupted by an unexpected visitor, Clarissa's old suitor Peter

Walsh. Feminine privacy, represented by her mending, is violated by male intrusiveness. Clarissa starts to hide her dress, "like a virgin protecting chastity" (*Mrs. Dalloway* 40), recalling the goddess Artemis alarmed in her bath by the hunter Actaeon. After they have shaken hands, Peter takes out a large pocketknife, which he tilts toward the green dress. "And what's all this?" he asks thinking, "Here she is mending her dress [. . .], here she's been sitting all the time I've been in India; mending her dress; playing about; going to parties" (40). All he sees in her sewing is the triviality of her life compared with his. Clarissa goes on sewing; the conversation turns to their youth, when Peter was courting her; he suddenly bursts into tears. But he is not transformed into a stag, like the mythological Actaeon. Still the hunter, he leaves Clarissa and walks down the street stalking an attractive woman, fingering his pocketknife.

Peter's interruption of Clarissa's sewing, his violation of her privacy, prefigures later, graver intrusions. Dr. Holmes pushes his way into Septimus's flat, where there is peace for the moment, prompting Septimus to plunge to his death through a window. News of this suicide interrupts Clarissa's triumph as a hostess: "Oh! thought Clarissa, in the middle of my party, here's death" (183).

In the 1930s the pleasures of sewing fade from Woolf's fiction. In *The Waves* (1931), Susan's sewing, briefly mentioned twice, represents stability and safety: She sees "others' lives eddying like straws" while she pushes her needle in and out (*The Waves* 192). The sewing that appears in *The Years* (1937) seems prompted not by authorial pleasure in the colors or feel of thread, but rather by a concern with historical change, both cultural and economic. One of the older characters wistfully recalls evenings when she would embroider a medieval design and "weave the after-dinner talk into a pleasant harmony" or reflect in wool her husband's reading aloud from Tennyson (*The Years* 79). Her daughter's indifference to this harmony of sewing and words signals a passing of generations. Sewing figures later in *The Years* in a reference not to needlework but to a sewing machine, evidence of financial decline. Two young women from a once-affluent family live on a "shabby street," cook their own food, and make their own clothes (162).

At the end of Woolf's last novel, *Between the Acts* (1941), sewing is dropped. The pageant is over; so is dinner at Pointz Hall. Isa, who prefigures the restless housewives of later fiction and film, sweeps up her sewing (not mentioned earlier in the novel) from the table and sinks into a chair, murmuring a few words she remembers from the pageant: "scraps and fragments" (*Between the Acts* 188). Alone at last, she and her husband face each other, with love, with hate, as the dog fox faces the vixen, "in the heart of darkness, in the fields of night. Isa let her sewing drop" (219). Civilization brings together, connects; so does sewing. Here connection of both kinds is abandoned.

What, now, does sewing signify in Virginia Woolf's novels? It's hard to say offhand because the women who engage in it differ so from each other. Do we conclude that in Woolf's fiction needlework is too varied to be "symbolical," to use Mrs. Browning's term?

Like Mrs. Browning before her, Woolf pays as much attention to the activity of sewing as she does to its products. But this activity does not stand for the subjection of women. Nor does it represent the ambiguity of work as Victorians construed it. Only Helen Ambrose, of all Woolf's needlewomen, shows anything approaching godlike creativity; yet not even Betty Flanders's pathetic mending suggests a punishment imposed on womankind by a patriarchal God. In Woolf sewing is an activity involving eye, hand, and intellect, thus connecting body and mind. Furthermore, it can serve as a metaphor for connecting within the mind. In *Orlando* the mind is called a "perfect rag-bag of odds and ends [. . .] lightly stitched together by a single thread. Memory is the seamstress, and a capricious one at that. Memory runs her needle in and out, up and down, hither and thither" (*Orlando* 78). The mind includes other seamstresses, more conscious and purposeful ones.

Sewing can be a metaphor for the work and play of the writer's mind, whose business it is to make and also to mend, to collect and connect. It is an activity that Woolf sees neither as a privilege nor as a punishment, but as something that belongs to women. In both its literal and its figurative forms we can contrast it with the activity of the masculine mind as Woolf caricatures it in *Mrs. Dalloway*, "[s]hredding and slicing, dividing and subdividing" (102). For Ruskin, the highest textile work was sewing, "directing the serviceable stitch, to draw the separate into the inseparable" (*The Works of John Ruskin* 29: 511). This was women's work.

Works Cited

Browning, Elizabeth Barrett. *Aurora Leigh and Other Poems.* Ed. John Robert Glorney Bolton and Julia Bolton Holloway. London: Penguin, 1995.

Hedges, Elaine. "The Needle or the Pen: The Literary Rediscovery of Women's Textile Work," *Tradition and the Talents of Women.* Ed. Florence Howe. Urbana: University of Illinois Press, 1991.

Rich, Adrienne. *Adrienne Rich's Poetry: Texts of the Poems: The Poet on Her Work: Reviews and Criticism.* Ed. Barbara Charlesworth Gelpi and Albert Gelpi. New York: W. W. Norton, 1975.

Ruskin, John. *The Works of John Ruskin.* Ed. E. T. Cook and Alexander Wedderburn. 39 vols. New York: Longmans, Green, and Co., 1903–12.

Woolf, Virginia. *Between the Acts.* San Diego: Harvest-Harcourt Brace Jovanovich, 1969.

---. *Collected Essays.* Ed. Leonard Woolf. 4 vols. New York: Harcourt, Brace & World, 1967.

---. *Jacob's Room.* San Diego: Harvest-Harcourt Brace & Company, 1978.

---. *The Letters of Virginia Woolf.* Ed. Nigel Nicolson and Joanne Trautmann. 6 vols. New York: Harcourt Brace Jovanovich, 1975–80.

---. *Melymbrosia: an Early Version of "The Voyage Out."* Ed. Louise A. DeSalvo. New York: New York Public Library, 1982.

---. *Mrs. Dalloway.* San Diego: Harvest-Harcourt Brace & Company, 1981.

---. *Night and Day.* London: Duckworth and Company, 1919.

---. *Orlando.* San Diego: Harvest-Harcourt Brace Jovanovich, 1973.

---. *Passionate Apprentice: The Early Journals, 1897–1909.* Ed. Mitchell A. Leaska. San Diego: Harvest-Harcourt Brace Jovanovich, 1990.

---. *The Voyage Out.* San Diego: Harvest-Harcourt Brace Jovanovich, 1968.

---. *The Waves.* New York: Harvest-Harcourt Brace Jovanovich, 1959.

---. *The Years.* San Diego: Harvest-Harcourt Brace & Company, 1969.

Part Three:
The Afterlife of Virginia Woolf

VANESSA BELL'S PORTRAIT OF VIRGINIA WOOLF
AT SMITH COLLEGE

by Frances Spalding

The painting of Virginia Woolf in the Smith College Museum of Art, which is reproduced on the front cover, is one of four portraits of her sister that Vanessa Bell painted between 1911 and 1912. It is indicative of just how close these sisters were that Vanessa Bell managed to snatch from Virginia these likenesses, for it is well known that she later developed a dislike of posing for official portraits. But the informality of these pictures may also relate to the artist's intention. Almost certainly, in these four images, Vanessa Bell is experimenting with postimpressionism in relation to portraiture, and in this way questioning the need for "likeness" or "correctness of representation."

Like other young artists, Vanessa Bell had dramatically changed her manner of painting after seeing, in the autumn of 1910, *Manet and the Post-Impressionists* at the Grafton Gallery, London. The impact of this exhibit had been reinforced during the winter of 1912–13 by a further display of recent French art in the *Second Post-Impressionist Exhibition,* again at the same venue. In the wake of these two events, Vanessa Bell began to experiment boldly in her art.

The Smith College *Virginia Woolf,* donated by Ann Safford Mandel in 2003, is one of the most attractive portraits of Woolf, while also being one of the most radical. In other paintings at this time, Vanessa Bell had begun to cut out detail in order to enhance the architecture or design of the picture. It is evident here, for instance, that Bell is not concerned with creating an illusion and makes no attempt to disguise the brush strokes, which in many places remain separated from each other, thereby insisting on their reality as paint. In the face, these parallel brush strokes, as they fall down over the face, seem to create a veil, which obscures rather than defines the facial features. More usually in a portrait our interest gathers to a climax when the eye engages with the face, with that which is usually regarded as an index to human character. But in this case, it is just at this point that we experience the greatest tension: For though the information we seek appears to have been withheld, the portrait remains powerfully haunting and even characterful.

It can be argued that by denying us access to what Virginia Woolf looked like at a specific age and at a certain moment in time, Vanessa Bell opens up the portrait to a larger narration, a greater duration. This "trap for the gaze," as Jacques Lacan once referred to painting, invites us, as spectators, to bring to the face our knowledge and imagination. We are offered not the fixity of a precise likeness, but an empty space through which can flow thought, fantasy, feeling, knowledge, and metonymical associations. In this way Bell opens up the formation of identity to both past and future, something that Woolf herself later tried to do in *Orlando,* writing on the title page of the manuscript: "the theory being that character goes on underground before we were born; and leaves something afterwards also."

Of course, the picture works as a likeness partly because the near-blank face sits within the recognizable syntax of a portrait, for we can see that Woolf is seated elegantly in a wing-backed armchair. Nevertheless, in that empty face the expected narrative has been suspended. It is possible that Bell wanted to acknowledge the inchoate, the fact that Woolf as a writer had scarcely begun, her novels remaining as yet unwritten. With the advantage of hindsight, today we can interpret this portrait as an eloquent symbol of the interiority that Woolf pursued in her writing. It evokes her unknowableness ("We do not know our own souls, let alone the souls of others," Woolf wrote in "On Being Ill"[1]); it evokes anonymity ("I must be private, secret, as anonymous and submerged as possible in order to write"[2]); it also is suggestive of hidden strata in the mind, something similar to the state for which Mrs. Ramsay yearns in *To the Lighthouse*: "To be silent; to be alone. All the being and the doing, expansive, glittering, vocal, evaporated" (62).

So this portrait, though painted in England at a certain moment in time, by an artist belonging to a particular social class, and which now hangs in Smith College Museum of Art, is not easily captured. Instead, it belongs to all those who engage with that obscured face, in the search for meanings that rest not on the surface but are discoverable over time and in dialogue, as memory, history, and association become inextricably woven into the act of looking.

Notes

1.   Virginia Woolf, "On Being Ill," in *Collected Essays*, ed. Leonard Woolf, vol. 4 (New York: Harcourt, Brace & World, 1967) 196.
2.   Virginia Woolf, "To Ethel Smyth," 17 Sept. 1938, letter 3443 of *The Letters of Virginia Woolf*, ed. Nigel Nicolson and Joanne Trautmann, vol. 6 (New York: Harcourt Brace Jovanovich, 1980) 272.

Works Cited

Woolf, Virginia. *Collected Essays*. Ed. Leonard Woolf. 4 vols. New York: Harcourt, Brace & World, 1967.
---. *The Letters of Virginia Woolf*. Ed. Nigel Nicolson and Joanne Trautmann. 6 vols. New York: Harcourt Brace Jovanovich, 1975-80.
---. *To the Lighthouse*. San Diego: Harvest-Harcourt Brace Jovanovich, 1981.

EDITING THE PALIMPSESTIC TEXT:
THE CASE OF VIRGINIA WOOLF'S "A SKETCH OF THE PAST"

by Elizabeth A. Shih and Susan M. Kenney

Virginia Woolf's longest and most significant autobiographical essay, "A Sketch of the Past," presents a singularly difficult editorial problem. Studying the three holograph manuscripts in the Monks House Papers at the University of Sussex (MH/A.5b, MH/A.5c, MH/A.5d), two typescripts (MH/A.5a and British Library additional manuscript 61973, both by Virginia Woolf), and four transcripts (MH/A.5a and MH/A.5b, both by Anne Olivier Bell; MH/A.5c and MH/A.5d by Leonard Woolf's anonymous typist) alongside the first published edition produced by Jeanne Schulkind in *Moments of Being* (Chatto and Windus for Sussex University Press, 1976), and the revised and enlarged second edition of *Moments of Being* (Hogarth Press, 1985), we have uncovered numerous gaps, conflicts, and editorial inconsistencies that bring into question the accuracy of the published text.[1]

We therefore perform in what follows a miniversioning of "A Sketch of the Past." *Versioning,* according to Donald Reiman in *Romantic Texts and Contexts,* is a critique of final intention as leading to authoritative, single-state texts. It involves the presentation of "enough different *primary* textual documents and states of major texts . . . so that readers, teachers, and critics can compare for themselves" the different versions and explore their "distinct ideologies, aesthetic perspectives or rhetorical strategies" (Reiman 169; qtd. in Silver 196). Such comparative reading presupposes the concept of a palimpsestic text—a text "whose surface designs" may "conceal or obscure deeper, less accessible [. . .] levels of meaning" that may conform to and subvert patriarchal literary standards (Gilbert and Gubar 73).

We are indebted to Susan Stanford Friedman for bringing feminist psychoanalytic insights to modernist textual study, particularly in her assertion that writing autobiographical fiction can be seen as a "writing cure" in which the present and past selves collaborate to reconstruct a narrative that undoes repression. In her analysis, the writer's constant return to the scene of autobiographical composition—through endless revision—reproduces the psychodynamic of transference and working through, which Freud identified as the movement from mere repetition to remembering (Friedman 145–46).

But in the case of "A Sketch of the Past," such numerous and complex textual changes occur simultaneously, so that textual evidence should guide and ground the process of theorization—in effect, allowing Woolf's revisions to modify the theory. Here the evidence is too multidirectional, contradictory, and even at times picayune to form a coherent argument of progress, regression, patterned repetition, and remembering that "reproduce the working through" of psychoanalysis—though it could at certain points be each of these things. The issues raised by the data are not sufficiently addressed by any particular theory.

To begin our versioning, we note major differences between the early text Schulkind published in *Moments of Being* (1976), using the MH/A.5a typescript and the MH/A.5d holograph housed in the Monks House Papers, and the revised version published in the second edition of *Moments of Being* (1985) that supplanted the sixty-four pages of manuscript notes of MH/A.5d with the seventy-seven-page typescript version discovered in 1980, cataloged in the British Library as additional manuscript 61973. Correspondence in the Monks House archive between Jeanne Schulkind and Quentin and Anne Olivier Bell shows that the copy texts for both editions were chosen in close consultation with them. The disposition of topics between the two editions is identical for the MH/A.5a sections, but differs between MH/A.5d and the British Library additional manuscript 61973 segments. In the second edition, the typescript from the British Library adds approximately nine pages to the material on Leslie Stephen that stress his authority and charisma and Woolf's ambivalence toward him. Some eight pages are devoted to the environment of 22 Hyde Park Gate, the effect of Stella's death is recalled in detail, the material on Thoby is somewhat altered, and Woolf expands some of her thoughts on consciousness and the writing process by the second edition. See Figure 1, below.

Developments and differences between MH/A.5d in the Monks House Papers and British Library additional manuscript 61973 demonstrate the possibility of various psychic conflicts for Woolf as well as an intensification of thought and recollection. Although Jeanne Schulkind and Katherine Hill-Miller suggest that Woolf's prose is more polished in the British Library typescript, in fact, her typing and handwriting deteriorate significantly as the typescript goes on, as she discusses increasingly painful material and as the blitz comes closer to home. But it is often impossible to distinguish "working through" from "repression" here, because of the scattershot nature of the textual evidence. Schulkind further complicates the process of textual recovery by obscuring what Woolf's psychic work may have been in the various draft versions of MH/A.5a and MH/A.5d in the name of a coherent narrative, often favoring Leonard Woolf's posthumous corrections (of MH/A.5a and BL/61973 typescripts) over Virginia's. See Figure 2, below.

Let's next consider some of the errors in Schulkind's editing that occur between the MH/A.5d manuscript and the first and second editions of *Moments of Being*. See Figure 3, below.

These gaps, inconsistencies, fissures, and reading errors for both halves of the published editions of "A Sketch of the Past," present substantial evidence of Schulkind's failure to reevaluate and represent such textual issues for the desultorily prepared second edition. Virginia Woolf made a number of superscript and marginal corrections or additions to the typescript in the British Library early on; however, the extensive marginal ones, especially from folio 54 on, are Leonard Woolf's much later changes, as he was preparing the transcript for publication when he was elderly and his tremor was quite bad. Schulkind's tendency here is to arbitrarily accept or reject these superscript or marginal corrections and additions, often without acknowledging them. See Figure 4, below.

Based on the examples exhibited in the four figures below, it is our contention that the posthumous editor or reader needs to be empathetic in order to be as sensitive as possible to the author's fragments, their connections, and their contradictions, but often fails to be so. In light of Schulkind's editorial inconsistencies, her imprecise or incorrect footnotes, silent arbitrary changes, questionable adoptions or omissions (particularly her haphazard disregard for most of Woolf's typed paragraph indentations and white jump spaces, which significantly alter the tone and pace of the work), it remains for our further study to explore in detail the precise nature of her editorializing (rather than editing) decisions, and what, if any, discernible agenda drives them.

However, what is clear from the evidence we have found is that in the first edition of "A Sketch of the Past" in *Moments of Being* (1976), Schulkind tends to rely too heavily on the MH/A.5a and MH/A.5d transcripts instead of returning to the manuscripts or Virginia Woolf's typescripts (in the case of MH/A.5a). Schulkind also arbitrarily but inconsistently restores material deleted by Woolf or omits contradictory material, which works to darken the depiction of Leslie Stephen. Her preface to the second edition refers to a restoration of Woolf's ambivalence from the earlier first edition, without acknowledging that it was her editing that intensified the "partial" and "misleading" depiction of Leslie Stephen (*Moments of Being* [1985] 6). And finally, Schulkind makes various reading errors that tend to be more outmoded than corrected by her adaptation of the British Library typescript in the second edition.

Apart from the British Library's additional manuscript 61973 (which is technically a typescript for MH/A.5.d with an additional twenty-seven pages filling in the time gap between the entries for 8 June and 11 October 1940 not represented in the MH/A.5.d ms.) and the eight-page holograph fragment "The tea-table . . . ." in the Henry W. and Albert A. Berg Collection at the New York Public Library—the entire text of which appears at times typed nearly word for word in folios 19–28 of these first twenty-seven pages of the British Library's additional manuscript 61973 and which we strongly suspect is a section of the lost manuscript of MH/A.5a that connects the two typescripts of MH/A.5a and MH/A.5.d—we have no paired sets of Woolf's manuscript and original typescript drafts for any substantial fragment of "A Sketch of the Past." This, in addition to the kinds of errors the editor makes, makes it doubly hard to measure the possibility that psychic "working through" occurs for Woolf. We are not, to be clear, suggesting that all we have is textual chaos, but only that the multifarious revisions and changes should not be papered over. "A Sketch of the Past" is not as stable a text as the existing editions imply. What we do have is a text whose previous manuscripts, typescripts, and transcripts each form different surfaces of the palimpsestic piece, in which one layer "erupts into the other" (Friedman 148). Different layers of the palimpsest critique different issues in different ways.

Beyond the issue of textual evidence, the psychic work of revision is hard to trace, since revisions are subject to intense transference and projective identification on the part of the person reading them; and since the psychoanalytic "talking cure—at least in a linear conception, as it is often oversimplified—may not be the best analogy for the process of revision. Woolf's psychic processes are more likely recurrent, and we offer as hypothesis that she was engaging in traumatic repetition and a depersonalized distancing from her own experience, instead of "working through" the past. Scrutiny of the obsessive, even painful repetitions and minute reworkings of the deeply disturbing material on pages 67–69 of the New York Public Library's holograph fragment "The tea table . . ." compared with its corresponding section in the typescript British Library's additional manuscript 61973 folios 27–28 (*Moments of Being* 1985, 123–124) does much to bear this out.

It is possible, however, that Woolf engaged in what Friedman has described as a dialogic process with herself—in effect, a self-analysis—in which she plays in a repetitive way roles like those of both analyst and analysand, in order to gain some degree of control over the material of her life. It is possible that the revision process of conducting thesauruslike searches, listing words, add-ons, and refinements may have functioned as a buffer for Woolf between the painful material and the emotion without actually blocking it—slowing and controlling the emotion, almost as an analyst would. However, the page has no empathetic response (and we read repeatedly in the letters and diaries of Woolf's pain at having lost her audience due to the war) so that the ostensibly therapeutic function of writing "A Sketch of the Past" did not ultimately prevent her suicide four months after the last entry (November 1940).

Before a hypertext edition, proposed by Julia Briggs, can be composed, we are planning to produce a variorum manuscript edition of "A Sketch of the Past," bringing to the project Susan Kenney's expertise in textual scholarship to balance Elizabeth Shih's hermeneutic strengths. Although by necessity we have limited our canvas here to the body of "A Sketch of the Past" itself (excluding contextual material for the period), we hope we have given you a taste of the complexities that a new edition would need to address.[2]

Figure 1: Some variants between MH/A.5d manuscript (ms.) andBL/61973 (ts.)— first versus second edition (ed.) of *Moments of Being.*

First ed. (MH/A. 5d ms.)	Second ed. (BL/61973 ts.)
Re: Thoby/Thoby's death A force of nature "respected me sufficiently to make me feel what was real" + marginal addition: "to make me wince; spin; ground between grind stones" (MH/A.5d 28; first ed. 118).	Second ed. reduces the addition to "to make me feel myself ground between grindstones" (137).
no entry	"[. . .] to have become critical and skeptical of the family—? Perhaps to have remained in the family, believing in it, accepting it, as we should, without those two deaths, would have given us greater scope, greater variety, and certainly greater confidence." (137)
"Brothers and sisters today talk quite freely together about—oh everything" (MH/A.5d 30; 120).	Second ed. adds to "everything": "Sex, sodomy, periods, and so on." (139)
Re: Woolf's father (negative) exhibitions "of self-pity, of self-dramatisation" (MH/A.5d 37; first ed. deletes MH/A.5d ms. 37, including this reference) Leslie Stephen's "dramatisation of self-pity, anger and despair" (first ed. 124) matches MH/A.5d ms. (38) and ts. (34-35)	"self pity, horror, anger" (144)
"But that does not explain the [. . .] the breast-beating; the groaning" + marginal: "which played so large a part, so disgusting a part in these scenes" (MH/A.5d 39). Cf. "But that does not explain the [. . .] breast beating, the groaning, which played so large a part, so disgusting a part in these scenes" (first ed. 25).	"But that does not explain [. . .] the breast beating, the groaning, the self-dramatisation." (145) [softens Leslie Stephen]

First ed. (MH/A. 5d ms.)	Second ed. (BL/61973 ts.)
He needed always a woman to sympathize [. . .]. Why? Because he was conscious of his failure as a philosopher, as a writer. But his creed"+marginal: "made him ashamed to confess this need of sympathy to men." (MH/A.5d 39-40; first ed. 125)	"He needed always some woman to act before; to sympathize with him, to console him ('He is one of those men who cannot live without us,' Aunt Mary whispered to me once. 'And it is very nice for us that it should be so.' Coming downstairs [. . .] I laid that remark aside for further inspection.)" (145)
no entry	Second ed. adds to the above: "If then, these suppressions and needs are combined, it seems possible that the reason for this brutality to Vanessa was that he had an illict need for sympathy, released by the woman, stimulated; and her refusal to accept her role, part slave, part angel, exacerbated him; checked the flow that had become necessary of self pity, and stirred in him instincts of which he was unconscious. Yet also ashamed. 'You must think me,' he said to me after one of these rages-I think the word he used was 'foolish.' I was silent. I did not think him foolish. I thought him brutal." (145-46) [Here the treatment of Leslie Stephen is not softened.]
Re: Family No entry: in Woolf's descriptions of George's motives for chaperoning her and Vanessa (to bring them "out" into society, to show them how to conform to it, etc.), there is no reference to his sexuality (MH/A.5d 51; first ed. 132-33).	"Here the other motive came in; his desire to make us share his views, approve of his beliefs. I cannot even now understand why it was that he attached so much emotion to his desire [. . .] and, as became obvious later, some sexual urge. At any rate this matter of taking us out became an obsession with him." (154)

Figure 2: Some variants between MH/A.5a ts. and first and second editions of "A Sketch of the Past" in *Moments of Being*.

MH/A.5a(ts)	First ed.	Second ed.
Re: Moment of being "I was looking at a plant with a spread of leaves; and it seemed suddnely plain that a part of the earth was part of the flower; that a ring enclosed the flower; and that was the real flower; part earth; part background part flower. It was a revelation: a thought put away as being likely to be very useful to me later" (MH/A.5a 12).	"[. . .] that the flower itself was a part of the earth; that a ring enclosed what was the flower; and that was the real flower; part earth; part flower. It was a thought I put away as being likely to be very useful to me later." (71; LW's revisions, silently adapted by Schulkind)	repeats first ed. (71) [The revised phrasing is more felicitous, but is not noted by Schulkind.]
Re: Allowing Thoby to hit her It was a feeling of hopelessness, [superscript:] sadness" (the "ness" of "hopelessness" is not crossed through) (MH/A.5a 12). LW has written "hopelessness" above.	"It was a feeling of hopeless sadness." (71)	repeats first ed. (71)

MH/A.5a(ts)	First ed.	Second ed.
Re: Stella and Jack's engagement "And next morning at brekfast [*sic*] there was excitement and emotion and gloom" (MH/A.5a ts. 61). MH/A. 5d ms. has "[. . .] there was/were gloom [x'd through] [superscript word:] ["high"?], emotion."	"[. . .] there was excitement and emotion and gloom." (101) Schulkind follows MH/A.5a ts. without acknowledging VW's revisions in MH/A.5d ms. [Woolf is conflicted about the degree of her father's severity.]	repeats first ed. (101) [Schulkind's editing comes down hard on Leslie Stephen here.]

Figure 3: Some methodological errors between MH/A.5d ms. and the first and second eds. of *Moments of Being*, including those created by an anonymous transcription of MH/A.5d (This is an especially rich source of errors and omissions, since Schulkind often overuses the anonymous transcript.)

MH/A.5d ms.	First ed.	Second ed.
Re: Leslie Stephen's miserliness MH/A.5d ms.: "a man to whom money was an [superscript:] obsession nightmare" (14)	"obscene nightmare" (109)	"obsession" (127)
Re: The owl beneath VW's window MH/A.5d ms.: "And then the little owl mak[es] a chattering noise." (22)	And then the little owl [makes] a chattering noise." (114) (Unclear use of [] from MH/A.5.d ms.)	"Then a little owl [chatters] under my window" (133; folio 39). Schulkind confusingly notes here that "[a] line has been drawn through 'chatters' and an indecipherable word has been pencilled in" in a superscript form (133). The word "qurrelling" is not indecipherable; it is perfectly clear but apparently a made-up word. VW may have written "qurreling" onomatopoetically, or it may simply be a spelling error. Schulkind keeps "chatters" instead of what VW superscripted.
Re: Climbing/walking near St. Ives "At Halestown bog, one jumped from hag to hag" (MH/A.5d 23).	"At Halestown bog, one jumped from hay to hay" (115). The transcript (MH/A.5d transcript 25) is left blank, which did not assist Schulkind; Bet Inglis recorded that Susan Kenney corrected the mistake in 1976 at the Monks House archive.	In that bog we sprang from hag to hag" (134; folio 40). Schulkind may have corrected the error via the Monks House archive, or relied on the typescript of BL/61973, which is clearer than the handwritten A.5d ms.

MH/A.5d ms.	First ed.	Second ed.
Re: Description of 12 Oct. 1940, a writing day amidst war "I recover then today (October 12th 1940): a sulky autum day" (MH/A.5d 26).	"a milky autum day" (117) First ed. here repeats the MH/A.5d transcript (27).	Using the BL/61973, Schulkind changes the phrase to "a mild Autumn day" (136; folio 43). This is LW's correction to VW's typed "mily." We believe that the correct reading is in fact "milky."
Re: Walking near 46 Godon Square "I would see (after Thoby's death) two great grindstones (as I walked around Godn Sqe) and myself between them" (27).	"I would see (after Thoby's death) two great grindstones (as I walked around *Goode Tye*) and myself between them." (118, emphasis added) MH/A.5d transcript also makes the error (which Schulkind seems to have copied). Bet Inglis recorded that Susan Kenney also corrected this error in 1976 at the Monks House archive.	"I would see (after Thoby's death) two great grindstones (as I walked round *Gordon Square*) and myself between them." (137, emphasis added) Schulkind relied on either the correction to MH/A.5d ts. by Susan Kenney, or on the BL ts., which is clearer than VW's handwriting.
Re: Contest against Thoby to demonstrate drama is "antipathetic" MH/A.5d ms. says "I opened ____ to prove this; I opened at 'If music be the food of love, play on . . .' I was downed that time." (29)	First ed. cites *Twelfth Night* and repeats the phrasing of MH/A.5d ms. Schulkind fails to note that the anonymous MH/A.5d transcript has incorrectly cited *As You Like It* here, and that VW did not know the title, although Schulkind notes (in a footnote) that the ms. leaves a blank space for the title. (119)	Second ed. changes phrasing slightly: "To prove it I opened [*Twelfth Night*] and read 'If music be the food of love, play on . . . I was downed that time." (138)
Re: VW's relation to LS VW says "I so like him in excitability" or "exasperation" (37, illegible) In the consecutive versions VW has for the check writing scene in MH/A.5d (the first of which is crossed out), each describes Leslie Stephen as having "some pity" for Virginia and as ahving "some ['regret' x'd through:] regret remorse." (37)	First ed. (124-25) omits p. 37 of MH/A.5d ms. because of repetition and roughness (p. 38 addresses the same material but omits this refernce)	The second ed. that supposedly details VW's relationship with her father in more sympathetic detail should but does not acknowledge the degree of ambivalence of the suppressed p. 37 of MH/A.5d ms.

Figure 4: Some issues between BL/61973 and the second ed. of *Moments of Being*.

BL/61973	Second ed.
N/A	**Re: Errors in Schulkind's editorial notes (61-62, 125)** In her "Editor's Note" to "A Sketch of the Past," Schulkind reports that "[t]he text that follows is based on two seperate typescripts, one in the University of Sussex Library (MH/A.5d) and the other in the British Library (BL/61973). They were clearly intended to run consecutively" (62). The last sentence is incorrect. She perhaps meant to refer to "MH/A.5a," as it is the one that preceeds both MH/A.5d and BL/61973. Schulkind writes oddly in a footnote to the section dated 18 August 1940 that "[t]he material that follows is a revision of the manuscript MH/A.5d, which was transcribed on pages 107-137 in the original edition of *Moments of Being*" (125). The difficulty with this note is that it seems to have been misplaced, since evidence indicates that Schulkind began using BL/61973 on page 107 of the second edition. The error or contradiction is not resolved.
Re: Leslie Stephen's character VW gives a right-hand-side marginal comment on Leslie Stephen that "[h]e never used his hands." Beth Daugherty and Elizabeth shih were able to deduce "never did anything helpful in his time" to follow it, which Schulkind did not even try (folio 59).	In the second ed. Schulkind observes that the rest of the sentence after this clause is "illegible because of the deterioration of the paper" (146). Some investigation into the housing of the drafts before publication would be helpful.
Re: Leslie Stephen's character around the tea table Schulkind uses MH/A.5d ms. pages (44-45) (misrecorded as "A.5a" [second ed. 149]). But on MH/A.5d ms. 49, there are several lines in addition ot those of the BL/61973 ts., which describe LS's social behavior at Hyde Park Gate.	Schulkind takes unprecedented care in citing these lines (MH/A.5d ms. 49) in the second ed. in a footnote, but with the effect only of intensifying the sense of Leslie Stephen's pessimistic and demanding character: "Florence Bishop had said that she thought him looking remarkably well. This was an insult—a breach of the code: it was essential that he should receive sympathy. And so we must brush up our talk with that." (149) By comparison, in a snetence that Schulkind does not seem to adapt for the second ed., but which is present in the first ed. (128), VW writes: "The conversation would be lighter than now; more mannered; jokes would be laughed at [. . .]." (MH/A5d. ms. 44)
Re: Renovations to 22 Hyde Park Gate; Leslie Stephen's study VW's handwritten superscript says "that storye had been build on" (folio 20, line 1).	Schulkind reads the word "storey" as "study" (119), which makes no sense in context: that the reference is to the entire third floor is clear from the previous description of "three roomed storeys" (118).

Notes

1. The new edition of *Moments of Being*, introduced and revised by Hermione Lee (Pimlico, 2002), while welcome as a further addition to the oeuvre, does not materially address the problems in the text of "A Sketch of the Past" we have presented.
2. We gratefully acknowledge Dorothy Sheridan and the special collections staff of the University of Sussex Library; the staff of the Manuscripts Reading Room at the British Library; and the staff of the E. J. Pratt Library at the University of Toronto, for their helpful assistance in viewing archival materials. Thanks also to Anne Olivier Bell and Julia Briggs, and to Nick Hubble for his research assistance. We are especially grateful to Hilary Clark, Beth Daugherty, and Bet Inglis for generously sharing their insight, knowledge, and enthusiasm.

Works Cited

Friedman, Susan Stanford. "The Return of the Repressed in Women's Narrative." *The Journal of Narrative Technique*. 19.1 (1989): 141–56.

Gilbert, Sandra M., and Susan Gubar, eds. *The Madwoman in the Attic: The Woman Writer and the Nineteenth-Century Literary Imagination*. New Haven: Yale University Press, 1979.

Hill-Miller, Katherine C. "Leslie Stephen Revisited: A New Fragment of Virginia Woolf's 'A Sketch of the Past.'" *Faith of a (Woman) Writer*. Ed. Alice Kessler Harris and William McBrien. New York: Greenwood Press, 1988. 279–83.

Reiman, Donald. *Romantic Texts and Contexts*. Columbia: University of Missouri Press, 1987.

Silver, Brenda R. "Textual Criticism as Feminist Practice: Or, Who's Afraid of Virginia Woolf Part II." *Representing Modernist Texts: Editing as Interpretation*. Ed. George Bornstein. Ann Arbor: University of Michigan Press, 1991. 193–222.

Woolf, Virginia. *Moments of Being*. Ed. Jeanne Schulkind. 2d ed. London: Hogarth Press, 1985.

---. *Moments of Being: Autobiographical Writings*. Ed. Jeanne Schulkind. Introd. and rev. Hermione Lee. New ed. London: Pimlico, 2002.

---. *Moments of Being: Unpublished Autobiographical Writings*. London: Chatto and Windus for Sussex University Press, 1976.

---. "A Sketch of the Past." Typescript by Virginia Woolf with manuscript corrections by Virginia and Leonard Woolf, n.d., 69 pages. Monks House Papers, A.5a, University of Sussex Library, Sussex, England.

---. "A Sketch of the Past." Holograph notes, n.d., 64 pages. Monks House Papers, A.5d, University of Sussex Library, Sussex, England. Accompanied by a typed transcript by Leonard Woolf's typist.

---. "A Sketch of the Past I." Typescript by Virginia Woolf, 19 June–15 Nov. 1940, 77 pages. Additional manuscript 61973, British Library, London, England.

---. "The tea table was the center of Victorian family life. . . ." Holograph fragment, n.d., 8 pages, bound in *Articles Essays Fiction Reviews* 9.1 (1940): 55-69. Henry W. and Albert A. Berg Collection of English and American Literature, New York Public Library, Astor Lennox and Tilden Foundations, New York, New York, USA.

The Paris Press Publication of *On Being Ill*

by Jan Freeman

One June day in 2001 Karen Kukil, the associate curator of rare books at Smith College, visited me at my office and home in Ashfield, Massachusetts. She talked with me about the lives and works of Virginia Woolf and Sylvia Plath and about my life as a poet and a publisher. During the visit, Karen invited me to participate in the upcoming conference on Virginia Woolf at Smith College, and that invitation launched the most magical adventure that Paris Press has embarked on—a project that began as a seemingly impossible wish as I walked with Karen through my garden. "Do you think," I asked as we strolled past the lupine, the columbine, and the forget-me-nots, "that anything by Virginia Woolf has ever been neglected? Wouldn't it be amazing to publish something by Woolf in time for the conference in 2003?" "Come visit the rare book room," Karen responded. "Perhaps you'll find something in Smith's collection."

A month later, after releasing Elizabeth Cady Stanton's last speech, *Solitude of Self,* I compiled a short list of books by Virginia Woolf that were out of print, and I passed the titles on to Karen. The following week, I stepped into that enchanted sanctum, the Mortimer Rare Book Room. On the table were the books that I'd asked to see, as well as manuscripts with Woolf's purple-inked edits. Looking at her handwriting was exhilarating. Then, among the books, I saw *On Being Ill,* with its unusual cover by Vanessa Bell, yellow and gray with the circles and the grid. It had been published as an individual volume by the Hogarth Press in 1930 in an edition of 250 copies, signed by Woolf in that purple ink, and I soon discovered it was typeset by her as well. As a poet, this was critical information—it meant that *On Being Ill* was a book Woolf wanted in print. And yet, as an individual volume, it had disappeared seventy years before. Almost no critical attention had been given to it during that time, even though it was later included in two collections of her essays: *The Moment and Other Essays* (1947) and volume four of the *Collected Essays* (1967).

At the time I read *On Being Ill,* sitting at a library table in the rare book room, I had been sick for two years following an injury. Illness was a central part of my daily life. As I read the first sentence of the essay, I was filled with relief and covered in goose bumps:

> Considering how common illness is, how tremendous the spiritual change that it brings, how astonishing, when the lights of health go down, the undiscovered countries that are then disclosed, what wastes and deserts of the soul a slight attack of influenza brings to view, what precipices and lawns sprinkled with bright flowers a little rise of temperature reveals, what ancient and obdurate oaks are uprooted in us by the act of sickness, how we go down into the pit of death and feel the waters of annihilation close above our heads and wake thinking to find ourselves in the presence of the angels and the harpers when we have a tooth out and come to the surface in the dentist's arm-chair and confuse his "Rinse the mouth—rinse the mouth" with the greeting of the Deity stooping from the floor

of Heaven to welcome us—when we think of this, as we are so frequently forced to think of it, it becomes strange indeed that illness has not taken its place with love and battle and jealousy among the prime themes of literature. (9-10)

The taboo of illness was something I had become very familiar with. Illness had educated me, and I had experienced its transforming ways, including the intricacies of isolation. What was luscious about *On Being Ill* was Woolf's humor, as well as her pathos and her truth telling. The essay was funny:

[L]et a sufferer try to describe a pain in his head to a doctor and language at once runs dry. There is nothing ready made for him. He is forced to coin words himself, and, taking his pain in one hand, and a lump of pure sound in the other (as perhaps the people of Babel did in the beginning), so to crush them together that a brand new word in the end drops out. Probably it will be something laughable. For who of English birth can take liberties with the language? To us it is a sacred thing and therefore doomed to die, unless the Americans, whose genius is so much happier in the making of new words than in the disposition of the old, will come to our help and set the springs aflow. (13)

And the language of *On Being Ill* was magnificent. In fact, the *Los Angeles Times* later included it among the best poetry books published in 2002. Woolf says:

Human beings do not go hand in hand the whole stretch of the way. There is a virgin forest in each; a snow field where even the print of birds' feet is unknown. Here we go alone, and like it better so. Always to have sympathy, always to be accompanied, always to be understood would be intolerable. But in health the genial pretense must be kept up and the effort renewed—to communicate, to civilise, to share, to cultivate the desert, educate the native, to work together by day and by night to sport. In illness this make-believe ceases. Directly the bed is called for, or, sunk deep among pillows in one chair, we raise our feet even an inch above the ground on another, we cease to be soldiers in the army of the upright; we become deserters. They march to battle. We float with the sticks on the stream; helter-skelter with the dead leaves on the lawn, irresponsible and disinterested and able, perhaps for the first time for years, to look round, to look up—to look, for example, at the sky. (18-19)

That day in the Mortimer Rare Book Room, I felt as though Virginia Woolf had offered me the ultimate gift of companionship, affirmation, and solace. I needed the essay. And I realized that if *On Being Ill* was useful to me, perhaps it might be equally helpful to others.

Karen made a photocopy of the essay, and I took it home and read and reread it over the next several weeks, since, as Woolf points out, illness affects our ability to read. When we are ill, she notes, we can read poetry and trashy novels; it is not the time for complex literature (25-26). I needed to read *On Being Ill* very slowly, and many times.

In September I contacted the Society of Authors to inquire if the rights were available for the republication of the 1930 Hogarth Press edition. Six months later, Paris Press and the Estate of Virginia Woolf signed the contract to bring this essential book back into the world.

In the meantime I had decided that an introduction would benefit the essay, and I contacted the writer who was my first choice—Hermione Lee. I deeply admire her biography of Woolf; I love her writing style. Hermione Lee was not familiar with Paris Press, and she asked to see a sampling of the books. I sent her a package containing every book I'd published, along with several reviews, and our catalog. I explained the mission of the Press (to publish neglected or misrepresented literature by women writers); and I described my interest in the design of the books, which I believe must be very beautiful inside and out, and must in all ways complement the text.

To my great joy, Hermione Lee said yes, she would write the introduction, and she wrote a perfect one, placing the essay in the context of Woolf's personal life, her writing life, and her publishing life.

I had decided to publish *On Being Ill* as a near facsimile of the Hogarth Press edition, and so I contacted Henrietta Garnett, Vanessa Bell's granddaughter and the executor of her estate, and asked if Paris Press might replicate the Vanessa Bell cover art, while making a few necessary additions that the publishing business now requires.

Henrietta and I had a conversation that was one of the high points for me of the winter of 2002. In the middle of a snowstorm, following the sunrise quilling of one of my dogs, Henrietta and I spoke of literature and humor and how pathos and humor highlight each other in the best of literature, including the work of Woolf. She was very happy that I wanted to reissue the book. *On Being Ill* was, she said, her favorite Woolf essay. Then she asked me where I was calling from, and I said, "Ashfield, a very small village in western Massachusetts." She had been to Massachusetts with her father a long time ago. "Where?" I asked, expecting that she'd say Boston. "To visit Mina Curtiss," she replied; and just as that first reading of *On Being Ill* covered me with goose bumps, so did this remarkable response—since Mina Curtiss had long ago taught at Smith College, and she had been the subject of a dinner conversation I'd had two nights before. Mina Kirstein Curtiss was a Proust scholar, who also wrote about correspondence in a book called *Other People's Letters,* a book Henrietta loved—a book that was, as of two nights before, now sitting on my living-room table. Mina Curtiss had lived down the path behind my home, through the woods—the path on which my dog was quilled that morning at sunrise.

In the course of the conversation, Henrietta asked me to describe the back cover of the 1930 edition of *On Being Ill*. She could only remember the front. As I described the vase with the drooping flowers, she told me she was, that very moment, looking at the same sight, and a half hour later she faxed me the permission to reproduce the cover. In the margin of the permission was a drawing of the vase that was in front of her as we spoke on the telephone, a vase with tulips hanging down. She had just returned from a stay in the hospital, and the flowers had died while she was away.

The journey of publishing this book, even proofreading the text, was filled with vibrant moments of connection and revelation. I discovered that the closer you read *On Being Ill,* the more spectacular it becomes; reading every piece of punctuation aloud highlights the exquisite pacing and craft and brilliance of the essay.

I spent many months immersed in the Woolf text, reading and rereading the different versions of the essay. The first was written in 1925 for publication in T. S. Eliot's *New Criterion* and Woolf later revised that version for the Hogarth 1930 edition. Another version was included in the 1947 publication of *The Moment and Other Essays,* and in that Leonard Woolf corrected some typos from the 1930 edition. And yet another version was published in volume four of the *Collected Essays* (1967), and that one changed some punctuation. The Society of Authors asked that I use the first version written for T. S. Eliot. But I requested, and was permitted to use, the Hogarth edition as a baseline text, since Woolf herself made several changes to the Eliot version. And I ultimately decided to incorporate most of the changes that Leonard Woolf made in *The Moment,* and each one is mentioned in my publisher's note.

One passage in the essay that troubled me initially—and, in fact, prompted me to address the need for the introduction—is the last scene, in which Virginia Woolf paraphrases the ending of Augustus Hare's *The Story of Two Noble Lives.* And, characteristic of the transformations that occur when reading, what concerned me at first gradually became one of the many markers of Woolf's brilliance in the essay. That final scene has grown on me so that now it is the summation of the devastation of illness. And the last image—of Lady Waterford grasping the curtain as she looks out the window—mirrors an image in Leslie Stephen's photograph album of Julia Stephen standing between two curtains, before a window in the Bear at Grindelwald, Switzerland, in 1889. I considered including that image in the front and the back of the book. But finally I decided to publish *On Being Ill* as Woolf published it. I did not want to editorialize by framing the essay with that image—though the photograph is striking when viewed in correlation with the essay.

The decision to replicate the design of the 1930 Hogarth edition was informed directly by my life as a poet. As a poet and a publisher, I've had the good fortune, like Virginia Woolf, to publish some of my own work, such as my latest collection, *Simon Says.* By publishing it through Paris Press, I was able to avoid editorial compromise—something that Carolyn Heilbrun discussed during her interview at the conference in regard to Woolf and the Hogarth Press. Publishing one's own work permits the rare freedom of writing about any subject, in whatever style the text itself requires of the writer.

Like Woolf, I was able to physically shape my own collection, and include poems that a more conservative editor might have cut. I could use wide pages so that the long lines of many poems received the space they needed, and I was able to select the cover art that suited the work, a Paul Klee painting.

The fact that Woolf had been directly involved with the 1930 publication of *On Being Ill* was deeply meaningful to me. She created the text and helped to create the physical being of the book. When I read the essay in the rare book room, the fact that Woolf had held that volume in her own hands, signed it, and typeset it—spacing the letters, the words, and the lines herself—thrilled me. Even the errors, which she describes in a humorous letter of apology that Hermione Lee includes in the introduction, transformed the icon Virginia Woolf into the human being Virginia Woolf:

> As one of the guilty parties I bow to your strictures upon the printing of On Being Ill. I agree that the colour is uneven, the letters not always clear, the spacing inaccurate, and the word "campion" should read "companion".
>
> All I have to urge in excuse is that printing is a hobby carried on in the base-

ment of a London house; that as amateurs all instruction in the art was denied us; that we have picked up what we know for ourselves; and that we practise printing in the intervals of lives that are otherwise engaged. (qtd. in Lee xxi)

By preserving the original integrity of the Hogarth edition, I felt connected to Virginia and Leonard, and to Vanessa Bell. And I wanted to allow readers of the Paris Press edition to feel that connection as well.

So, I decided to closely replicate the overall design of the 1930 edition, using the same margins, the original Caslon typeface and the leading, and copying the title page as well. I worked with Michael Russem of Kat Ran Press on the design of the body of the book, and then Michael also printed the magnificent letterpress limited edition. I worked with Jeff Potter of Potter Publishing Studio on the cover of the trade edition of the book, and we spent close to one hundred hours matching our cover to the original Vanessa Bell cover. And I had the great delight of working with Claudia Cohen, who designed and created the unique pastepaper bindings of the limited editions of the book—a project that a supporter of the Paris Press made possible in order to raise funds to offset the cost of producing and promoting the trade edition.

Full immersion into the writing of Virginia Woolf has been an incredible gift of the last two years, and the critical response that the book has received has been immensely satisfying. On a par with the raves in publications, such as the *Los Angeles Times,* the *Philadelphia Inquirer,* the *New Yorker,* National Public Radio's *Fresh Air,* and an amazing feature in *Publishers' Weekly,* was the typed letter that Henrietta Garnett sent to me after she received a copy of the trade edition:

Dear Jan Freeman [handwritten],

I want to write at once to tell you how much pleasure your re-publication of Virginia Woolf's [essay] On Being Ill has given me. First of all, I think it an essay of the highest water, writing of superb quality which manages to encapsulate the misery endured by [an] invalid together with the absurd, macabre [business] of being ill. What was so typically brilliant of Virginia was not only did she realise that she was well qualified to write about the subject but that she actually DID it & because she knew of this condition removed from health, but still a part of life, she could only do it in the [intensely] intimate way in which she lent most of the writing she accomplished in that vein in her profoundly personal way. Nothing can really be more personal than illness, except, perhaps for being in love which often, but not always, is a reflection of health of mind & spirit, if not of body. But what has given me almost equal pleasure is how well you've done it. [It's] a beautiful little volume & these days that is unfortunately rarer & rarer. I love the type-face you have chosen and how it is printed on the page. The cover is beautiful, as most of my grandmother's dust-jackets are, and it is a relish to see it again. I think the shinyness of it (unlike the quality of the original) works very well indeed. & I am very impressed by Hermione's introduction which is full of insight [. . .].

Henrietta continues, and then along the top margin handwrites, "[Y]ou would love this autumnal Indian summer—after Biblical floods worthy of the Book of Moses, I have woken to a day suffused with yellow light & celestial skies the colour of morning glories." Which brought me full circle into the language of Woolf, her own description of the sky, and the gratitude that *On Being Ill* and its truths are now woven into my own life, as well as the life of Paris Press.

Works Cited

Garnett, Henrietta. Letter to Jan Freeman, 24 Oct. 2002. Paris Press Archives. Ashfield, MA.

Lee, Hermione. Introduction. *On Being Ill*. By Virginia Woolf. Ashfield, MA: Paris Press, 2002.

Stephen, Leslie. Photograph album of Leslie Stephen, 1856–1894. Mortimer Rare Book Room, MS 5, plate 39c, Smith College, Northampton, MA.

Woolf, Virginia. *On Being Ill*. [London]: Hogarth Press, 1930.

THE LIVING MEMES AND JEANS OF BLOOMSBURY AND NEO-PAGANISM

by William Pryor

Let me be clear: I am not an academic, nor a Woolfian scholar. I have slunk into these proceedings as a living relic of Bloomsbury and Neo-Paganism, an aging beatnik-publisher-author and I stand before you in a blatant and shameless act of self-advertisement. I am one of thirty-two great-great-grandsons of Charles Darwin and one of three grandsons of Jacques and Gwen Raverat,[1] who were friends of Virginia Woolf and founder members of Rupert Brooke's Neo-Paganism. The memes of Bloomsbury, Neo-Paganism, beatnikery, and bohemianism have shaped my life, the tea leaves of which may demonstrate my theme: The ideas that are memes have us, not we ideas.

This paper is a shameless act of self-advertisement in that it revolves around the first two books published by what is my homage to Hogarth Press, Clear Books. They are: *The Survival of the Coolest,* a memoir of my sixties neo-Dadaist, beatnik, addiction madness; and *Virginia Woolf & the Raverats,* a portrait of the friendship between Jacques and Gwen Raverat and Virginia Woolf in their letters, diary entries, other writings, paintings, photographs, and wood engravings.

Back to memes—I owe you an explanation. It is a word that the *Oxford English Dictionary* has only recently welcomed onto its hallowed divans, defining it as an element of a culture or system of behavior that may be considered to be passed from one individual to another by nongenetic means, especially imitation.[2] They are like viruses, you catch them. I caught Bloomsbury and Neo-Paganism from my grandmother—she made her wood engravings, her art was her life, and I was infected. I didn't understand the memes, you don't have to, but I had the illness. Memes are dangerous—they got me addicted, and here in the United State of Ascendancy, though my great-great-grandfather's star may be bright, the evolutionary meme has had people arrested.

Like genes, memes are selfish. Daniel Dennett has an interesting way of looking at them: "A scholar is just a library's way of making another library" (*Consciousness Explained* 202). A human being is a meme's way of making more memes. I could add: Virginia Woolf is Nicole Kidman's nose's way of making another film. If you weren't infected by the meme meme when I started, you should be by now and there's nothing you can do about it. We are doomed to do what our memes determine. Any success we may claim lies solely in the grace and elegance we bring to the memetic dance; not in the contents of the memes, which are not us, though they determine how we are.

Since we cannot shape our lives, it is up to us to find our art in exquisite and articulate expressions of our memes. They would speak, but it is we who give them voice. Virginia wrote in a letter to my grandfather: "Is your art as chaotic as ours? I feel that for us writers the only chance now is to go out into the desert and *peer* about, like devoted scapegoats, for some sign of a path. I expect you got through your discoveries sometime earlier" (*Letters* 2: 591). This paper is me peering about—as a scapegoat I am certainly devoted.

Memes need hosts in which they can work out their evolutionary purpose. If those hosts also bear genetic determinants of outré behavior then the effects of Neo-Pagan memes are doubly strong. Not only was my grandfather, Jacques Raverat, a close friend of Rupert Brooke and therefore a Neo-Pagan, but he was deeply infected by the Bloomsbury memeplex through his and Gwen's friendship with Virginia Woolf. This allows my favorite self-reference meme to have an outing: The Bloomsbury memeplex needs to reject itself so that it can be the truly revolutionary meme that it is.

"We will now discuss in a little more detail the struggle for existence," wrote Charles Darwin in *On the Origin of Species* (62). Only here it is the struggle for the existence of meaning, of purpose, of clarity as against madness (what is called "insanity" does seem to be an ingredient of the bohemian meme pudding), the struggle for the overthrow of encrusted order and academic enstranglement—sorry, we were told to avoid long words, let me rephrase—the struggle for the existence of creativity, which is bohemianism. It is my contention that Bloomsbury and Neo-Paganism were simply two species of a meme for bohemianism, as were its later variants: beatnikery and hippiedom. By "simply" I in no way impugn their importance, but merely stress the inevitability of the process of becoming bohemian. I couldn't help be a beatnik myself, so how could I impugn that holy state. As Jack Kerouac said: "[Beat is] a sort of furtiveness. Like we were a generation of furtives. You know, with an inner knowledge [. . .], a kind of beatness [. . .] and a weariness with all the forms, all the conventions of the world" (Holmes 107).

The followers of the church of meme (founded by Richard Dawkins, that devout disciple of Mr. Darwin) would have us believe that we don't have ideas (or memes); rather, ideas have us. We are mere vehicles in which ideas, memes, can work out their evolutionary destiny. However wrong the theory may be—and no one is too sure yet (nor will ever be)—the meme meme is attractive. It is our memes that are clever, brilliant, not us. The meme meme is attractive because it hints at a spiritual reality, the hegemony of interior authenticity (what a phrase!—it would have made a great title for a paper at such an august gathering), above and beyond the vast memeplex that is the mind and also thus helps develop more radical views of madness—two conditions that are not wholly disconnected. As Ginsberg wrote: "I saw the best minds of my generation destroyed by madness, starving hysterical naked" ("Howl" 9).

Virginia Woolf was a most successful meme generator—if volumes published, films made, and conferences organized are any measure. Not quite as successful as my great-great-grandfather's Darwin meme, which has gone as far as getting his face on the British ten-pound note. We are marinated in the mimsy of such memetic marvels, swimming in a Darwinian and Woolfian meme-pool.

What is it like to be a reliquary of such memes and genes, you might ask. My grandmother wrote: "Of course, we always felt embarrassed if our grandfather were mentioned, just as we did if God were spoken of. In fact, he was obviously in the same category as God and Father Christmas" (*Period Piece* 153).

In my memoir, *The Survival of the Coolest*, I wrote:

> The Darwin genes for observation and enquiry were to be put to the one-pointed service of my addiction. In March 1792, Charles' grandfather Erasmus Darwin wrote in a letter: *A fool . . . is a man who never tried an experiment in his life.*
>
> Charles Darwin was ours after all; we were of him. But Darwinian dogmas

do not encourage any challenges being made to the dysfunction endemic in his own family. Everything must fit their ideology, which has little to say about the joys and pains of being evolved or of the illuminations of art. [. . .] Ah! That lack of explanation, that lack of a family myth, of intimacy! We had no religion but Darwin and Bloomsbury, the gods of science and art, no structure of the heart. [. . .]

When sitting in the bath, with the steam around my ears, I would debate with myself why I, William, was not someone else. What on earth (or in heaven) determined that I should be 'I'? It was so lonely being William. Why couldn't I be someone else, why *wasn't* I someone else? (10–11)

My Bloomsbury memes were developing that particular sixties, Camus-esque alienation in me such that I would become fertile ground for the counterculture, beatnik, Dadaist memes that were to have their wicked way with me. Also a strong Woolfian meme is this: How can we know who we are? You'll have to read my book to find out who I was, but am no more.

In 1916 my grandmother Gwen Raverat, no doubt influenced by Virginia's success as a writer, began a novel of her own that drew on her experiences as a Neo-Pagan. I use this excerpt to set the scene in *Virginia Woolf & the Raverats*. The hero, Hubert, is clearly Rupert Brooke, while George is modeled on Jacques. She writes:

I remember those first two years as long days and nights of talk; talk, lying in the cow parsley under the great elms; talk in lazy punts on the river; talk round the fire in Hubert's room; talk which seemed always to get nearer and nearer to the heart of things. It was best of all in the evenings in Hubert's room. He used to lie in his great armchair, his legs stretched right across the floor, his fingers twisted in his hair; while George sat smoking by the fire, continually poking it; his face was round and pale; his hair was dark. We smoked and ate muffins or sweets and talked and talked while the firelight danced on the ceiling, and all the possibilities of the world seemed open to us.

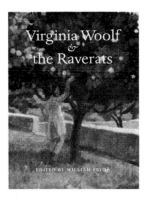

For a time we were very decadent. We used to loll in armchairs and talk wearily about Art and Suicide and the Sex Problem. We used to discuss the ridiculous superstitions about God and Religion; the absurd prejudices of patriotism and decency; the grotesque encumbrances called parents. We were very, very old and we knew all about everything; but we often forgot our age and omniscience and played the fool like anyone else. (30–31)

In 1909 this was, no doubt, shocking stuff, the direct equivalent of my smoking a joint at the age of fifteen in 1960 with Syd Barrett who was later to start that epitome of hippie entrepreneurship, Pink Floyd. In *The Survival of the Coolest* I wrote:

The Darwinian authority I had inherited, peering through an upper middle class desert of assumptions and muddled priorities, got me, at a very early age, questioning the mores of the Darwin-Bloomsbury nexus itself. They seemed such hypocrites. So much didn't make sense. I was, unconsciously, applying the principles they held most precious: question everything.

All male Pryors since gentry were gentry had been to Eton and Trinity Cambridge. To break the tradition would be to tempt the wrath of the gods and to suggest we didn't have domain over a reasonable chunk of the empire. To get into Eton you had to take the common entrance exam; common only in that all public schools used it. A key paper in the exam was Divinity: you had to demonstrate a fundamental understanding of the Bible to enter the ruling elite.

At one of my first enforced readings of the New Testament—I was eleven—I noticed that on one page this guy they were wittering on about was called Saul and on the next he was Paul. Obviously, a misprint! I took my biro and corrected all the 'Paul's, making them 'Saul's. If a Darwin can't know how to edit the Bible, what can he know? (13)

Nothing was sacred, not even the memetic gospel according to Saint Darwin. Bohemianism is about overthrow and rejection of the past. Virginia Woolf reinvented the novel; we beatniks adopted bebop and performed happenings. As Tristan Tzara said in his 1918 *Dada Manifesto*, we were new men, "uncouth, galloping, riding astride on hiccups. And there is a mutilated world and literary medicasters in desperate need of amelioration. I assure you: there is no beginning, and we are not afraid; we aren't sentimental" (7–8).

The evidence of the existence and power of the Bloomsbury meme in my life is not just my part in the first British poetry and jazz performances and the largest British poetry reading ever: *Wholly Communion* at the Albert Hall, when seven thousand people paid to share the beat poesy muse. No, it is that I am now starting a publishing venture, Clear Press, whose avowed aim is to create a direct, Internet-developed relationship with a new audience, memetically empowered by the Woolfs' Hogarth Press.

Without Charles Darwin, Richard Dawkins would not have been able to develop the concept of the meme. Without Darwin's granddaughter, Gwen Raverat, and her connections with Neo-Paganism and the Woolfs, I would not have been infected by the Bloomsbury memeplex.

A subject we have no time for is the relationship between the memes of bohemianism and maturity, or, what happens to old rebellion? In 1925, just before Jacques's death, Gwen Raverat wrote about Neo-Paganism to Virginia:

Anyhow it's all over long ago; it died in 1914 I should think, though it was sick before—Neo Pagans, where are they? Here's Jacques & me very old in Vence, & Ka so pathetic & lost in Cornwall; & do the Oliviers exist or not? Frances

[Cornford] I believe carries on the tradition in the fields of Cambridge — at least as far as neo-paganism can be combined with evangelical christianity, (which I think any one but Frances would find difficult.) And all the others are dead or have quarrelled or gone mad or are making a lot of money in business. It doesn't seem to have been a really successful religion, though it was very good fun while it lasted.

And what about Bloomsburyism? From here the front looks still firm; but is it solid behind? Is it only a front, concealing earthquakes & chasms? You must tell me. (*Virginia Woolf & the Raverats* 114–15)

From the heights of my old age I would say bohemianism in the twenty-first century is far from solid behind, but is riddled with earthquakes and chasms. There's a sense that the memes of art as business and as academic endeavor have devoured the beatnik counterculture memeplex. Look at British art!

Virginia wrote back to Gwen:

One could say anything to Jacques. And that will always be the same with you and me. But oh, dearest Gwen, to think of you is making me cry—why should you and Jacques have had to go through this? As I told him, it is your love that has forever been love to me—all those years ago, when you used to come to Fitzroy Square, and I was so angry and you were so furious, and Jacques wrote me a sensible manly letter, which I answered, sitting at my table in the window. Perhaps I was frightfully jealous of you both, being at war with the whole world at the moment. Still, the vision has become to me a source of wonder—the vision of your face; which, if I were painting I should cover with flames, and put you on a hill top. Then, I don't think you would believe how it moves me that you and Jacques should have been reading Mrs Dalloway, and liking it. I'm awfully vain I know; and I was on pins and needles about sending it to Jacques; and now I feel exquisitely relieved; not flattered: but one does want that side of one to be acceptable—I was going to have written to Jacques about his children, and about my having none—I mean, these efforts of mine to communicate with people are partly childlessness, and the horror that sometimes overcomes me.

There is very little use in writing this. One feels so ignorant, so trivial, and like a child, just teasing you. But it is only that one keeps thinking of you, with a sort of reverence, and of that adorable man, whom I loved. (*Letters* 3: 171–72)

I will be holding memetic counseling sessions straight after this panel.

Notes

1. The city of Cambridge, England, has begun to redress the university's poor record apropos women by unveiling an English Heritage Blue Plaque for Gwen Raverat, its first for a woman, next to the front door of her birthplace, Newnham Grange, now Darwin College.

2.   According to the *Oxford English Dictionary* (2005), *meme* is a "cultural element or behavioural trait whose transmission and consequent persistence in a population, although occurring by non-genetic means (esp. imitation), is considered as analogous to the inheritance of a gene."

Works Cited

Darwin, Charles. *On the Origin of Species.* London: John Murray, 1859.

Dennett, Daniel C. *Consciousness Explained.* Boston: Little, Brown and Company, 1991.

Ginsberg, Allen. *Howl, and Other Poems.* San Francisco: City Lights Books, 1959.

Holmes, John Clellon. *Nothing More to Declare.* New York: E. P. Dutton & Co., 1967.

Pryor, William. *The Survival of the Coolest: An Addiction Memoir.* Bath: Clear Press, 2003.

Raverat, Gwen. *Period Piece.* New York: W. W. Norton & Company, 1953.

Tzara, Tristan. *Seven Dada Manifestos and Lampisteries.* Trans. Barbara Wright. London: John Calder, 1977.

Virginia Woolf & the Raverats: A Different Sort of Friendship. Ed. William Pryor. Bath: Clear Books, 2003.

Woolf, Virginia. *The Letters of Virginia Woolf.* Ed. Nigel Nicolson and Joanne Trautmann. 6 vols. New York: Harcourt Brace Jovanovich, 1975–80.

THE LIGHTLY ATTACHED WEB: THE FICTIONAL VIRGINIA WOOLF

by Drew Patrick Shannon

The novelist or playwright who chooses to write about a living historical figure is obligated to deal in some fashion with the historical record. Faced with either a scarcity or surplus of information, writers must in either case make the decision regarding what to leave out and what to include. The choice may at times be an ethical one, as the temptation to "overlook" material that does not correspond to the writer's vision of the character must be great. As noted by Mark C. Carnes in *Novel History*, writers often feel free to invent in cases where the historical record is lacking, or are compelled to write about events and their characters' involvement only when adequate documentation exists (19–23). The writer who uses Virginia Woolf as a fictional character must apprehend the voluminous record of her life; Michael Cunningham has stated that one can find out what Woolf did "on almost every day of her life" (Schiff 117). The debate in Woolf circles surrounding both Cunningham's novel *The Hours* and the film version highlights the questions that haunt all works of fiction featuring Woolf as a character: Exactly whose Virginia Woolf is the piece portraying? What function does she serve? What process of selection has the writer used in the formation of the character? Is there an "appropriate" Woolf to put before the larger public? How much knowledge of Woolf is necessary on the part of the reader or viewer in order to "get" the character? What obligation does a work of fiction have to attempt fidelity to the historical record? Is it possible to depict the real Woolf on the page or screen, and how close can we come?

In "The Reanimators: On the Art of Literary Graverobbing," Jonathan Dee claims that the tendency of fiction writers to base their characters on historical figures represents a weakening of the novelistic art, one that does not allow writers the full play of their imaginations, since it provides them with, as it were, ready-made characters to drop into their narratives. For Dee, this is a "lowering of the literary bar. Creating a character out of words and making him or her as vivid and memorable as a real person might be is perhaps the hardest of the fundamental tricks a novelist has to perform" (83–84). Dee implies a kind of laziness on the part of such writers, as they have the ability to dip into the historical record for their characters' pasts, interests, and loves; thus, if characters create plot, a good deal of the writer's job is done. In the case of Virginia Woolf, this problem, if it is one, is exacerbated by the sheer volume of material available, a body of writing that has led to a group of readers who are in a position to question nearly every detail of a fictional Woolf. In addition, the use of a writer as a character in a work of fiction amounts to a kind of interpretation, an act of literary criticism, and just as opinions differ wildly about Woolf's work and its meaning, so will the depiction created by fiction writers provoke argument. As will be seen in each of the following cases, writers make selections, take fragments of Woolf that serve their purposes, and build a character upon those fragments. As Brenda Silver has shown in *Virginia Woolf Icon*, even a photograph of Woolf can be representative, and some fiction writers have used Woolf to stand in simplistically for something, a kind of embodied shorthand, while others have attempted a greater degree of felicity. Thus the wide array of Woolfs available in fiction—and she may be the most fictionalized of modern writers—serve up split-off pieces of the whole.

Woolf has been presented on the stage and screen with varying degrees of success and accuracy. One of the earliest fictional Woolfs appears in Peter Luke's 1974 play, *Bloomsbury*, in which Woolf appears onstage alone, talking dreamily to the audience about her writing and her use of her Bloomsbury friends as characters. She thus narrates and frames the piece, which suggests that she is the animating force behind all other activity, while remaining separate from it. When she is first seen, she is writing at her desk, bathed in light described as "gently oscillating blues and greens, giving a subaqueous effect"; speakers produce "the sound of waves regularly pounding on a rocky shore"; and she writes "as if she were at the bottom of the sea" (7). Luke takes an episode from the Quentin Bell biography—Woolf bathing naked with Rupert Brooke—and has his Woolf strip down to nothing and dance offstage to piano music (16). More distressing is the melodrama of the ending, in which Woolf, in the throes of madness, rocks back and forth and cries "hysterically," "the sea rises, rises, and then—the waves, the waves . . ." Looking over the side of her chair, she "lets out a terrified scream as of someone about to fall from a great height" (93). Luke might be excused some of his more egregious misconceptions due to his reliance on the Bell biography, with which several Woolf scholars took issue upon its publication. But Luke's depiction also fits in with some of the then-current, Q. D. Leavis–influenced impressions of Woolf as the delicate madwoman of Bloomsbury, prone to hysteria, obsessed with death.

A slightly broader perspective is seen in two plays that focus on the relationship between Woolf and Vita Sackville-West. Edna O'Brien's *Virginia* was performed in London in 1981 with Maggie Smith in the lead. O'Brien's script is an attempt to give an impressionistic view of Woolf's life, and Regina Marler suggests that O'Brien "must have known she risked offending a good portion of her audience" (189) because this approach, drawn almost exclusively from diaries, letters, and memoirs, reinforces the notion of a dreamy, ethereal Woolf. Much would depend on staging—the play contains almost no stage directions, and reading it, one can visualize the actors gazing out into the auditorium, reading their admittedly beautiful lines without any kind of dramatic momentum. Marler states that the actors could very well read "into microphones from distant corners of the theater" and produce the same effect as the staged piece (189). To her credit, O'Brien admits that the multiple perspectives on Woolf could result in "fifty plays about her" (qtd. in Marler 190), and that hers is merely one interpretation.[1]

Eileen Atkins's *Vita & Virginia,* produced in 1992 with Atkins as Virginia Woolf and Vanessa Redgrave as Vita Sackville-West, covers much of the same ground as O'Brien's play; some of the quoted Woolf material is identical. What distinguishes Atkins's piece is its focus on the dynamic relationship between the two women. Unlike *Virginia*, which perhaps covers too much time and makes the relationship with Vita a less interesting strand, *Vita & Virginia* is a tighter piece that does not omit the witty repartee from the writers' letters. Here, Woolf interacts with Vita; her words seem less like monologue and more like dialogue, thus emphasizing Woolf's quick tongue and quicker pen. The result is a more vibrant character—not surprising, given Atkins's feisty powerhouse performance on stage and screen as Woolf in *A Room of One's Own*. While both *Virginia* and *Vita &*

Virginia allow Woolf to exist as a full person rather than a stand-in (unlike Luke's play), the difference in the plays' effectiveness proves that the process of selection and arrangement can create utterly different Woolfs, even when using much the same material.

Brian Gilbert's 1994 film, *Tom & Viv,* about the troubled relationship between T. S. Eliot and Vivienne Haigh-Wood, delivers the image of the biting, snobbish Woolf so close to anti-Bloomsbury hearts. Though she does not appear in Michael Hastings's play *Tom and Viv,* in Gilbert's film Woolf turns up at a dinner party at which she tells Tom Eliot that Viv is doing damage to his career. At the other end of the table, Viv mocks Virginia, saying that she knows that Virginia has called her a "bag of ferrets" around Tom's neck. Her impossible knowledge of a phrase that only appeared in Woolf's diary on 8 November 1930 (*Diary* 3: 331) points out the filmmaker's need for a Woolf that represents the nastier aspects of Bloomsbury. When Woolf runs into Viv on a London street and Viv denies that she is Mrs. Eliot, Woolf snaps, "Don't be silly. You are Vivienne Eliot," and is promptly threatened by Viv with a knife. Though loosely based on an actual incident reported by Woolf in a letter (*Letters* 5: 207, Silver 178), the incident serves to render Bloomsbury, with Woolf as its representative, as insular, exclusive, and malicious, and the film fails to acknowledge the many sympathetic feelings Woolf had for Viv, as shown elsewhere in her writings.

In Christopher Hampton's *Carrington* (1995), Woolf is mentioned only in conversation between Lytton and Carrington, in a comment designed to get a laugh. After Lytton mentions that he once foolishly asked Virginia Woolf to marry him, Carrington asks, "She turned you down?" Lytton replies, "No, no, she accepted. It was ghastly" (Hampton 24). The line operates on two levels: The audience at this point knows that Strachey's marriage to any woman is unlikely to be a success, but the joke also relies on audience knowledge of Woolf, and is in keeping with Bloomsbury behavior—friends often made fun of one another mercilessly—and it renders Woolf a mockable but formidable figure. Her absence from the film is odd, however, given her close relationships with both Lytton and Carrington.

It is in fiction, with its greater ability to enter the minds of its characters, that Dee's warnings are more applicable. Ellen Hawkes and Peter Manso's *The Shadow of the Moth: A Novel of Espionage with Virginia Woolf* (1983) reflects the changes in Woolf scholarship in the 1970s. Scholars were challenging the image of the delicate lady novelist, and Hawkes herself published "The Virgin in the Bell Biography" (1974), a critique of Bell's presentation of his aunt. Her novel, as Regina Marler notes (280), is perhaps a response to Bell's version, for her Woolf is a plucky, feisty, intellectually curious heroine, willing to join forces with a female American reporter named Bobbie to uncover a conspiracy that might have serious implications for the course of World War I. The hardcover's dust jacket features a tinted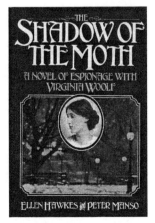
Beresford photograph that suggests a rouged and lipsticked Woolf—a woman flushed and ready for adventure. *The Shadow of the Moth* is diverting and entertaining, and knowingly implausible, not necessarily for its Woolf, who, despite the detective elements, seems quite

like the vigorous person shown in her diaries and letters, but for the details of its plot having worldwide implications. Hawkes and Manso's version is a refreshing change from the Bloomsbury shrew or wilting neurotic.

Surprisingly, one of the more balanced portrayals of Woolf in fiction appears in *Mitz: The Marmoset of Bloomsbury* by Sigrid Nunez (1998). Loosely inspired by Woolf's *Flush*, it depicts the Woolfs' marriage through the eyes of the eponymous monkey, from the years 1934 to 1939. Extremely well researched, *Mitz* attains its balanced portrait of Woolf by examining her over an extended period, and in varying moods. Woolf is shown as playful, perplexed by Leonard's fascination with Mitz, devoted to family, friends, and writing, and mournful over the losses of Roger Fry and Julian Bell. Unlike O'Brien's play, Virginia's despair or happiness is rendered in *Mitz* from the outside, and as the reader is not privy to Woolf's thoughts, only to her external behavior, the novel takes on the semblance of biography. Nunez perhaps wisely avoids trying to figure Woolf out, but achieves a sense of authenticity by quoting liberally from the Woolfs and their friends and by writing passages in imitation of *Mrs. Dalloway*, *To the Lighthouse*, and *Orlando*.

Much of the criticism leveled at Michael Cunningham's *The Hours* (1998) accuses it of being a regression to the prefeminist version of Woolf—a troubled, neurotic, suicidal genius obsessed with death. While Luke uses his Woolf to represent the dreamy, solemn side of the Bloomsbury Group, his depiction also illustrates his basic lack of sympathy with his subject. Cunningham, on the other hand, frequently quoted as being devoted to Woolf, gives his character a greater depth and complexity than any of the other fictional presentations. Easily the most complicated and controversial fictional portrait of Woolf to date, *The Hours* is noteworthy in that it is the only fictional rendering that attempts to enter Woolf's mind as she is writing. Much of the controversy thus lies in the audacity of a writer daring to guess what went through Woolf's mind on the day she began one of her masterpieces. It is significant that much of the controversy surrounding *The Hours* lies in the 2002 screen version: While the novel could present Woolf's thoughts, however imperfectly, the film, with its lack of voiceovers, relies on looks, mannerisms, and dialogue to convey Woolf to the audience. Many scholars have argued that a moviegoer unfamiliar with Woolf will come away from the film believing that Woolf was constantly depressed, often mad, given to gazing vacantly into the middle distance, and saying bizarre and inappropriate things to children.[2] What these responses overlook are the fleeting but discernible flashes of wit and pleasure in Nicole Kidman's performance—her gentle chiding of Vanessa and her brood as "barbarians," her knowing glance at Leonard when she declares, "I believe I may have a first sentence."

The Hours (both novel and film) leaves itself open to the charge that it depicts Woolf as depressed and mad by beginning with her suicide. It can be argued that the Woolf character is thereafter read as a woman who will ultimately die by her own hand, making the later flashback scenes more poignant. The demand that Cunningham examine other aspects of Woolf's personality would require that he radically alter the nature of his project. In other words, Cunningham needs a Woolf who is recovering from illness, who is making tentative steps toward mental, physical, and artistic recovery, in order to fill out the pattern established by the rest of the book in the "Mrs. Dalloway" and "Mrs. Brown" stories. He is further hindered by the limitation of the single-day, *Dalloway*-inspired plot. A Woolf who is witty, charming, literate, and funny as well as irritable, sullen, and depressed over the course of one day would be unbelievable to Woolf scholars and common readers alike. This structural limitation is all too frequently ignored when critics find fault with *The Hours*. Cunningham's Woolf is shown on one day—his choice of a bad day has led many to insist that he sees Woolf as a victim. The film's final image—of Kidman once again walking into the river—has perplexed many, for it seems to reinforce failure over triumph, if one reads Woolf's suicide as a failure. But as the scene fades to black, Woolf looks upriver, and her head is still above water.

What is probably most vexing to those who are displeased by Cunningham's Woolf is the fact of *The Hours*' remarkable success. No one is concerned with Luke's Woolf in *Bloomsbury*, for the play is out of print and rarely, if ever, produced. But *The Hours* has reached a mass audience, and there is some fear that this Woolf will be the Woolf for thousands of readers and moviegoers. But consider the case of the common reader or student (of whom I was one) who does not receive any academic instruction in Woolf. A text like *The Hours* provides a viable if not ideal entry point into Woolf and her life, and if the reader is serious and interested, he or she will continue to read more, will be led to the real writer's works, to the biographies and letters and diaries. Paramount Pictures makes a step in this direction by including on the DVD of *The Hours* a documentary called "The Mind and Times of Virginia Woolf," featuring interviews with Hermione Lee, Frances Spalding, and Nigel Nicolson, with readings from Woolf's works by Eileen Atkins. From the hearty applause this program received at the Woolf conference at Smith College the night before this paper was delivered, it would seem that Woolfians are pleased by this biographical addendum to the film.

While there is a great deal of validity to Jonathan Dee's argument about the use of real people in fiction, he strays off the mark when he suggests that the fictional Woolf can never be as interesting or compelling as the fictional Laura Brown (84). What this assertion ignores is that in the case of Woolf, who, as Brenda Silver has so effectively shown has become a commodified, iconic figure, only fiction has the ability at this point to restore her to human proportions. This exercise is doomed to imperfection, for everyone has "their" version of Woolf, but to suggest that fiction should not deal in real people is to ignore its very real power to chip away at the critical edifice in which many of these figures reside. Inadvertently, Jonathan Dee uses precisely the right phrase in his title "The Reanimators," for it is the intention of these texts, at their best, to infuse new life, to thaw these figures from the block of critical ice in which they are entombed.

In *A Room of One's Own*, Woolf says that "fiction is like a spider's web, attached ever so lightly, but still attached to life at all four corners" (41). However lightly attached these works might be, they nevertheless add up to a portrait, and reveal their writers' biases, likes, dislikes, and allegiances. Biographers understand the futility of trying to sum up a life in the pages of a book, and fiction can be expected to do little more. But fiction can fill in some of the gaps left by biography—it can give us Woolf's triumph at writing the first few sentences of *Mrs. Dalloway* and it can reveal her own doubts and fears in a way that biography can only suggest through citation and speculation. In reading a fictional Woolf, we can, for a brief, heady time, *become* Virginia Woolf, in the same way that we can become any fictional character who is well written and grabs at our consciousness. The works examined here all have some attachment to the immense record of Virginia Woolf's life, and perhaps, read and seen together, they can begin to approach, or at least to suggest, the real complexity of the living, breathing writer.

Notes

1. A revised version of the play was published in 1985, presumably taking into account changes to the script made in performance. Among the many minor changes, Woolf's response to Leslie Stephen's grief after Julia's death is changed from a resistant "No, no" (O'Brien 1981, 5) to a resistant "Shut up" (O'Brien 1985, 4).
2. See Patricia Cohen's "The Nose Was the Final Straw" in the *New York Times,* 15 February 2003, for a sampling of the varied critical reactions of Woolf scholars to the film and Kidman's performance.

Works Cited

Atkins, Eileen. *Vita & Virginia: Adapted from the Correspondence between Virginia Woolf and Vita Sackville-West.* New York: Samuel French, 1995.

Carrington. Dir. Christopher Hampton. Perf. Emma Thompson, Jonathan Pryce, Steven Waddington, Rufus Sewell, and Jeremy Northam. Videocassette. PolyGram, 1996.

Cohen, Patricia. "The Nose Was the Final Straw." *New York Times* 15 Feb. 2003, late ed.: B9.

Cunningham, Michael. *The Hours.* New York: Farrar, Straus, Giroux, 1998.

Dee, Jonathan. "The Reanimators: On the Art of Literary Graverobbing." *Harper's* 298 (June 1999): 76–84.

Hampton, Christopher. *Carrington.* London: Faber and Faber, 1995.

Hastings, Michael. *Tom and Viv.* London: Royal Court Theatre, 1984.

Hawkes, Ellen and Peter Manso. *The Shadow of the Moth: A Novel of Espionage with Virginia Woolf.* New York: St. Martin's/Marek, 1983.

The Hours. Dir. Stephen Daldry. Screenplay by David Hare. Perf. Nicole Kidman, Meryl Streep, Julianne Moore, Stephen Dillane, Ed Harris, Miranda Richardson, and Toni Collette. 2002. DVD. Paramount, 2003.

Luke, Peter. *Bloomsbury: A Play in Two Acts.* New York: Samuel French, 1976.

Marler, Regina. *Bloomsbury Pie: The Making of the Bloomsbury Boom.* New York: Henry Holt, 1997.

"The Mind and Times of Virginia Woolf." Dir. Tony Steyger. Perf. Hermione Lee, Frances Spalding, Nigel Nicolson, Alistair Upton, and Olivier Bell. *The Hours.* DVD. Paramount, 2003.

Novel History: Historians and Novelists Confront America's Past (and Each Other). Ed. Mark C. Carnes. New York: Simon & Schuster, 2001.

Nunez, Sigrid. *Mitz: The Marmoset of Bloomsbury.* New York: Harper Flamingo, 1998.

O'Brien, Edna. *Virginia: A Play.* New York: Harcourt Brace Jovanovich, 1981.

---. *Virginia: A Play.* Rev. ed. San Diego: Harvest-Harcourt Brace Jovanovich, 1985.

Rogat, Ellen Hawkes. "The Virgin in the Bell Biography." *Twentieth Century Literature* 20 (1974): 96–113.

Schiff, James. "An Interview with Michael Cunningham." *Missouri Review* 26.2 (2003): 111–27.

Silver, Brenda R. *Virginia Woolf Icon.* Chicago: University of Chicago Press, 1999.

Tom & Viv. Dir. Brian Gilbert. Screenplay by Michael Hastings and Adrian Hodges. Perf. Willem Dafoe, Miranda Richardson, Rosemary Harris, and Tim Dutton. 1994. Videocassette. Miramax, 1995.

Woolf, Virginia. *The Diary of Virginia Woolf.* Ed. Anne Olivier Bell. 5 vols. New York: Harcourt Brace Jovanovich, 1977–84.

---. *The Letters of Virginia Woolf.* Ed. Nigel Nicolson and Joanne Trautmann. 6 vols. New York: Harcourt Brace Jovanovich, 1975–80.

---. *A Room of One's Own.* San Diego: Harcourt Brace & Company, 1981.

In the Footsteps of Virginia Woolf:
The Hours by Michael Cunningham

by Laura Francesca Aimone

When looking at the literary panorama of the most recent years, one reaches the unavoidable conclusion that Virginia Woolf continues to play a major role and that her legacy lives on. In a sense, her body is still curling against one of the pilings of the bridge at Southease, absorbing the noise of the busy world above it, to borrow an effective visual image from Michael Cunningham's novel, *The Hours*.

Cunningham's novel is an excellent example of the interplay between Woolf and a contemporary writer. In *The Hours,* the British author and her novel *Mrs. Dalloway* are not only often referenced, but also enter the narration directly. For this reason, the relationship between the two novels is not linear, but rather multilayered.

This relationship can be summarized in three major categories: Cunningham's novel can be considered an "original rewriting" of *Mrs. Dalloway,* a dialogue with Woolf's novel, and a modern version of it. I will focus in particular on the last category (i.e., *The Hours* as a modern version of *Mrs. Dalloway*), as I believe it best represents how Virginia Woolf continues to engage "real world" issues in the twenty-first century.

Firstly, Cunningham's novel is an "original rewriting"[1] of *Mrs. Dalloway*. As a rewriting, it maintains a strong tie to an earlier work. One can discern this bond simply by looking at the title; "The Hours" was the working title used by Woolf while writing *Mrs. Dalloway*. Its originality lies in its overlapping of genres; Cunningham's novel is not only a work of fiction like Woolf's, but it can also be read as a special kind of biography and a literary reflection[2] concerning the writing and the reading process. Most of the narration is fictional and both the sections[3] "Mrs. Dalloway" and "Mrs. Brown" are dedicated to fiction. However, the third section of the novel, "Mrs. Woolf," takes on a biographical slant in that its characters, although fictionalized, are drawn with accuracy from real life. The three sections that constitute *The Hours* are all scattered with references concerning the processes of writing and reading. In so doing, Cunningham manages not only to analyze the meaning of creativity in general, but also to describe in detail what being a writer or an active reader implies.

Secondly, *The Hours* can be considered a dialogue with *Mrs. Dalloway*. In his novel, Cunningham elaborates on some of Woolf's themes, extending her discourse over a century. While focusing on certain issues already posed by Woolf, Cunningham offers many more examples of how various people react when facing similar existential questions in different periods. This is especially true when considering some of the main themes in both novels, such as the choice between an ordinary life and an adventurous one, the restrictions that society imposes onto its members, and the question of how to make sense out of life and death. It is appropriate to characterize the relationship between the two novels as dialogue not only because Cunningham, like every good conversation partner, contributes to the interchange with his own experience, but also because in many ways *The Hours* is complementary to and intertwined with *Mrs. Dalloway*. Its sections "talk to each other" and together communicate with *Mrs. Dalloway*.

Among the examples scattered throughout the novel, I singled out one of particular interest. If we analyze in depth the relationships among the main characters of the section "Mrs. Dalloway," we perceive that Cunningham builds on Mrs. Dalloway's story, giving his Clarissa the relationship with Sally that had been forbidden to the Woolfian Clarissa. While a relationship with Sally would have exceeded the bounds of ordinariness for the Woolfian Clarissa, for Mrs. Vaughan it simply represents the safety of everyday life. Likewise, a relationship with Richard, whom for Clarissa Dalloway represents security, would have implied taking the risk and exceeding the bounds of ordinariness for Clarissa Vaughan. The following diagram clearly shows that Cunningham's rewriting is more than a mere addition. Represented in dotted lines are the passionate relationships the two women decided to interrupt and in solid lines the stable ones for which they finally opted. As the direction of the arrows emphasizes, the two stories are intertwined and complementary.

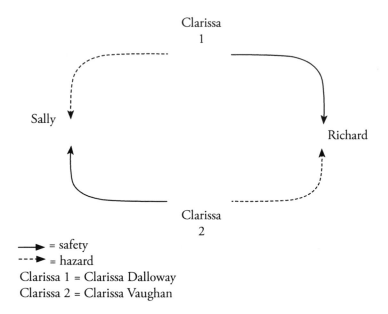

Clarissa 1

Sally

Richard

Clarissa 2

⟶ = safety
---▸ = hazard
Clarissa 1 = Clarissa Dalloway
Clarissa 2 = Clarissa Vaughan

Finally, *The Hours* can be read as a modern version of *Mrs. Dalloway*. While Virginia Woolf did choose the ordinariness of everyday life as the subject of many of her works, we should not forget that through those details she was also looking at the bigger picture. On the one hand, Cunningham's task while writing *The Hours* was, in his own words, "to take Woolf's insistence that right now is the stuff of literature and to bring that into the present."[4] On the other hand, and this is true if we consider the section of *The Hours* that most closely resembles *Mrs. Dalloway*, he had to create an updated version of some of the "big events" Woolf addressed. If we concentrate exclusively on the section of *The Hours* set in contemporary New York, we can interpret Cunningham's novel as a modern version of *Mrs. Dalloway*.

Beginning with some of the real-world issues posed by Woolf, I decided to analyze how Cunningham transposed them into the present. In so doing, I identified three main thematic pairs that I would like to discuss in the rest of this paper: the First World War and the AIDS epidemic, the new social order in the 1920s and in the 1990s, and the attitudes toward sexuality at the beginning and at the end of the twentieth century.

Although the Great War ended five years before "that day in June in 1923," references to it appear throughout *Mrs. Dalloway*. Tombs of the Unknown Warrior, orphans, widows, and planes, which still "bore ominously in the ears of the crowd" (*Mrs. Dalloway* 21), are just some of the examples. Most notably, Woolf decided to assign to one of her characters, the shell-shocked Septimus Warren Smith, the role of representing the tragic aftermath of war. In *The Hours*, AIDS takes on this legacy and Richard becomes its main representative.

Cunningham organizes *The Hours* in such a way that its three sections are set right after the First World War, right after the Second World War, and in the 1990s when the HIV virus is spreading. This structure further emphasizes the association of war to AIDS. In one interview, Cunningham uses the word "shell-shocked"[5] to refer to his situation as an AIDS survivor. As the critic Michael Sherry points out, the language of war is recurrent in AIDS discourse, as evidenced by the titles of the most important books dealing with AIDS. *Reports from the Holocaust* by Larry Kramer and *Ground Zero* by Andrew Holleran are just two examples (Sherry 39). By transposing the First World War with AIDS, Cunningham locates his novel in the canon of AIDS literature.

Cunningham's narrative choice is also particularly meaningful for another reason. If we consider the two characters who symbolize the First World War and AIDS in the two novels, it is immediately apparent that they are both male subjects who experienced a profound trauma. What we can witness in *The Hours*, therefore, is a sort of shifting from a shocking event, the First World War, which threatened masculine identity, to AIDS, which further destabilized it. In Septimus's and Richard's homosexuality (supposed in the first case, open in the second) a link emerges between the lives of the two characters. In the passage from one novel to the other, homoeroticism turns from latent to explicit, but it doesn't lose its problematic aura. Although being gay or lesbian in the New York of the 1990s no longer necessarily implies being an outsider, by extensively describing the trauma caused by AIDS Cunningham seems to suggest that, at least unconsciously, homosexuality is still considered a fault to be punished. The parallel between war and AIDS that Cunningham establishes gives us "an exquisite and haunting reflection on AIDS through the prism of Virginia Woolf's masterpiece."[6]

Another real-world issue that appears in *Mrs. Dalloway* is the new social order characterizing the 1920s. With the death of Queen Victoria in 1901, a century of economic stabilities and strict hierarchy of social classes came to an end. The sense of liberation and renewal already present in the first years of the 1920s reached its apex only after the First World War. In *Mrs. Dalloway*, which is set in the postwar period, people find themselves facing new values that demand to be integrated in the normal flow of life.

Among the characters, Peter Walsh, who spent five years in India, is the most apt to notice that something has changed during his absence. Through his words, and through those of Elizabeth and Miss Kilman, Virginia Woolf describes a new society where men can write "quite openly in respectable weeklies about water-closets" (*Mrs. Dalloway* 78) and women are allowed to put on makeup in public. As David Bradshaw notes in his introduction to *Mrs. Dalloway*, the fact that Clarissa offers to help her waitress and buy the flowers for the party herself, or that she sleeps in an attic room, space usually intended for servants, signals a major shift in attitude (Bradshaw 41).

Similarly, the most recent part of *The Hours* is set in a period full of social changes. Out of all the issues with which Cunningham could have dealt, he decided to focus on the growing number of nonbiological families, which characterized the 1990s in America. The basis for the growth of this phenomenon dates back to the 1960s. As a consequence of the Stonewall Rebellion, nonheterosexual relationships acquired a new visibility in society. It is only with the diffusion of AIDS, however, that the standard family model entered a period of crisis, and people were drawn to form new groups finding the support that their biological families denied them.[7]

In *The Hours* this alternative family is represented by Clarissa, her lover Sally, and their daughter Julia, who was conceived by artificial insemination. In a way, Richard can also be considered part of this enlarged family, since it seems that, without Clarissa, no one would have taken care of him.

While Woolf decided to analyze the changes occurring in 1920s London from a primarily hierarchical point of view, Cunningham examined the changes in 1990s New York from a sociological perspective. Although Woolf's interest in hierarchies predominates, it is possible to glimpse in her novel some hints that help us better understand Cunningham's choices. The latent homosexuality that permeates the whole narration of *Mrs. Dalloway* can signify an always-unspoken desire for new family groups beyond those existing in the 1920s. After all, we should not forget that one of the founding principles of Bloomsbury was that of support for freer associations among its members.

The last real-world issue I would like to discuss is attitudes toward sexuality. After deconstructing unitary concepts such as those of "narration" and "identity," which had characterized the works of her predecessors, Virginia Woolf shows us that sexuality itself cannot be interpreted as a monolithic block. In *Mrs. Dalloway*, she gives us examples of the different nuances sexuality can display.

Throughout the text, Clarissa is the character who most frequently lingers on reflections regarding her sexuality. Although she initially describes herself as lacking sexual responsiveness, the more we read, the more we realize that Clarissa has in the past felt and can indeed still feel "something central which permeated" (*Mrs. Dalloway* 34). However, she has only experienced this erotic feeling in the presence of other women. As Joseph Boone suggests, these recollections can escape self-censorship only because they are inserted in a comforting heterosexual framework. When thinking about them, Clarissa tells herself she is only describing what "men felt [toward women]" (*Mrs. Dalloway* 34). At the same time, her infatuation for Sally was made psychologically possible only because the two girls both knew their ineluctable destiny involved getting married to a man (Boone 191).

We can perceive the same "repressed feelings" if we analyze Miss Kilman's veiled love for Elizabeth and Septimus Smith's for Evans. Woolf gives us very subtle descriptions of their struggles toward their sexual instincts, but once again she portrays how both had to conceal their real ego and find refuge in religious fanaticism, in the case of Miss Kilman, and in an arid marriage, in the case of Septimus Smith.

Although in *Mrs. Dalloway* Woolf offers us an array of sexual responses, at the same time she shows us how her characters had to repress them in order to conform to the ruling principles of heterosexuality. The message she seems to convey, borrowing the last lines of Forster's *Passage to India,* is that of "No, not yet. No, not there" (317).

Cunningham's novel is more candid. In the most recent part of *The Hours,* the writer deals openly with the theme of sexuality. He presents a series of characters who are experiencing, or have experienced in the past, a gay, lesbian, or bisexual relationship without restrictions imposed by the heterosexual world. As the author himself stated in one interview, one of his goals in writing *The Hours* was to explore many different kinds of love.[8]

What stands out at once, though, is that the different relationships Cunningham presents in his novel are equal and its characters do not feel the need to define them. What lies at the basis of these relationships is something strong—it does not matter what that something is. According to the critic Reed Woodhouse, it is this characteristic that links Cunningham to a new generation of gay writers hardly imaginable at any time before the mid-1980s. His characters never deny their sexual orientation, as happened in the "closet literature" of the 1960s, but they never glory in it either, as was the case with the "ghetto literature" of the 1970s (Woodhouse 84–85). Exceeding the bounds of heterosexual relationships has plainly become undramatic, although, as discussed earlier, some unconscious and eradicated misbeliefs still emerge from time to time.

Finally, in creating the characters for the most recent part of *The Hours,* Cunningham changed the sexual orientations of almost all of Woolf's original characters, with Miss Kilman and Mary Krull, both lesbians, being the only exception.[9] This element is particularly interesting because it shows how heterosexuality and homosexuality are actually two sides of the same coin. The fact that one can prevail over the other often depends on the context in which people find themselves living. In so doing, Cunningham further emphasizes the concept already addressed by Woolf that sexuality is something fluid, with nearly invisible borders, and, for this reason, easily expandable.

As I explained in the course of this brief analysis, *The Hours* demonstrates how Virginia Woolf's legacy lives on. Most of all, the novel shows how Woolf, already able to address real-world issues while alive, continues to engage real-world issues through Cunningham's contemporary words. As the Indigo Girls would say, Woolf "weathered the storm of cruel mortality."[10] The river that eclipsed her life sent her soul to us like a message in a bottle, offering its temporary holders moments of rebirth before disappearing again among the waves.

Notes

1. These two words could seem contradictory. The mere fact of rewriting implies "saying again" what other people already said, a concept that is in contrast with the notion of originality. However, as Christian Moraru clearly points out in his book *Rewriting: Postmodern Narrative and Cultural Critique in the Age of Cloning,* we should not be mislead by the prefix "re." "Numerous rewrites are anything but repetitive, epigonic-imitative and shallow recyclings" and contemporary writers "do not borrow from others because they have exhausted, in an unpleasantly decadent fashion, nonliterary sources of inspiration, [. . .] because there is nothing left for them to do." On the contrary, "in an age that notwithstanding its pose of superiority, remains troubled by the myth of originality, contemporary writing finds means to make the old new by rewriting it, [. . .] to make it new all over again" (Moraru 7–9). In such a context, it is still possible to talk about originality. We simply have to keep in mind that every innovation is to be measured starting from the shared assumption of a rewritten text.
2. The word "literature," from which the adjective "literary" derives, is to be interpreted in its oldest meaning, that is as "the art of reading and writing."
3. I have chosen this word to define the three parts in which Cunningham divides his novel. The cohesive meaning of the word, however, is to be considered on the thematic level (that is, as that group of chap-

ters dedicated to a certain character), but not on a structural one. The chapters "Mrs. Dalloway," "Mrs. Brown," and "Mrs. Woolf" are, in fact, intertwined throughout the narration, and they do not represent a "homogeneous block" as the word "section" might suggest.

4. Charlotte Innes, "Shades of Virginia Woolf; Michael Cunningham Examines the Creative Process in his Latest Novel, Based on *Mrs. Dalloway*," *Los Angeles Times* 22 Feb. 1999 E:1. 1 Jan. 2002 <http://pqasb. pqarchiver.com/latimes/main/doc/000000039175443.html>.

5. Joy Episalla, "Dances With Woolf." *Poz* Feb. 2000. 8 Jun. 2002 <http://www.poz.com/archive/february2000/columns/litchat.html>.

6. *Ibid.*

7. Cunningham's opinion about this issue can be found in: Philip Gambone, *Something Inside: Conversations With Gay Fiction Writers*. Madison: University of Wisconsin Press, 1999: 148.

8. Elizabeth Farnsworth, "The Pulitzer for Fiction." *PBS Online NewsHour* 20 Apr. 1999. 8 June 2002 <http://www.pbs.org/newshour/bb/entertainment/jan-june99/pulitzer_4-13.html>.

9. The following list makes this point clear by pairing a character from *Mrs. Dalloway* with its corresponding character in *The Hours* and by indicating their sexual orientations between brackets: Clarissa Dalloway (lesbian) / Clarissa Vaughan (bisexual), Richard (heterosexual) / Sally (lesbian), Sally Seton (lesbian) & Septimus (probably gay) / Richard (bisexual), Peter Walsh (heterosexual) / Louis (gay), Miss Kilman (lesbian) / Mary Krull (lesbian), Elizabeth (lesbian) / Julie (heterosexual), Hugh Whitbread (heterosexual) / Walter Hardy (gay), Lady Bruton (more likely lesbian) / Oliver (gay).

10. Indigo Girls, "Virginia Woolf." *Rites of Passage*. Epic Records, 1992.

Works Cited

Boone, Joseph Allen. *Libidinal Currents: Sexuality and the Shaping of Modernism*. Chicago: University of Chicago Press, 1998.

Bradshaw, David. "Introduction" to *Mrs Dalloway*. Oxford: Oxford University Press, 2000. 11–45.

Episalla, Joy. "Dances With Woolf." *Poz* Feb. 2000. 8 June 2002 <http://www.poz.com/archive /february2000/columns/litchat.html>.

Farnsworth, Elizabeth. "The Pulitzer for Fiction." *PBS Online NewsHour* 20 April 1999. 8 June 2002 <http://www.pbs.org/newshour/bb/entertainment/jan-june99/pulitzer_4-13.html>.

Forster, E. M. *Passage to India*. Harmondsworth, Eng.: Penguin Books, 1974.

Gambone, Philip. *Something Inside: Conversations With Gay Fiction Writers*. Madison: University of Wisconsin Press, 1999.

Indigo Girls. "Virginia Woolf." *Rites of Passage*. Epic Records, 1992.

Innes, Charlotte. "Shades of Virginia Woolf; Michael Cunningham Examines the Creative Process in His Latest Novel, Based on *Mrs. Dalloway*." *Los Angeles Times*, 22 Feb. 1999 E:1. 1 Jan. 2002 <http://pqasb.pqarchiver.com/latimes/main/doc/000000039175443.html>.

Moraru, Christian. *Rewriting: Postmodern Narrative and Cultural Critique in the Age of Cloning*. Albany: State University of New York Press, 2001.

Sherry, Michael S. "The Language of War in AIDS Discourse." *Writing AIDS: Gay Literature, Language, and Analysis*. Eds. Timothy F. Murphy and Suzanne Poirier. New York: Columbia University Press, 1993. 39–53.

Woodhouse, Reed. "Michael Cunningham." *Contemporary Gay American Novelists: a Bio-Bibliographical Critical Sourcebook*. Ed. Emmanuel S. Nelson. Westport, CT: Greenwood, 1993. 83–88.

Woolf, Virginia. *Mrs. Dalloway*. London: Penguin Books, 1992.

"What Are Novelists For?":
Writing and Rewriting Reality from Woolf to McEwan

by Doryjane Birrer

In his letter rejecting an aspiring woman writer's first novella, *Horizon* magazine editor Cyril Connolly critiques the work by saying that it perhaps "owed a little too much to the techniques of Mrs. Woolf." Although Connolly says the narrative's shifting perspectives help capture "something unique and unexplained," he thinks the impressionistic style would be more engaging with "an underlying pull of simple narrative." The letter I'm quoting, interestingly enough, isn't a lost part of the critical oeuvre of the man Woolf called a "smartyboots" (Lee, *Virginia Woolf* 662); it appears in Ian McEwan's recent novel *Atonement* (294). If anyone, however, believed a moment ago that the letter was really Connolly's, perhaps that highlights once more our eternal questions about the relationship between art and life. When Woolf asked in "Mr. Bennett and Mrs. Brown," "[W]hat is reality? And who are the judges of reality?" (*Collected Essays* 1: 325) perhaps she little knew how vexing these questions would remain nearly a century afterward. Woolf's questions are taken up yet again in *Atonement,* an obviously metafictional novel in Patricia Waugh's sense of "explor[ing] a *theory* of fiction through the *practice* of writing fiction" (2). The novel's focus is writer figure Briony Tallis's attempt to tell the story of a day in 1935 from the perspectives of several characters—including herself—and of the day's events, which have consequences beyond the imaginations of those involved. Yet McEwan also engages in metafiction through *Atonement*'s intertextuality; he essentially initiates a dialogue with other writers of fiction not only within the novel—Woolf is one of several novelists overtly mentioned—but also through his engagement with, and transformation of, their different modes of writing what I'll still call (for lack of a better term) "reality."

Though I'm appearing to set up a formalist comparison of techniques or catalog of inheritances, that's not really my interest. What I'm intrigued by is what McEwan thinks the novel can do, or as Briony puts it, "What are novelists for?" especially as these concerns are inflected by McEwan's somewhat peculiar novel; it's ostensibly a "realist" novel, in more or less the nineteenth-century sense, yet reviewer Geoff Dyer pinpoints *sine qua non* experimentalist Woolf as *Atonement*'s chief literary influence. I want, then, to take up some questions about fiction, representation, and "reality" through a brief consideration of the allusions to Woolf in *Atonement,* and by extension, to explore Woolf's influence on a contemporary British novel enlivened by a reimagined realism. First, however, for those unfamiliar with McEwan's novel (it was published in 1999 and shortlisted for the Booker Prize), a lightning plot summary should be helpful.

The novel opens with Briony Tallis, aged thirteen, who considers herself a writer. After witnessing an inexplicable scene between her older sister Cecilia and family friend Robbie Turner, Briony believes she has glimpsed "the real, the adult world," and plans to "write the scene three times over, from three points of view" using an "impartial psychological realism" (37, 38). However, by the end of that day—which encompasses 175 pages, or roughly half of McEwan's novel—Briony has instead told a different kind of story; she has falsely accused Robbie of a crime. More disturbing is that she tells this false tale because what "really" happened does not suit what she sees as the reality of her developing story. As a result, Robbie is incarcerated, Cecilia is devastated, and the two are perhaps irrevocably separated, first by prison and later by World War II. During this latter separation, in 1940, a guilt-ridden Briony comes to understand that Robbie and Cecilia's future has been doomed by the plot she set in motion. The novella that Briony submits at this time to *Horizon* magazine, and that Cyril Connolly rejects as overly "Woolf-ish," is Briony's first, and failed, attempt to capture what she sees as the realities of that day. The novella's ultimate incarnation nearly sixty years later as a thoroughly revised full-length novel is Briony's final attempt at atonement for her part in Cecilia and Robbie's ruined lives, and turns out to be the story we've just read.

As Hermione Lee says in her review of *Atonement*, "[t]his quite familiar fictional trick allows McEwan to ask some interesting questions about writing, in what is a highly literary book." I would add that one of the questions the book begs is McEwan's relationship to Woolf. The bulk of McEwan's novel is set while Woolf is still alive, publishing, and being reviewed, and McEwan's literary Briony submits her first piece of what is apparently modernist fiction not long after Woolf has solidified her reputation with *To the Lighthouse, Mrs. Dalloway,* and *The Waves.* The direct references to Woolf make it clear that these convergences aren't coincidental, but to what end are they employed? In the letter mentioned earlier, McEwan's fictional Connolly criticizes the fact that Briony's attempt to adopt Woolf's techniques involves "dedicat[ing] scores of pages to the quality of light and shade, and to random impressions." He follows with, "[y]our most sophisticated readers might be well up on the latest Bergsonian theories of consciousness, but I'm sure they retain a childlike desire to be told a story, to be held in suspense, to know what happens" (295, 296). Briony's (that is, McEwan's) final novel does tell this story, and clearly eliminates much of the early novella's purported experimentation. As a result, it's hard not to wonder whether McEwan, like both real and fictional Connollys, rejects Woolf's experimentalism. Yet more than one review suggests, among other literary echoes, strong echoes of Woolf, and McEwan himself acknowledges debts to Woolf, as well as to friends and contemporaries Rosamond Lehmann and Elizabeth Bowen (McEwan, "Interview"). Additionally, despite the stronger narrative drive of Briony's revision, the shifting perspectives of the opening half of the novel, with their differing reactions to and interpretations of the same events, evoke Woolf's highly experimental novel *The Waves. The Waves* was published in 1931, roughly a decade before Briony's first submission to *Horizon,* and we learn that Briony herself has read *The Waves* several times and thought it brilliant. Further, Briony echoes Woolf's famous declaration about human character changing; as a result of reading Woolf's work, Briony believes in "a great transformation [. . .] in human nature," and that "only fiction, a new kind of fiction, could capture the essence of the change." "Plots," thinks Briony, "were like rusted machinery whose wheels could no longer turn," and she conceives of her initial novella in the light of "an artistic triumph," rather than as a "story" (265).

Yet a story is just what we're told Connolly most desires in Briony's work. It may be that McEwan is establishing Connolly as a slightly later incarnation of the sort of conventional "tyrant" of Woolf's "Modern Fiction," who insists upon "plot" (*Collected Essays* 2: 106). Yet it's not just Connolly whom McEwan evokes with his faux letter; Connolly says Briony's work found an "avid reader" in "Mrs. Elizabeth Bowen," whose notes on the novel have been worked into Connolly's letter (296). It's also implied that Bowen shares at least some of Connolly's views. Now, we know from Lee's biography of Woolf that Connolly didn't admire Woolf's work any more than she liked him (603); we also know, however, that not only Bowen and Connolly, but Bowen and Woolf were on visiting terms (641). More importantly, Bowen certainly didn't disparage Woolf's work. In fact, Bowen was recently called "a less experimental heir" to Woolf (Kershner 68), which would jibe with the fact that despite the (fictional) Bowen's critique of Briony's work, "she was 'hooked for a while'" (*Atonement* 296) by the novella. She also sees Briony—as, to be fair, does Connolly—as a promising writer who shouldn't be discouraged by their initial rejection.

So where do we stand now? I'd say with regard to McEwan's novel, as well as with regard to Briony's, we stand smack in the middle of yet another realism versus experimentalism debate not just alluded to in, but enacted by, *Atonement* itself. Briony receives her rejection letter in the midst of World War II—in other words, in the early forties, a time that not only witnessed Woolf's death, but also, as Andrzej Gasiorek outlines, "witnessed fierce debates about the present and future direction of the novel" (2). These polemics were one primary incarnation of the realism/experimentalism debates that appear in retrospect to have been cyclical in the twentieth century, with "experimentalists" panning the widespread return to realism as regression, and "realists" decrying experimentalism as heralding the "death of the novel." And while I put provisional quotes around the supposed antonyms "realism" and "experimentalism," given their generally reductive formal definitions, the limiting binary posited between them isn't dead. In fact, it's still being tied to the fate of the novel, at least with regard to some assessors of British literature. In a 2001 essay, Ulrich Broich argues that British literature over the last decade "has lost some of its creative energy and vitality,"and attributes this to "a turning away from experimentation with different forms of perspective and narrative and a return to more traditional ways of storytelling" (33). By this he means social realism—with the adjective "naïve" implicit. "To sum up," he says, "postmodernism and experimentation"—he equates the two—"seem to be over, as far as British fiction is concerned" (34).

Well, Jeremiah, I just don't buy it—especially not on those terms. Lee says that *Atonement* "asks what the English novel of the twenty-first century has inherited, and what it can do now" ("Memories"). I'd say the answer is, particularly with the literary and commercial success of McEwan's novel, quite a lot—that is, if we can conceive of modes of realism that aren't naïve retrenchments, if we can accept writers of "realist" fiction as potentially innovative artists who, as Gasiorek puts it, "do not reject realism outright but who write with the legacy of modernism at their backs" (15), as McEwan so clearly does. One crucial aspect of the modernist legacy is, of course, an understanding not only of the complexities of fiction and representation, but also of reality as in some sense a fiction. Woolf's work, for example, suggests that reality can be continually written and rewritten by people of both genders and widely varying nationalities and cultures. We also know from Woolf that life isn't always orderly like a tidy series of gig lamps, that life might be found in a pattern as well as at a tea party. And to quote Bernard in *The Waves*, "there are so many, and so many [stories . . .] and none of them are true" (238). Briony's final story is also one of many different versions she's written, and is also, in the same sense as

Bernard's, not true, despite the seductive realism of its form. Both Briony and McEwan remain highly aware of the fictionality of their fictions, even given their connections with what appear to be "truths," such as Briony's personal and familial histories, and McEwan's detailed research for his novel at the Department of Documents in Britain's Imperial War Museum.

That realism as a form has been interrogated and reconceived since the time of Woolf is one of the ways in which a contemporary "realist" novel like *Atonement* can demonstrate the problematics of realism as a form even while employing some of its techniques to tell a "good story" (*Atonement*, in fact, is an international best seller—score one for the "common reader"). Yet how revolutionary is this idea? Even a mention of McEwan's novel that crops up in a pop magazine suggests the point is banal: In her editorial on the prevalence of "meta" in contemporary fiction, television, and film, Laura Miller is exasperated by *Atonement* and says that "going on about how fiction is a 'lie' is one of the more irritatingly arch affectations novelists are prone to" (27). Here's a similar argument: "[T]here can surely be no more mileage to be had from demonstrating yet again through self-enclosed 'fictions' that reality is words and words are lies. There is no need to be strangled by that particular loop—the artifice of fiction can be taken for granted" (51). That last quote is straight from McEwan, who said it in 1978 when assessing the state of fiction in the 1970s incarnation of the realism/experimentalism debates. Though McEwan was referring to the more overtly metafictional and highly experimental self-begetting novels of the period, we might still give McEwan a bit more credit than to think that "fiction equals lies," a proposition he thought could be taken for granted twenty-five years ago, is all he was interested in exploring via *Atonement*.

Before I conclude with my necessarily brief ideas on what McEwan might be exploring instead, I want to make a last comment or two with regard to McEwan and Woolf. First, yes, maybe it's true that we now take for granted many of the points Woolf so effectively made about the relationship between fiction and reality, but it's important to remember, as McEwan does via his novel, that Woolf did make these incredible contributions both to the path of the novel beginning in the early twentieth century, and to the ways in which we still talk about fiction and representation. And not only did she famously remark that human character changed, but, as one reviewer of *Atonement* points out, she helped to bring about this change (Dyer, par. 14). McEwan, too, may be helping to bring about a change already begun by those contemporary writers who reimagine realism, a change that responds to the exigencies of our new century as Woolf responded to those of hers. And just as Briony negotiates with Woolf in creating her story, McEwan negotiates with Woolf while creating his. That McEwan, while retaining some of Woolf's polyphony and impressionism, decides to tell his story in a more "traditionally" realist mode may be his own promotion of the power of storytelling, of our own, as his fictional Connolly put it, "childlike desire to be told a story"—perhaps our desire to participate in making our own stories. If we as individuals are fundamentally overwritten by social forces, as we're perpetually reminded in our postmodern/poststructuralist age, just who is telling the stories of our lives?

This question suggests the power of stories to be used, as Michael Hanne recently argued, for good or for ill. "Storytelling," he asserts, "is always associated with the exercise, in one sense or another, of power" (8). Granted, the words that make up stories are unstable; in the wake of modernism and postmodernism, we realize, like Bernard, that it's difficult "to foretell the flight of a word[. . . .] To speak of knowledge is futile" (*The Waves* 118). Yet we also realize, like both Bernard and Briony, that despite these linguistic and epistemological uncertainties, words do have power: both the power of ordering reality, and, as Briony realizes, the power of creating it. The story Briony tells to the police about Robbie exercises dramatically negative power over him (she essentially rewrites the story of his, and by extension Cecilia's, life through her lie). Later, Briony realizes the implications of this power, and wants to use it for good, so she rewrites Robbie and Cecilia's life to give them the happier ending she thinks they would wish to have. "I know," says Briony, "[that] there's always a certain kind of reader who will be compelled to ask, But what *really* happened? The answer is simple: the lovers survive and flourish." This will be true, she says, "[a]s long as there is a single copy, a solitary typescript of my final draft" (350).

Ultimately, of course, Briony's story is only a consolation for herself despite its offer of literary transcendence for Cecilia and Robbie, for we know (or at least we think we know) what the fates of Robbie, Cecilia, and Briony herself actually are, and they're not what we've in some cases been led to believe. Nor do we know whether Briony's final story is in fact the story the lovers would have wanted; they're not around to say. In these concessions, perhaps, is where we best understand Briony's negotiations with fictional form. Her early experimentalism is actually not, like Woolf's, a commitment to a deeper engagement with reality, but an evasion of reality, a failure to engage with the truth of her involvement in ruined lives. Her ultimate realism, despite its manipulation of reality, is less a further evasion than Briony's individual "stand against oblivion and despair" (351). For someone who lives through words and stories as Briony does (and as Woolf has been described as doing), an atonement through storytelling might well be a form of consolation and transcendence, much like the transcendence Woolf sought through her own novels. Further, McEwan has demonstrated that the "pull of simple narrative" has the power to lure us with the hope of imaginative possibilities. Like Briony, we cannot truly rewrite the past, at least in the sense of remedying material injustices; however, we can rewrite certain narratives of the past. Perhaps better still, we can envision what stories might be able to do to rewrite the present and shape a more livable future. This is certainly a more interesting proposition than remaining focused on what stories can't do. However, whether stories will be used for good or for ill, to evade or to engage, remains to be seen. Whatever the case, McEwan reevaluates, as Woolf did a century earlier, the tools of fiction available to him to tell the kinds of stories he wants to tell and perhaps thinks we need to hear. Ultimately, the questions *Atonement* raises about the efficacy of any form of fiction to create new realities are not only indebted to Woolf's creativity and insight, but reveal Woolf's continued positive influence through writers, fiction, and the power of story in what is popularly known as "the real world."

Works Cited

Broich, Ulrich. "Introduction Two: English Language and British Literature at the Turn of the Century." *Britain at the Turn of the Twenty-First Century*. Ed. Ulrich Broich and Susan Bassnett. *European Studies* 16. Amsterdam: Rodopi, 2001. 25–37.

Dyer, Geoff. "Who's afraid of influence?" Rev. of *Atonement*, by Ian McEwan. *Guardian* 22 September 2001. 5 January 2003 http://books.guardian.co.uk/reviews/generalfiction/0,6121,555614,00.html>.

Gasiorek, Andrzej. *Post-War British Fiction: Realism and After*. London: Edward Arnold, 1995.

Hanne, Michael. *The Power of the Story: Fiction and Political Change*. Providence, RI: Berghahn Books, 1994.

Kershner, R. B. *The Twentieth-Century Novel: An Introduction*. Boston: Bedford Books, 1997.

Lee, Hermione. "If your memories serve you well . . ." Rev. of *Atonement*, by Ian McEwan. *Observer* 23 September 2001. 5 January 2003 <http://books.guardian.co.uk/reviews/generalfiction/0,6121,556327,00.html>.

---. *Virginia Woolf*. New York: Alfred A. Knopf, 1997.

McEwan, Ian. *Atonement*. New York: Anchor Books, 2003.

---. "Life was clearly too interesting in the war." Interview with John Sutherland. *Guardian* 3 January 2002. 5 January 2003 <http://books.guardian.co.uk/departments/generalfiction/story/0,6000,627239,00.html>.

---. "The State of Fiction: A Symposium." *New Review* 5.1 (Summer 1978): 50–51.

Miller, Laura. "This Is a Headline for an Essay about Meta." *New York Times Sunday Magazine* 17 November 2002: 22–27.

Waugh, Patricia. *Metafiction: The Theory and Practice of Self-Conscious Fiction*. London: Methuen, 1984.

Woolf, Virginia. *Collected Essays*. 4 vols. New York: Harcourt, Brace & World, 1967.

---. *The Waves*. New York: Harcourt, Brace and Company, 1931.

In Search of the Self: Virginia Woolf's Shadow across Sylvia Plath's Page

by Pamela St. Clair

Cold glass, how you insert yourself // Between myself and myself.
—Sylvia Plath, "The Other"

Sylvia Plath's journals reveal her affinity for Virginia Woolf, both the writer and the woman. In Woolf's creative vision, Plath reads her own experiences, as writer and woman. Plath's underscores and marginalia in her copies of *Mrs. Dalloway* and *Jacob's Room* manifest her writerly interest in Woolf's craft, and particularly in Woolf's methods for unfolding identities haunted by feelings of selflessness. Informing Plath's work is her empathy with Woolf. In Esther Greenwood, the frangible self of *The Bell Jar*, Plath creates the literary descendent of Clarissa Dalloway and Jacob Flanders. Through characters' feelings of alienation from themselves and from others, Plath, like Woolf, exploits the female position in a patriarchal system as "other," a secondary self, defined by Simone de Beauvoir as measured against the absolute self, the male.[1] Like Woolf, Plath uses tropes of invisibility and duality to emphasize this disconnected self. A literary double, an "other," manifests a female creative vision divided between an inherent sense of self and a socially constructed self. Arguably, Woolf and Plath sought to reconcile their disparate selves through their art. The page becomes a mirror, the "cold glass" in which Woolf and Plath envision an authentic, rather than an "other" self. They use their fiction to declare "I am," rather than "I am not."

In Woolf's writing, Plath discerns a creative vision that parallels her own: a disciplined approach to art and explorations of the self that resonate for Plath with her own experiences. When Plath reads of Woolf working through the despair of rejection by cleaning out her kitchen or cooking haddock and sausage, Plath's prose rushes along with dashes and exclamation marks in her enthusiasm for discovering a female literary predecessor who alleviates Plath's fears of "falling headfirst into a bowl of cookie batter" (*The Journals of Sylvia Plath* 269) to the exclusion of falling headfirst into her writing. Later, Plath shies away from Woolf, complaining of her "dull old women who have never spilt blood" (*Journals* 494). For although Woolf celebrates women's experiences, she does not define herself by them. Whereas Plath wants to have it all, the "Books & Babies & Beef stews" (*Journals* 269), Woolf acknowledges a friction between domestic demands and the creative impulse. In a book review for the *Guardian*, Woolf writes, "The world might, perhaps, be considerably poorer if the great writers had exchanged their books for children of flesh and blood" (Lee 230). But for Plath, one act of creation complements the other. Nevertheless, she acknowledges Woolf's influence: "Virginia Woolf helps. Her novels make mine possible" (*Journals* 289). Learning from Woolf that even the most quotidian (female) experiences are the lifeblood of her art, Plath feels "linked to her, somehow" (*Journals* 269). A web of connection threads Plath's creative vision to Woolf's.

One thread is poetry. In "A Letter to a Young Poet," Woolf suggests that the novelist should "re-think human life into poetry" and that characters should not be "spun out at length in the novelist's way, but condensed and synthesised in the poet's way" (*Collected Essays 2*: 191). Plath is drawn to the poetry of Woolf's prose. In her journal, Plath refers to Woolf's "luminousness" (342, 485). A number of passages Plath underlines in *Mrs. Dalloway* and *Jacob's Room* illustrate Woolf's "luminosity," her manipulation of poetic devices to underscore meaning. In *Mrs. Dalloway*, for example, Plath marks, "So on a summer's day waves collect, overbalance, and fall; collect and fall; and the whole world seems to be saying 'that is all' more and more ponderously, until even the heart in the body which lies in the sun on the beach says too, that is all" (44–45). Repetition, rhyme, and a languid stretch of prepositional phrases lull Clarissa into a trancelike state, where she floats along the waves of memory.

A close reading of the passage unravels another thread of association between Plath and Woolf—a vision of a creative self disadvantaged by lack of opportunity. Having rejected Lucy's offer to help with the mending, Clarissa takes up the needle and sews her dress and her own narrative, stitching together memories of events that have brought her to this moment marked by contentment, as signaled by the clause "that is all." Yet within a sentence, Woolf repeats "that is all" (*Mrs. Dalloway* 45). The emphasis juxtaposes contentment with lost opportunity. Not only is Clarissa comfortable and needing nothing more, but also nothing more is available to or required of her. Plath underlines in *Mrs. Dalloway* where for Clarissa "there [is] no more marrying, no more having children now" (13). Clarissa personifies Plath's fear "of making early choices which close off alternatives" (*Journals* 445). Plath assigns this concern to Esther Greenwood in *The Bell Jar*. Unlike Clarissa, Esther can choose a career, *or* she can choose marriage. However, as the women in Esther's life—her mother, Philomena Guinea, Jay Cee—teach her, she cannot have both. Culturally scripted gender roles and expectations hem her in, as they have Clarissa.

Plath's interest in how selves are shaped or misshaped directed her own writing and her reading of Woolf. Her first marked passages in *Jacob's Room* and *Mrs. Dalloway* reveal her attention to Woolf's depictions, early on, of identities delineated by selflessness. In *Jacob's Room*, Plath underlines "He was lost" (8). In *Mrs. Dalloway*, Plath underlines "She knew nothing; [. . .] she would not say of Peter, she would not say of herself, I am this, I am that" (11). Next to this passage in *Mrs. Dalloway*, one of Plath's few marginal notes—"problem: identity: unfixed"—echoes an anxiety voiced in her journal—"I must not be selfless: develop a sense of self" (*Journals* 446)—and transferred to Esther, who opens *The Bell Jar* announcing, "I didn't know what I was doing in New York" (5). Instead of taking command, "steering New York like her own private car," Esther reflects, "I wasn't steering anything, not even myself" (6). Alongside Jacob and Clarissa, Esther stands in a continuum of unfixed selves seeking definition.

Woolf believed that identity is defined, in part, by a nucleus of uniqueness, by an 'irreducible core [. . .], which exists independently of other people" (Hawthorn 43). In *Mrs. Dalloway*, Woolf likens this core to a diamond or gem. Plath underscores the passage in which Lady Bruton considers her soul to be "half looking-glass, half precious stone" (*Mrs. Dalloway* 120). But Woolf also maintained that the self was not simply a static, "irreducible core," but a self in flux, too, dependent on "a nexus of relationships and influences without which it cannot emerge from the background [. . .]" (Naremore 59). After all, the ego is born in others' eyes; the diamond remains hidden unless external gazes shine on it. Yet if the gazes prove too intense, the diamond must be, according to Lady Bruton, "carefully hidden in case people should sneer at it" (*Mrs. Dalloway* 120). If the self remains buried for too long, its diamond "luminosity" dulled, it becomes hidden from others and from oneself. Plath notes a passage where Clarissa obeys her husband's and her doctor's orders that she rest in the afternoon:

> But—but—why did she suddenly feel, for no reason that she could discover, desperately unhappy? As a person who has dropped some grain of pearl or diamond into the grass and parts the tall blades very carefully, this way and that, and searches here and there vainly, and at last spies it there at the roots, so she went through one thing and another. (*Mrs. Dalloway* 133)

The phallic blades of grass, those patriarchal definitions, intervene and prevent Clarissa from recognizing a core self.

Woolf and Plath suggest this fragmented self by reflecting it across multiple mirrored surfaces. Clarissa's image bounces from one glassy perfume bottle to the next. Plath marks a passage where Clarissa's creative vision empowers her to gather the disparate images into a complete vision: Clarissa is "the woman who was that very night to give a party; of Clarissa Dalloway; of herself" (*Mrs. Dalloway* 42). Clarissa's success as hostess will allow her to see the diamond sparkling among the blades of grass. Esther similarly acknowledges her power to merge the pieces into a whole. She sees a "million little replicas" of herself in a glassy ball of mercury and thinks, "[I]f I pushed them near each other, they would fuse, without a crack, into one whole again" (*The Bell Jar* 173). But the "if" implies that Esther, unlike Clarissa, remains distanced from a creative vision that would grant her completeness. These kaleidoscopic visions hint at the fragmented self's *potential* to gather into a whole.

Terms of invisibility also highlight characters' selflessness, as if the mirror reflects no self at all. In *Mrs. Dalloway*, Plath underlines the passage in which Clarissa feels as if she is "nothing at all. She had the oddest sense of being herself invisible; unseen; unknown" (13). Like light passing unimpeded through a transparent diamond, society gazes through Clarissa. Plath suggests invisibility through negatives and shadows. Esther feels herself "melting into the shadows like the negative of a person I'd never seen before in my life" (*The Bell Jar* 13). She shares Clarissa's sense of worthlessness, of being "nothing at all." The depiction of an invisible self culminates with the very structure of *Jacob's Room*, in which Jacob remains largely out of view. Presented in glimpses and filtered through a third-person narrator, Jacob's story is of an unknowable self. As Plath marks, "Nobody sees anyone as he is [. . .] they see all sorts of things—they see themselves. . . ." (*Jacob's Room* 28–29). Through others' assorted impressions, Jacob remains out of focus; like a cubist portrait, he is a disembodied assortment of shapes suggesting a complete image, yet remaining disjointed nonetheless. By marginalizing his presence, Woolf articulates the female struggle as "other" to be seen rather than overlooked. Jacob's absence overshadows his presence. Twice in *Jacob's Room* Woolf writes, "It is no use trying to sum people up. One must follow hints, not exactly what is said, nor yet entirely what is done" (29, 153). Not only does Plath note both passages, but she similarly defines Esther through absence. When Esther is rejected for a writing class, any remaining vestiges of a self fall away. Like

Septimus Smith, Esther becomes disconnected and numb. She attempts to drown herself but cannot because her heart pounds, "I am I am I am" (*The Bell Jar* 149). No commas separate this string of declarations. Esther cannot distinguish a self; she has become invisible, a blank page she cannot read.

Plath's and Woolf's "selfless" characters also reflect the female artist's desire to transcend the patriarchal construct equating femininity with the selflessness of self-sacrifice and subjugation. In "Professions for Women," Woolf labels this submissive self the "sympathetic," "charming," "unselfish," and "pure" angel in the house (*Collected Essays 2*: 285). Woolf was well acquainted with this angel self. From the ages of thirteen to twenty-two, she abnegated her own interests to meet the demands of a father who, as Hermione Lee writes, "darkened" his daughters' youth "with his selfish grief and his assumptions of their servitude to him" (73). Plath similarly struggled under conformity's yoke. Tim Kendall writes that "Plath's conformist ambitions existed alongside a profound dissatisfaction with such roles" (50). When Buddy dismisses poetry, Esther's (and Plath's) passion, as nothing but dust, Esther complains, "My trouble was I took everything Buddy Willard told me as the honest-to-God truth" (*The Bell Jar* 56). Esther voices the angel self's dictum, "Never let anybody guess that you have a mind of your own" (*Collected Essays 2*: 285).

Extending Woolf's angel metaphor, Sandra Gilbert and Susan Gubar write that male authors have imposed on the female writer "the extreme images of 'angel' and 'monster'" (17). Woolf and Plath use the double trope, the Clarissa/Septimus and Esther/Joan pairings, to reify this psychic split, which Woolf references in *A Room of One's Own*: "Again if one is a woman one is often surprised by a sudden splitting off of consciousness, say in walking down Whitehall, when from being the natural inheritor of that civilisation, she becomes, on the contrary, outside of it, alien and critical" (97). As "other," the woman is duplicitous, firstly, in that she is divided and, secondly, in that her angel self deliberately masks the monster beneath. When Esther is rescued from her suicide attempt, she requests a mirror. The third-person voice she adopts distances her from the monster reflection: "One side of the person's face was purple, and bulged out in a shapeless way, shading to green along the edges, and then to a sallow yellow" (*The Bell Jar* 165). Later, when Esther protests being transferred to another hospital, her mother admonishes, "You should have behaved better, then" (166). But that Esther, the compliant angel, died in the basement crawl-space. The monster self prevails. As Woolf writes of her own angel, "Had I not killed her she would have killed me" (*Collected Essays 2*: 286). One self must be sacrificed for the other to survive. Hence, Septimus and Joan, the shadow others, must die.

Survival is possible, yet the novels deny characters their fully realized completeness. An early death renders Jacob forever unknowable. *Mrs. Dalloway* ends with an image of Clarissa, not as her socially constructed self, Mrs. Dalloway, wife and mother, but simply as Clarissa, as herself. Yet Woolf frames Clarissa through Peter's eyes. She remains a vision of the male gaze. When Esther prepares to leave the hospital, her heart again thrums "I am, I am, I am" (*The Bell Jar* 228), commas now establishing boundaries around the declarative statements. The sense of self is no longer blurred. But Esther is not seamlessly whole. The self she was not steering in New York is dubiously "patched, retreaded and approved for the road" (*The Bell Jar* 229). Self-definition is possible, but obstructions, those blades of grass, are rooted firmly.

Like many writers, Plath and Woolf defined themselves through their writing. Woolf writes in her diary of how "nothing makes a whole unless I am writing" (*Diary 4*: 161). Plath, reading through Woolf's "blessed diary" writes, "Only I've got to write. I feel sick, this week, of having written nothing lately" (*Journals* 269). The page is the mirror in which each writer seeks a reflection through *her* gaze alone. Thus, the literary double functions outside of the text, too, as a metaphor for the writer's split self. In *Negotiating with the Dead*, Margaret Atwood writes of the duplicity inherent in all writers: "And who is the writing 'I'? A hand must hold the pen or hit the keys, but who is in control of that hand at the moment of writing? Which half of the equation, if either, may be said to be authentic?" (45). If, as Plath writes in *The Magic Mirror*, the literary double allows for "man's eternal desire to solve the enigma of his own identity" (1), writing, likewise, allows a writer to peel back the selves veiling her elusive authentic self. Woolf and Plath dissolve the border, passing through the mirror to confront that self waiting on the other side. Naremore posits that one of Woolf's leitmotifs, the lack of boundary between her characters, evinces a lack of boundary between author and material. The extensive biographical elements in *The Bell Jar* reveal an equally fluid boundary between Plath and her material. These permeable margins suggest that the selflessness haunting fictional identities adumbrates similar tensions within Woolf and Plath.

Although both writers shared a palimpsest of personal histories defining and undermining each writer's sense of self—an authoritarian father, severe depression, and, at an early age, the loss of a parent—the strands shaping each writer are tied in a Gordian knot. The threads knitting their similar visions are not easily unraveled. Nevertheless, their fiction suggests that the female imaginative life is split by the struggle for self-definition. Gilbert and Gubar write that "the creative 'I am' cannot be uttered if the 'I' knows not what it is. But for the female artist the essential process of self-definition is complicated by all those patriarchal definitions that intervene between herself and herself" (17). Those patriarchal definitions shroud the self, and, as Plath writes in "The Birthday Present," those shrouds suffocate: "If you only knew how the veils were killing my days" (*Collected Poems* 207). By writing, Woolf and Plath shed those veils. Atwood suggests that "writing has to do with darkness, and a desire or perhaps a compulsion to enter it, and, with luck, to illuminate it, and to bring something back out to the light" (xxiv). Plath learned from Woolf the value of entering the shadowy depths to "bring something back out to the light," that multifaceted diamond self.

Note

1. Simone de Beauvoir, *The Second Sex*, trans. H. M. Parshley (New York: Alfred A. Knopf, 1989) xxii.

Works Cited

Atwood, Margaret. *Negotiating with the Dead: A Writer on Writing*. Cambridge: Cambridge University Press, 2002.

Beauvoir, Simone de. *The Second Sex*. Trans. H. M. Parshley. New York: Alfred A. Knopf, 1989.

Gilbert, Sandra M., and Susan Gubar. *The Madwoman in the Attic: The Woman Writer and the Nineteenth-Century Literary Imagination*. New Haven: Yale University Press, 1984.

Hawthorn, Jeremy. "Together and Apart." *Clarissa Dalloway*. Ed. Harold Bloom. New York: Chelsea House Publishers, 1990. 41–45.

Kendall, Tim. *Sylvia Plath: A Critical Study*. London: Faber and Faber, 2001.

Lee, Hermione. *Virginia Woolf.* New York: Alfred A. Knopf, 1997.

Naremore, James. *The World without a Self: Virginia Woolf and the Novel.* New Haven: Yale University Press, 1973.

Plath, Sylvia. *The Bell Jar.* Introd. Diane Wood Middlebrook. New York: Alfred A. Knopf, 1998.

---. *The Collected Poems.* New York: Harper & Row, 1981.

----. *The Journals of Sylvia Plath, 1950–1962.* Ed. Karen V. Kukil. London: Faber and Faber, 2000.

---. *The Magic Mirror: A Study of the Double in Two of Dostoevsky's Novels.* Rhiwargor, [Wales]: Embers Handpress, 1989.

---. "The Other." *The Collected Poems.* New York: Harper & Row, 1981. 201–202.

Woolf, Virginia. *Collected Essays.* Ed. Leonard Woolf. 4 vols. New York: Harcourt, Brace & World, 1967.

---. *The Diary of Virginia Woolf.* Ed. Anne Olivier Bell. 5 vols. New York: Harcourt Brace Jovanovich, 1977–84.

---. *Jacob's Room.* Uniform ed. 8th impression. London: Hogarth Press, 1954. Sylvia Plath's copy, Mortimer Rare Book Room, Smith College.

---. *Mrs. Dalloway.* Uniform ed. 8th impression. London: Hogarth Press, 1954. Sylvia Plath's copy, Mortimer Rare Book Room, Smith College.

---. *A Room of One's Own.* San Diego: Harcourt Brace & Company, 1981.

FILMING FEMINISM:
A ROOM OF ONE'S OWN ON *MASTERPIECE THEATER*

by Kristin Kommers Czarnecki

Virginia Woolf's *A Room of One's Own* (1929) addresses women, fiction, and the historical conditions that prevented any woman from writing the plays of Shakespeare. Stemming from two lectures Woolf read at Newnham and Girton, women's colleges at Cambridge, in October 1928, the book concludes that in order for a woman to be a successful writer of fiction, she must have financial independence and a private place to work. Long considered a quintessential feminist tract, *A Room of One's Own* assumes another dimension in its 1990 film version on *Masterpiece Theater,* starring Eileen Atkins as Woolf. Atkins first performed the role on stage, yet the Public Broadcasting Service (PBS) production brought the work to a much wider audience. Omitting passages, changing and adding words, even abandoning Woolf's principal narrative framework, Atkins attempts to convey the heart of the piece for contemporary audiences. I would like to consider the film's potential impression upon viewers unfamiliar with the source material and whether *A Room's* feminism is enhanced or diminished in this translation from book to film.

Films often take liberties with their subject matter. In her 1926 essay "The Cinema," Woolf grimly notes that "the picture-makers seem dissatisfied with such obvious sources of interest as the passage of time and the suggestiveness of reality" (182), perhaps skeptical that her own writing could be suitably represented on film. Regarding literary adaptations, she writes, "The cinema fell upon its prey [the text] with immense rapacity [. . .]. But the results are disastrous to both. The alliance is unnatural. Eye and brain are torn asunder ruthlessly as they try vainly to work in couples" (182). Yet unwavering fidelity to a text is not necessarily desirable in a film, which, as Michelle N. Mimlitsch explains, "revises its original in ways that reflect its creator's interpretation of the source text" (284).[1] Brenda Silver, for one, is more intrigued by the cultural sensibilities shaping contemporary representations of Virginia Woolf than in whether those representations reflect Woolf and her writing accurately. In Silver's view, stage and film performances are active, fluid engagements of Woolf's writing at the nexus of current and past cultural concerns.[2]

Atkins's performance aligns well with Silver's argument, for while it dispenses with some of Woolf's more arcane observations, it maintains her matrix of historical fact and hypothetical scenario to communicate *A Room's* key points. Atkins is deeply interested in Virginia Woolf as a writer, thinker, social activist, and feminist, and has dealt extensively with her life and writing. "I find her the most endlessly fascinating character I think I've ever played," she states. "I would like to have known her more than anybody else" (qtd. in Riedel 54). Her conversion of *A Room of One's Own* from print into film bears the added twist that *A Room* began as oration. It may be said, then, that Atkins returns the work to its original form, although Woolf's Cambridge lectures were by all accounts rather uninspiring,[3] containing "none of the sparkle of the finished piece" (Colburn 61). One student regretted having fallen asleep during the talk: "If only I had known it was to become *A Room of One's Own!*" she later lamented (qtd. in Lee 557). Woolf's material only came to life in the ensuing text's intricate and powerful rhetoric.

A Room of One's Own begins with the narrator anticipating a challenging but sensible question from her audience: "But, you may say, we asked you to speak about women and fiction—what has that got to do with a room of one's own?" (3) Interrupting the flow of her thoughts before even beginning to speak, Woolf's narrator establishes a dialogue with the Fernham undergraduates. Atkins, on the other hand, says the book's opening line after a male voice-over at the start of the film announces, "Virginia Woolf was invited to Cambridge to give a lecture about women and fiction." Atkins responds, then, not to a female audience but to an imperious male voice, the voice Woolf resisted throughout her life and oeuvre, the voice thwarting women's creativity. Significantly, Atkins presents herself as Virginia Woolf rather than the narrator of a Woolfian text, availing herself of the hazy distinction between the two in *A Room of One's Own.*

In the text of *A Room of One's Own,* the disparity between meals at the fictional men's college of Oxbridge and women's college of Fernham prompts the narrator's foray into women in/and literature. She thinks "of the safety and prosperity of the one sex and of the poverty and insecurity of the other" (24). She invokes the male literary tradition to emphasize that women, too, require a literary history and a space in which their talents may flourish without ridicule or interruption. She discusses women's exclusion from educated circles and urges the women of Fernham to resist and rectify their own society's arbitrary and artificial gender divisions. Atkins does all of this, too, yet with notable adjustments.

In the film of *A Room,* Woolf's premise—an afternoon and evening spent at fictional colleges—is rejected in favor of situating the talk at Cambridge itself. Initially surprised by such a deviation, because Woolf's point is that women were barred from such institutions for centuries, I believe Atkins's rendition compels contemporary viewers to consider the ongoing causes and effects of sexism. Locating herself at Cambridge, Atkins signifies that although women in universities are a given these days, they continue to suffer subordination and belittlement once there. *A Room's* narrator prods her audience in a roundabout fashion to investigate why this is so: "What one wants, I thought—and why does not some brilliant student at Newnham or Girton supply it?—is a mass of information" (47); "the value that men set upon women's chastity and its effect upon their education [. . .] might provide an interesting book if any student at Girton or Newnham cared to go into the matter" (67). Atkins, on the other hand, looks directly into the camera and says "you" and "your," enjoining an audience of males and females to seek the answers.

Forceful at times, Atkins retreats from some of Woolf's more rigorous rhetorical stances. She omits the description of the sumptuous Oxbridge lunch followed by the meager dinner at Fernham, presenting instead a pantomime of dinner at Girton, the actual women's college where Woolf delivered her talk. Only afterward does Atkins-as-Woolf discuss the men's lavish environs, so that while the women's meal is dissatisfying, it is not quite the catalyst it is in the text for investigating the unfair distribution of resources to women and men. However, Atkins emphasizes to an equal degree the other amenities men have always enjoyed, such as scholarships, libraries, cigars, books, and privacy, while women's colleges can barely raise enough money for buildings. Woolf's point, projected differently yet effectively by Atkins, is that only when offered the best of what men have had for centuries can women compete and succeed in education and fiction writing.

Chapter two of *A Room of One's Own* finds Woolf's narrator heading toward the British Museum for explanations to the questions raised the previous day, such as why men drink wine and women water, and why men are wealthy and women poor. Atkins poses the same questions yet leaves out a critical detail. Woolf's narrator ironically regards the British Museum as a source of answers, for "[i]f truth is not to be found on the shelves of the British Museum, where, I asked myself, picking up a notebook and a pencil, is truth?" (25–26). The truth lies in writing, in a woman's determination and opportunity to create her own fiction, for the books within the museum contain prejudice and falsity. Atkins omits not only the gesture of lifting the pencil but also the concurrent phrase, sacrificing Woolf's injunction for women to start writing *now*. For Woolf, the notebook and pencil are the tools with which women can respond to a specious and exclusionary male literary tradition. In the film, they are mainly for jotting down scraps of information.

The film of *A Room of One's Own* alters another important sentence. In the text, Woolf's narrator explains that Lady Bessborough, "with all her passion for politics, must humbly bow herself and write to Lord Granville Leveson-Gower" that because she is just a woman, she will refrain from participating in politics "or any other serious business" (57). Atkins, however, has Lady Bessborough writing not to Lord Granville but to Lady Lucenborough. With this change, Lady Bessborough buckles under not to male hostility but to female pressure, a gender switch jarring to those familiar with the text, yet helpful to those who are not. By telling of an intelligent, politically savvy woman caving to female pressure, Atkins engages an issue of paramount importance to Woolf: women's oppression of women, resulting in a dubious sisterhood modeled on proscriptive male practices. Rather than depict a woman deferring to a male, Atkins shows, as does Woolf throughout her works, how patriarchy engenders women's aggression toward each other. Both Woolf and Atkins go on to admit with pleasure that they like women, that women are of course often wonderful to each other.

After careful research and reflection, Woolf's narrator discovers the discrepancies between women in fiction and women in fact. Atkins-as-Woolf does the same, also picking up a book by a renowned professor to read: "[W]omen have burnt like beacons in all the works of all the poets from the beginning of time [. . .]. But this is woman in fiction. In fact [. . .] she was locked up, beaten and flung about the room" (44–45). As Jane Marcus notes, "[b]y quotation [Woolf] sought to rob history of its power over women" (3). Citing illustrious male professors, Woolf and Atkins reveal the patriarchy's abuse of women in real life and hypocritical deification of them in literature. Offering examples from Shakespeare and Greek plays—fictional women seemingly not without personality and character—effectively demonstrates the extent to which women are subordinated in patriarchal society.

A Room's narrator then discusses the forgotten women who paved the way for future female writers,[4] noting, "Jane Austen and the Brontës and George Eliot could no more have written than Shakespeare could have written without Marlowe, or Marlowe without Chaucer" (68). In the film, Atkins rattles off the names of women writers at a rapid-fire pace, accessing a female literary tradition every bit as rich as the male. Woolf's narrator then discusses the fate of women deigning to have literary interests, embarking on the third chapter's tale of Shakespeare's doomed sister, which Atkins relates in its entirety. Atkins also maintains Woolf's thoughts on how life for women might have been different had their mothers gone into business and left a legacy to women's colleges. And she keeps the text's later section on women who did succeed in earning their living by writing. She drives the point home by adding details about the domestic duties undertaken by such women, like kneading dough and baking bread. Atkins's changes stress what might not be immediately obvious to a late twentieth-century audience. Austen, Brontë, Eliot, and their ilk did not have hours of leisure to hone their craft, only brief moments snatched between endless, exhausting domestic chores that automatically fell to them as women, leaving men free to do as they pleased.

Atkins links this information with Woolf's conclusion, which states sarcastically that for women in 1928, "the excuse of lack of opportunity, training, encouragement, leisure and money no longer holds good" (117) because they have now had access to them for nearly ten years. Both Woolf and Atkins reiterate the fate of Shakespeare's sister, and with this final image in the audience's mind, Atkins concludes the production by repeating a line already spoken, from the conclusion of chapter four. "Lock up your libraries if you like," Atkins says, glaring fiercely into the camera, referring not only to the beadle driving women off the turf at Cambridge but also to anyone who would threaten women's intellectual lives. "[T]here is no gate, no lock, no bolt that you can set upon the freedom of my mind" (79).

Brenda Silver believes Atkins's alteration compromises Woolf's tenet that "women's writing, women's creativity, has been and will remain different from men's" (Silver, *Icon* 217). According to Silver, the film effects a seismic shift from Woolf's concept of gendered literature to an overarching theme of the universality of art.[5] In fact, Atkins's reiteration of the male beadle's scorn for women reinforces Woolf's own statement that neither he nor any male so inclined may ever again impinge upon a woman's mind. The film's change (although these are in fact Woolf's words, just repeated) stresses for modern audiences that women were uniformly discouraged from and abused for having literary ambitions. The film of *A Room of One's Own* accommodates a contemporary audience that may never have read the text, as do recent film adaptations of *Orlando* and *Mrs. Dalloway*.[6]

Some of Atkins's choices may seem drastic. She displaces the fictional colleges with a real one, neglects to mention that "Chloe liked Olivia" (86), and dispenses with several of the Marys, including the fifth chapter's naturalist-novelist, would-be poet Mary Carmichael.[7] Gone are the allusions to Radclyffe Hall's *The Well of Loneliness* and the obscenity trial overseen by Sir Chartres Biron, lurking behind the curtains in Woolf's text. Atkins does not stick to the book line by line because doing so would have sabotaged her project (and lengthened the film to several hours, risking the chance of its even being aired). Contemporary audiences are likely unfamiliar with many of Woolf's sophisticated asides and allusions. Additionally, the book's ellipses, parenthetical remarks, and interruptions, which communicate the fluidity of human thought and history, and, as Judith Allen points out, disrupt traditions, boundaries, and rigidity, are not discernible to film viewers.[8] For Atkins to have attempted to convey them in speech or gesture would likely have confused and alienated viewers when her purpose is to draw them into Woolf's discourse.

In her suit jacket, loosely tied scarf, and short hair, Atkins bears an uncanny resemblance to Man Ray's 1934 photographs of Woolf. Regina Marler states that for a public television-watching audience, "[t]he new face of Virginia Woolf may indeed be that of Eileen Atkins" (252), although critic John Simon believes, "Miss Atkins, sturdier by far, could have blown Mrs. Woolf with one breath from Bloomsbury to Billingsgate" (qtd. in Silver, *Icon* 126). Of her own performance, Atkins concedes that hers is indeed a one-sided depiction of Woolf, displaying her brilliance and imaginative power rather than "her vulnerability, the unstable mind, her emotion or her relationships with other people. In fact, I felt extremely guilty," Atkins says, "that I had to whip up that lecture and deliver it in a way to hold the audience's attention in a manner which Virginia herself would probably have abhorred" (Atkins 16).

Yet surely Woolf would approve Atkins's emphasis on women's restrictions to education and art, their lack of access to intellectual society, their physical abuse within patriarchy, and the extraordinary emergence of the Austens, Brontës, and Eliots of the world. Atkins eulogizes Judith Shakespeare and exhorts her audience to contemplate women in/and fiction. Ultimately, Atkins offers viewers a provocative, clear, and graspable rendition of *A Room of One's Own*, crucial to any discussion, in any time, of women, literature, and the social construction of gender.

Notes

1. In "Envisioning/Revisioning Woolf in Film at the End of the Twentieth Century," *Virginia Woolf: Turning the Centuries: Selected Papers from the Ninth Annual Conference on Virginia Woolf*, eds. Ann Ardis & Bonnie Kime Scott (New York: Pace University Press, 2000) 284–85, Mimlitsch says, "as scholars of literature we seem always tempted to use the standard of faithfulness in judging an adaptation" when "insistence upon fidelity simply isn't useful, and can obscure more productive approaches to comparing an adaptation and its source."
2. Brenda R. Silver, "Tom & Viv & Vita & Virginia & Ottoline & Edith . . ." *Woolf Studies Annual* 2 (1996): 161.
3. Hermione Lee, *Virginia Woolf* (New York: Alfred A. Knopf, 1997) 556.
4. Alice Fox points out, "Woolf's original audiences for the talks on women and literature which formed the basis of *A Room* were educated young women at Cambridge, women Woolf would assume to be 'up' on their literature and therefore able to recognize whatever allusions she chose to use." "Literary Allusion as Feminist Criticism in *A Room of One's Own*," *Philological Quarterly* 63:2 (1984): 147.
5. Brenda Silver, *Virginia Woolf Icon* 218. Frances L. Restuccia would likely concur, given her statement, "Despite accumulated clichés fostering the notion of Woolf's dedication to androgyny, *A Room of One's Own* actually places more emphasis on the difference between the sexes than on their androgynous mergence." "'Untying the Mother Tongue': Female Difference in Virginia Woolf's *A Room of One's Own*," *Tulsa Studies in Women's Literature* 4:2 (1985): 254–55.
6. See Mimlitsch for a discussion of Sally Potter's *Orlando* and Marleen Gorris's *Mrs. Dalloway*.
7. According to Krystyna Colburn, the Marys in Woolf's text invoke the oral folk "Ballad of the Four Marys," which Woolf attributes to a woman writer and identifies most strongly with Mary Queen of Scots and her ladies-in-waiting named Mary. Colburn believes the "Ballad" "forms the structural underpinnings of *A Room of One's Own*" (59).
8. Judith Allen, "The Rhetoric of Performance in *A Room of One's Own*," *Virginia Woolf and Communities: Selected Papers from the Eighth Annual Conference on Virginia Woolf*, eds. Jeannette McVicker and Laura Davis (New York: Pace University Press, 1999) 292.

Works Cited

Allen, Judith. "The Rhetoric of Performance in *A Room of One's Own*." *Virginia Woolf & Communities: Selected*

Papers from the Eighth Annual Conference on Virginia Woolf. Ed. Jeanette McVicker and Laura Davis. New York: Pace University Press, 1999. 289–96.

Atkins, Eileen. "Playing Virginia." *The Charleston Magazine* 16 (1997): 13–18.

Colburn, Krystyna. "Women's Oral Tradition and *A Room of One's Own.*" *Re:Reading,Re:Writing, Re:Teaching Virginia Woolf.* Ed. Eileen Barret and Patricia Cramer. New York: Pace University Press, 1995. 59–63.

Fox, Alice. "Literary Allusion as Feminist Criticism in *A Room of One's Own.*" *Philological Quarterly* 63:2 (1984): 145–61.

Lee, Hermione. *Virginia Woolf.* New York: Alfred A. Knopf, 1997.

Marcus, Jane, ed. *New Feminist Essays on Virginia Woolf.* Lincoln: University of Nebraska Press, 1981.

Marler, Regina. *Bloomsbury Pie: The Making of the Bloomsbury Boom.* New York: Henry Holt, 1997.

Mimlitsch, Michelle N. "Envisioning/Revisioning Woolf in Film at the End of the Twentieth Century." *Virginia Woolf: Turning the Centuries: Selected Papers from The Ninth Annual Conference on Virginia Woolf.* Ed. Ann Ardis & Bonnie Kime Scott. New York: Pace University Press, 2000. 283–90.

Restuccia, Frances L. "'Untying the Mother Tongue': Female Difference in Virginia Woolf's *A Room of One's Own.*" *Tulsa Studies in Women's Literature* 4:2 (1985): 253–64.

Riedel, Michael. "A Play of One's Own." *Mirabella* 6:7 (1994): 52–54.

A Room of One's Own. By Virginia Woolf. Dir. Patrick Garland. Perf. Eileen Atkins. Videocassette. Cantor, 1990.

Silver, Brenda. "Tom & Viv & Virginia & Ottoline & Edith . . ." *Woolf Studies Annual* 2 (1996): 160–74.

---. *Virginia Woolf Icon.* Chicago: University of Chicago Press, 1999.

Woolf, Virginia. *A Room of One's Own.* 1929. New York: Harcourt, Brace, Jovanovich, 1957.

---. "The Cinema." *The Captain's Death Bed and Other Essays.* New York: Harcourt Brace Jovanovich, 1950. 180–86.

Doing the Splits:
Outsider/Insider as Women's Historian and Feminist Activist

by Joyce Avrech Berkman

Since the mid-1960s Virginia Woolf has beamed as my intellectual and moral light-house. Her fiction and nonfiction formed part of my research for my Yale disser-tation on the history of "Pacifism in England, 1914–1939" and influenced my anti-Vietnam War activism. Woolf's questions in *Three Guineas*—what causes war, what perpetuates aggressive and violent behavior, what promotes peace—nagged me daily. In the early 1970s as I began to teach women's history, Woolf's writings inspired my criti-cal understanding of European and American society. Through her nonfiction and even her fiction, such as *Orlando,* Woolf strengthened my conviction that those illiterate in women's history are severely handicapped in their analysis of women's experience and the conditions of social change. I responded to Woolf's call that we illuminate "that vast chamber where no body has yet been. [. . .] All these infinitely obscure lives remain to be recorded" (*A Room of One's Own* [1929], 1957, 88, 93). Her feminist ideals became my ideals, both as professor and as political activist. Despite my serious reservations about some of her gender assumptions and strategies for change, she exerted a vital and enduring influence on my life.

Now again we are in the midst of war, with individual freedoms at risk both here and abroad. I return to Woolf's examination of war and join her inquiry: What kind of educa-tion can instill hatred of war and promote peace, human equality, freedom, and integrity? We are also again at the crossroads of feminist development. Since Woolf assumes that only truly liberated human beings can prevent war, another vital question ensues: What is a liberated woman and how is she educated? Though teaching history since 1965, I've really been teaching the liberal arts, that is, the meaning and methods of becoming free ourselves and fighting for societal changes that enable everyone to be free.

The title of my talk, "Doing the Splits: The Outsider/Insider as Women's Historian and Feminist Activist," reflects my nearly forty years of struggle to reconcile the tension between my outsider experiences, ideals, and values and my insider position as tenured full professor of history, a comfortably upper middle-class, white, heterosexual married woman and mother of two, member of many same-sex and mixed-sex insider professional organizations.

As a child I envied my next-door neighbor who easily did the splits. I spent hours a day trying to loosen my hamstrings, to no avail. Given my physical constitution, it simply was not possible. As an adult, my success in doing the splits between outsider and insider has been uneven, some of the tensions simply unresolvable.

Today, after reviewing briefly Woolf's outsider ideals and insider possibilities as set forth in both *A Room of One's Own* and *Three Guineas,* I will examine my leg sprain in doing the splits.

Woolf presents two visions: one, pure or utopian radical and the other pragmatic radical. She ultimately opts for her pragmatic radicalism, but her heart, her eloquence, her brilliance surge through her pure radicalism. In *Three Guineas,* she lambastes the lives and mores of most educated men and their professional cultures: "There they go, our brothers who have been educated at public schools and universities, mounting those steps, passing in and out of those doors, ascending those pulpits, preaching, teaching, administering justice, practising medicine, transacting business, making money. Great-grandfathers, grandfathers, fathers, uncles—they all went that way, wearing their gowns, wearing their wigs, some with ribbons across their breasts, others without" (*Three Guineas* 60–61). The "titles before, or letters after" professional names, Woolf warns, "are acts that rouse competition and jealousy" (*Three Guineas* 21), emotions that predispose individuals to warfare. Eager for advancement, college and university professors are slaves, "piling words into books, piling words into articles, as the old slaves piled stones into pyramids [. . .] while the lilac shakes its branches in the garden free" (99). After the 1919 Sex Disqualification Act most professions opened to women, which leads Woolf to inquire, "We too can leave the house, can mount those steps [. . .] wear wigs and gowns, make money [. . .] do we wish to join that procession, or don't we? [. . .] where is it leading us?" (61–62). Woolf asks women whether they want to become

> human cripples, [. . .] to make the same incomes from the same professions that those men make you will have to accept the same conditions that they accept. [. . .] You will have to leave the house at nine and come back to it at six. That leaves very little time for fathers to know their children. [. . .] That leaves very little time for friendship, travel or art. [. . .] Sight goes. [. . .] no time to look at pictures. Sound goes. [. . .] no time to listen to music. Speech goes. [. . .] no time for conversation. [. . .] Humanity goes. [. . .] Health goes. [. . .] What then remains of a human being who has lost sight, sound, and sense of proportion? Only a cripple in a cave. (*Three Guineas* 69–70, 72)

Even if this odious outcome is somewhat overstated, professional cultures have not changed since Woolf's day. I hear over and over again faculty lament being time-poor, no time for evenings with friends, for exercise, for attending concerts and theater, for reading a variety of periodicals to stay adequately informed, and for contemplation on perennial questions of human existence.

For Woolf, the truly educated woman's world has a wide circumference that extends beyond human relationships, social, economic, and political issues and probes the "world of reality" (*A Room of One's Own* 118). She asks: What is the nature of the thing itself, be it a tree or simply the phenomenon of being? The educated woman knows the landscape of her own soul. The metaphorical brightly lit inner room is as important as the outer room. It is this dual illumination that Woolf intends when she exclaims: "Light up the windows of the new house, daughters! Let them blaze!" (*Three Guineas* 83).

But can education, as she and we know it, build a new house and provide those lamps? Woolf's pure radical solution envisions colleges open to everyone regardless of sex, social class, religion, and race. These colleges, experimental and adventurous, foster learning for its own sake, stir the joy of grappling with issues of truth and beauty, cultivate the whole person, integrate fields of study, and offer instruction in the arts of communication and social understanding. Ideal colleges are structures without stone and stained glass, without chapels and museums and libraries that protect items behind glass cases, without ceremonies, hoods, and degrees, without sermons and examinations, and without lectures because lectures perpetuate passive, uncritical, and uncreative minds, whet faculty vanity and authority, and impose noxious traditions (*Three Guineas* 33–35, 39).

But Woolf steps back and acknowledges that a woman needs a degree to enter a profession. She modifies her radicalism. Since intellectual freedom and economic independence are interwoven, we must support existing colleges, however flawed they may be. She believes women can do the splits, can advocate outsider values, while staying insiders as professors. She believes educators and members of other professions can resist narcissism and self-aggrandizement, can refuse to prostitute their minds for money and fame, can be a citizen of the whole world, putting humanity's well-being above national self-interest. Woolf comforts herself naively with the thought that professors can refuse to lecture on or teach any art or science that abets war, can "pour mild scorn" (*Three Guineas* 37) upon ceremonies and honors and upon the value of examinations, and can refuse honors and degrees for themselves (*Three Guineas* 100, 109–114, 143). Can they really?

In mid-May I attended the University of Massachusetts's annual awards dinner. Since 1980 when I was honored with and accepted the university's Distinguished Teaching Award, I have attended this event almost every year. Should I have accepted the award? Should I continue to attend this event? Should I display my plaque, even in the privacy of my home? In the end, does my doing so abet false pride, competition, jealousy, pugnacity, and the toxins that breed submission to the state? My right leg says yes: By participating in this event I applaud a system that pits people against one another, and that implies that teaching and the pursuit of understanding are not sufficiently their own reward. But my left leg affirms such an honor: Dedicated teaching at research universities and at many so-called liberal arts colleges gets the short end of the stick, and this form of obscurity does not promote personal integrity but anger, the snake that Woolf abhors in *A Room of One's Own*. At most institutions, teaching is inflected "female," while research and administration are inflected "male." By rewarding teachers, we sustain the positive nurturing female tradition, a precarious tradition when productivity in the form of many published works is the criteria of employment and tenure. Then my right leg balks and warns: Joyce, don't deceive yourself. This is a token event that gives the illusion of the importance of teaching, a classic example of institutional deflection of critical protest. You are buying into that tokenism. Think, Joyce, of the recent external review of our history department. Our distinguished evaluators and consultants recommended that we hire big-name celebrities to bolster our doctoral program to give our department greater national visibility. This presumably to ensure our recruitment of outstanding graduate students. Now how are *big name* and *celebrity* defined? Certainly, these eminent outside reviewers and most faculty, for that matter, define faculty celebrities as scholars engaged foremost in path-breaking research and heralded for their prodigious publications. Then my left leg rebuts: If I had turned down the Distinguished Teacher Award and if I did not attend this annual event, what good would I have done? Even if my dramatic act received sterling publicity, no reforms would follow, no betterment of the academic profession; I would have even less chance than I currently do to exert influence as an insider toward some modest improvements.

Another personal example of the splits strain concerns my civic organizational work. About five years ago two other women and I launched the Valley Women's History Collaborative, composed of academic and nonacademic volunteers whose mission was to find, preserve, and generate documents, including oral history tapes and transcripts, of the history since the mid-1960s of feminist and lesbian activism in our Pioneer Valley, Hampshire, Hampden, and Franklin counties. One of our three co-founders, like Woolf, disdained all organizational titles, insisting that we designate ourselves coordinators, not directors, make decisions by consensus, and jointly undertake most of our tasks. Within a year of our inception, we applied for a grant from the Massachusetts Foundation for the Humanities (MFH). Simultaneously we sought nonprofit status. National requirements for nonprofit status involved our filling out forms that list our organization's officers. The MFH expects the language of application to conform to conventional prose. All this our radical co-director found elitist and repugnant. Shall we fake officers? Shall we use old terms rather than invent new? Are we not perpetuating the usual binary between the status-driven academy and the community of poor and less-educated women? Yes, my right leg agreed. All three of us wanted to bring into our organization radical straight and lesbian feminists. We did not want to alienate women on marginal incomes with fewer academic skills than ours. Yet if we were to garner the resources to do our work, such as tape recorders and transcribers, we needed grants, we needed to collaborate with faculty and archivists and librarians, with potential donors, and with lawyers. We needed to speak their language, which, for two of us, as insiders of colleges, was also our language. During the first two years, we convinced our anti-academic colleague of the wisdom of these sacrifices, but she resented them anyway. Many further arguments occurred over the tensions between protecting our shared outsider convictions, yet respecting our insider perspectives that would accommodate the external demands of granting agencies, and discerning how best to collaborate with area libraries and archives. With deep divisions of opinions on other matters as well, ultimately, we cast consensus decision-making aside and outvoted our purist radical from her coordinator position. She withdrew completely from the collaborative. The collaborative thrives today, but at the cost of a key founder and with some loss of credibility among a certain segment of the area women's movement. We couldn't manage the outside/insider splits as successfully as we originally envisioned and hoped.

I can cite countless other examples of the insider/outsider challenge of Woolfian ideals. I have also grown critical of some of her analysis. She insufficiently appreciated the extent to which human beings depend upon others' acceptance of them and upon external recognition for their motivation and sense of well-being. We will continue to struggle with the splits. Perhaps, in time, with good enough parenting, good enough education, and good enough collective efforts to shape a more egalitarian and less violent world, women can become reasonably free and whole, with their two legs limber and strong.

Works Cited

Woolf, Virginia. *A Room of One's Own*. 1929. New York: Harcourt, Brace, and World, 1957.
---. *Three Guineas*.1938. New York: Harcourt, Brace, and World, 1966.

CAROLYN HEILBRUN: THE LAST INTERVIEW

by Susan C. Bourque

Carolyn Heilbrun's last visit to Smith College was for the thirteenth annual conference on Virginia Woolf in June of 2003. It was in every respect a splendid visit: Carolyn was engaging, insightful, and humorous in her public interview; charming and spunky in her social interactions; challenging in her intellectual exchanges; and generous in her praise for younger scholars and conference speakers. She especially respected delegates who were willing to take risks and challenge standard interpretations and received dogma.

Carolyn was the founding president of the Virginia Woolf Society (now the International Virginia Woolf Society) in 1976. During her term as president of the Modern Language Association (MLA) in 1984, the society became an affiliated group of the MLA. A special exhibition at the conference commemorated Carolyn's role in the Woolf society. The display of original typewritten documents and newsletters from the society underscored for all of us the tremendous technological changes in how we write and communicate as well as how Virginia Woolf's stature has changed since Carolyn's first efforts to celebrate her genius. It reminded all of us again of what a startling pioneer Carolyn Heilbrun had been with her insistence on the excellence of Woolf's work, assigning Woolf the appropriate acclaim in American literary circles.

It was equally gratifying to measure the growth of interest in Woolf, apparent not only by the growth of the society and by the numbers attending the conference, but also by the vibrancy of the graduate students and younger scholars participating in the sessions, always a sign of the intellectual energy in a field. Carolyn met Woolf biographer

Hermione Lee for the first time in a pleasant instance of serendipity. Carolyn had been given Lee's conference packet by mistake and it led them to one another—Carolyn immediately decreed this was not a mistake, but an example of superb planning by the conference organizers to ensure that everyone got to know each other.

By all appearances, it was a good conference for Carolyn—she was surrounded by friends, colleagues, and admirers. She rekindled her friendship with Jill Ker Conway (president of Smith from 1975 to 1985); she met the new president of Smith, Carol T. Christ; and she attended the opening speeches by Christ and Conway. They gave two synchronized and synthetic presentations, which elicited Carolyn's praise in her comments the next day during our interview. She admired Carol Christ's discussion of women's education and applauded Woolf's critique of women's exclusion from the academy. She found Jill Conway's interpretation of autobiography and Woolf's struggle to find a language appropriate to tell the story of women's lives resonant with her own sense of the fictional nature of both biography and autobiography.

Carolyn Heilbrun's association with Smith began in the 1980s when Jill Conway convinced Carolyn to serve as a senior scholar and advisor to the Smith Project on Women and Social Change. That began a series of conversations in Northampton, Massachusetts, as Carolyn became a regular visitor to Smith during Conway's presidency. She continued to visit Smith during Mary Maples Dunn's presidency and was awarded an honorary degree in 1988. Carolyn spent a summer in the early 1990s living in Northampton and using the Sophia Smith Collection, a world-renowned repository of women's archives, for her work on Gloria Steinem's biography. Carolyn often remarked on her affection for Smith and its leaders. She was firmly committed to the importance of friendship among women who were attempting new and difficult roles in the public sphere. She felt a kindred spirit with women leading women's colleges and, fortunately, Carolyn decided to donate her papers to Smith where they reside in the Sophia Smith Collection.

Thus, when Smith organizers Karen Kukil and Stephanie Schoen began to plan for the 2003 international conference on Virginia Woolf, they looked forward to welcoming back a friend of the college. With respect to the conference, Carolyn was clear that she did not wish to prepare a formal paper. Rather, it was her request to be interviewed and, given our long-standing friendship, she asked if I would conduct it. I was delighted to be asked.

I sent her a few preliminary questions via email in the May preceding the conference. My favorite was, "What influence did Virginia Woolf have on Kate Fansler?" (Fansler is Carolyn's marvelous invention, the female academic/quasi-sleuth in her Amanda Cross series.) I was thinking, in particular, of the appearance of a *Freshwater* performance and her reference to Woolf's appearance in a similar spoof of Tennyson in the plot line of one of her Amanda Cross books, *Honest Doubt* (2000). To my question Carolyn shot back an immediate electronic conversation stopper: "The answer is simple: none, no influence whatsoever."

But I didn't want to let go of that question. I remained convinced that Carolyn used the Kate Fansler stories to convey connections to Woolf's insights, or at least Carolyn's version of those insights. During the interview at the Woolf conference, I abandoned the Tennyson allusion and instead pointed out Woolf's insistence on the importance of understanding the past if we are to sort out the "cotton wool of daily life" (*Moments of Being*

72). I noted that Carolyn's most recent Fansler volume, *The Edge of Doom* (2002), makes just this point. Carolyn deflected my question once again and took our conversation in a different direction, speaking of Woolf's enormous capacity to convey complexity in a new and revolutionary form—her invention of the modern novel.

Reconsidering the interview in hindsight, I realize my questions were all softballs, which gave her freedom to range and comment and be as outrageous as she chose. And she was wonderful, holding the audience firmly in her sway throughout the afternoon. Among her more memorable comments that afternoon was a stirring defense of Leonard Woolf. She did not see him as an overbearing, highly controlling gatekeeper, despite what she acknowledged as the legitimate criticism of some of his decisions with respect to Virginia's medical treatments. She pointed out that Leonard's decisions were based on the best medical advice available at the time and that he had Vanessa's concurrence in his decisions. Carolyn argued in our interview that Leonard was the individual who enabled Woolf's genius to flourish and provided her with stability, companionship, and compass. Carolyn commented that Leonard Woolf was the rare sort of man who possessed the quality she most admired—the capacity and desire to live with a woman as highly accomplished as, and perhaps more accomplished than, he.

This led Carolyn to speak about what she said was one of her most misunderstood statements on marriage. Carolyn noted again her firm belief that Leonard and Virginia Woolf had what she viewed as a revolutionary marriage, one in which both individuals—and most critically, the woman—could work and flourish. Carolyn has written and spoken at length of the difficulty of finding examples of successful partnerships, but she argued that the Woolfs were just such an example. Further, she argued in our interview that to deny Leonard's critical contributions to the success of that unique arrangement was to deny that there might be successful marriages between men and women of accomplishment.

We were all eager to hear Carolyn's assessment of the recently released film *The Hours*, which conference participants had been able to view prior to the interview. She stated firmly that she liked the book *The Hours*, but found the film portrayal of Virginia Woolf on the whole disappointing. In Carolyn's opinion, it dwelt too long on her illness, missed her work life entirely, and left the viewer without the slightest sense of Woolf's humor, irony, and conversational acuity. In other words, it depicted a deadened, heavy, and decidedly unappealing Woolf. This Carolyn could not abide and she gave us some hilarious examples of Woolf's astute observations of her contemporaries.

I asked Carolyn to speak about the influence of Woolf on her own, Carolyn's, scholarly writing, in particular on Carolyn's thinking about androgyny. To this Carolyn spoke about the difficulty for all accomplished women writers to find a way to convey their life stories in a language and plot structures that have been shaped to tell the stories of men's lives. This is a theme Carolyn addressed frequently and in particular depth in *Writing a Woman's Life*. In our interview, she elaborated on her concern that we still have not found a language and plot line adequate to convey the challenge of leaving the conventional, the costs of that decision, as well as the rewards for both men and women of doing so. She reminded us of the vast changes between the world of the 1940s and 1950s when she lived with the weight of conventional roles and expectations. She reiterated the challenge faced by adventurous or "questing" women who live out different life plots and then try to tell their stories in conventional language that forces them to deny their own motivations. She argued that our language has been shaped to tell men's stories and that women like Woolf were struggling to find a way to express the truth of women's lives, to create a more honest account of the stifling consequences of a life plot that reduces a woman's life to end in marriage and children. She argued that such a controlling convention led even the most adventurous of women to deny in the telling of their lives their motivations for power and control, and led them to mask their quests for adventure, daring, and pleasure.

I wanted to know which of Woolf's books had been the most memorable for Carolyn over the years. Was there one that she returned to or was it a different book at distinct moments in her life? In response Carolyn mentioned *To the Lighthouse, Mrs. Dalloway*, and *Between the Acts*—in each finding a component of Woolf's insight into the restrictions of conventional gender roles and evidence of Woolf's need to write a new story of women's lives. She also noted her pleasure at the reevaluation of Woolf's overtly feminist volumes, *A Room of One's Own* and *Three Guineas*. In these volumes it is the attention to the significance of women's friendships and women's solidarity that she found profoundly important.

Thinking back to the interview in light of subsequent events, I wondered that we made no mention of Woolf's suicide. It certainly did not loom large in the discussion, though of course *The Hours* opens with Woolf's suicide and sets Woolf in a context that focuses attention on her mental instability. The subject never came up and no one in the audience made mention of it, nor of Carolyn's well-known statements on suicide and the need for an explicit choice to live once one has reached the age of seventy. But that afternoon, suicide was not a topic.

Among Carolyn's memorable events at Smith, one in particular stands out in my mind— 28 January 1990, Super Bowl Sunday. Instead of the traditional day of football, we organized a program at Smith in which Carolyn and Jill Conway appeared to a standing-room-only crowd. The title of the session was "In Our Own Voices: Reflections on Women's Biography and Autobiography." This was a topic Carolyn and Jill had developed in a workshop at Smith during the summer of 1983 entitled: "New Approaches to Women's Biography and Autobiography." That summer workshop was followed by stellar autobiographical writing by both women. It also led to a number of insights about women's writing, which Carolyn published in *Writing a Woman's Life* (1988).

Throughout this discussion with Jill in 1990, Carolyn alluded to the issue of control and how a sense of control had been critical to her own life, explaining why she had taken up a secret life of mystery writing while a young tenure-track professor at Columbia University. Her standard explanation was that if the department had known about her mystery-writing career, she would have been dismissed as an academic and she would have failed to get tenure. But, she added, concern about tenure was not the only reason. There was in her use of a pseudonym a desire for a secret, and the desire to have a life of her own, in the midst of the myriad demands upon her as a mother also involved in a demanding career. She sought in her secret career a sense of control—the need to control some space and to control some aspect of her life, free of the multiple demands of others. She saw the quest for control as a feminist act, one that underscored the right to live an independent life, with its own purpose and demands, free of the claims of convention. Among her statements about control on that Super Bowl Sunday was the following:

All human beings need to be, to feel in control of their lives. They need to feel there is something one controls and I think you're best off if you're more or less in control of yourself and the decisions you make about your life. For many of us women that meant control of the kitchen and the firm conviction that only you could properly load the dishwasher. But of course it must mean much more than that. And that, I have come to understand is what, in part, writing the mystery stories represented for me.[1]

Carolyn found a measure of that control in her secret writing—and understood it in retrospect as part of her effort to create a sphere she could control. But Kate Fansler and her marriage to the perfect partner was also Carolyn's attempt to explore how to write a different sort of marriage and life plot for a woman. Was it possible to write about a marriage where the woman did not disappear into a subordinate wifely role, to essentially be written out of the adventure, which, she argued, Dorothy Sayers had done to Harriet Vane? Carolyn's Kate does prevail and gives voice to the feminist conflicts of the 1980s and 1990s. Each story can be read as Carolyn's accounts from the field, or briefings on debates in the feminist movement. She used all her considerable literary power to try to tell us where we had come from, to recall for us the oppressive world she found in the 1940s and 1950s, to describe the claustrophobic atmosphere she encountered in the academy, and to remind us of all we had to lose by not seeking to learn a new way to live our lives and to tell the truth about those lives. She saw Woolf as struggling to find a way to unmask the oppressive nature of the conventional plot for women in *Mrs. Dalloway* and in *To the Lighthouse*. She admired Woolf's own struggles to live a different life and to tell a different story.

Carolyn never failed to emphasize the importance of women's friendships to feminism and to women's happiness. She felt the centrality of this need profoundly, both personally and politically. She spoke of it often and with deep feeling. She distinguished what she meant by women's friendship from the world of female love and ritual described by Carroll Smith-Rosenberg. In her insightful article on "The Female World of Love and Ritual," Smith-Rosenberg described how women's friendship and love in nineteenth-century America helped them endure their private lives, but, critically, did *not* challenge the prevailing expectations about women's lives. Indeed, these women prepared their daughters to lead the same lives they had led.

What Carolyn longed for was a redefinition of friendship in the lives of women, where women would support one another in their private lives and in the public sphere. She argued that women needed to develop friendships that not only consoled one another and supported one another in their private and family lives, but also helped them in public struggles. She felt women needed to talk not only about how one endures, but also about how one prevails. Carolyn longed for women's friendship and support for one another as they challenged prevailing norms, roles, and expectations. She wanted support for women living public lives—new lives that had not been previously scripted to be subordinate to those of men. She felt her own aloneness as she challenged the treatment of women and searched for new ways for women to live in the world, and she was clear about her own desire for support from other women. She was explicit in her belief that without such public support for one another, the women's movement would fail and we would all return to isolation and loneliness in our individual homes.

I am comforted by the memory that during her days at the Smith Woolf conference Carolyn was surrounded by friends and public acclaim. Her comments at the interview were met with enthusiasm and a standing ovation of pleasure and acknowledgment of her public leadership and her efforts to write a new story. Carolyn resurrected Woolf for American literature in the 1970s and blazed a trail through both her literary scholarship and her popular inventions. She lived her commitment to other public women and, in private and in public, attempted to emotionally and politically support other women attempting to break the mold and to live lives that mattered in some larger sense. At the Woolf conference there was public acknowledgment of how much both had meant to so many.

Note

1.   Quoted from author's personal notes, 28 Jan. 1990.

Works Cited

Smith-Rosenberg, Carroll. "The Female World of Love and Ritual: Relations between Women in Nineteenth-Century America." *Signs: Journal of Women in Culture and Society* 1.1 (1975): 1–29.

Woolf, Virginia. *Moments of Being.* Ed. Jeanne Schulkind. 2d ed. San Diego: Harvest-Harcourt Brace & Company, 1985.

Notes on Contributors

LAURA FRANCESCA AIMONE majored in English literature at the Università del Piemonte Orientale A. Avogadro of Vercelli, Italy, writing a final thesis about the relationship between *The Hours* and *Mrs. Dalloway*. She received a bachelor of arts in July 2002. Her research interests are gender and literature.

MICHÈLE BARRETT is a feminist sociologist and professor of modern and cultural literary theory at Queen Mary and Westfield College, University of London. Her publications include *Ideology and Cultural Production* (ed. 1979); *Women's Oppression Today: Some Problems in Marxist Feminist Analysis* (1980); *Virginia Woolf, Women and Writing* (ed. 1980); *The Anti-Social Family* (ed. with M. McIntosh, 1982); *The Politics of Diversity* (ed. with Roberta Hamilton, 1986); *Women's Opposition Today: The Marxist/ Feminist Encounter* (1988); *The Politics of Truth: From Marx to Foucault* (1991); *Destabilizing Theory: Contemporary Feminist Debates* (ed. with Anne Phillips, 1992); and *Imagination in Theory: Essays on Writing and Culture* (1999). She is also the editor of the Penguin edition of Woolf's feminist essays *A Room of One's Own* and *Three Guineas* (2000).

JOYCE AVRECH BERKMAN, professor of history and adjunct professor of women's studies at the University of Massachusetts at Amherst, authored *The Healing Imagination of Olive Schreiner: Beyond South African Colonialism* (1989) and edited a forthcoming volume of essays, *Contemplating Edith Stein* (2005). As co-director of the Valley Women's History Collaborative, she has engaged in oral history and archival projects to reconstruct and preserve the path-breaking history of second-wave feminism in western Massachusetts.

DORYJANE BIRRER is an assistant professor at the College of Charleston, South Carolina, where she teaches contemporary British literature and literary criticism. Her research explores the interactions among literature, literary criticism/theory, and academic culture, particularly with regard to the post-1960 British novel. She has also recently co-edited, with Diane Gillespie, a Broadview Press edition of Cicely Hamilton's *Diana of Dobson's*.

SUSAN C. BOURQUE is the provost and dean of the faculty at Smith College, Northampton, Massachusetts. She is also the Esther Booth Wiley Professor of Government at Smith and, prior to becoming provost, served as the director of the Smith Project on Women and Social Change through which she first met Carolyn Heilbrun in the 1980s. She is a devotee of the work of Heilbrun, Amanda Cross, and Virginia Woolf.

JULIA BRIGGS is a research professor at De Montford University, Leicester, and emeritus fellow of Hertford College, Oxford, England. She has written on Renaissance literature and children's literature, and acted as general editor of the Penguin 1992 reprint of the works of Virginia Woolf. Professor Briggs has recently completed a major new account of Woolf, entitled *A Life in Books* (Penguin, 2005) and a biography of Woolf's creative life, entitled *Virginia Woolf: An Inner Life* (Allen Lane, 2005). Briggs is bringing out an edition of Hope Mirrlees's *Paris: A Poem* in Bonnie Kime Scott's sequel to *The Gender of Modernism*.

CORNELIA BURIAN is originally from Germany. She is currently finishing her Ph.D. at the University of Saskatchewan, Canada. Her research interests are modernist literature and gender studies.

CAROL T. CHRIST began her tenure as president of Smith College in June 2002, following a career as an English professor and administrator at the University of California at Berkeley from 1970 to 2000. A scholar of Victorian literature, Christ is an editor of *The Norton Anthology of English Literature* and is the author of *Victorian and Modern Poetics* (1984). Her current scholarly project involves literary representations of death in the Victorian period.

KRISTIN KOMMERS CZARNECKI recently completed her Ph.D. in English at the University of Cincinnati, Ohio. Her research interests include Anglo and African American modern women writers, including Virginia Woof, Jean Rhys, Nella Larsen, and Zora Neale Hurston. Currently she teaches courses in modern British fiction and African American literature at the University of Cincinnati and at Xavier University, in Cincinatti, Ohio.

JAN FREEMAN is the author of three collections of poetry: *Simon Says, Hyena,* and *Autumn Sequence.* She is publisher of Paris Press and a contributing editor to the *American Poetry Review.* Her poetry and essays have appeared in numerous journals and anthologies. She lives in Ashfield, Massachusetts.

LYNDALL GORDON was born in Cape Town, South Africa. She has been an assistant professor at Columbia University, New York; a lecturer at Jesus College, Oxford, England; lecturer in English at Oxford; and Dame Helen Gardner Fellow at St Hilda's College, Oxford. Since 1995 she has been senior fellow at St Hilda's College. Her biographies have won numerous awards. They include: *Eliot's Early Years* (1977), *Eliot's New Life* (1988), *T. S. Eliot: An Imperfect Life* (1998), *Virginia Woolf: A Writer's Life* (1984), *Shared Lives* (1992), *Charlotte Brontë: A Passionate Life* (1994), *A Private Life of Henry James: Two Women and His Art* (1998), and *Vindication: A Life of Mary Wollstonecraft* (2005).

SUSAN RUBINOW GORSKY teaches part-time at the University of California at Santa Cruz and at Cabrillo College, after many years of full-time work, primarily on the English faculty at Cleveland State University, Ohio, and as dean of students at the Punahou School, Hawaii. She is the author of books on Woolf and on women in nineteenth-century fiction, as well as the co-author (with her husband) of a text on medical hypnosis.

ELIZABETH HIRSH, associate professor of English at the University of South Florida, has published articles and book chapters on Virginia Woolf, H. D., Luce Irigaray, and Adrienne Rich, among others, and is the co-author of *Women Writing Culture* (1995). Her current project approaches Woolf's writing in terms of the relationship it suggests between fiction, biography, and history writing.

CATHERINE W. HOLLIS is an assistant professor of English at Lawrence University in Appleton, Wisconsin. She'll be teaching an undergraduate seminar on Bloomsbury in twenty-first century culture at the University of California at Berkeley in the autumn of 2005.

Maggie Humm is a professor of cultural studies at the University of East London and the author of many award-winning books on feminism. Her most recent publication, *Snapshots of Bloomsbury: The Private Lives of Virginia Woolf and Vanessa Bell* (2005), contains the first catalog of Woolf's Monk's House albums.

Dianne Hunter, professor of English at Trinity College in Hartford, Connecticut, editor of *Seduction and Theory* (1989) and *The Makings of Dr. Charcot's Hysteria Shows* (1998), has published essays in the journals *American Imago,* the *Psychoanalytic Review, Feminist Studies,* and *Partial Answers.*

Erica L. Johnson is an assistant professor at Chatham College in Pittsburgh, Pennsylvania, where she teaches British and world literature. She is the author of *Home, Maison, Casa: The Politics of Location in Works by Jean Rhys, Marguerite Duras, and Erminia Dell'Oro* (2003), as well as articles on Virginia Woolf, Helene Cixous, George Sand, and Dionne Brand. Her current project, *Haunted Empires,* links modernist and postcolonial writing through the transnational theme of hauntings.

Susan M. Kenney is a novelist and short story writer as well as a scholar and critic of twentieth-century and contemporary literature. Her fiction, particularly the novels *In Another Country* and *Sailing,* has been greatly influenced by her longtime interest in Virginia Woolf. Her scholarly articles on Woolf include "Two Endings: Virginia Woolf's Suicide and *Between the Acts*" (*University of Toronto Quarterly,* 1975) and "Virginia Woolf and the Art of Madness" (*Massachusetts Review,* 1983). She is currently the Charles A. Dana Professor of English and Creative Writing at Colby College in Waterville, Maine.

Jennifer-Ann DiGregorio Kightlinger is a former assistant dean of undergraduate and graduate studies at St. John's University in New York City. She is currently a Ph.D. candidate at the State University of New York at Stony Brook, where she teaches Italian American literature and international modernism.

Joseph Kreutziger resides in New York City, where he teaches English and writing at the Birch Wathen Lenox School. His dissertation from Washington University, on Virginia Woolf and temporal aesthetics, is scheduled for completion in 2005.

Karen V. Kukil curates the Virginia Woolf and Sylvia Plath collections at Smith College, where she holds a split appointment in the Mortimer Rare Book Room and the Sophia Smith Collection. She edited *The Unabridged Journals of Sylvia Plath* (2000) and is the co-author of *"No Other Appetite": Sylvia Plath, Ted Hughes, and the Blood Jet of Poetry* (2005).

Eleanor McNees is an associate professor of English at the University of Denver, Colorado, where she teaches Victorian and early twentieth-century British literature. She is the author of *Eucharistic Poetry: The Search for Presence in the Writings of John Donne, Gerard Manley Hopkins, Dylan Thomas, and Geoffrey Hill* (1992), and editor of *Virginia Woolf: Critical Assessments* (1994) and *The Brontë Sisters: Critical Assessments* (1996).

MARY C. MADDEN teaches at the University of South Florida, Tampa. She has been published in the *Virginia Woolf Miscellany, Style, Sunscripts, Kalliope,* and the *Florida English Journal* among other publications, and is currently researching class issues in the work of Virginia Woolf. Madden is also a published and performance poet.

CHERYL MARES is a professor of English at Sweet Briar College in Virginia. Her research interests focus on works by modernist writers, especially Virginia Woolf and Marcel Proust, on whom she has published a number of articles. Currently, she is working on an article on Virginia Woolf and Gertrude Stein and on a larger project exploring Woolf's relationship with American culture, from which her paper is drawn.

WILLIAM PRYOR is an entrepreneur and a publisher, writer, and speaker on mysticism and drugs issues. He is currently writing a popular philosophy of man's relationship with psychosomatics, while also producing a feature film based on his memoir, *The Survival of the Coolest.*

PAMELA ST. CLAIR is a part-time English instructor and a full-time student in the M.F.A. poetry program at Vermont College. Her research interests include twentieth-century and contemporary British and American literature. She has presented or published papers on Virginia Woolf, Sylvia Plath, and A. S. Byatt.

DREW PATRICK SHANNON is a doctoral candidate at the University of Cincinnati, where he is specializing in Victorian and twentieth-century British literature. He has published articles on Virginia Woolf, David Leavitt, and Doris Lessing, and is currently working on a novel.

ELIZABETH A. SHIH, most recently of the Graduate Studies Program at the University of Toronto, is the author of numerous papers and scholarly articles on Virginia Woolf, H. D., and other prominent women writers of the twentieth century. She most recently published an article in *The Virginia Woolf Miscellany* entitled "When Woolf Goes Missing (From Herself)," a critique of David Hare's film *The Hours* and the surfeit of popular newspaper articles that accompanied its release.

LORRAINE SIM recently completed her Ph.D. in English, communication, and cultural studies at the University of Western Australia, Perth, where she currently lectures. Her dissertation is entitled "'An Ordinary Mind on an Ordinary Day': Virginia Woolf's Reconstruction of Common Experience."

KATHRYN SIMPSON is lecturer in English at the University of Birmingham, England, where she teaches nineteenth- and twentieth-century fiction and film. Her research interests focus on the interrelationships of sexuality and creativity in the work of Virginia

Woolf, H. D., and Gertrude Stein. Her current research is concerned with exploring the operation of the gift economy as it works in conjunction with market and libidinal economies.

FRANCES SPALDING is an art historian, critic, and biographer. Her books include *British Art since 1900* as well as a centenary history of the Tate Gallery (1998). A new edition of her biography of the poet Stevie Smith, first published in 1988, appeared in 2002. She is also a well-known authority on Bloomsbury, having published biographies of Roger Fry, Vanessa Bell, and Duncan Grant. For eight years she edited the *Charleston Magazine,* also sitting on the Council for the Charleston Trust. Her most recent books are *Gwen Raverat: Friends, Family and Affections* (2004), *The Bloomsbury Group* (2005), and *John Milton: Dance Till the Stars Come Down* (2005). She is a Fellow of the Royal Society of Literature; a Fellow of the Royal Society of Arts, Manufacture and Commerce; and an Honorary Fellow of the Royal College of Art. She is currently Reader in Twentieth-Century British Art at the University of Newcastle, England.

ELIZABETH GALLAHER VON KLEMPERER, the Esther Cloudman Dunn *professor emerita* of English at Smith College, received her doctorate from Harvard University, Cambridge, Massachusetts, after graduating from Smith, where she returned to teach for over forty years. Her interests have ranged over various areas of British and comparative literature, centering on the Victorian period. Besides teaching Woolf in classes and seminars she has directed numerous honors theses on her work.

MCKENZIE L. ZEISS received her bachelor of arts in literature and in women's studies from the University of California, Santa Cruz, in 1996. She is currently at the University of California, Irvine, where she completed her master of arts in 2002 and is currently working on her dissertation.

Conference Program

Woolf in the Real World
Thirteenth Annual Conference on Virginia Woolf
Smith College, 5–8 June 2003

Conference at a Glance

Wednesday, June 4

10:00 a.m.	Registration opens for on-campus delegates (24 hours—Laura Scales House)
12:00–6:00 p.m.	Information table (Neilson Browsing Room)
6:00–7:30 p.m.	Reception for early arrivals (King/Scales House courtyard)
8:00 p.m.	*Woolf in the Reel World* (film series): *Mrs. Dalloway* (Wright Hall Auditorium)
10:00 p.m.	Informal discussion/cookies and milk (Jordan House Common Room)

Thursday, June 5

24 hours	Registration for delegates staying on campus (Laura Scales House)
7:30–8:45 a.m.	Breakfast for delegates staying on campus (King/Scales Dining Room)
8:00 a.m.–9:00 p.m.	Registration for delegates staying off campus (Neilson Library)
9:00 a.m.–3:00 p.m.	Field trip to the Mount (meet bus at 8:30 a.m. in front of John M. Greene Hall)
3:30–4:30 p.m.	Performance: *A Room of One's Own,* with Clare Dalton (Wright Hall Auditorium)
5:00–6:30 p.m.	Conference opening Welcome and plenary session: Carol T. Christ and Jill Ker Conway
6:45–8:45 p.m.	Gala reception for conference delegates, viewing of exhibition *Woolf in the World: A Pen and a Press of Her Own,* and book arts demonstrations (Neilson Library, third floor)
8:30–11:00 p.m.	Film series: *The Hours,* including sneak preview of extras from the DVD
10:00 p.m.	Informal discussion/cookies and milk (Jordan House Common Room)

Friday, June 6

Book and art fair is open 10:30 a.m.–2:00 p.m. and 3:30–5:30 p.m., Neilson Library, third floor.

24 hours	Registration for delegates staying on campus (Laura Scales House)
7:30–8:45 a.m.	Breakfast for participants staying on campus; *Miscellany* breakfast meeting (King/Scales Dining Hall)
8:00 a.m.–6:00 p.m.	Registration for delegates staying off campus (Neilson Library, first floor)
9:00–10:30 a.m.	Concurrent panels, session #1
10:30–11:00 a.m.	Morning refreshments (Neilson Library, third floor)
11:00 a.m.-12:30 p.m.	Concurrent panels, session #2
12:30–2:00 p.m.	Lunch (not provided—Davis Student Center is open) and reception for Suzanne Bellamy exhibit at Northampton Center for the Arts
2:00–3:30 p.m.	Concurrent panels, session #3
3:30 p.m.	Refreshment break (Neilson Library, third floor)
4:00–5:00 p.m.	Plenary session: Carolyn Heilbrun interviewed by Susan C. Bourque (Wright Hall Auditorium)
5:15–6:15 p.m.	International Virginia Woolf Society Reception (Atrium of the Brown Fine Arts Center) and viewing of exhibition *Vanessa Bell and Bloomsbury* (Smith College Museum of Art)
6:30–7:50 p.m.	Plenary session: Gretchen Holbrook Gerzina and Frances Spalding (Wright Hall Auditorium)
8:00 p.m.	Dinner (delegates are free to make their own arrangements)
8:15 p.m.	Film series: Sally Potter's *Orlando* (Wright Hall Auditorium)
10:00 p.m.	Informal discussion/cookies and milk (Jordan House Common Room)

Saturday, June 7

Book and art fair is open 10:30 a.m.–2:00 p.m. and 3:30–5:30 p.m., Neilson Library, third floor.

24 hours	Registration/check out for on-campus delegates (Laura Scales House)
7:30–8:45 a.m.	Breakfast for delegates staying on campus; International Virginia Woolf Society breakfast meeting (King/Scales Dining Hall)
8:00 a.m.–6:00 p.m.	Registration for delegates staying off campus (Neilson Library, first floor)
9:00–10:00 a.m.	Plenary session: Lyndall Gordon (Wright Hall Auditorium)
10:00–10:30 a.m.	Morning refreshments (Neilson Library, third floor)
10:30 a.m.-12:00 p.m.	Concurrent panels, session #4

12:00 p.m.–1:00 p.m.	Lunch on your own (preordered boxed lunches may be picked up at the Neilson Library, third floor)
1:00–2:30 p.m.	Concurrent panels, session #5
2:30–3:00 p.m.	Afternoon refreshments (Neilson Library, third floor)
3:00–4:30 p.m.	Concurrent panels, session #6
4:30–5:30 p.m.	Break
5:30–6:45 p.m.	Keynote Address: Hermione Lee (Sage Hall)
7:00–9:00 p.m.	Banquet (King/Scales Dining Room)
9:00–10:30 p.m.	Reception, viewing of exhibition *Woolf: A Botanical Perspective*, illumination of botanic gardens, and Hermione Lee book signing of *On Being Ill* (Lyman Plant House)
10:00 p.m.	Informal discussion/cookies and milk (Jordan Common Room)

Sunday, June 8

Book and art fair is open 10:30 a.m.–12:30 p.m., Neilson Library, third floor.

7:30–8:45 a.m.	Breakfast for delegates staying on campus; Conference 2004 meeting (King/Scales Dining Room)
8:00 a.m.–4:00 p.m.	Information table (Neilson Browsing Room)
9:00–10:30 a.m.	Concurrent panels, session #7
10:30–11:00 a.m.	Refreshment break (Neilson Library, third floor)
11:00 a.m.–12:30 p.m.	Concurrent panels, session #8
12:30–1:30 p.m.	Lunch on your own (preordered boxed lunches may be picked up at Neilson Library, third floor)
1:30–2:30 p.m.	Performance: *Lytton and Virginia,* a staged reading of the Woolf–Strachey correspondence (Wright Hall Auditorium)
4:00–7:00 p.m.	Trip to Emily Dickinson sites (meet vans at 3:30 p.m. in front of Neilson Library)
7:00 p.m.	Dinner (delegates are free to make their own arrangements)
8:30–10:00 p.m.	Film series: *Carrington,* introduced by Gretchen Holbrook Gerzina (Wright Hall Auditorium)
10:00 p.m.	Informal discussion/cookies and milk (Jordan Common Room)

Monday, June 9

Midnight–noon	Checkout (Laura Scales House)
7:15–8:30 a.m.	Breakfast for delegates staying on campus (King/Scales Dining Room)
12:00 noon	Final checkout time for delegates staying in Smith housing (Laura Scales House)

Full Schedule

PRE-CONFERENCE EVENTS

Wednesday, June 4

10:00 a.m.	Registration opens for delegates staying on campus (Laura Scales House)
12:00 p.m.–6:00 p.m.	Information table (Neilson Browsing Room)
6:00–7:30 p.m.	Reception for early arrivals (King/Scales House courtyard)
8:00 p.m.	*Woolf in the Reel World* (film series): *Mrs. Dalloway* (Wright Hall Auditorium)
10:00 p.m.	Informal discussion/cookies and milk (Jordan House Common Room)

Thursday, June 5

7:30–8:45 a.m.	**Breakfast** for delegates staying on campus (Laura Scales House)
8:00 a.m.	**Registration** opens (Neilson Library—8:00 a.m.–9:00 p.m. for off-campus delegates; Laura Scales House—24 hours for on-campus delegates)
9:00 a.m.–3:00 p.m.	**Field trip** to the Mount (meet bus at 8:30 a.m. in front of John M. Greene Hall)
3:30–4:30 p.m.	**Performance:** *A Room of One's Own,* with Clare Dalton

CONFERENCE SESSIONS BEGIN

5:00–6:30 p.m.	**Welcome** (Wright Hall Auditorium)
	Plenary session: Carol T. Christ, "Virginia Woolf and Education" and President *emeritus* Jill Ker Conway, "My Present Distance of Time"
6:45–8:45 p.m.	**Gala buffet reception:** viewing of exhibition *Woolf in the World: A Pen and a Press of Her Own* and book arts demonstrations (Neilson Library, third floor)
8:30 p.m.	**Film series:** *The Hours,* introduced by Brenda Silver (Dartmouth College), preceded by a sneak preview of some of the DVD extras, courtesy Paramount Pictures (Wright Hall Auditorium)

Friday, June 6

24 hours	**Registration** for delegates staying on campus, Laura Scales House
7:15–8:45 a.m.	**Breakfast** for delegates staying on campus (King/Scales Dining Room)
8:00 a.m.–6:00 p.m.	**Registration** for delegates staying off campus, Neilson Library

10:30 a.m.–2:00 p.m. **Book and Art Fair** (Neilson Library, third floor)
& 3:30–5:30 p.m.

9:00–10:30 a.m. **CONCURRENT SESSIONS #1**

1A: **The Electronic Woolf.** Chair: Robin Kinder (Smith College)
Location: Neilson Library Electronic Classroom
Robin Kinder (Smith College): "Woolf On-line Resources at Smith College"—
Demonstration
Kathryn Holland (University of Alberta): "Virginia Woolf, Writing Women, and the
Orlando Project"
Stuart Clarke (Virginia Woolf Society of Great Britain): "Virginia Woolf and Bloomsbury:
A Bibliography"—Demonstration

1B: **The Education of Women.** Chair: Catherine Sandbach-Dahlström (Stockholm
University)
Location: Seelye 201
Ann Murphy (Assumption College): "Freedom from Unreal Loyalties: An Imaginary Con-
versation between Emily Davis and Virginia Woolf on the Formation of the College for
Women"
Sara Hoover (Dickinson College): "Educating the Outsiders: Re-Writing War Narratives
in *Three Guineas*"
Judith Robertson (University of Ottawa): "Objects of Desire in Narrative Treatments of
Education: The Uncanny Sisterhood of Virginia Woolf and Sylvia Ashton-Warner"
Joyce Berkman (University of Massachusetts, Amherst): "Doing the Splits: Outsider/
Insider as Women's Historian and Feminist Activist"

1C: **Hogarth Press I.** Chair: Debra Sims (Independent Scholar)
Location: Graham Hall—Brown Fine Arts Center
Carol Shloss (Stanford University): "Virginia Woolf's Composing Room: Movable Types
and the Modernist Novel"
Alice Staveley (Stanford University): "Woolf's Q Factor: 'Kew Gardens' 1927"
Susan Waterman (Rutgers University): "'There Is a Great Deal to Be Said for Small Books':
The Hogarth Press and the Short Story as Catalysts in the Development of Virginia
Woolf's Voice"

1D: **Woolf: Walking and Stalking.** Chair: Suzanne Bellamy, Artist-in-Residence
Location: Seelye 106
Elisa Kay Sparks (Clemson University): "A Rose Burning Between Marches: Walking
Pictures in *Mrs. Dalloway*"
Diane Gillespie (Washington State University): "Woolf and Walking: Mapping a Rural
Flaneuse"
Sheila Deane (University of Winnipeg): "'Take Back the Night': Stalking and Trespassing
in Woolf's Fiction"

1E: **Woolf and Illness.** Chair: Martha Greene Eads (Valparaiso University
Location: Seelye 101
Lorraine Sim (University of Western Australia): "Ailing Dualisms: Woolf's Revolt against Rationalism in the 'Real World' of Influenza"
Susan Gorsky (Cabrillo College/Foothill College): "The Mask/Masque of Food: Illness and Art"
Jo Ann Circosta (University of Kentucky): "Time Disrupted: Virginia Woolf's Phenomenology of Psychosis"

1F: **National Identity.** Chair: Mark Hussey (Pace University)
Location: Seelye 107
McKenzie L. Zeiss (University of California, Irvine): "The Political Legacy of the Garden: (Anti) Pastoral Images and National Identity in Virginia Woolf and Vita Sackville-West"
Erica Johnson (Chatham College): "Writing the Land: The Geography of National Identity in *Orlando*"
Renée Dickinson (University of Colorado): "Mrs. Dalloway's Corporeum: Body, Land, Nation, and Text in the Worlds of Patriarchy and Imperialism"

1G: **Reading and Writing.** Chair: Elizabeth von Klemperer (Smith College)
Location: Neilson Browsing Room
Jane de Gay (Trinity and All Saints College): "Dynamic Encounters: Virginia Woolf as Active Reader"
Jennifer Arends (University of Regina): "Life? Literature? Virginia Woolf and T. S. Eliot in Form"
Cornelia Pearsall (Smith College): "Woolf and the Poetry of the Real World"
Doryjane Birrer (College of Charleston): "What are Novelists For?: Writing and Rewriting Reality from Woolf to McEwan"

10:30 a.m. **Morning refreshments** (Neilson Library Periodical Room, third floor)

11:00 a.m.–12:30 p.m. **CONCURRENT SESSIONS #2**

2A: **Diverse Appeal of Virginia Woolf and Bloomsbury.** Chair: Margaret Bruzelius (Smith College)
Location: Seelye 101
Justyna Kostkowska (Middle Tennessee State University): "'Scissors and Silks,' 'Flowers and Trees,' and 'Geraniums Ruined by War': Sociology and Ecology in Virginia Woolf's *Mrs. Dalloway*"
Sally Jacobson (Northern Kentucky University): "Woolf's Emblematic Women Meet the Real World in *Between the Acts:* Sexual Dynamics and Christianity"
Sarah Kersh (Muhlenberg College): "Lily's Porthole to the Past: Painting and the Subversion of Gendered Energy Flow in *To the Lighthouse*"
William Pryor (Independent Scholar): "The Living Memes and Jeans of Bloomsbury and Neo-Paganism"

2B: Trauma and Rupture in Woolf. Chair: Susan Gorsky (Cabrillo College/Foothill College)
Location: Seelye 107
Cornelia Burian (University of Saskatchewan): "Modernity's Shock and Beauty: Trauma and the Vulnerable Body in Virginia Woolf's *Mrs. Dalloway*"
Anne Wettersten (Rutgers University): "'And I Will Make It Real by Putting It into Words': Moments of Rupture, Moments of Being in the Literary Landscapes of Woolf and H.D."
David Eberly (John F. Kennedy School of Government, Harvard) "Face to Face: Incest and Audience in the Work of Virginia Woolf"

2C: *The Hours* (Discussion). Chair: Brenda Silver (Dartmouth College)
Location: Wright Hall Auditorium
Leslie Hankins (Cornell College)
Michèle Barrett (University of London)
Daniel Mendelsohn (*New York Review of Books*)
Mary Desjardins (Dartmouth College)

2D: Politics in Woolf's Early Novels. Chair: Elicia Clements (York University)
Location: Seelye 106
Justine Dymond (University of Massachusetts, Amherst): "'Filled Her Eyes with Sights': Intersubjectivity and Empire in Virginia Woolf's *Melymbrosia* and *The Voyage Out*"
Heather Lusty (University of Nevada): "What Exactly Did [She] Mean?: Pacifism and Anti-Colonial Sentiment in *The Voyage Out*"
Michael Whitworth (University of Wales, Bangor): "*Night and Day* and National Efficiency"

2E: Featured Panel. Chair: Brenda Lyons (Greenfield Community College)
Location: Graham Hall—Brown Fine Arts Center
David Bradshaw (Oxford University): "Carlyle's House and Other Sketches"
Emily Dalgarno (Boston University): "Woolf and Proust: The Intermittances of the Heart"

2F: The Biographical Woolf. Chair: Cornelia Pearsall (Smith College)
Location: Neilson Browsing Room
Catherine Sandbach-Dahlström (Stockholm University): "Virginia Woolf and the Question of Fact: Re-Visiting the Biographical Legend"
Bruce Gilman (La Sierra University): "This 'Business of Intimacy': Reading Mrs. Woolf, Reading Mrs. Brown"
Drew Patrick Shannon (University of Cincinnati): "The Lightly Attached Web: The Fictional Virginia Woolf"
Patricia Laurence (City University of New York): "Biography and Fiction: Virginia Woolf's *Orlando*, Michael Cunningham's *The Hours*, and Hong Ying's *K: The Art of Love*"

2G: Books. Chair: Barbara Blumenthal (Smith College)
Location: Seelye 201

David Porter (Williams College): "'Riding a Great Horse': Virginia Woolf and the Hogarth Press"

Carolyn Byrd (Independent Scholar): "French Impressionism and *To the Lighthouse*: An Altered Book Experience"

12:30–2:00 p.m. **Lunch** (Delegates are free to make own arrangements—Davis Student Center is open; reception at Northampton Center for the Arts for exhibition by Suzanne Bellamy, Conference Artist-in-Residence.)

2:00–3:30 p.m. **CONCURRENT SESSIONS #3**

3A: **Woolf's Influence on Plath.** Chair: Karen V. Kukil (Smith College)
Location: Neilson Browsing Room
Melissa Maday (Emory University): "'A Heap of Unrelated Articles': Objects of Desire and Revulsion in the Fiction of Virginia Woolf and Sylvia Plath"
Pamela St. Clair (Salem State College) "In Search of the Self: Virginia Woolf's Shadow across Sylvia Plath's Page"
Amanda Golden (University of Massachusetts, Amherst): "Virginia Woolf's Influence on Sylvia Plath's Abandoned Novel, *Falcon Yard*"
Wayne Chapman (Clemson University): "Last Respects: The Posthumous Editing of Sylvia Plath and Virginia Woolf"

3B: **Memories.** Chair: Leslie Werden (University of North Dakota)
Location: Seelye 107
Robert Reginio (University of Massachusetts, Amherst): "'Perpetually Contradicted': Private Memories and History: A Reconsideration of Freud and Virginia Woolf"
Ravit Reichman (Yale University): "Memory-Work and Traumatic Inheritance: Woolf's Practical Legacy"
Victoria Blythe (New York University): "True Memoir, Real Fiction: Virginia Woolf and the Mimesis of Memory"

3C: **War and Pacifism.** Chair: Naomi Black (York University)
Location: Wright Hall Auditorium
Kathleen Wall (University of Regina): "'Listen Not to the Bark of the Guns but to the Voices of the Poets': The Aesthetics of *Three Guineas*"
Todd Avery (University of Massachusetts, Lowell): "Our Lives in Relation to the Outside World: Woolf, Maynard Keynes, and Utopian Visions on the Brink of War"
Michèle Barrett (University of London): "Virginia Woolf and Pacifism"
Jean Moorcroft Wilson (University of London/Cecil Woolf Publishers): "Woolf and Sassoon"

3D: **Construction of Englishness.** Chair: Sowon Park (Lucy Cavendish College, Cambridge)
Location: Graham Hall—Brown Fine Arts Center
Raphaël Ingelbien (Université catholique de Louvain, Belgium): "Between Englands: A

New Look at Virginia Woolf and Nationhood"
Heidi Stalla (Exeter College, Oxford): "Elvedon and the Fisher King in *The Waves*"
Shelly Auster (State University of New York, Stony Brook): "Representations of 'Britishness': Shifting National Identity and Colonial Discourse in Virginia Woolf's *Mrs. Dalloway*"
David Bradshaw (Oxford University): "*Jacob's Room* and 'The Complexity of Things'"

3E: **Gendered Feminisms.** Chair: Marilyn Schuster (Smith College)
Location: Seelye 201
Amy Borders (Clemson University): "Criticism of Masculinity in the Manuscript Version of *Mrs. Dalloway*: The Reaction to Animosity towards Women in the Manuscript Version of 'The Waste Land'"
Jennifer-Ann Kightlinger (State University of New York, Stony Brook): "Sex Costumes: Signifying Sex and Gender in Woolf's 'The Introduction' and *The Years*"
Emily Blair (University of California, Davis): "Poetry the Wrong Side Out"
Victoria Longino (Massachusetts College of Pharmacy and Health Science): "Virginia Woolf's Legacy in Philip Larkin's Work"

3F: **Life Writing I: Writing and Revision.** Chair: Kimberly Lamm (Pratt Institute/ University of Washington)
Location: Seelye 106
Stacey Floyd (University of Kentucky): "Becoming *A Room of One's Own*: A Textual and Socio-historical Look at Virginia Woolf's Process"
Wyatt Bonikowski (Cornell University): "'Mak[ing] It Real': Writing and Experience in 'A Sketch of the Past' and *The Waves*"
Elizabeth Shih (University of Toronto): "Editing the Palimpsestic Text: The Case of Virginia Woolf's 'A Sketch of the Past'"

3G: **Diverse Sciences and Social Sciences.** Chair: Holly Henry (California State University, San Bernardino)
Location: Seelye 101
Brenda Lyons (Greenfield Community College): "Platonic Sketches: Literary Appreciation and Revolutionary Resistance in the Shorter Fiction"
Holly Henry (California State University, San Bernardino) "That 'Fin in the Waste of Waters' and an Outsider's View of Science"
Joseph Kreutziger (Washington University) "Darwin's Temporal Aesthetics: A Brief Stretch in Time from Pater to Woolf"
Akemi Yaguchi (University of Nottingham): "'(Rezia Warren Smith Divined It)': *Mrs. Dalloway* and 'The Schreber Case'"

3:30 p.m. **Afternoon refreshments** (Neilson Library, third floor)

4:00 p.m. **Plenary session:** Carolyn Heilbrun interviewed by Smith College Provost Susan C. Bourque (Wright Hall Auditorium)

5:15 p.m. **International Virginia Woolf Society Reception:** viewing of exhibition *Vanessa Bell and Bloomsbury* (Atrium of Brown Fine Arts Center/Smith College Museum of Art)

6:30 p.m. **Plenary session:** Gretchen Holbrook Gerzina (Vassar College), "Bloomsbury and Race" and Frances Spalding, "When Are Words Not Enough?: Roger Fry and Virginia Woolf" (Wright Hall Auditorium)

8:00 p.m. **Dinner** (delegates are free to make own arrangements)

8:15–10:00 p.m. **Film series:** Sally Potter's *Orlando* (Wright Hall Auditorium)

10:00 p.m. **Informal discussion/cookies and milk** (Jordan House Common Room)

Saturday, June 7

24 hours **Registration** for delegates staying on campus (Laura Scales House)

7:15–8:45 a.m. **Breakfast** for delegates staying on campus; International Virginia Woolf Society breakfast meeting (King/Scales Dining Hall)

8:00 a.m.–6:00 p.m. **Registration** for off-campus delegates (Neilson Library)

9:00 a.m. **Plenary session:** Lyndall Gordon (St. Hilda's College, Oxford), "'This Loose Drifting Material of Life': Virginia Woolf and Biography" (Wright Hall Auditorium)

10:30 a.m. **Refreshment break** (Neilson Library, third floor)

10:30 a.m.–2:00 p.m. and 3:30–5:50 p.m. **Book and Art Fair** (Neilson Library, third floor)

10:30 a.m.–12:00 noon **CONCURRENT SESSIONS #4**

4A: **Featured Session.** Chair: Karen V. Kukil (Smith College)
Location: Mortimer Rare Book Room, Neilson Library
Julia Briggs (De Montfort University): "'Printing Hope': Virginia Woolf, Hope Mirrlees, and the Iconic Imagery of *Paris*"

4B: **Foreign Places.** Chair: Michael Gorra (Smith College)
Location: Seelye 201
Steve Putzel (Penn State University): "Invisible City: Woolf's Real and Imagined Venice"
Eleanor McNees (University of Denver): "The Guidebook and the Dog: Virginia Woolf and Italy"
Clare Morgan (Kellogg College, Oxford University): "Woolf and Wales"
Cheryl Mares (Sweet Briar College): "Woolf and the American Imaginary"

4C: **Teaching** *Mrs. Dalloway* **in the 'Real World' of our Classrooms.** (Roundtable discussion)
Co-chairs: Eileen Barrett (California State University, Hayward) and Ruth Saxton (Mills College)
Location: Neilson Browsing Room
Beth Rigel Daugherty (Otterbein College)
Martha Greene Eads (Valparaiso University)
Leslie Hankins (Cornell College)
Mark Hussey (Pace University)
J. J. Wilson (Sonoma State University)

4D: **Woolf's Literary Afterlife.** Chair: Sherry Zivley (University of Houston)
Location: Graham Hall—Brown Fine Arts Center
Jody Rosen (City University of New York, Graduate Center): "Mrs. Dalloway's Afterlife"
Linda Westervelt (University of Houston): "Virginia Woolf as Literary Model"
Laura Aimone (Independent Scholar) "In the Footsteps of Virginia Woolf: *The Hours* by Michael Cunningham"
James Smith (Armstrong Atlantic State University): "Virginia Woolf's *Mrs. Dalloway* and Michael Cunningham's *The Hours*: When to Throw a Party in London or New York"

4E: **Woolf and Class.** Chair: Diana Royer (Miami University)
Location: Seelye 110
Mary Madden (University of South Florida): "Woolf's Interrogation of Class in *Night and Day*"
Diana Royer (Miami University): "Woolf and Flush's 'Brush . . . with Low Life': The Depiction of Whitechapel in *Flush*"
Catherine Mintler (University of Illinois, Chicago): "The 'Mermaid Dress' and the 'Mackintosh Coat': Social Class and Concealed Female Bodies in *Mrs. Dalloway*"
Rebecca McNeer (Ohio University Southern): "'Help Wanted': Virginia Woolf's Real Life as an Employer"

4F: **Novelistic Historiography.** Chair: Elizabeth Hirsh (University of South Florida)
Location: Seelye 101
Elaine Pigeon (Université de Montreal): "Remembering History: *Orlando* at the Dawn of the Twenty-First Century"
Sarah Alexander (Rutgers) "'The Body of Time': Historiography and the Body in Virginia Woolf's *Orlando*"
Lorelei Ormrod (Jesus College, Oxford University): "*The Waves*, Carlyle and 'Clothes': Virginia Woolf's Vision of History"

4G: **Life Writing II: From Private to Public.** Chair: Leena Kore-Schroder (University of Nottingham)
Location: Seelye 106
Alexandra Pett (Mount Royal College): "'Weevil in a Biscuit': Woolf's Diary Entries of the Early 1930s"

Stephen Barkway (Virginia Woolf Society of Great Britain): "'What Tiara Did You Wear?': Mrs. Woolf and Lady Aberconway"
Rebecca Blasco (University of Alberta): "'The Space Between Us': Epistolary and Dramatic Forms in *The Waves*"

12:30 p.m. **Lunch** (prepurchased boxed lunches may be picked up in the Neilson Library Periodical Room, third floor)

1:30–2:30 p.m. **CONCURRENT SESSIONS #5**

A: The Hogarth Press and Its Legacy. Chair: Karen V. Kukil (Smith College)
Location: Seelye 106
Jan Freeman (Paris Press): "The Paris Press Publication of *On Being Ill*"
Debra Sims (Independent Scholar): "Independence through Self-Publication: Virginia Woolf Discovers Her Voice with the Hogarth Press"
Marie Umeh (John Jay College, City University of New York): "Flora Nwapa Meets Virginia Woolf in the Publishing Industry"
Catherine Hollis (Lawrence University): "Virginia Woolf's Double Signature"

5B: Creative Session Inspired by Woolf. Chair: Ellen Watson (Smith College)
Location: Neilson Browsing Room
William Buckley (Indiana University): "Sylvia's Bells" (poetry)
Su Smallen (Hamline University): "Three Poems Inspired by Virginia Woolf"
George Ella Lyon (Independent Scholar): "Poems from Talland House"
Patrick Horrigan (Long Island University, Brooklyn): "Alone at Talland House"

5C: Landscape, Place, and Subjectivity. Chair: Richard Millington (Smith College)
Location: Seelye 201
Leena Kore-Schroder (University of Nottingham): "Virginia Woolf and the English Landed Estate: Hours in a (Country House) Library"
Lesley Higgins (York University): "'Something So Varied and Wandering': The Possibilities of a 'Restless' Subjectivity"
Annette Oxindine (Wright State University): "Woolf's Geographies of Longing: Mapping the Metaphysics of St. Ives and London"
Vera Eliasova (Rutgers University): "The 'Army of Anonymous Trampers': Women's Writing of Urban Collective Identity"

5D: Visual Aesthetics. Chair: Kathleen Wall (University of Regina)
Location: Graham Hall—Brown Fine Arts Center
Maggie Humm (University of East London): "Virginia Woolf and Vanessa Bell as Photographers: 'The Same Pair of Eyes, Only Different Spectacles'"
Leslie Hankins (Cornell College): "When 'The Cinema' was in *Vogue*: Situating Woolf's Essay on Cinema within Film Writing in British *Vogue*"
Steve Ellis (University of Birmingham): "Oil–Gas–Electricity: Woolf and Lighting"

5E: **Orlando, Gender, and Androgyny.** Chair: Patricia Feito (Barry University)
Location: Seelye 110
Lisa Suter (Miami University, Oxford, Ohio): "'A Little Language Such as Lovers Use':
Color-Coding and Secret Ciphers to Vita in Virginia Woolf's *Orlando*"
Joanna Lackey (Wellesley College): "The Nature of Homosexuality in Woolf's *Orlando*
and Plato's *Symposium*"
Tamara Slandard (State University of New York, Stonybrook): "'Chasing the Wild Goose':
Androgyny, Hermaphrodism, and the 'Truth' About *Orlando*"
Katie MacNamara (Indiana University): "Virginia Woolf's *Orlando*: Negotiating Camp
Camps"

5F: **Woolf and Forms of Trauma.** Chair: Clifford Wulfman (Tufts University)
Location: Seelye 107
Clifford Wulfman (Tufts University): "The Cryptonymy of Woolf's Little Language"
Patricia Moran (University of California, Davis): "Memory and Desire in Narratives of
Abuse: Jean Rhys and Virginia Woolf"
Nick Smart (College of New Rochelle): "This Is What She Loved . . . and Hated: The
Production of Real Life in *Mrs. Dalloway*"

5G: **Through the Generations: Presentations by Woolf Seminar Teachers at Smith
College.** Chair: Stephanie Schoen (Smith College)
Location: Seelye 101
Elizabeth von Klemperer (Smith College): "'The Works of Women Are Symbolical':
Needlework in Virginia Woolf"
J. J. Wilson (Sonoma State University): "Early Days Teaching Woolf in the Hampshire
Valley"
Robert Hosmer (Smith College): "Cannibalizing Woolf"

2:30–3:00 p.m. **Afternoon refreshments** (Neilson Library, third floor)

3:00–4:30 p.m. **CONCURRENT SESSIONS #6**

6A: **An Edition of One's Own: A Roundtable Discussion of Blackwell's Shakespeare
Head Press Edition of Virginia Woolf.** Chair: Pat Rosenbaum (University of Toronto)
Location: Neilson Browsing Room
Edward Bishop (University of Alberta): "Mind the Gap"
Naomi Black (York University): "The Edition's Daughter"
David Bradshaw (Oxford University): "Some with Their Corners Turned Down"
Diane Gillespie (Washington State University): "Annotation and Audience"
James Haule (University of Texas, Edinburg): "Texts, Reception, and Teaching"
Mary Millar (Queen's University): "'Ten Minutes of Present Time': Topical Allusions in
Between the Acts"

6B: **Unexpected Pleasure: Teaching Beyond Students' Initial Fear of Virginia Woolf.**
Chair: Ruth Saxton (Mills College)

Location: Seelye 106
Martha Greene Eads (Valparaiso University): "In League Together: Taking *Mrs. Dalloway* into a Women's Prison"
Patricia Feito (Barry University): "'The Ebbs and Flows Are a Reality of Life': Non-traditional Students Reading Virginia Woolf's *Mrs. Dalloway*"
Andrea Adolph (Kent State University): "Virginia Woolf at the A & P: Students Respond to the Cotton Wool of Life"
Jessica de Courcy Hinds (Brooklyn College): "A Teaching Journey: Immigrant Students Search for a Room of Their Own at Brooklyn College"

6C: **Woolf and Daly: The Outsider Highway Revisited (Plus Maps)**. Chair: Suzanne Bellamy (Artist-in-Residence)
Location: Seelye 110
Eileen Barrett (California State University, Hayward): "Virginia Woolf and Mary Daly: Dismantling the Real World of Patriarchy"
Suzanne Bellamy (Artist-in-Residence): "Virginia Woolf, Mary Daly, and the BIG BAD MAD RAD FEM COW CODE Battles"
Mark Hussey (Pace University): "The Personal Is Still the Political: Woolf, Daly, Pornography"
Krystyna Colburn (University of Massachusetts, Boston): "Virginia Woolf. Mary Daly. 1984"

6D: **Life-Cycles**. Chair: Elizabeth Hirsh (University of South Florida)
Location: Seelye 107
Stephanie Porcaro (St. John's College): "An Exploration of *The Waves*, as Encapsulated through the Journey of the Sun"
Janine Utell (City University of New York, Graduate Center): "Little or Nothing but Life: Real World Ritual in *The Waves*"
Elizabeth Hirsh (University of South Florida): "Mrs. Dalloway's Menopause: Encrypting the Female Life Course"

6E: **Art Objects and Aesthetics**. Chair: Laura Quinn (Smith College)
Location: Graham Hall—Brown Fine Arts Center
Elizabeth Cruse (Lucy Cavendish College, Cambridge): "The Window as Significant Form in the Voyage Out to the Lighthouse 1925–1927"
Kathryn Benzel (University of Nebraska, Kearney): "Pen and Paintbrush: Virginia Woolf and Walter Sickert"
Georgette Fleischer (Columbia University): "Fiction and Fact, or Woolf and the Autonomy of the Art Object"
Leslie Werden (University of North Dakota): "Visual Storytelling: Virginia Woolf's Representations of Memory"

6F: **Women Writers and Their Influence on Woolf**. Chair: Robert Hosmer (Smith College)
Location: Seelye 201

Michele Bala (Smith College): "Death and the Maiden: Why Rachel Vinrace Must Die"
Sherry Zivley (University of Houston): "Mansfield's 'At the Bay' and Woolf's *The Waves*"
Emily Bowles (Emory University): "'I Am by No Means Confining You to Fiction': Fictions of Aphra Behn in the Works of Virginia Woolf"

6G: Woolf as a Political Thinker. Chair: Todd Avery (University of Massachusetts, Lowell)
Location: Seelye 101
Jamie Carr (University of Rhode Island): "The Leaning Tower and a Critique of Fascism: Virginia Woolf's Influence on Christopher Isherwood"
Joyce Karpay (University of South Florida): "The Power of the Local: Virginia Woolf's Influence on the Political Novels of Nadine Gordimer"
Judith Allen (University of Pennsylvania): "Resisting 'Patriotism': Virginia Woolf's 'Thinking against the Current'"

4:30–5:30 p.m. **Break**

5:30 p.m. **Keynote address:** Hermione Lee (Oxford University): "Undiscovered Countries: Woolf, Illness, and Reading" (Sage Hall). A version of this talk, entitled "On Being Ill," is published in *Body Parts: Essays in Life-Writing* by Hermione Lee (London: Chatto & Windus, 2005).

7:00 p.m. **Dinner:** Banquet (optional) with entertainment by the Virginia Woolf Players (King/Scales Dining Room)

9:00 p.m. **Reception:** Viewing of exhibition *Virginia Woolf: A Botanical Perspective,* illumination of the botanic gardens, and Hermione Lee book signing of Paris Press edition of *On Being Ill* (Lyman Plant House)

10:00 p.m. **Informal discussion/cookies and milk** (Jordan House Common Room)

Sunday, June 8

7:30–8:45 a.m. **Breakfast** for delegates staying on campus (King/Scales Dining Room)

10:30 a.m.–12:30 p.m. **Book and Art Fair** (Neilson Library, third floor)

9:00–10:30 a.m. **CONCURRENT SESSIONS #7**

7A: Featured Panel: The Art of the Essay. Chair: Michael Whitworth. (University of Wales, Bangor)
Location: Seelye 101
Beth Rigel Daugherty (Otterbein College): "Virginia Woolf's Apprenticeship: Becoming an Essayist"

Randi Saloman (Yale University): "'Here Again Is the Usual Door': Street Haunting and the Permeability of the Essay"

7B: **Gender and Feminism.** Chair: Krystyna Colburn (University of Massachusetts, Boston)
Location: Seelye 201
Jennifer Toole (University of California, Berkeley): "Stella Now, Stella Then"
Dianne Hunter (Trinity College, Connecticut): "Objects Dissolving in Time"
Kathryn Simpson (University of Birmingham): "The Paradox of the Gift: Gift Giving as a Disruptive Force in Woolf's Writing"

7C: **Forward and Retreat: Woolf's Home Fronts.** Chair: Rishona Zimring (Lewis and Clark University)
Location: Seelye 101
Rishona Zimring (Lewis and Clark University): "Retreating from Peace in 'The String Quartet'"
Margaret Bruzelius (Smith College): "Two Steps Backward: *The Voyage Out* and the Tradition of Adventure"
Jay Dickson (Reed College): "'The Crying Game': Woolf and the 'Retreat' of Sentimentality"

7D: **Fashionable Bloomsbury.** Chair: Laura Quinn (Smith College)
Location: Graham Hall—Brown Fine Arts Center
Maria Day (University of Maryland): "Modernism à la Mode: Woolf, Bell, and Fashions at Omega Workshops"
Ruth Hoberman (Eastern Illinois University): "Aesthetic Taste and Things in *The Years*"
Alastair Upton (Charleston Trust): "Charleston in the Real World"

7E: **Woolf's Continuing Influence.** Chair: Robert Hosmer (Smith College)
Location: Neilson Browsing Room
Ann Norton (Saint Anselm College): "'I Have Taken the Name of Virginia Woolf in Vain': Woolfian Irony in Anita Brookner's *Hotel du Lac*"
Kevin Stemmler (Clarion University): "Merged Worlds: Virginia Woolf's Legacy to Jeanette Winterson"
Kimberly Lamm (Pratt Institute/University of Washington): "Painting the Language and Writing the Landscape of the Maternal: Claudia Rankine's Plot and *To The Lighthouse*"
Kristin Czarnecki (University of Cincinnati): "Filming Feminism: *A Room of One's Own* on *Masterpiece Theater*"

7F: **The Writing Process.** Chair: Elizabeth Harries (Smith College)
Location: Seelye 106
Jennifer Sikes (Shorter College): "Virginia Woolf and Lytton Strachey in the Shadow of the Victorians"
Bill Goldstein (City University of New York, Graduate Center): "'Horribly in Debt' to Proust: Virginia Woolf's Reading of *In Search of Lost Time* and Its Influence on *Mrs. Dalloway*"

Lynn Langmade (San Francisco State University): "Blasting through Homogenous Time: Being, Bergsonism, and Empancipatory Strategies in Virginia Woolf's *Orlando*"

Courtney Carter (Hood College): "Imitations of 'Reality' in Virginia Woolf's *Between the Acts*"

7G: **Textual Subversions.** Chair: Elicia Clements (York University)
Location: Seelye 110
Virginia Costello (State University of New York, Stony Brook): "An Ethical Inquiry: Relational Autonomy in Virginia Woolf's *Three Guineas* and *Moments of Being*"
Maria Glade (University of Rhode Island): "A Medley: The Ethical Practice of Freedom as Performed by Woolf's *Between the Acts*"
Carolyn Tilghman Bitzenhofer (University of Texas, Tyler): "The Subject, the Ordinary, and Parody in *Three Guineas*"
Vicki Tromanhauser (Columbia University): "Given Freely: Sacrificial Economics in *Three Guineas*"

10:30 a.m. **Refreshment break** (Neilson Library Periodical Room, third floor)

11:00 a.m.–12:30 p.m. **CONCURRENT SESSIONS #8**

8A: **Roundtable: Teaching Woolf to High School Students.** Chair: Ellen Reich (Amherst Regional High School)
Location: Graham Hall—Brown Fine Arts Center
Sara Just, Kristin Iverson, Madeleine Hunter, Jani Baer-Leighton, and Kristen Barlow (Amherst Regional High School)

8B: **Politics and Feminism:** Chair: Cornelia Ratt (University of Saskatchewan)
Location: Seelye 201
Sowon Park (Lucy Cavendish College, Cambridge): "Tea, Suffrage, and Woolf's Critique of Feminist Judgment"
Geneviève Brassard (University of Connecticut): "'To Make It Whole, Beautiful, Entire': The Luminous Shadow of the War Over *The Years*"
Deborah Gerrard (De Montfort University): "A 'Literary Prostitute' Writes Back: Storm Jameson and Virginia Woolf"

8C: **Reading the Newspapers.** Chair: Stuart Clarke (Virginia Woolf Society of Great Britain)
Location: Seelye 106
Stuart Clarke (Virginia Woolf Society of Great Britain): "The Lord Chief Justice and the Woolfs"
Karin Westman (Kansas State University): "'Steadily More Feminist, Owing to the Times': Newspapers and New Realities in the Novels of Virginia Woolf"

8D: **Performing Woolf (Discussion).** Chair: Elizabeth Harries (Smith College)
Location: Seelye 107

Maryna Harrison (Independent Artist): "Performance of *The Waves:* A Work in Progress"
Clare Dalton: "Performing *A Room of One's Own*"
Tod Randolph: "Performing as Woolf"

8E: Movement, Dance, and Theatre. Chair, Mary Ramsay (Smith College)
Location: Seelye 101
Holly Messitt (Berkeley College): "Waltzing Virginia: Rhythm, Movement, and Meaning"
Toni Jaudon (Cornell University): "Visual Time and Bodily Experience in *The Waves* and *The Years*"

8F: Prosopopoeia and Pop Culture: Representing the Lost Other in the Real World.
Chair: Madelyn Detloff (Miami University of Ohio)
Location: Seelye 110
Keri Barber (California State University, Los Angeles): "The Body and the Brain: Woolf's Humanistic and Ever-Changing Vision of the Soldier from Jacob Flanders to Abel Pargiter"
Madelyn Detloff (Miami University of Ohio): "'Fear No More the Heat of the Sun': Septimus, AIDS, and *The Hours*"

12:30 p.m. Lunch (preordered boxed lunches available in the Neilson Library Periodical Room, third floor)

1:30–2:30 p.m. Lytton and Virginia: Staged reading of the Woolf-Strachey correspondence. Adapted by Sean Smith. Directed by Ellen Kaplan, associate professor, Smith College Theatre Department. Introduced by Paul Levy, editor of *The Letters of Lytton Strachey.* With Meghan Flaherty as Virginia Woolf, Shawn Dempewolf-Barrett as Lytton Strachey, and Sean Coté as Leonard Woolf.

POST-CONFERENCE EVENTS

4:00–7:00 p.m. Emily Dickinson homestead and Dickinson sites (optional field trip—meet vans at 3:30 p.m. in front of Neilson Library)

7:00 p.m. Dinner: Delegates are free to make their own arrangements

8:30–10:00 p.m. Film series: *Carrington,* introduced by Gretchen Holbrook Gerzina (Wright Hall Auditorium)

Monday, June 9

7:30–8:45 a.m. Breakfast for delegates staying on campus (King/Scales Dining Hall)

12 noon Final checkout time for delegates in Smith housing

ONGOING AND SPECIAL EVENTS

Exhibitions

NEILSON LIBRARY:

• *Woolf in the World: A Pen and a Press of Her Own,* curated by Karen V. Kukil. Highlights from the Elizabeth P. Richardson Bloomsbury Iconography Collection and the Frances Hooper Collection of Virginia Woolf Books and Manuscripts.(Book Arts Gallery, Neilson Library, third floor)

• *"The Politics of Mind": Writing on Woolf, Teaching Woolf,* curated by Kathleen Banks Nutter and Anne Lozier. Includes material from the Carolyn Heilbrun Papers, Sophia Smith Collection, and the papers of various Smith College faculty members in the Smith College Archives. (Alumnae Gym)

• *"Her Novels Make Mine Possible": Virginia Woolf's Influence on Sylvia Plath,* curated by Amanda Golden. (Mortimer Rare Book Room, Neilson Library, third floor)

• *A Story of Their Own: Virginia Woolf, Sylvia Plath, and Gloria Steinem,* curated by Karen V. Kukil. (Mortimer Rare Book Room, Neilson Library, third floor)

LYMAN CONSERVATORY:

• *Virginia Woolf: A Botanical Perspective,* curated by Madelaine Zadik. Includes photographs and multimedia presentations on the gardens of Virginia Woolf and her friends and family, including Monks House, Sissinghurst, and Charleston Farmhouse.

BROWN FINE ARTS CENTER:

• *Vanessa Bell and Bloomsbury,* curated by Linda Muehlig. This exhibition gathers a number of works of art associated with the Bloomsbury Group, including the writing desk once used by Virginia Woolf and several of the museum's paintings by Vanessa Bell; the exhibition also includes ceramics by Quentin Bell and works on paper by Vanessa Bell and Duncan Grant. Some items in the show were graciously loaned by private owners. (Smith College Museum of Art)

NORTHAMPTON CENTER FOR THE ARTS:

• *Suzanne Bellamy.* A one-woman art exhibition featuring the work of Suzanne Bellamy (conference Artist-in-Residence). The Northampton Center for the Arts is located in Sullivan Square just outside the gates of Smith College at the corner of Main Street and South Street.

Woolf in the Reel World: Film Series

Nightly, except Saturday, Wright Hall Auditorium

- *Mrs. Dalloway*—Wednesday, June 4, 8:00–10:00 p.m.
- *The Hours,* including sneak preview of DVD extras—Thursday, June 5, 8:30–11:00 p.m.
- *Orlando*—Friday, June 6, 8:15–10:00 p.m.
- *Carrington*—Sunday, June 8, 8:30–10:00 p.m.

Silent Auction

Many thanks to Krystyna Colburn for her ongoing generosity and hard work in providing this auction. All proceeds are donated to the Travel Scholarship Fund of the International Virginia Woolf Society. (Mortimer Rare Book Room, Neilson Library, third floor.)

Performances

A Room of One's Own with Clare Dalton—Thursday, June 5, 3:30–4:15 p.m. (Wright Hall Auditorium)
Clare Dalton is Matthews Distinguished University Professor of Law at Northeastern University and Executive Director of Northeastern's Domestic Violence Institute. Her career in the theater began during her undergraduate years at Oxford, as a member of the Oxford University Dramatic Society. Recently, she has performed with her husband, Robert Reich, in several productions of *Love Letters* in Wellfleet, Boston, Waltham and Lenox, Massachusetts. (Wright Hall Auditorium)

Lytton and Virginia—Sunday, June 8, 1:30–2:30 p.m. (Wright Hall Auditorium)
Premier of a dramatic reading selected from the Woolf–Strachey correspondence (140 original letters are in the collection of Smith's Mortimer Rare Book Room). Adapted by Sean Smith. Produced and directed by Ellen Kaplan, Associate Professor, Smith College Theatre Department. Introduced by Paul Levy, editor of *The Letters of Lytton Strachey* (2005) and co-executor of the Strachey literary estate. With Meghan Flaherty as Virginia Woolf, Shawn Dempewolf-Barrett as Lytton Strachey, and Sean Coté as Leonard Woolf.

Book Arts Demonstrations

Book artists from the Pioneer Valley demonstrate letterpress printing, wood engraving, paste paper design, and bookbinding. Artists include: Hosea Baskin, Art Larson, Michael Russem, Abigail Rorer, Claudia Cohen, and Barbara Blumenthal, who also organized the event. Friday, June 5, Mortimer Rare Book Room, Neilson Library, 6:45–8:45 p.m.

Book and Arts Fair

Hard-to-find books and electronic media relating to Woolf and the Bloomsbury Group; books by presenters; fine press editions; works of art by Suzanne Bellamy, Elisa Kay Sparks, and others are for sale. Hours: Friday and Saturday, 10:30 a.m.–2:00 p.m. and 3:30–5:50 p.m., and Sunday 10:30 a.m.–12:30 p.m. (Neilson Library, third floor)

Late-Night Discussions

Gather at 10 p.m. (or later) any night in the Jordan House Common Room for informal chats about topics of interest. This wonderful new tradition was started at the 2002 conference at Sonoma State by J. J. Wilson as "Cookies and Milk."

Conference Details

The **William Allan Neilson Library** is at the heart of the conference. Neilson Library will be open: Wednesday 8:00 a.m.–midnight; Thursday, 9:00 a.m.–midnight; Friday, 8:00 a.m.–6:00 p.m.; Saturday, 8:00 a.m.–6:00 p.m.; Sunday, 10:00 a.m.–midnight.

Registration takes place in two places: Neilson Library for those staying off campus; Laura Scales House in the dormitory complex called the "Quad" for those staying on campus (corner of Elm Street and Paradise Road). The registration table at Neilson Library is the main information site for the conference.

Plenary Sessions take place in Wright Hall Auditorium (adjacent to the library) and in Sage Hall on Green Street and College Lane.

Concurrent Panels take place in Seelye Hall (right angles to library), Neilson Library (Browsing Room and Mortimer Rare Book Room) and Graham Hall (downstairs in Hillyer Hall in the Brown Fine Arts Center).

Smith College Attractions
• The **Smith College Museum of Art** is one of the best art museums at any college or university in America.
• The **Sophia Smith Collection** is an internationally recognized repository of manuscripts, photographs, periodicals, and other primary sources in women's history.
• The **Smith Botanic Garden** includes the beautiful Lyman Conservatory, many gardens, as well as Smith's 150-acre campus, landscaped by Frederic Law Olmstead who designed Central Park in New York City.
• The **Mortimer Rare Book Room** is a teaching collection, available to students, scholars, and common readers. It houses 40,000 rare books and literary manuscripts, including the papers of Virginia Woolf and Sylvia Plath.
• The **Smith College Libraries** include **Neilson Library**, **Hillyer Art Library**, **Josten Library of the Performing Arts**, and **Young Science Library**.

Northampton is a wonderful town with many bookstores, arts and crafts galleries, unique boutiques, and venues for the arts and entertainment.

Acknowledgments

This conference and the many Woolf-related events at Smith College have truly been a collaborative effort among a great number of people. None of this would have been possible without the help, support, and talents of many staff and faculty colleagues and departments at Smith College.

We are grateful to Marilyn Schwinn Smith for organizing the program and for bringing forward the suggestion that Smith College host the thirteenth annual conference on Virginia Woolf. We thank Alyson Shaw, student intern extraordinaire, and alumnae conference assistant Michele Bala—both Ada Comstock Scholars—for all the days and nights they put into making the conference happen.

Thanks to the Smith steering committee members who helped guide the conference and keep things running smoothly: Elizabeth Harries, Chair of the English Department; Christopher Loring, Director of the Libraries; Laura Quinn, Director of Donor Relations and Special Events, and Elizabeth von Klemperer, Professor Emeritus of English. We thank the program committee members who carefully read and evaluated over 200 paper submissions: Beth Daugherty, Vara Neverow, Mark Hussey, Robert Hosmer, Cornelia Pearsall, Elizabeth von Klemperer, Marilyn Schwinn Smith, and Jeanne Dubino.

We are very grateful for financial support from numerous departments and funds at Smith College: the Provost's Office, the Lecture Fund Committee, the Ruth Mortimer Rare Book Room Fund, the Friends of the Smith College Libraries, the Advancement Office, the Botanic Garden, the Project on Women and Social Change, the English Department, the Smith College Museum of Art, and the Women's Studies Department—and we are grateful to all the individuals associated with these groups who offered that support. We also appreciate support received from the International Virginia Woolf Society, both financial and advisory.

We are grateful to Smith College President Carol T. Christ and Provost Susan C. Bourque for their enthusiastic support of the conference, and also for their participation in the plenary sessions.

Many staff members made exceptional contributions: Madelaine Zadik's creative work resulted in the beautiful exhibition *Virginia Woolf: A Botanical Perspective*. Barbara Blumenthal's efforts and talents made the book arts demonstrations and book and arts fair a reality. Thank you to Marilyn Woodman who worked behind the scenes on many pieces of the conference. Linda Muehlig, associate director of the Smith College Museum of Art, Kathleen Banks Nutter, reference archivist in the Sophia Smith Collection, Anne Lozier, associate archivist of the Smith College Archives, and guest curator Amanda Golden mounted special exhibitions. Betsy Baird of the Alumnae Association organized the Alumnae College sessions "Virginia Woolf in Place and Time," which drew a record number of alumnae to campus. Diane Jacobs at Summer Programs has been enormously helpful. We appreciate the talents of the colleagues who have helped with technology, especially Heather Morgan for creating a wonderful database that can be passed on to future conference organizers; to Debra Diemand for her help in envisioning that database; and to Bill Weakley for setting up a secure server for online registrations. We are deeply grateful to the many colleagues from Physical Plant and Residence and Dining Services for setting up everything, feeding everyone, and keeping things going, especially Matt Gawron and Betse Curtis.

Faculty have contributed in many wonderful ways. Great thanks to Ellen Kaplan of the Theatre Department for her boundless enthusiasm in helping with many aspects of conference performances, and especially for producing and directing *Lytton and Virginia*. We appreciate Robert Hosmer for the two-credit special studies course on Virginia Woolf, which made it possible for a number of Smith undergraduates to attend the conference. Thanks to Cornelia Pearsall for leading the Kahn Institute faculty seminar "The Sensual Woolf" (and to all the staff of the Kahn Institute). We also want to thank Alexandra Keller for her work on the film festival and all the Smith faculty members who chaired panels, presented papers, and introduced speakers, including Michael Gorra, Richard Millington, and Ellen Watson.

Thank you to Marilyn Schwinn Smith for organizing the "Woolf in the Valley" lecture series for faculty and students of the five colleges.

A special thank you to Lisa Baskin, Janice Carlson Oresman, Patricia Oresman, and David Porter.

We thank several artists who have been helpful and inspiring. We love the designs created by Lisa Carta (conference publications, poster, and T-shirt). We thank the inimitable Suzanne Bellamy for her "Woolf in the Reel World" cover design and for the countless other ways she has helped. We are grateful for the generosity and talents of Elisa Kay Sparks in contributing to the botanical exhibit and we are grateful to Pamela McMorrow for her beautiful Monks House photographs.

Stephanie particularly wants to thank her many colleagues in the Advancement Office for encouraging her to pursue her interest in Virginia Woolf and for supporting her work on the conference in countless ways—for helping, listening, meeting, and volunteering. Thanks, too, to friends and family outside of Smith who have done the same, and those of who traveled from great distances to help out. Eventually, I hope to find ways to appropriately thank each of you individually for being so wonderful. An added thank you to Elizabeth von Klemperer for being a superb teacher and mentor.

Karen wants to thank Martin Antonetti, curator of rare books, and Sherrill Redmon, coordinator of special collections, for their support. In addition, she would like to thank Jill Ker Conway, Gloria Steinem, and Carolyn Heilbrun for reading and commenting on the exhibition labels of *A Story of Their Own: Virginia Woolf, Sylvia Plath, and Gloria Steinem*. Smith alumnae Paula Deitz, Ann Pflaum, and Sarah Thomas also deserve special recognition for their contributions.

Smith colleagues in the library, museum, art department, and physical plant who have been particularly generous with their time and skills include Susan Barker, Joan Brink, Jane Clayton, Marit Cranmer, Phyllis Cummings, David Dempsey, Jolene de Verges, Jack Doherty, Arthur Dunn, Suzannah Fabing, Craig Felton, Mary Irwin, Robin Kinder, Peter-Michael Kinney, Elisa Lanzi, Mimi Lempart, Eric Loehr, Cindy Rucci, Kelcy Shepherd, Molly Twarog, Nanci Young, Shirley Zachazewski, and Marlene Znoy. The professional expertise of Alison Bell, Jim Gipe, Bohdan Kukil, and Paula Panich has been invaluable.

The participation of the local book arts community in printing demonstrations at the conference is greatly appreciated along with the special broadside published by Enid Mark at the ELM Press and Jan Freeman's Paris Press edition of *On Being Ill*. Roxie Mack of the Broadside Bookshop deserves recognition for providing scholarly texts for sale at the conference.

Colleagues from other institutions have also contributed to the intellectual vibrancy of the conference. They included Daria D'Arienzo (Amherst College), Elisabeth Fairman (Yale Center for British Art), Amanda Golden (University of Massachusetts, Amherst), and Dianne Hunter (Trinity College). Finally, a special thank you to student assistants Jessica Bumpous, Rachel Dwyer, Barbara Joo, Sonora Miller, and Joanna Patterson.

Together, we created an exciting conference. Additional information and photographs of the conference are available on the conference website: www.smith.edu/woolfconference.

Karen V. Kukil and Stephanie Cooper Schoen, Conference Co-chairs

ↅↄ

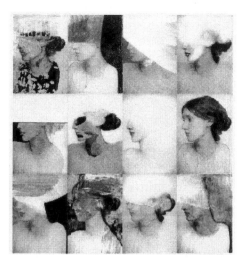

Linda Stein
Detail of *Virginia Woolf 370*, 1976/2002
Limited Edition Fine Art Print, Edition of 85
Unique water coloring on each
Signed in pencil
Numbered 11/85
12.5 x 11.5 inches, unframed
MORTIMER RARE BOOK ROOM, SMITH COLLEGE

American sculptor, painter, and printmaker Linda Stein is best known for her feminist, androgynous, and antiwar art. After 9/11, unable to do sculpture for almost a year, Stein was drawn back to her two-dimensional work dating from the 1970s: a long-standing exploration of the facial profile as a study of classical idealism and private fantasy. She reimmersed herself in these myriad drawings, collages, prints, and paintings of the face created over three decades.

Stein was again drawn to the provocative head studies, frequently in grid formation, and to the time when she first romanced prominent facial features to develop a personal language from her seductive notations. In her profile writing, abstractions of angular nose, curvilinear lips and chin were repeated to form a personal calligraphy, a cryptic text.

So, in 2002, when she came upon a 1976 watercolor series of facial profiles of Virginia Woolf, Stein found herself, once again, entranced by the facial arcs and areas she had created so long ago. She described it as falling in love again, and decided to combine these watercolors of Woolf profiles into a limited edition print, further water coloring by hand after printing, making each print one-of-a-kind.

Print number 11 was exhibited in *Linda Stein—The Face: An Obsession, Three Decades,* a 2004 exhibition in the William Allan Neilson Library. A catalog accompanied the show. The print is now part of the Elizabeth P. Richardson Bloomsbury Iconography Collection in the Mortimer Rare Book Room. A detail of the print appears on the back cover, courtesy of the artist.